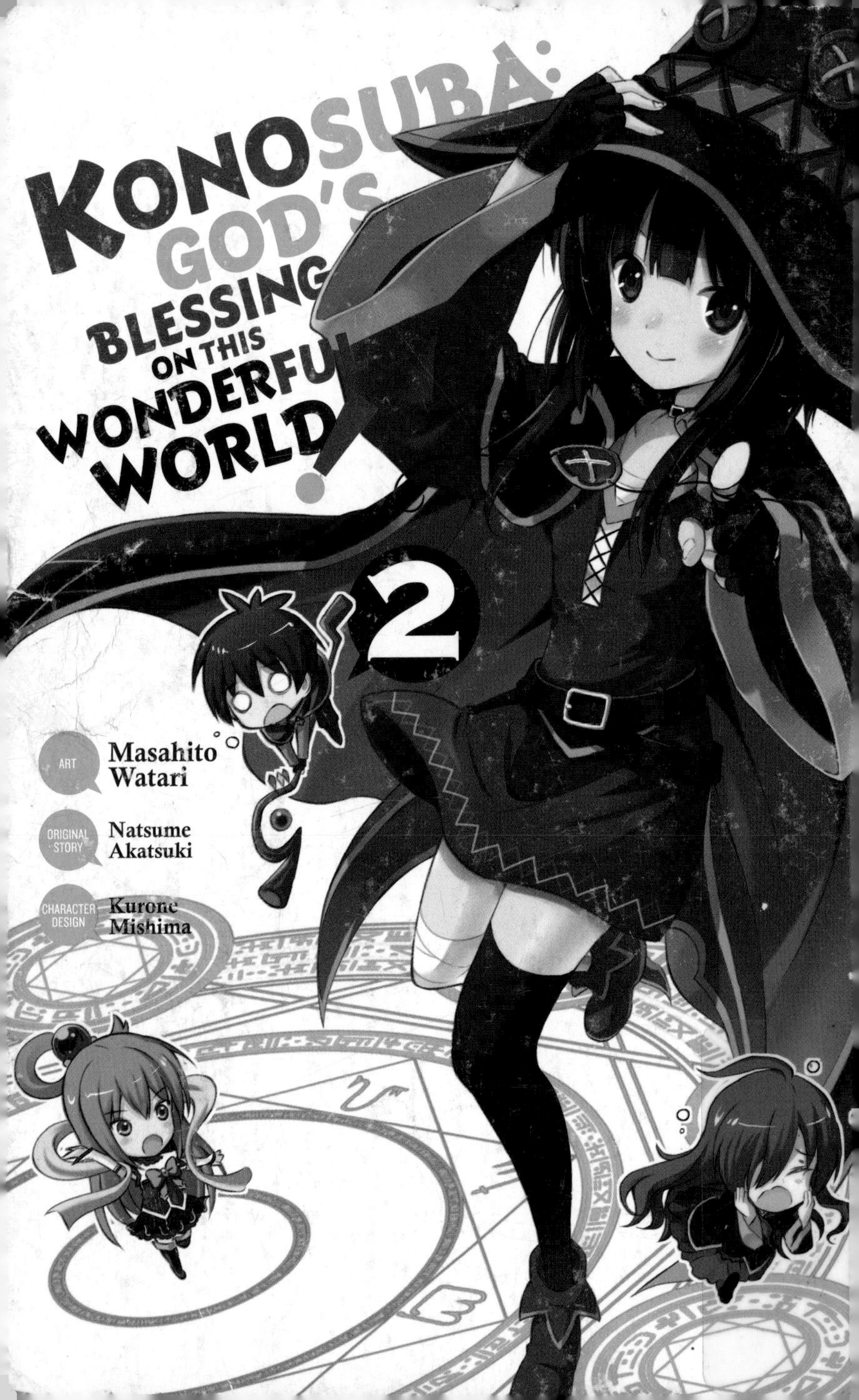
Konosuba: God's Blessing on This Wonderful World!
2
ART Masahito Watari
ORIGINAL STORY Natsume Akatsuki
CHARACTER DESIGN Kurone Mishima

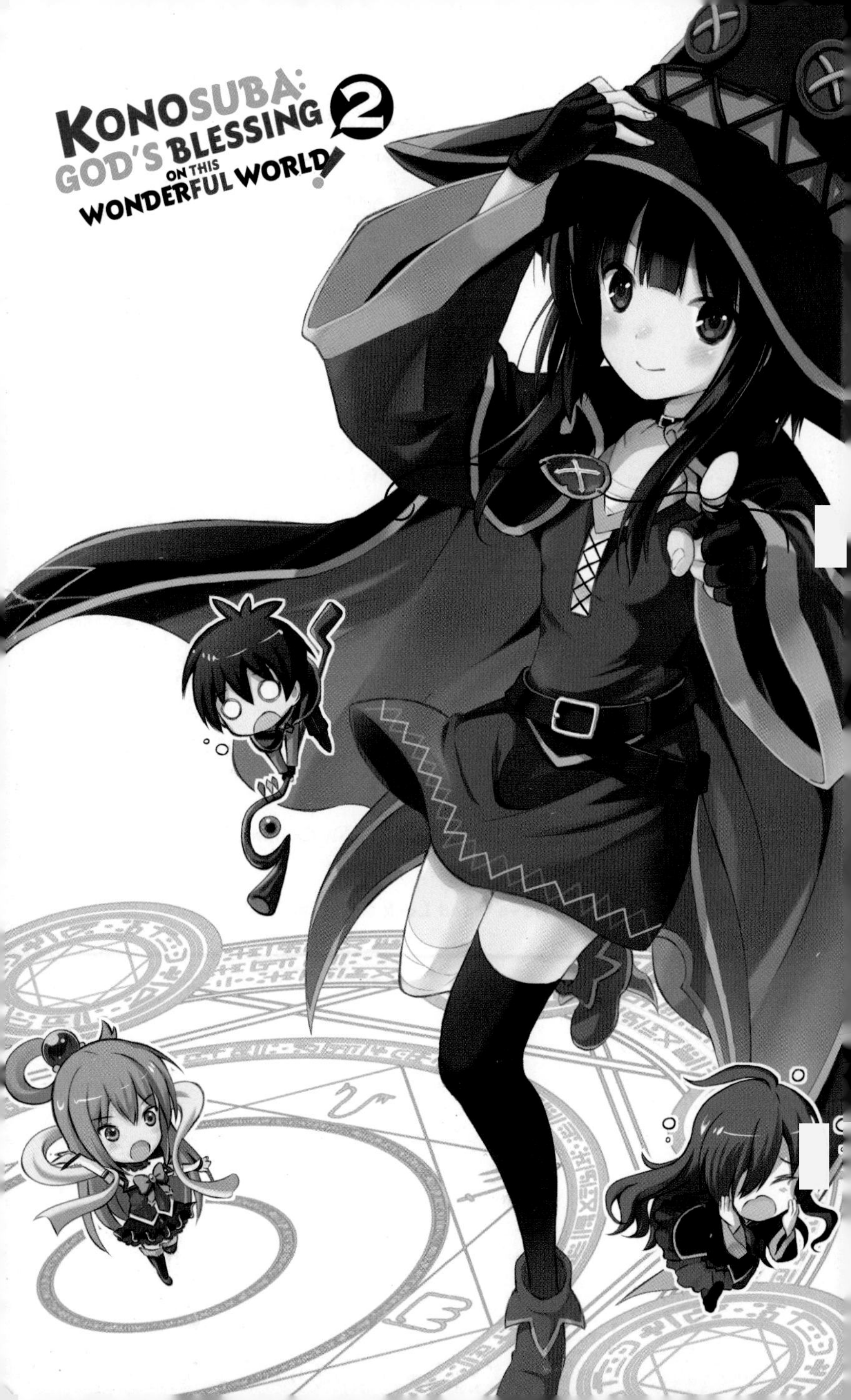
KONOSUBA:
GOD'S BLESSING
ON THIS
WONDERFUL WORLD!
2

2

GOD'S BLESSING ON THIS WONDERFUL WORLD! CONTENTS

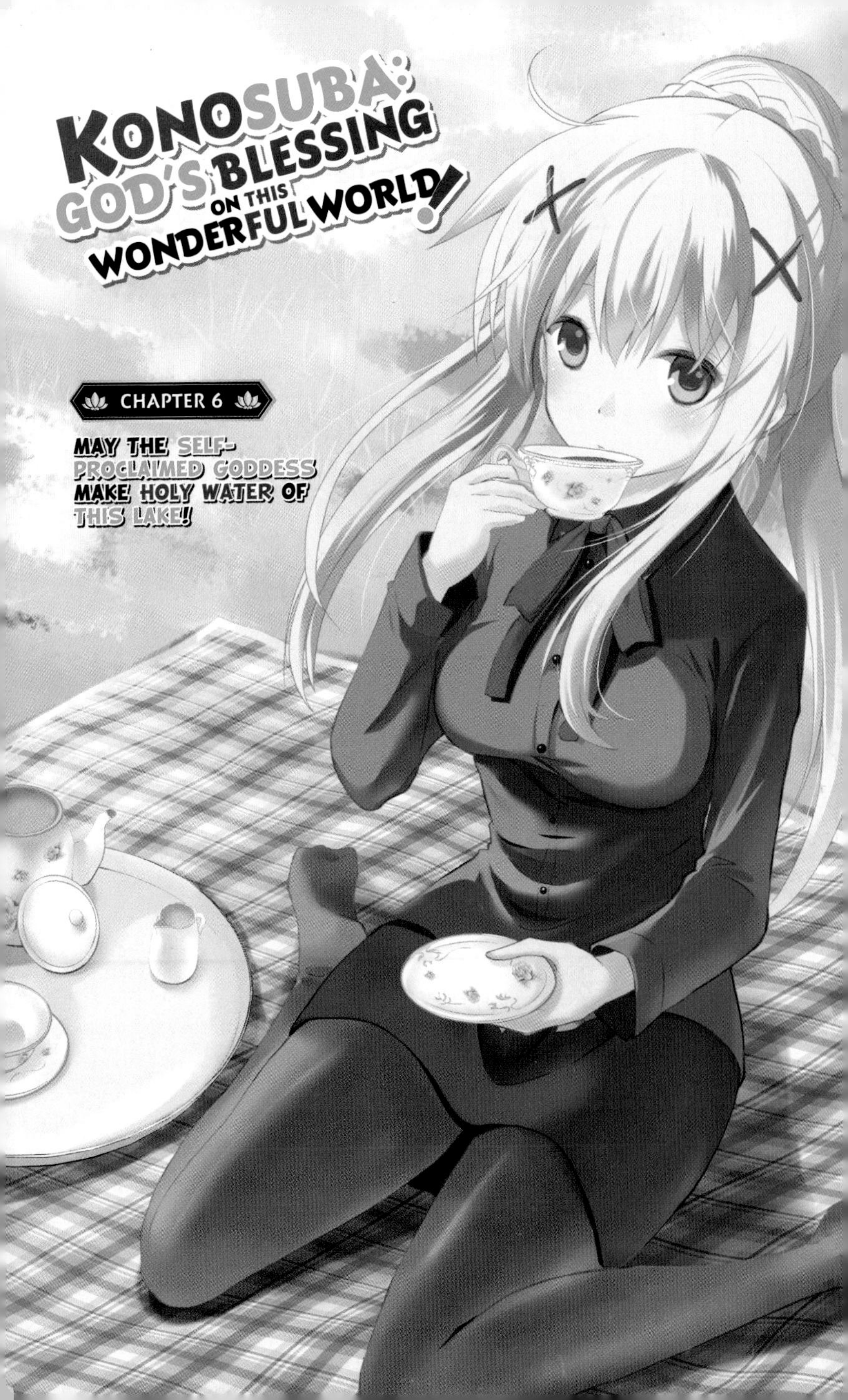
KONOSUBA: GOD'S BLESSING ON THIS WONDERFUL WORLD!
CHAPTER 6
MAY THE SELF-PROCLAIMED GODDESS MAKE HOLY WATER OF THIS LAKE!

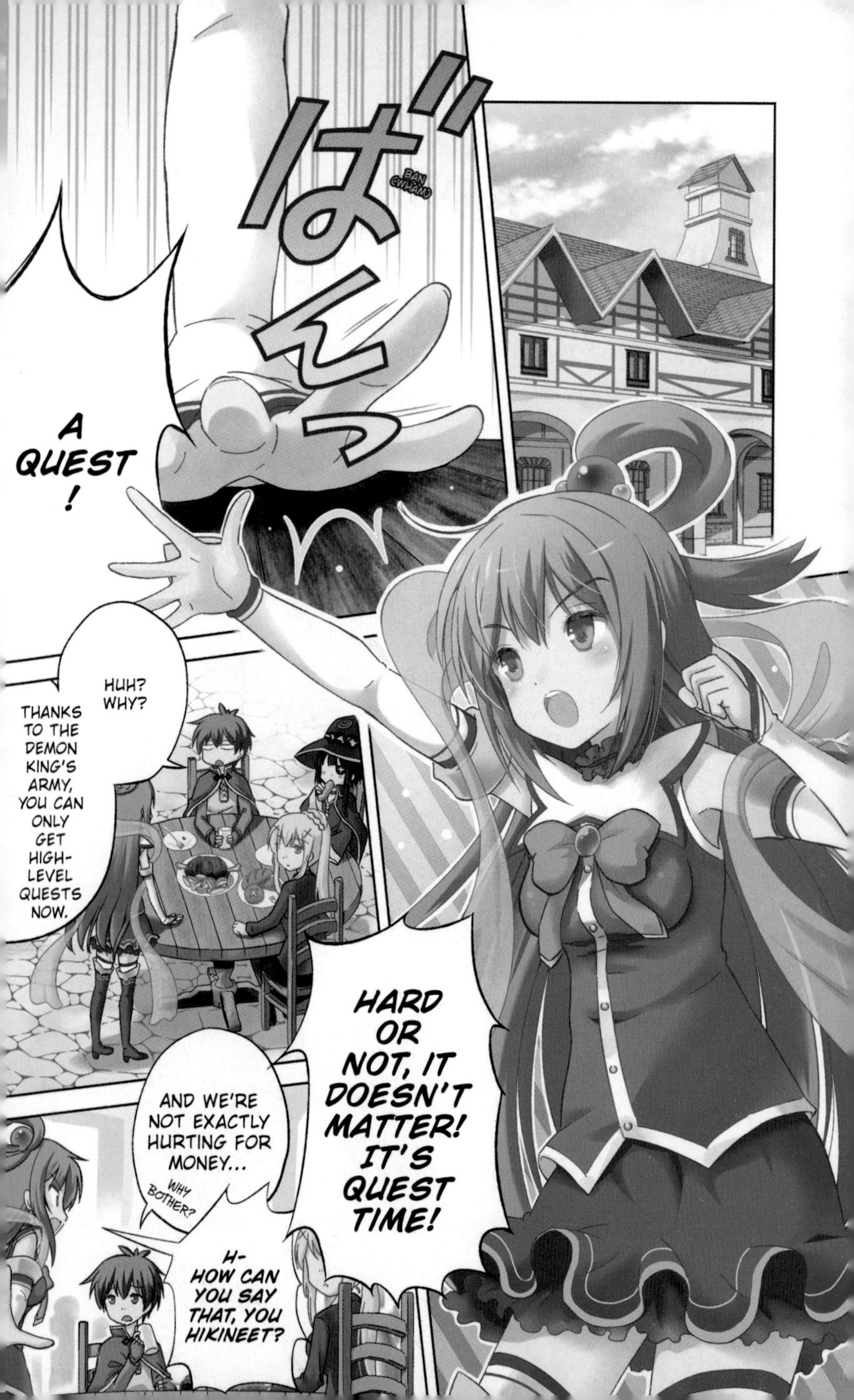
ばんっ
BAN (WHAM)
A QUEST!
HUH? WHY?
THANKS TO THE DEMON KING'S ARMY, YOU CAN ONLY GET HIGH-LEVEL QUESTS NOW.
AND WE'RE NOT EXACTLY HURTING FOR MONEY...
WHY BOTHER?
H-HOW CAN YOU SAY THAT, YOU HIKINEET?
HARD OR NOT, IT DOESN'T MATTER! IT'S QUEST TIME!

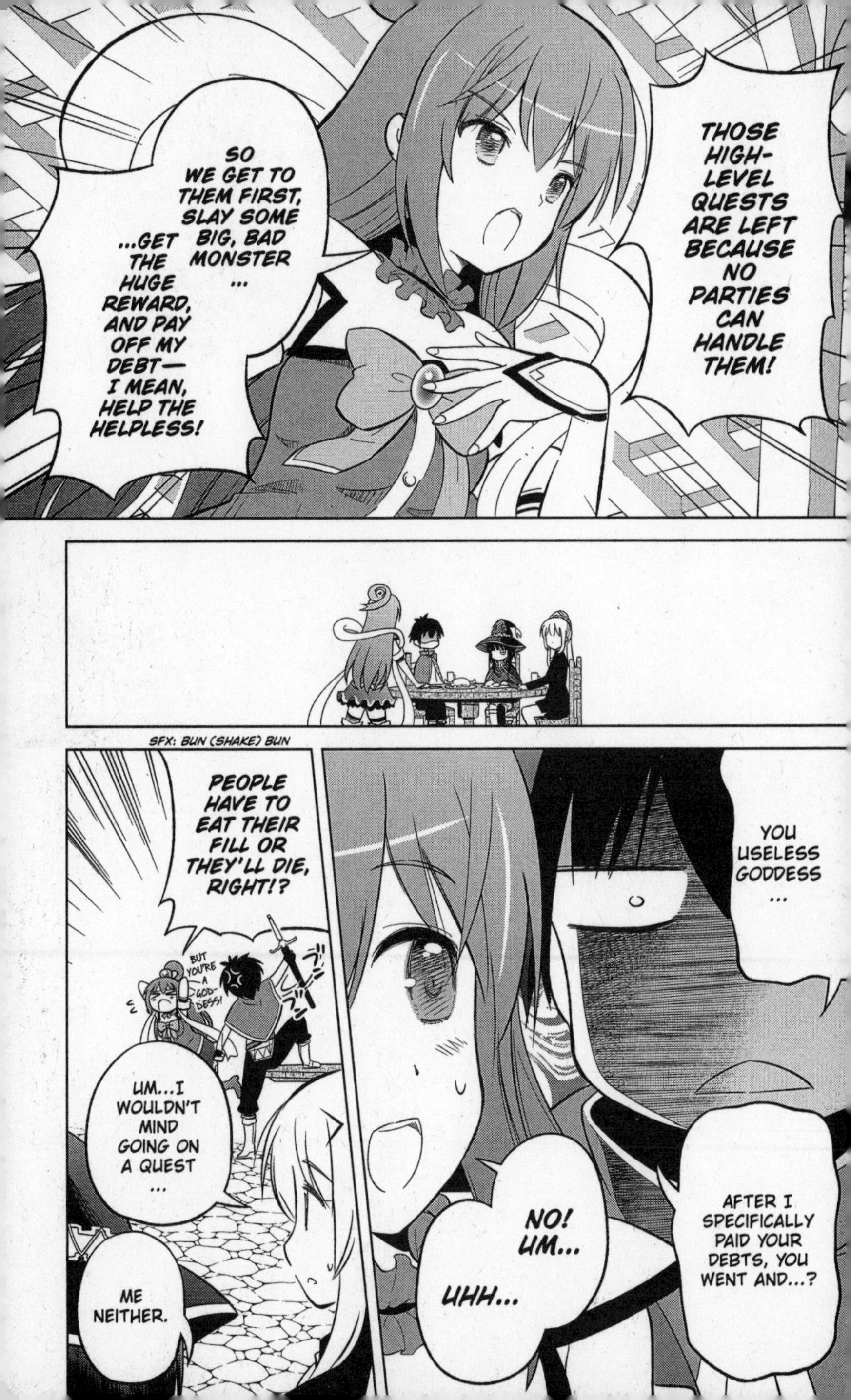
THOSE HIGH-LEVEL QUESTS ARE LEFT BECAUSE NO PARTIES CAN HANDLE THEM!
SO WE GET TO THEM FIRST, SLAY SOME BIG, BAD MONSTER ...
...GET THE HUGE REWARD, AND PAY OFF MY DEBT— I MEAN, HELP THE HELPLESS!
SFX: BUN (SHAKE) BUN
YOU USELESS GODDESS ...
AFTER I SPECIFICALLY PAID YOUR DEBTS, YOU WENT AND...?
NO! UM...
UHH...
PEOPLE HAVE TO EAT THEIR FILL OR THEY'LL DIE, RIGHT!?
BUT YOU'RE A GOD-DESS!
UM...I WOULDN'T MIND GOING ON A QUEST ...
ME NEITHER.

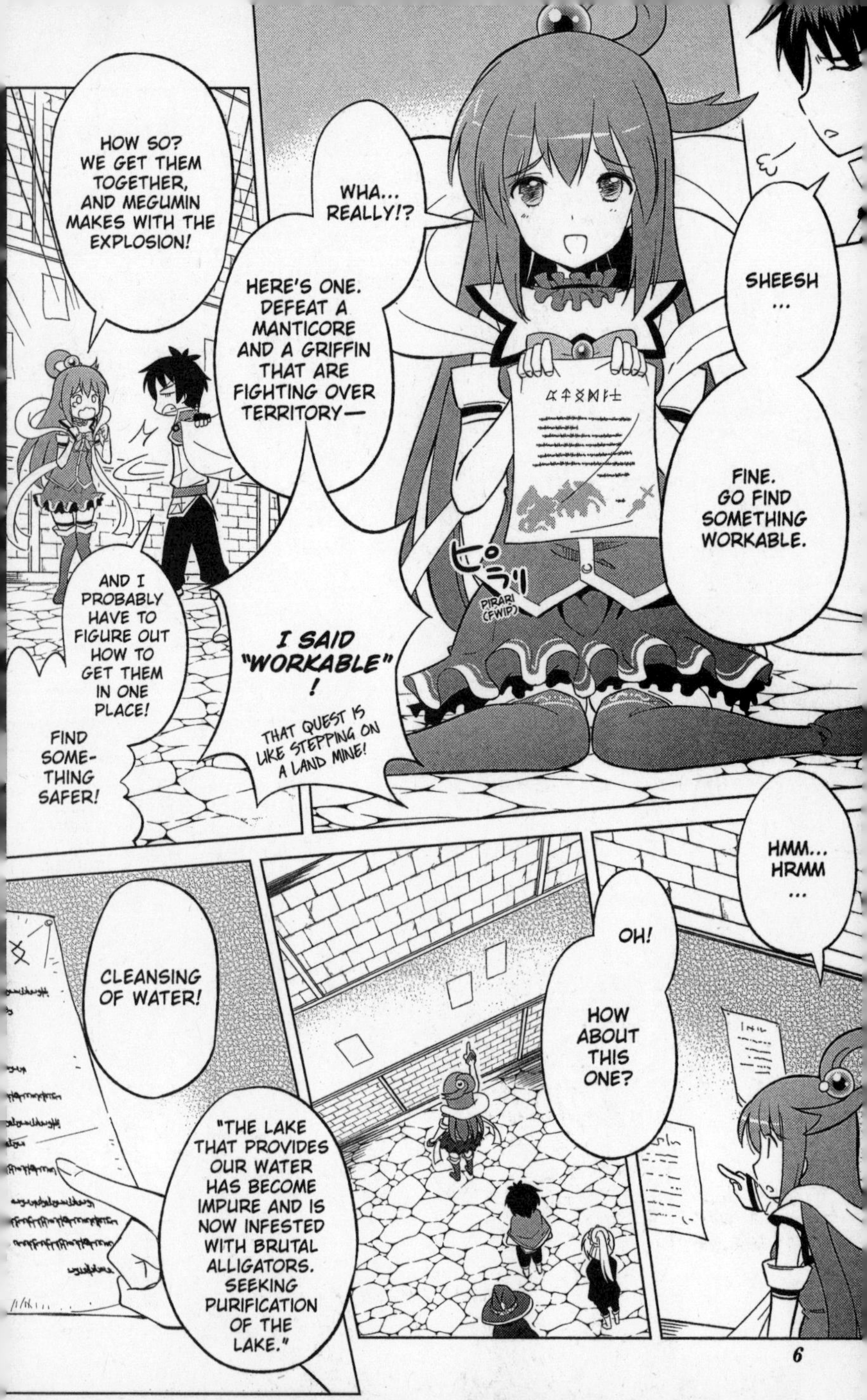
SHEESH ...
FINE. GO FIND SOMETHING WORKABLE.
WHA... REALLY!?
HERE'S ONE. DEFEAT A MANTICORE AND A GRIFFIN THAT ARE FIGHTING OVER TERRITORY—
ピラリ
PIRARI (FWIP)
I SAID "WORKABLE" !
THAT QUEST IS LIKE STEPPING ON A LAND MINE!
HOW SO? WE GET THEM TOGETHER, AND MEGUMIN MAKES WITH THE EXPLOSION!
AND I PROBABLY HAVE TO FIGURE OUT HOW TO GET THEM IN ONE PLACE!
FIND SOME- THING SAFER!
HMM... HRMM ...
OH!
HOW ABOUT THIS ONE?
CLEANSING OF WATER!
"THE LAKE THAT PROVIDES OUR WATER HAS BECOME IMPURE AND IS NOW INFESTED WITH BRUTAL ALLIGATORS. SEEKING PURIFICATION OF THE LAKE."

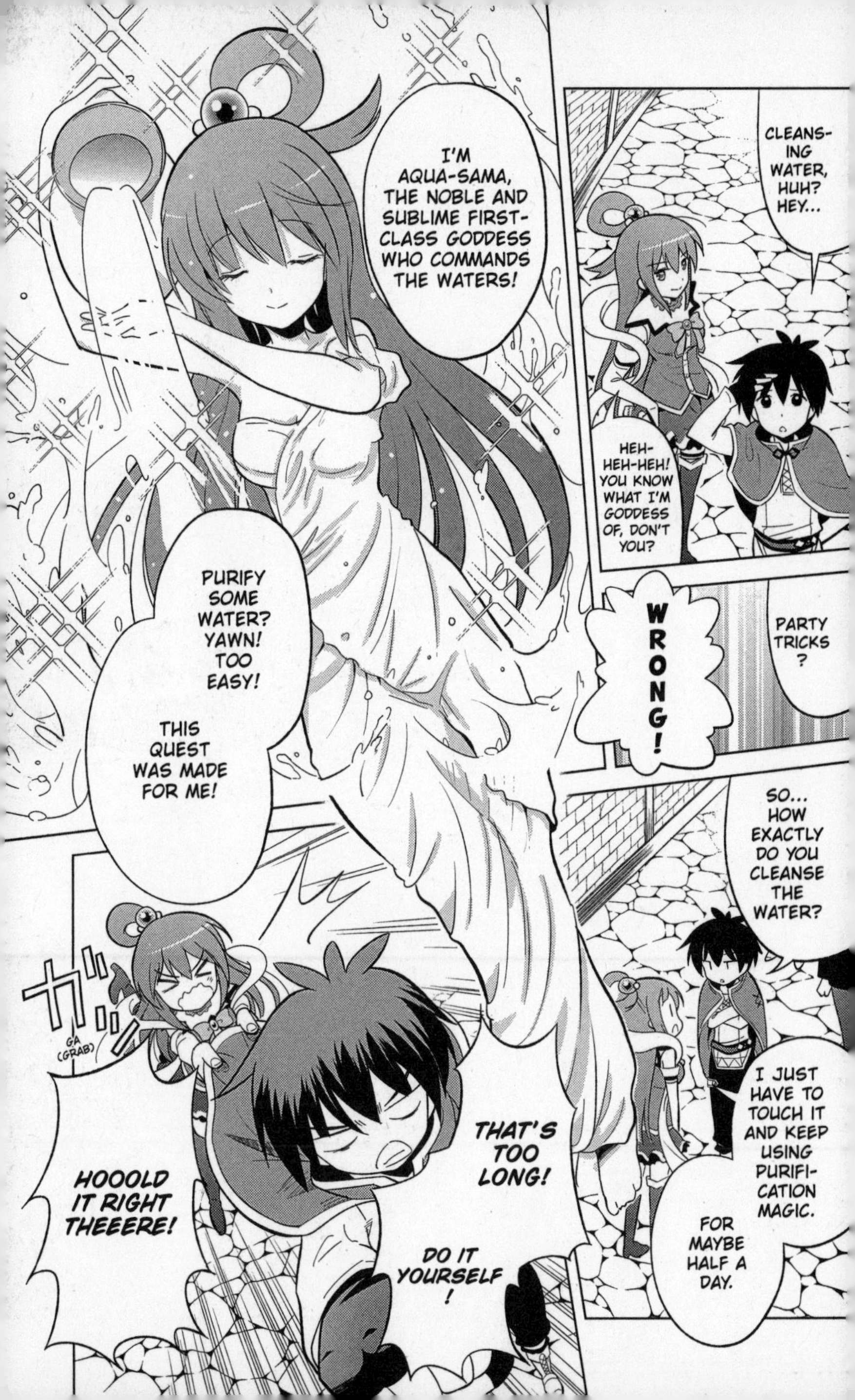
CLEANS-ING WATER, HUH? HEY...
HEH-HEH-HEH! YOU KNOW WHAT I'M GODDESS OF, DON'T YOU?
PARTY TRICKS?
WRONG!
I'M AQUA-SAMA, THE NOBLE AND SUBLIME FIRST-CLASS GODDESS WHO COMMANDS THE WATERS!
PURIFY SOME WATER? YAWN! TOO EASY!
THIS QUEST WAS MADE FOR ME!
SO... HOW EXACTLY DO YOU CLEANSE THE WATER?
I JUST HAVE TO TOUCH IT AND KEEP USING PURIFI-CATION MAGIC.
FOR MAYBE HALF A DAY.
THAT'S TOO LONG!
DO IT YOURSELF!
GA (GRAB)
HOOOLD IT RIGHT THEEERE!

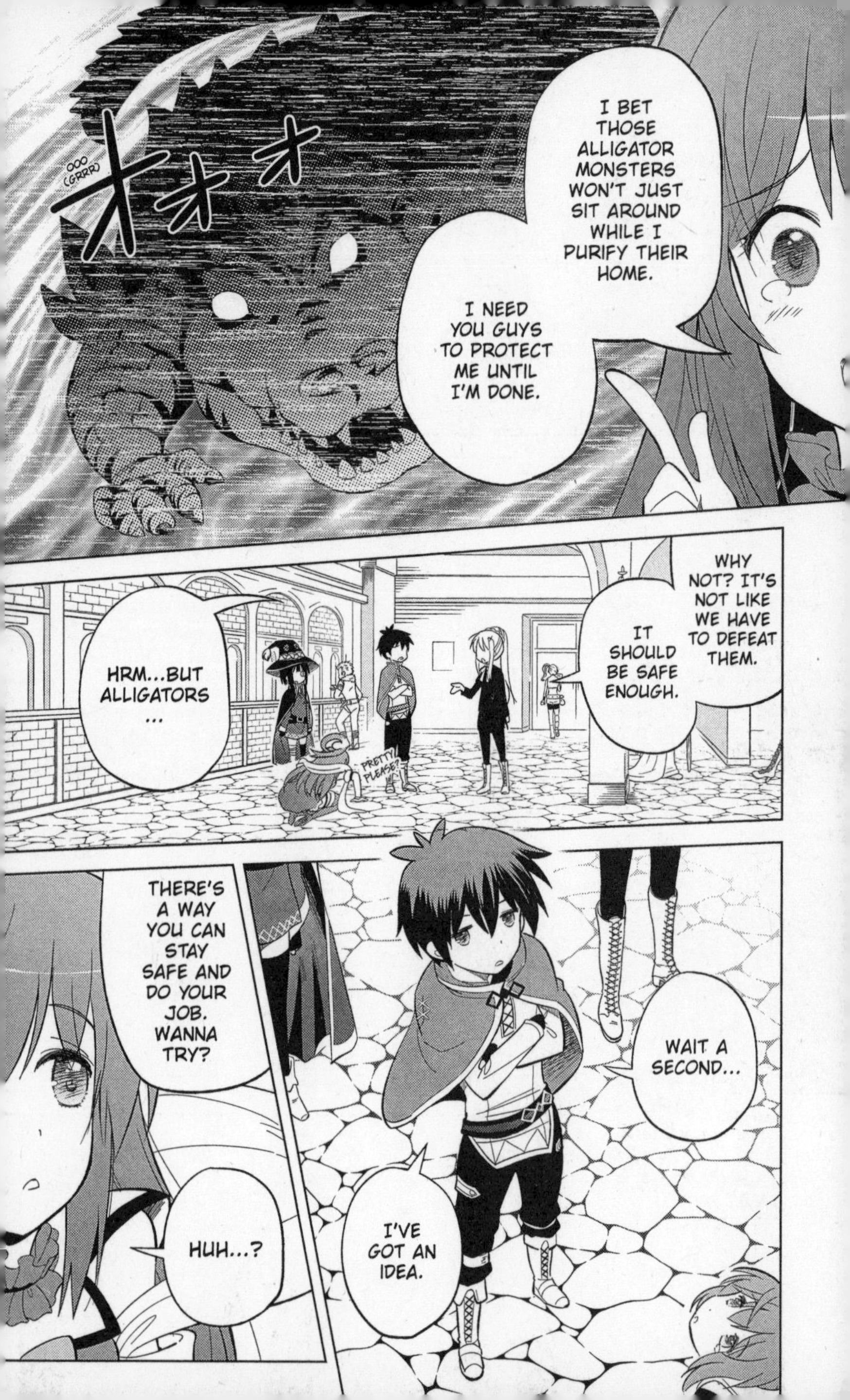
I BET THOSE ALLIGATOR MONSTERS WON'T JUST SIT AROUND WHILE I PURIFY THEIR HOME.
I NEED YOU GUYS TO PROTECT ME UNTIL I'M DONE.
OOO (GRRR)
WHY NOT? IT'S NOT LIKE WE HAVE TO DEFEAT THEM.
IT SHOULD BE SAFE ENOUGH.
PRETTY PLEASE?
HRM...BUT ALLIGATORS ...
WAIT A SECOND...
THERE'S A WAY YOU CAN STAY SAFE AND DO YOUR JOB. WANNA TRY?
I'VE GOT AN IDEA.
HUH...?

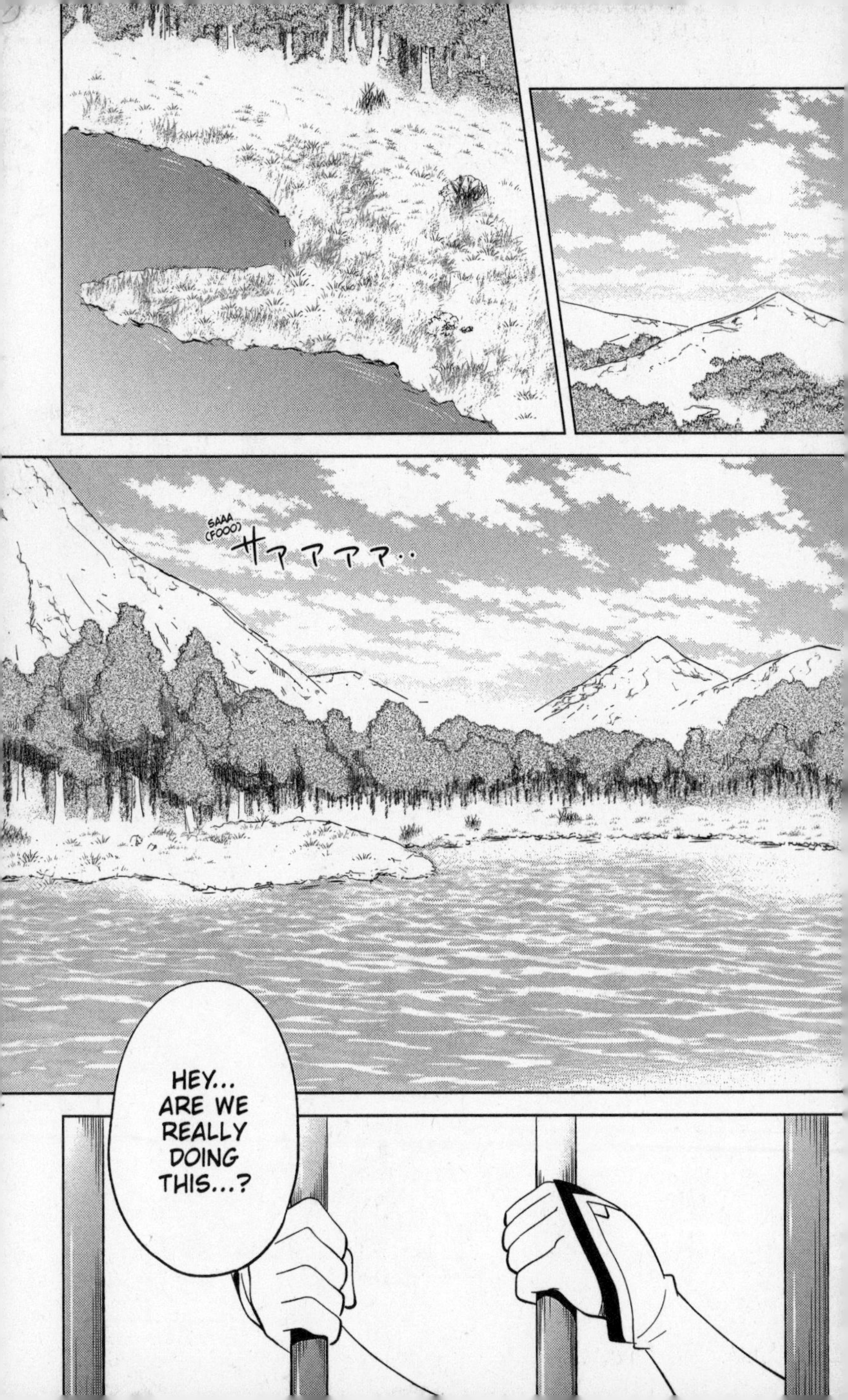
SAAA (FOOO)
サアアアア・・
HEY... ARE WE REALLY DOING THIS...?

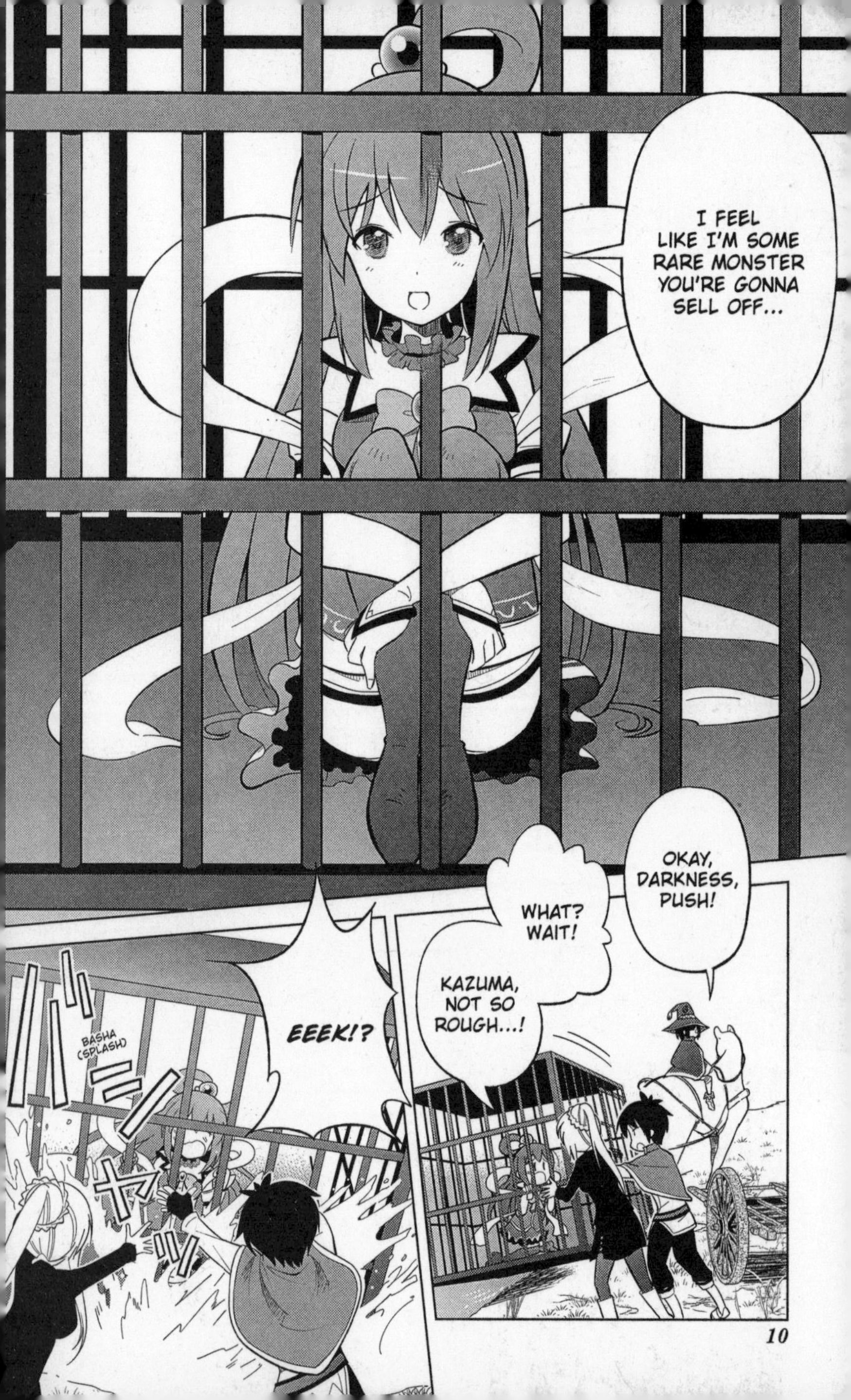
I FEEL LIKE I'M SOME RARE MONSTER YOU'RE GONNA SELL OFF...
OKAY, DARKNESS, PUSH!
WHAT? WAIT!
KAZUMA, NOT SO ROUGH...!
EEEK!?
BASHA (SPLASH)

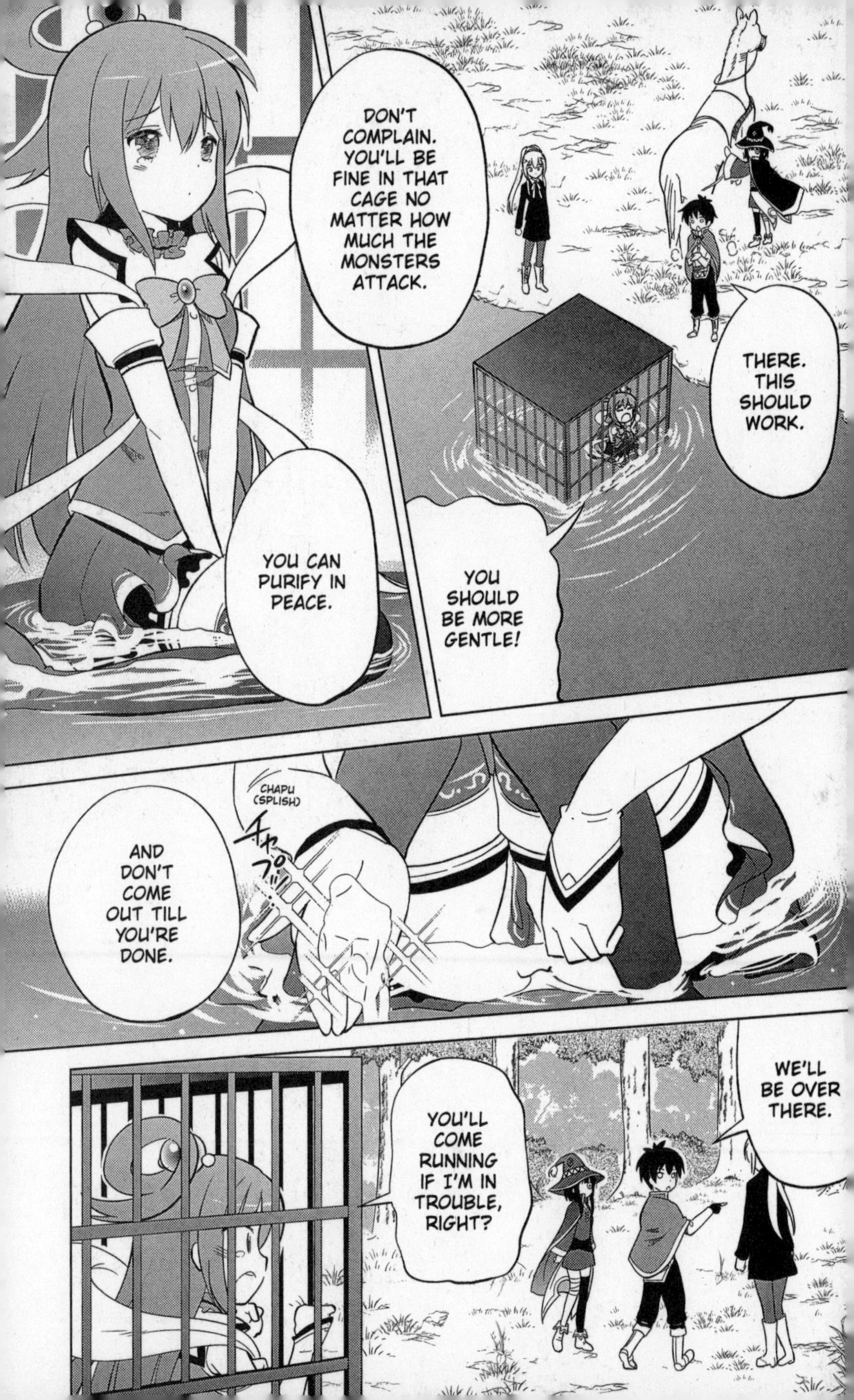
THERE. THIS SHOULD WORK.
YOU SHOULD BE MORE GENTLE!
DON'T COMPLAIN. YOU'LL BE FINE IN THAT CAGE NO MATTER HOW MUCH THE MONSTERS ATTACK.
YOU CAN PURIFY IN PEACE.
CHAPU (SPLISH)
AND DON'T COME OUT TILL YOU'RE DONE.
WE'LL BE OVER THERE.
YOU'LL COME RUNNING IF I'M IN TROUBLE, RIGHT?

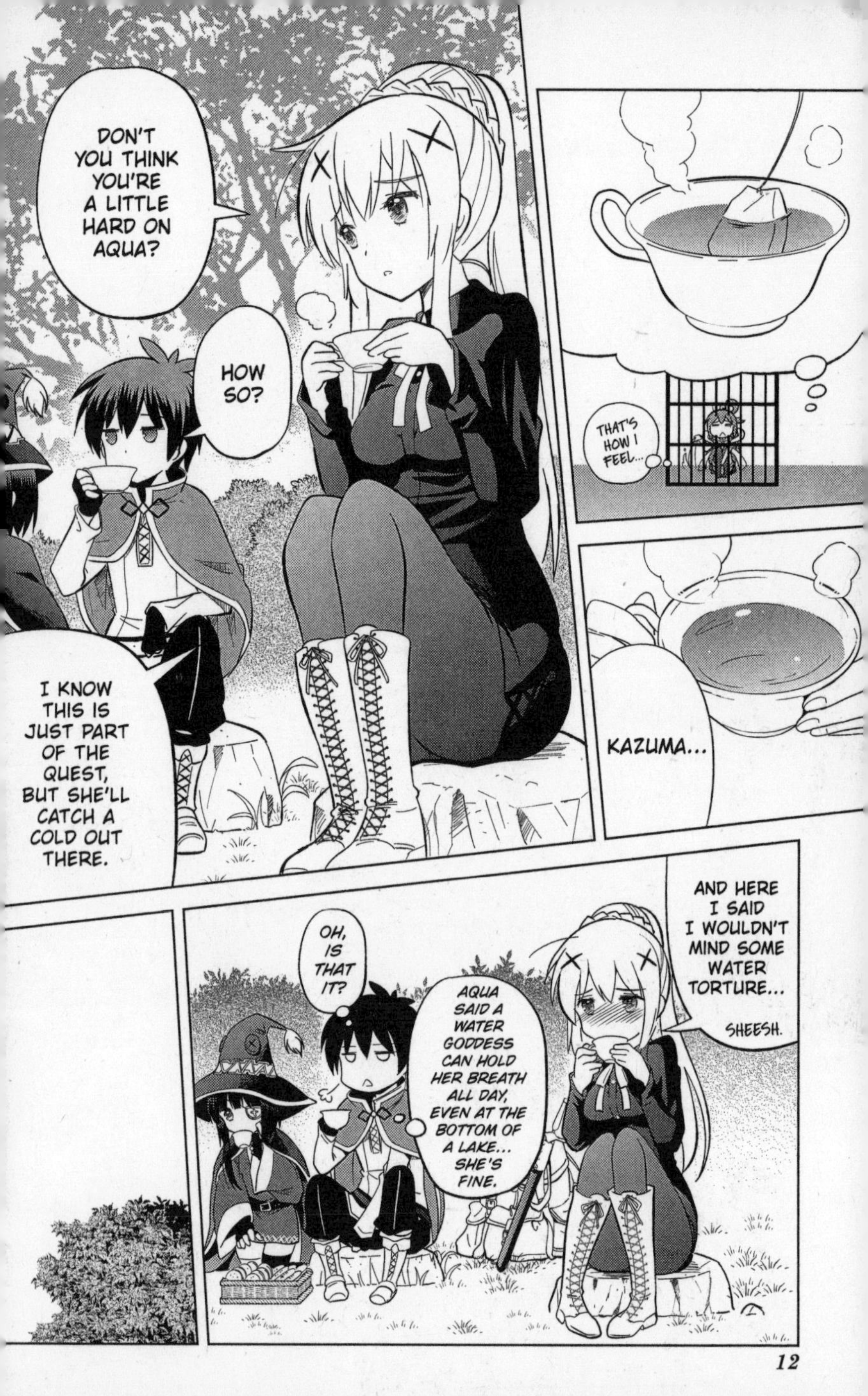
THAT'S HOW I FEEL...
KAZUMA...
DON'T YOU THINK YOU'RE A LITTLE HARD ON AQUA?
HOW SO?
I KNOW THIS IS JUST PART OF THE QUEST, BUT SHE'LL CATCH A COLD OUT THERE.
AND HERE I SAID I WOULDN'T MIND SOME WATER TORTURE...
SHEESH.
OH, IS THAT IT?
AQUA SAID A WATER GODDESS CAN HOLD HER BREATH ALL DAY, EVEN AT THE BOTTOM OF A LAKE... SHE'S FINE.

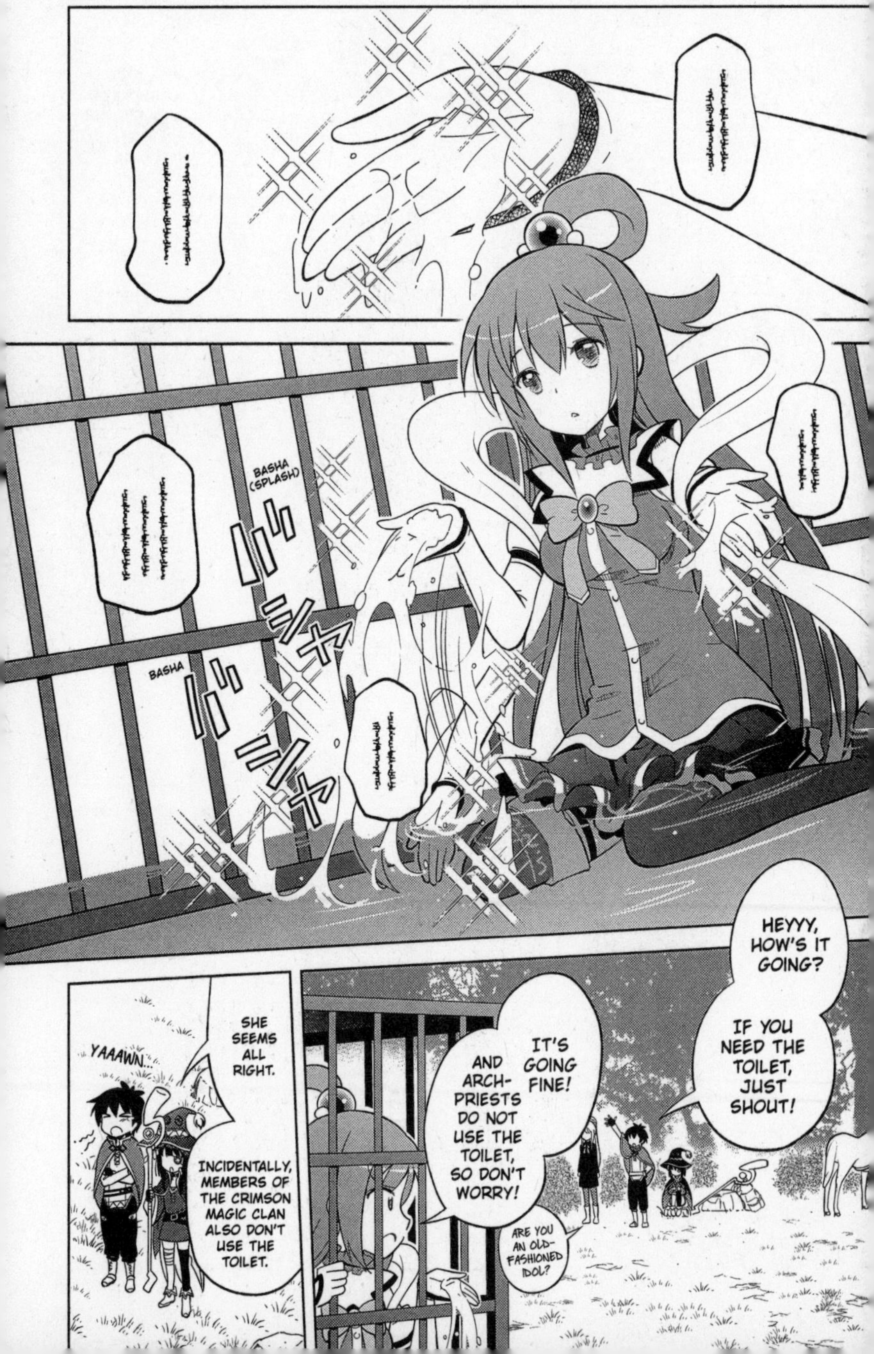
BASHA (SPLASH)
BASHA
HEYYY, HOW'S IT GOING?
IF YOU NEED THE TOILET, JUST SHOUT!
IT'S GOING FINE!
AND ARCH-PRIESTS DO NOT USE THE TOILET, SO DON'T WORRY!
ARE YOU AN OLD-FASHIONED IDOL?
SHE SEEMS ALL RIGHT.
YAAAWN...
INCIDENTALLY, MEMBERS OF THE CRIMSON MAGIC CLAN ALSO DON'T USE THE TOILET.

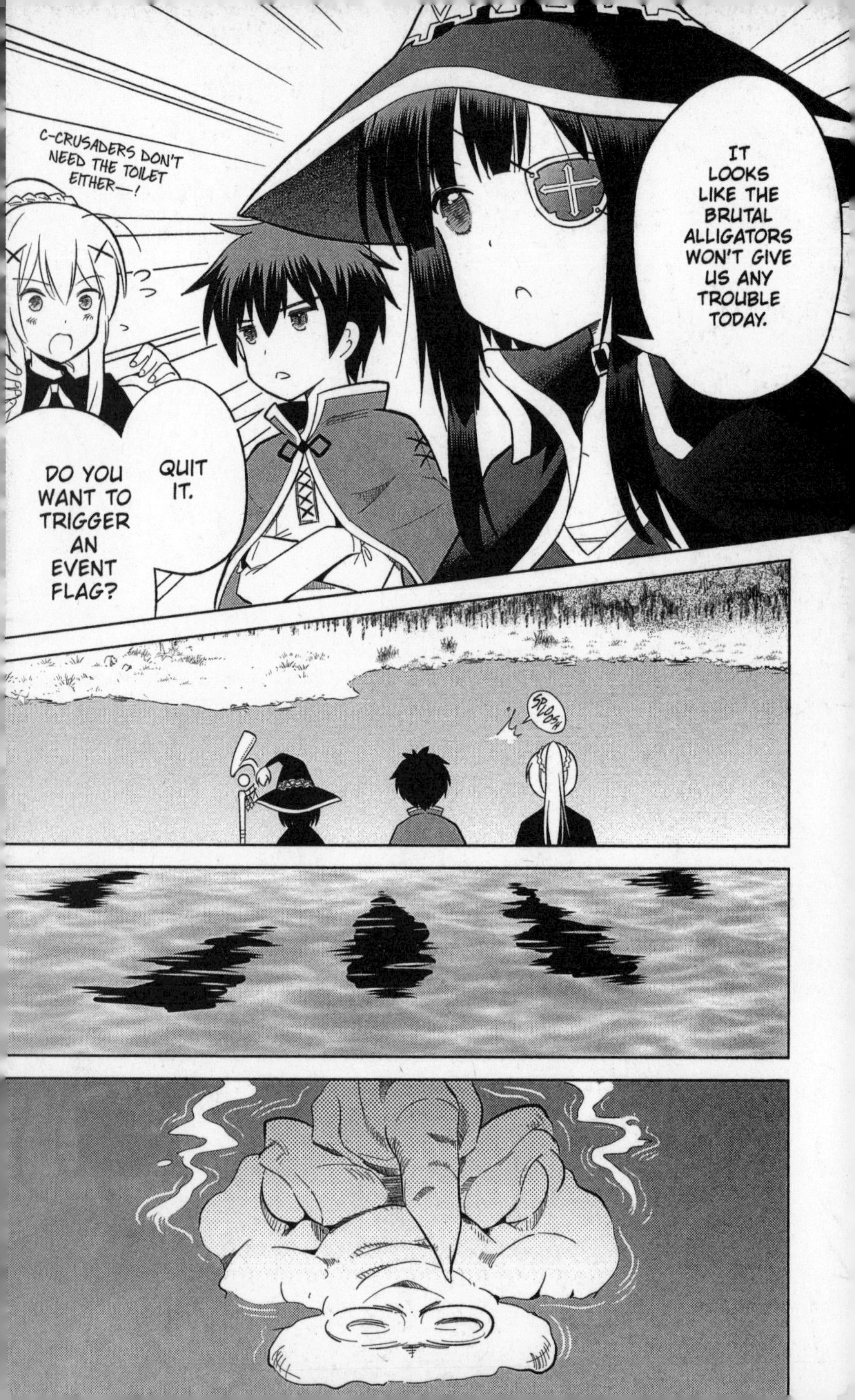
IT LOOKS LIKE THE BRUTAL ALLIGATORS WON'T GIVE US ANY TROUBLE TODAY.
C-CRUSADERS DON'T NEED THE TOILET EITHER—!
QUIT IT.
DO YOU WANT TO TRIGGER AN EVENT FLAG?
SPLOOSH

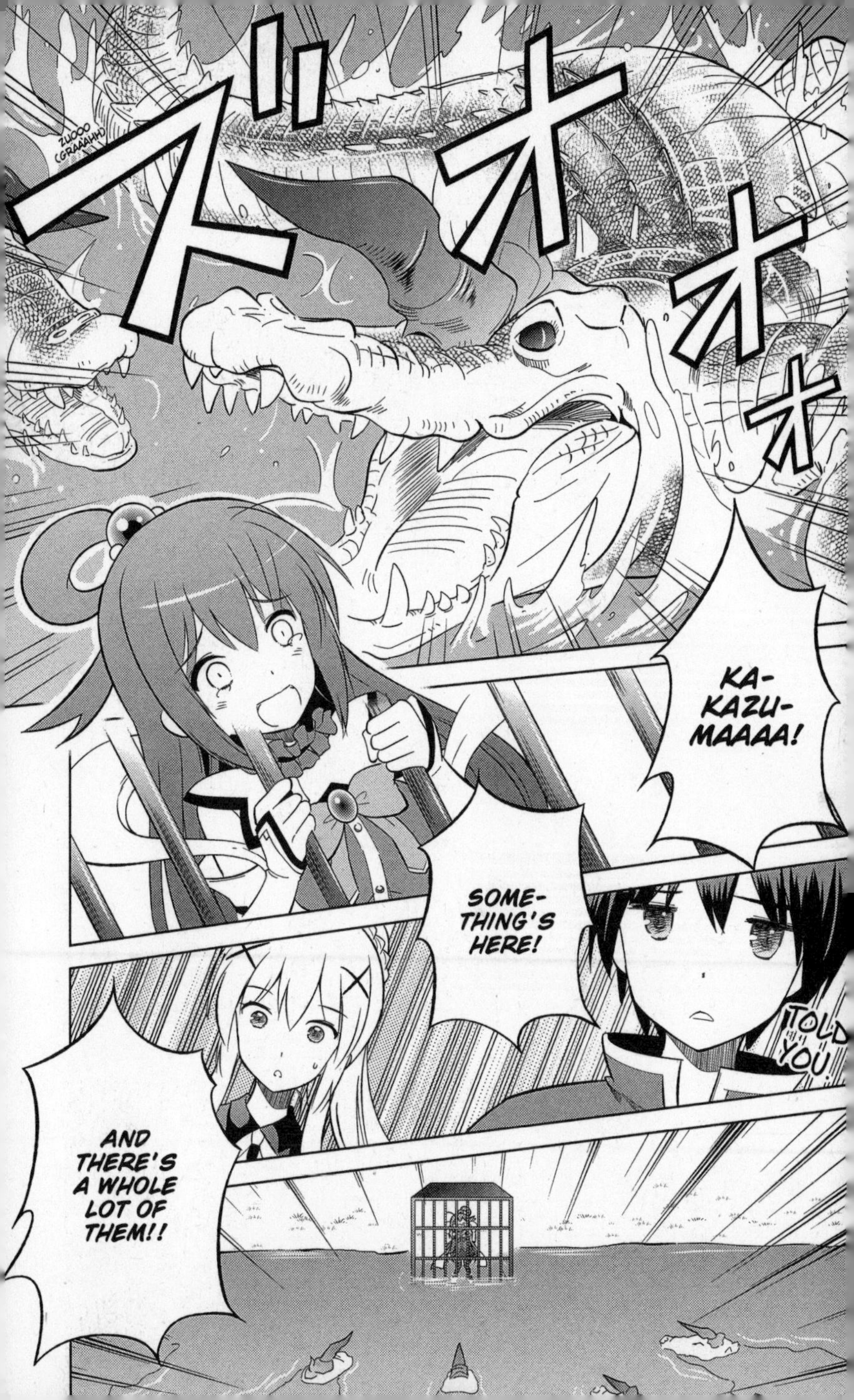
ズオオォ
ZUOOO (GRAAAHH)
KA-KAZU-MAAAA!
SOME-THING'S HERE!
TOLD YOU.
AND THERE'S A WHOLE LOT OF THEM!!

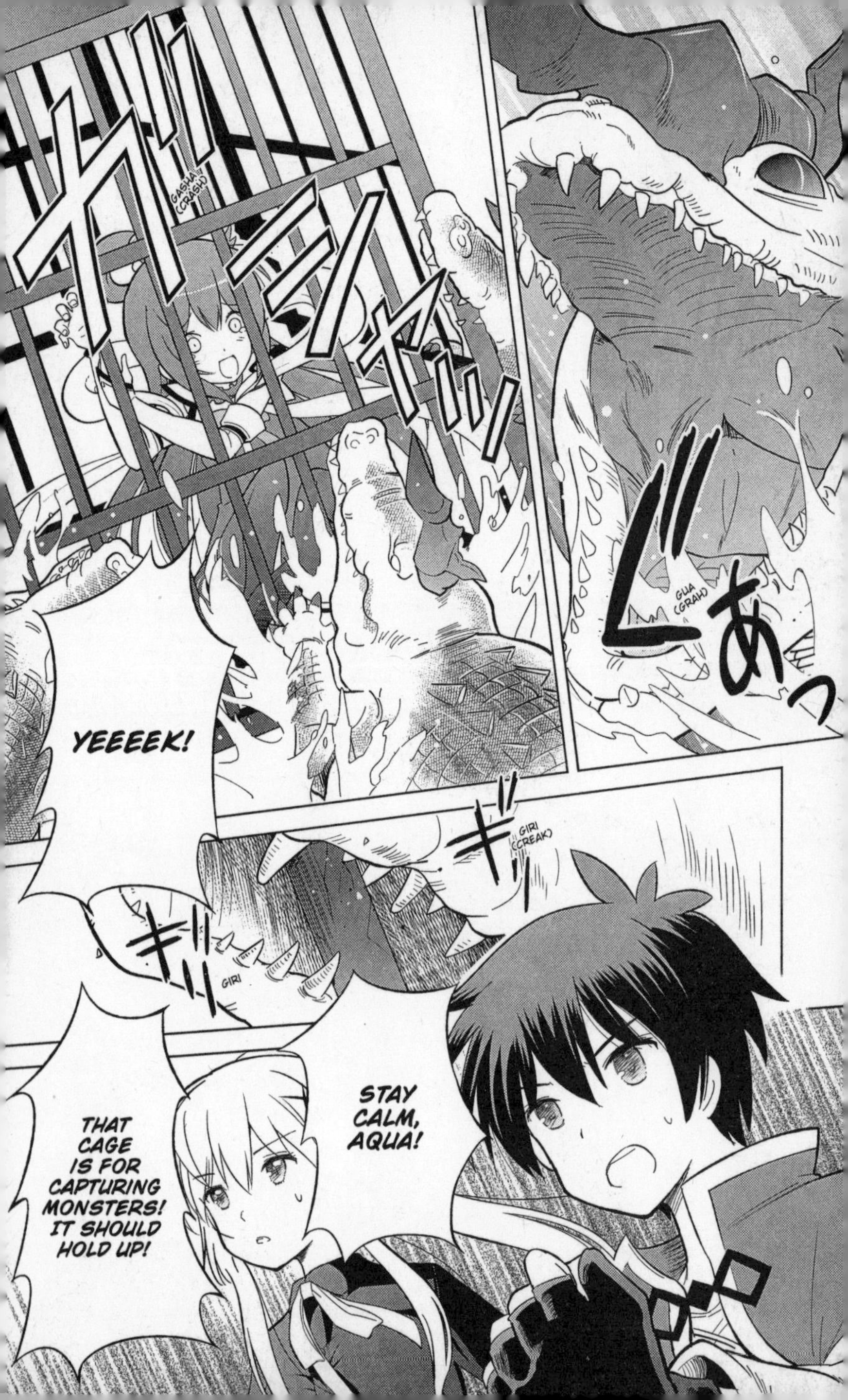

ぐあっ
GUA (GRAH)
GASHA (CRASH)
YEEEEK!
GIRI (CREAK)
GIRI
STAY CALM, AQUA!
THAT CAGE IS FOR CAPTURING MONSTERS! IT SHOULD HOLD UP!

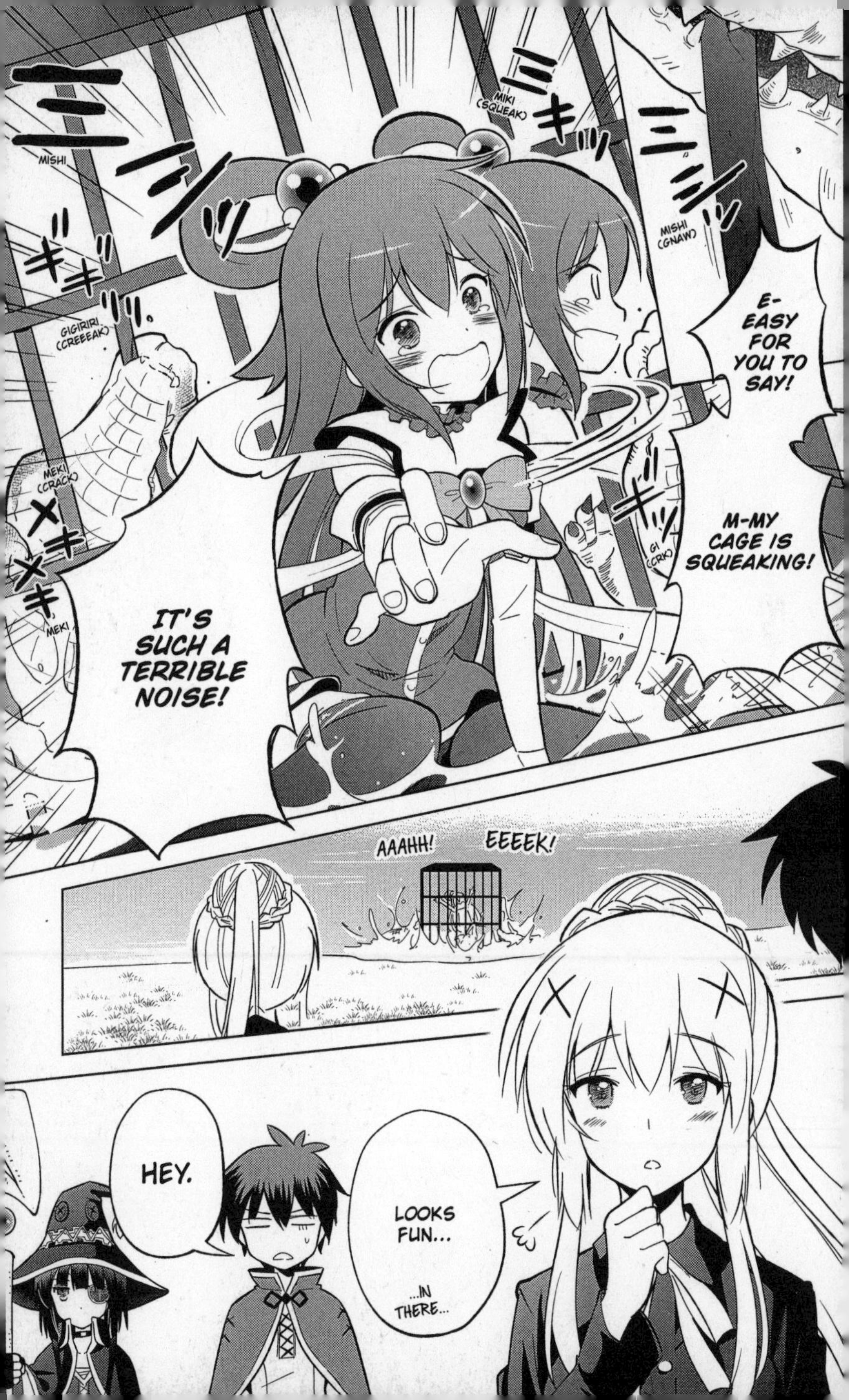
MISHI (GNAW)
MIKI (SQUEAK)
E-EASY FOR YOU TO SAY!
M-MY CAGE IS SQUEAKING!
GI (CRK)
MISHI
GIGIRIRI (CREEEAK)
MEKI (CRACK)
MEKI
IT'S SUCH A TERRIBLE NOISE!
EEEEK!
AAAHH!
LOOKS FUN...
...IN THERE...
HEY.

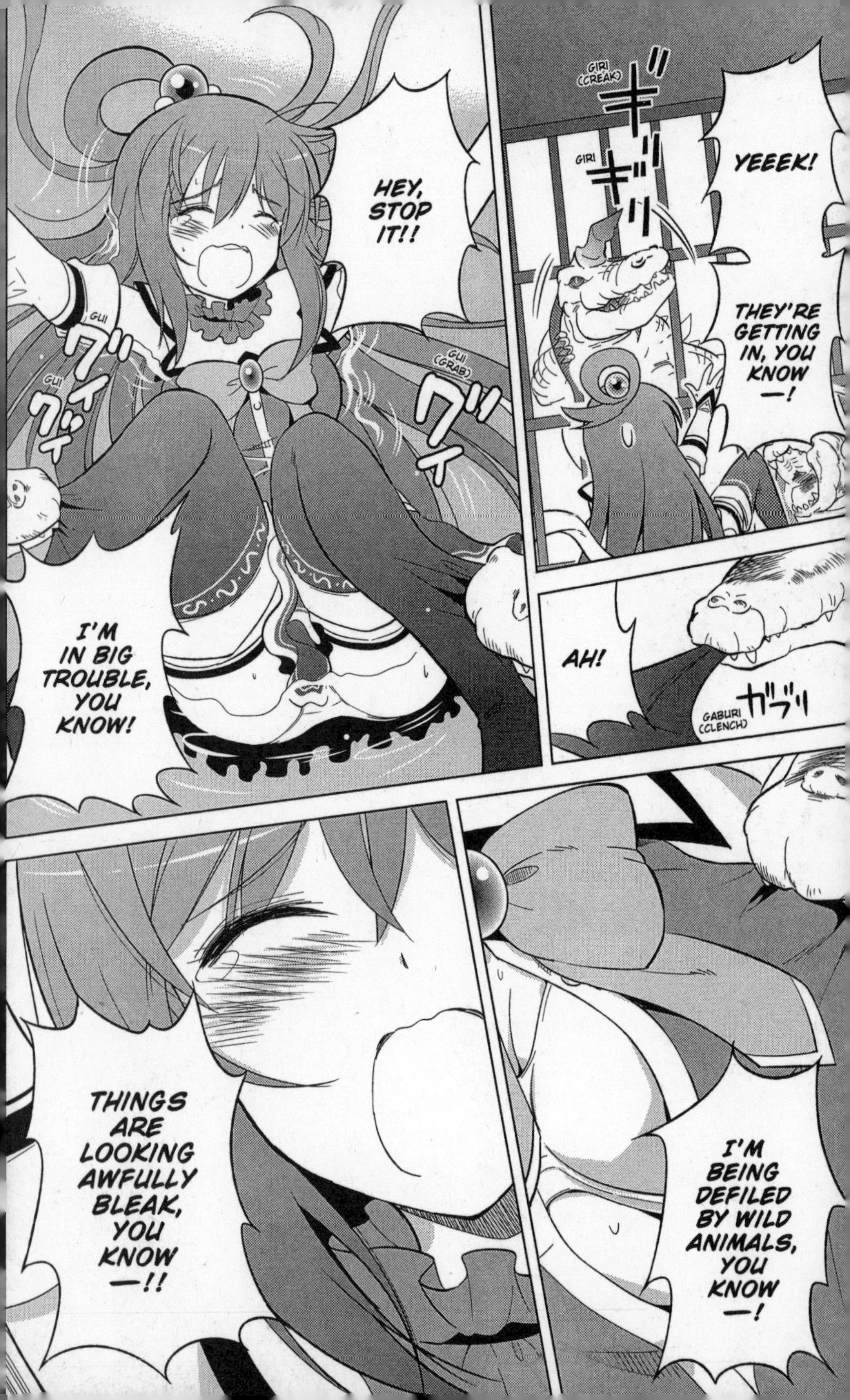
YEEEK!
GIRI (CREAK) ギ
GIRI ギリ
THEY'RE GETTING IN, YOU KNOW—!
AH!
GABURI (CLENCH) ガブリ
HEY, STOP IT!!
GUI (GRAB) グイ
GUI グイ
GUI グイ
I'M IN BIG TROUBLE, YOU KNOW!
I'M BEING DEFILED BY WILD ANIMALS, YOU KNOW—!
THINGS ARE LOOKING AWFULLY BLEAK, YOU KNOW—!!

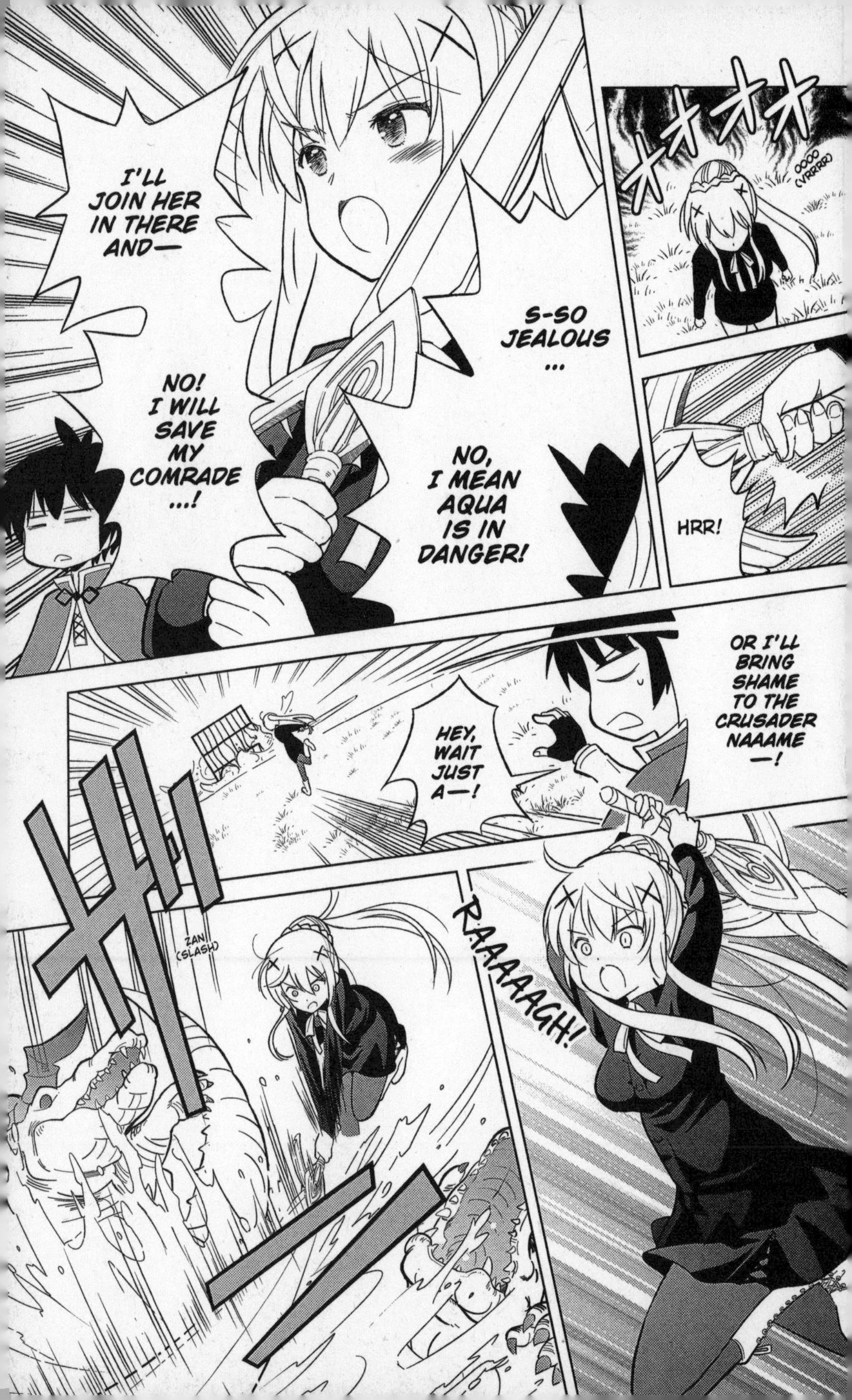
オオオオ
OOOO (VRRRR)
HRR!
S-SO JEALOUS ...
I'LL JOIN HER IN THERE AND—
NO, I MEAN AQUA IS IN DANGER!
NO! I WILL SAVE MY COMRADE ...!
OR I'LL BRING SHAME TO THE CRUSADER NAAAME—!
HEY, WAIT JUST A—!
RAAAAAGH!
ザン
ZAN (SLASH)

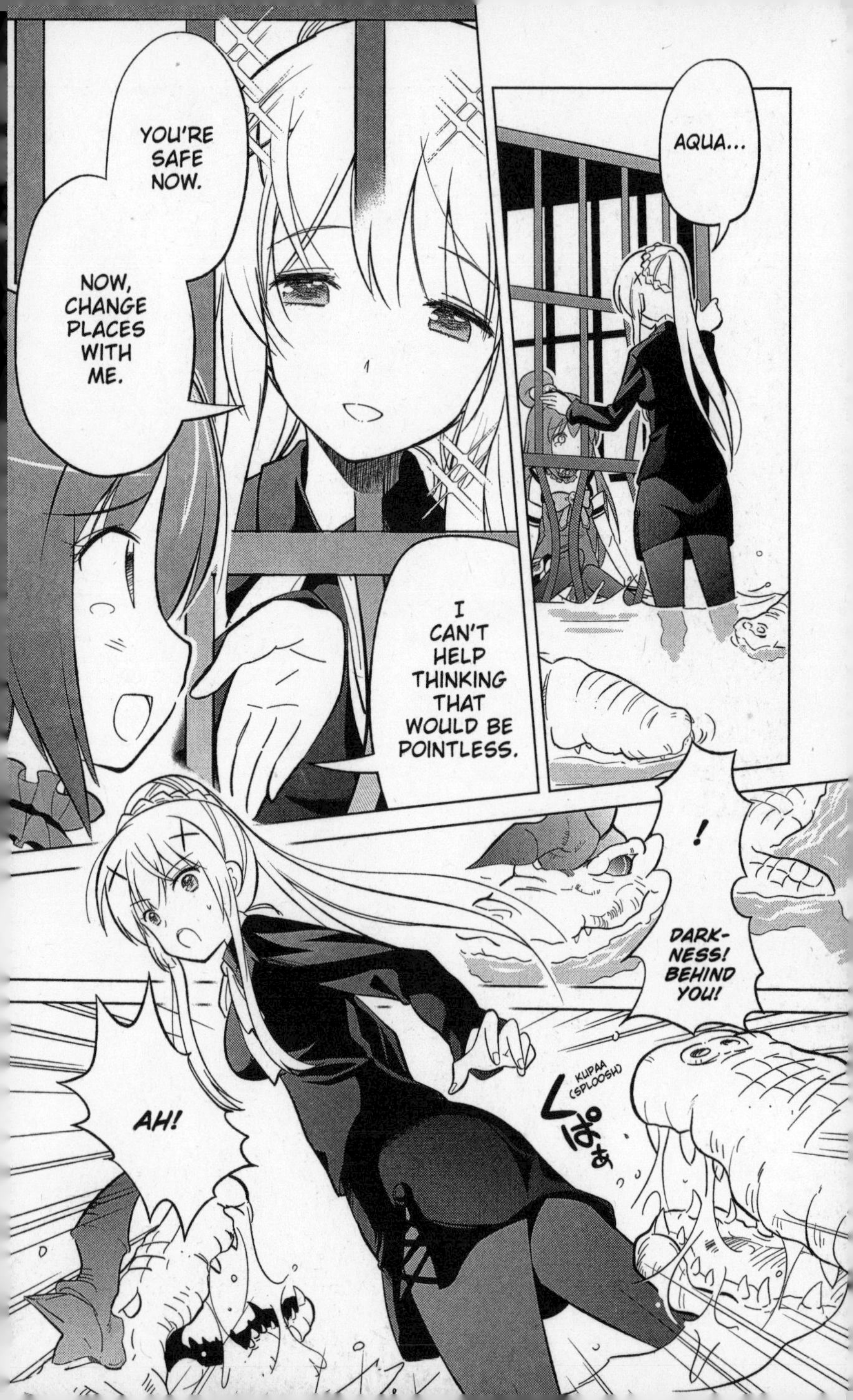
AQUA...
YOU'RE SAFE NOW.
NOW, CHANGE PLACES WITH ME.
I CAN'T HELP THINKING THAT WOULD BE POINTLESS.
!
DARKNESS! BEHIND YOU!
KUPAA (SPLOOSH)
AH!

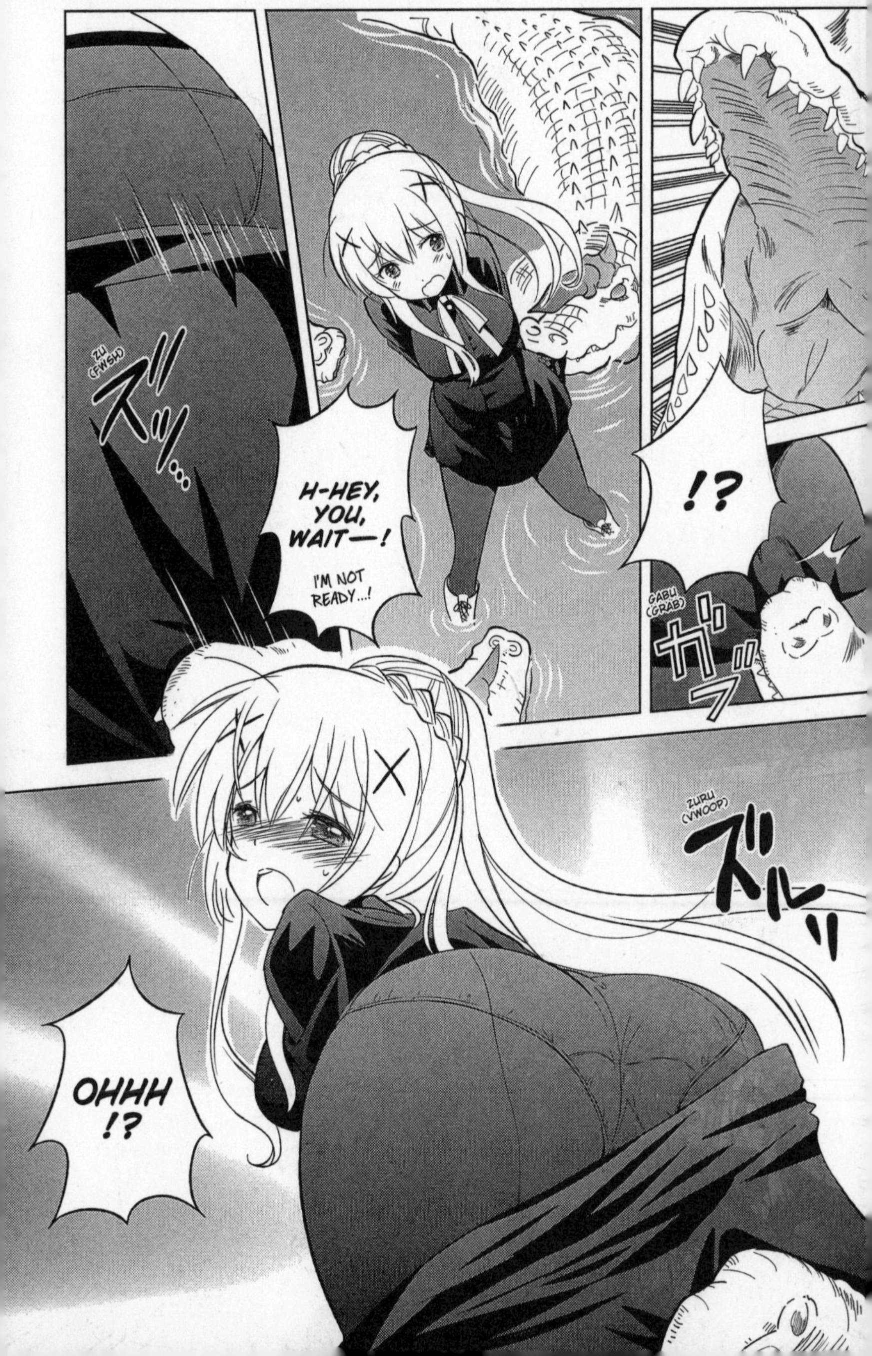
!?
GABU (GRAB)
H-HEY, YOU, WAIT—!
I'M NOT READY...!
ZU (FWSH)
ZURU (VWOOP)
OHHH !?

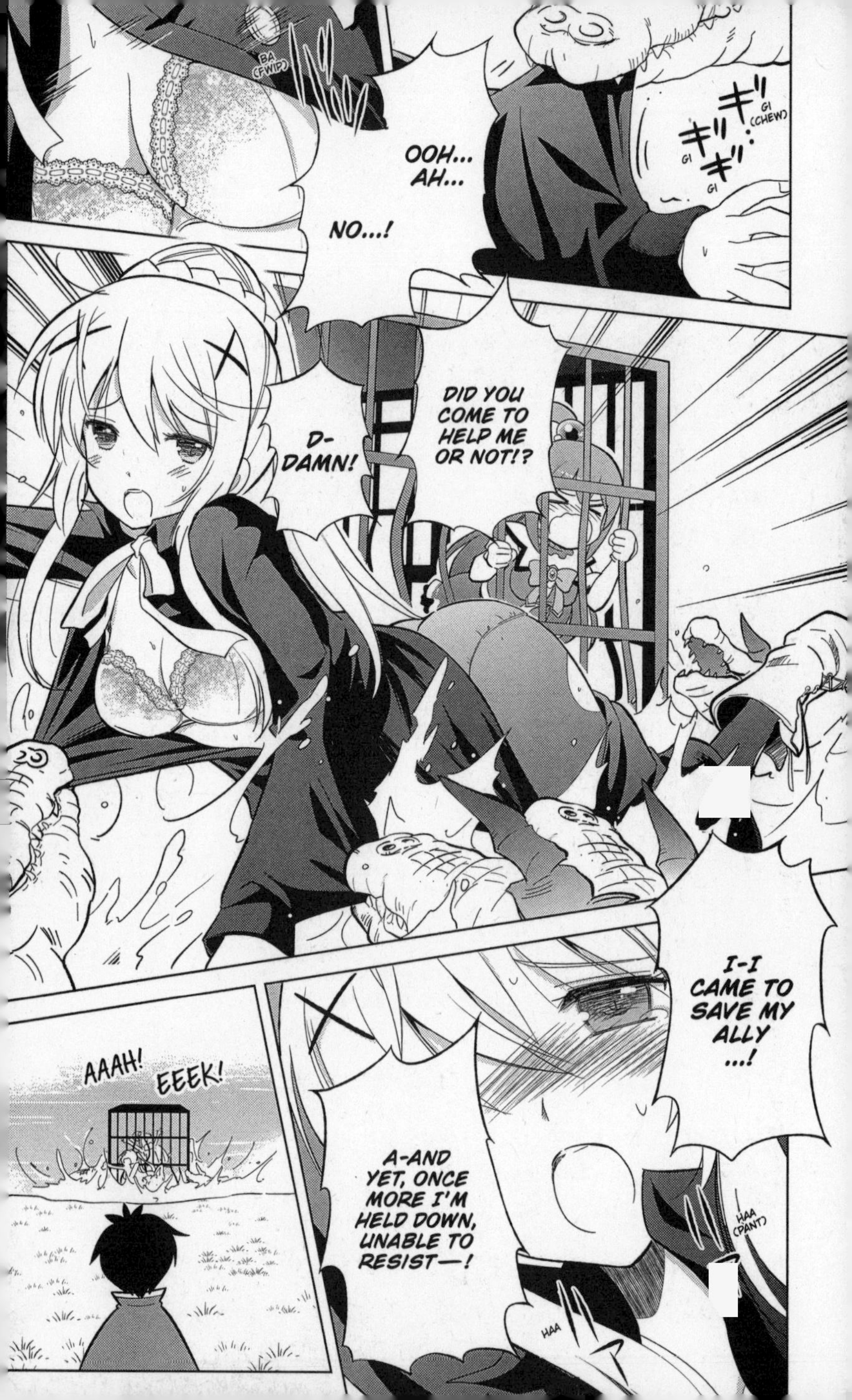

ギリギリ
GI GI
GI (CHEW)
OOH... AH...
NO...!
BA (FWIP)
DID YOU COME TO HELP ME OR NOT!?
D-DAMN!
I-I CAME TO SAVE MY ALLY ...!
A-AND YET, ONCE MORE I'M HELD DOWN, UNABLE TO RESIST—!
HAA (PANT)
HAA
AAAH!
EEEK!

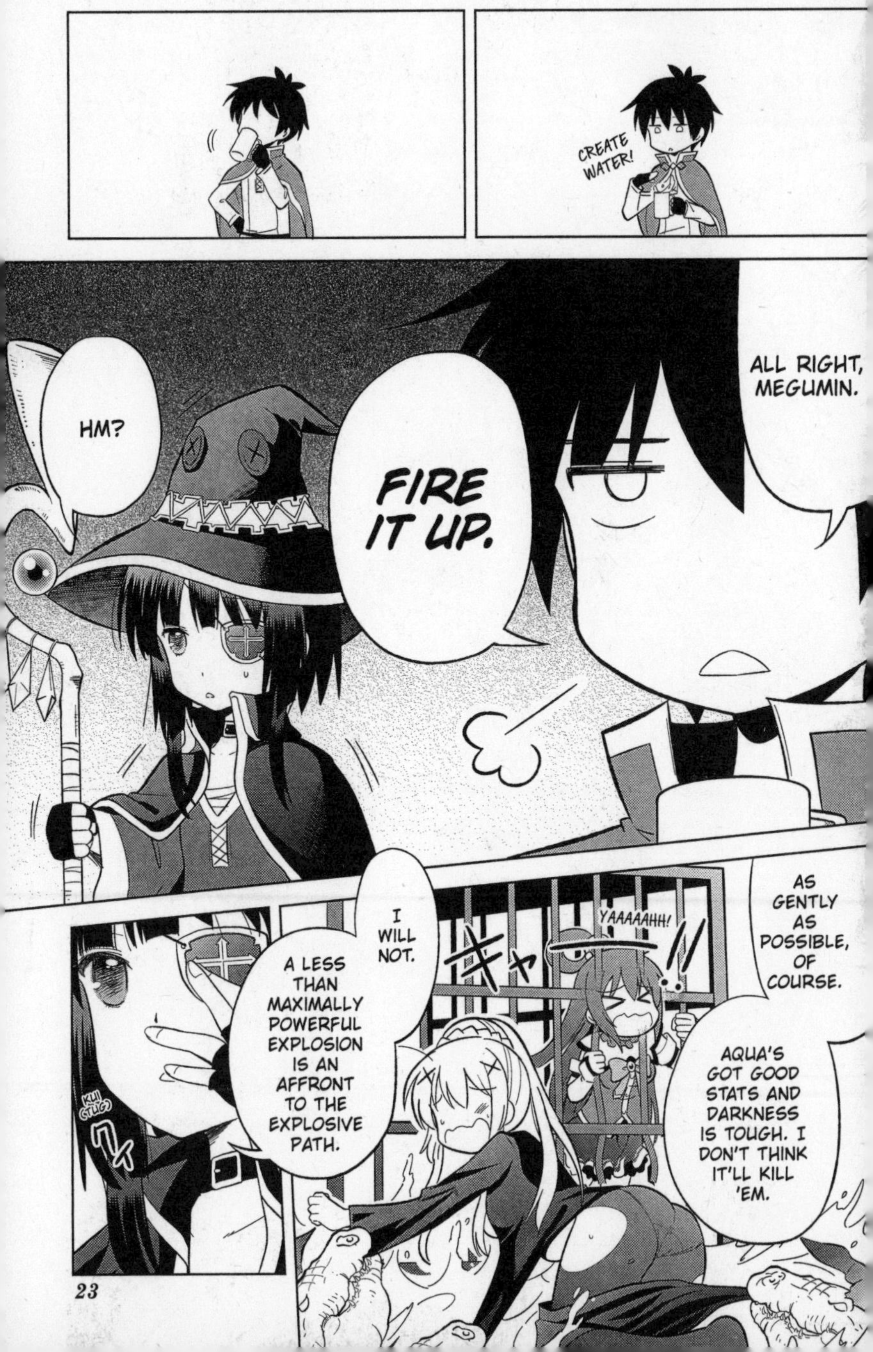
CREATE WATER!
ALL RIGHT, MEGUMIN.
FIRE IT UP.
HM?
AS GENTLY AS POSSIBLE, OF COURSE.
AQUA'S GOT GOOD STATS AND DARKNESS IS TOUGH. I DON'T THINK IT'LL KILL 'EM.
YAAAAAHH!
I WILL NOT.
A LESS THAN MAXIMALLY POWERFUL EXPLOSION IS AN AFFRONT TO THE EXPLOSIVE PATH.
KUI (TUG)

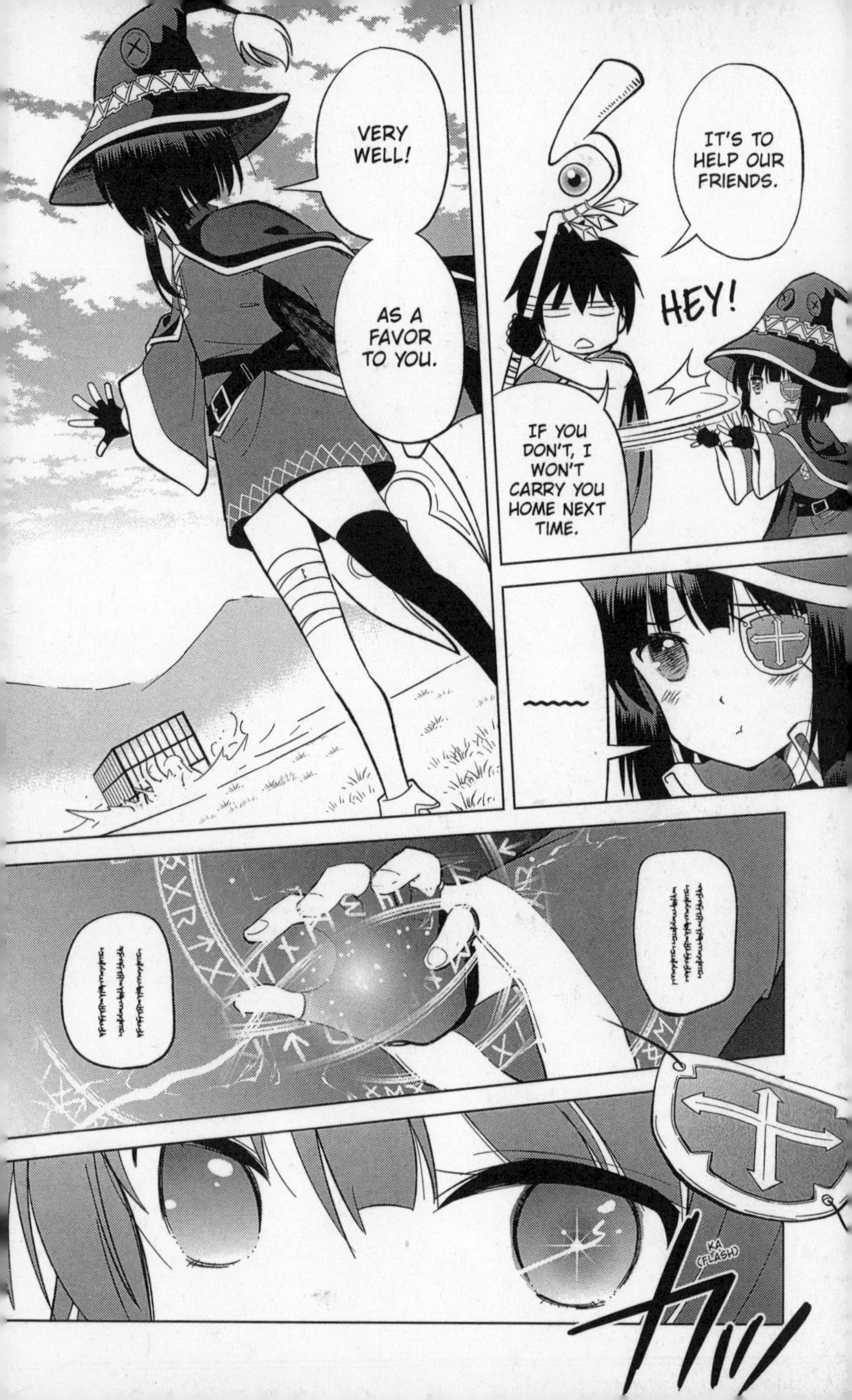

IT'S TO HELP OUR FRIENDS.
HEY!
IF YOU DON'T, I WON'T CARRY YOU HOME NEXT TIME.
~~~~
VERY WELL!
AS A FAVOR TO YOU.
KA (FLASH)
~~~~

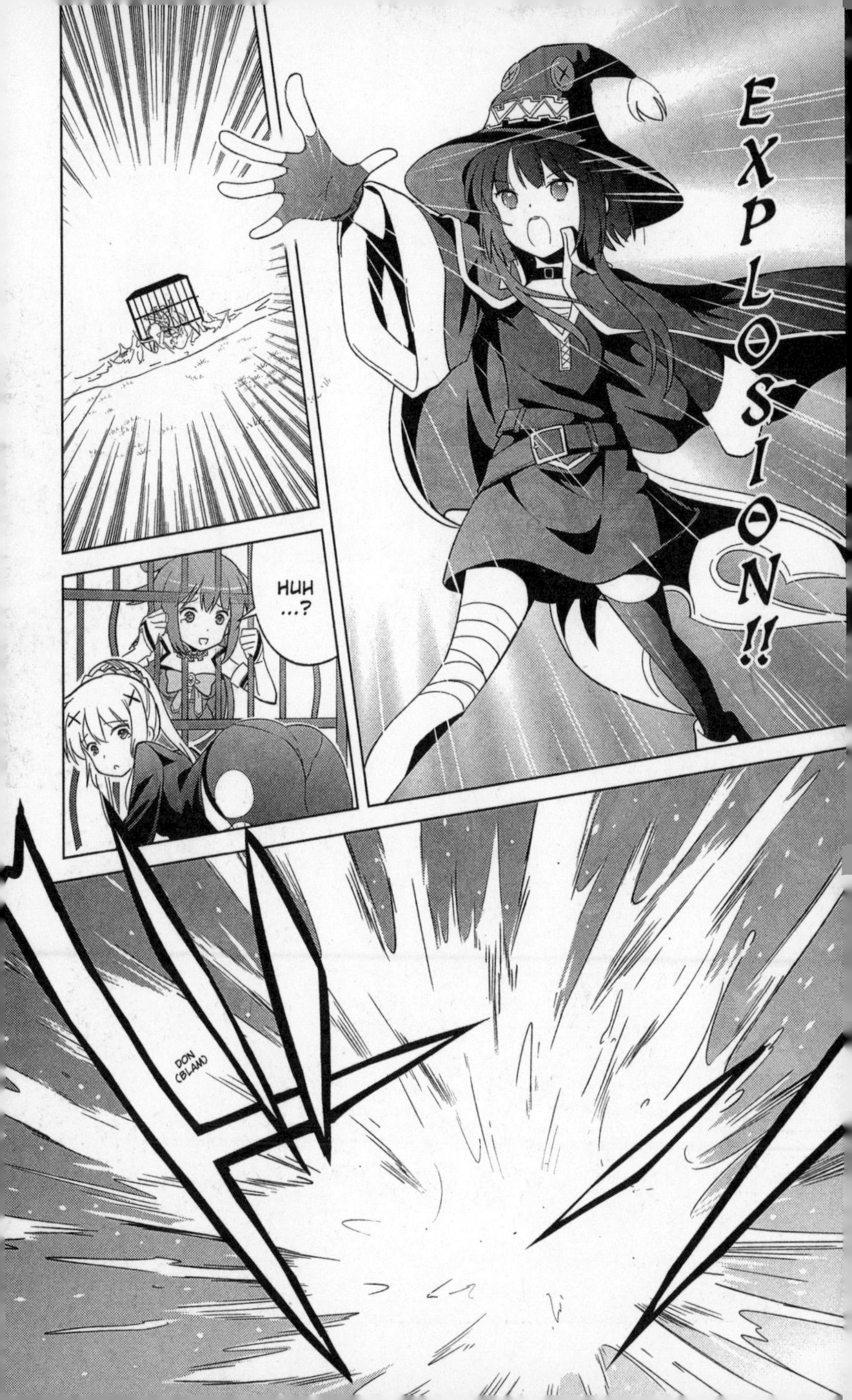
EXPLOSION!!
HUH ...?
DON (BLAM)

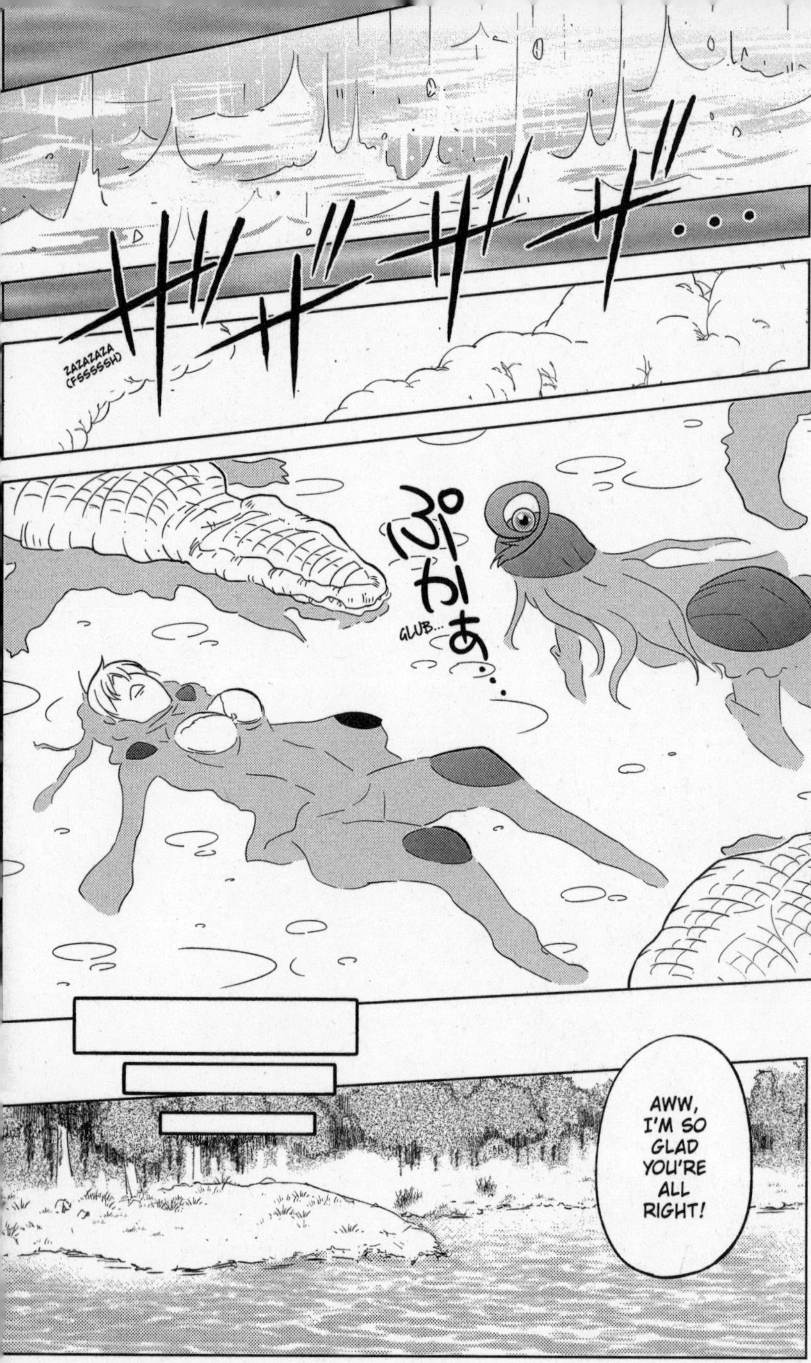
ザザザザ…
ZAZAZAZA (FSSSSSH)
ぷかあ…
GLUB…
AWW, I'M SO GLAD YOU'RE ALL RIGHT!

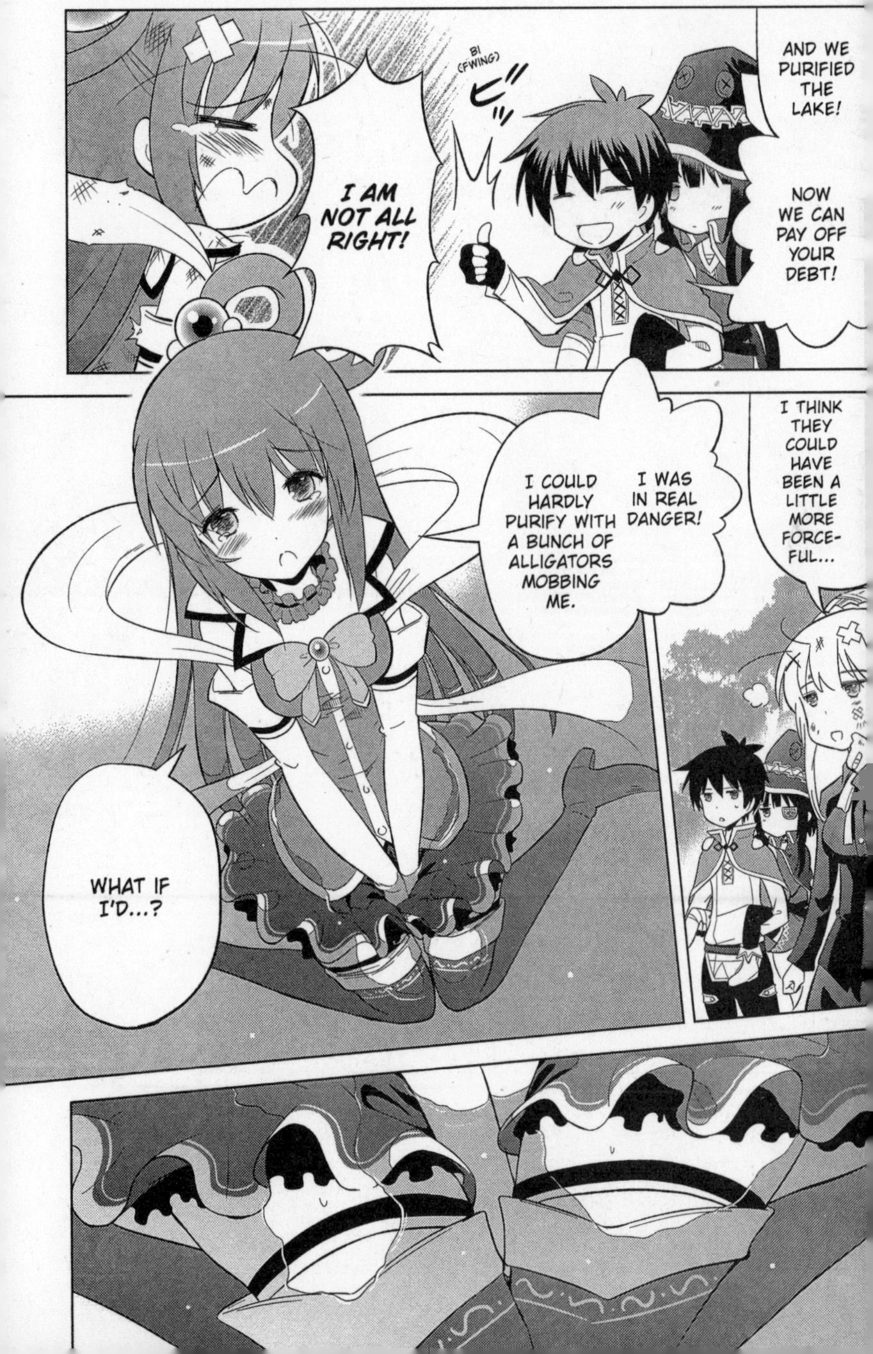
AND WE PURIFIED THE LAKE!
NOW WE CAN PAY OFF YOUR DEBT!
ビッ
BI (FWING)
I AM NOT ALL RIGHT!
I THINK THEY COULD HAVE BEEN A LITTLE MORE FORCE-FUL...
I WAS IN REAL DANGER!
I COULD HARDLY PURIFY WITH A BUNCH OF ALLIGATORS MOBBING ME.
WHAT IF I'D...?

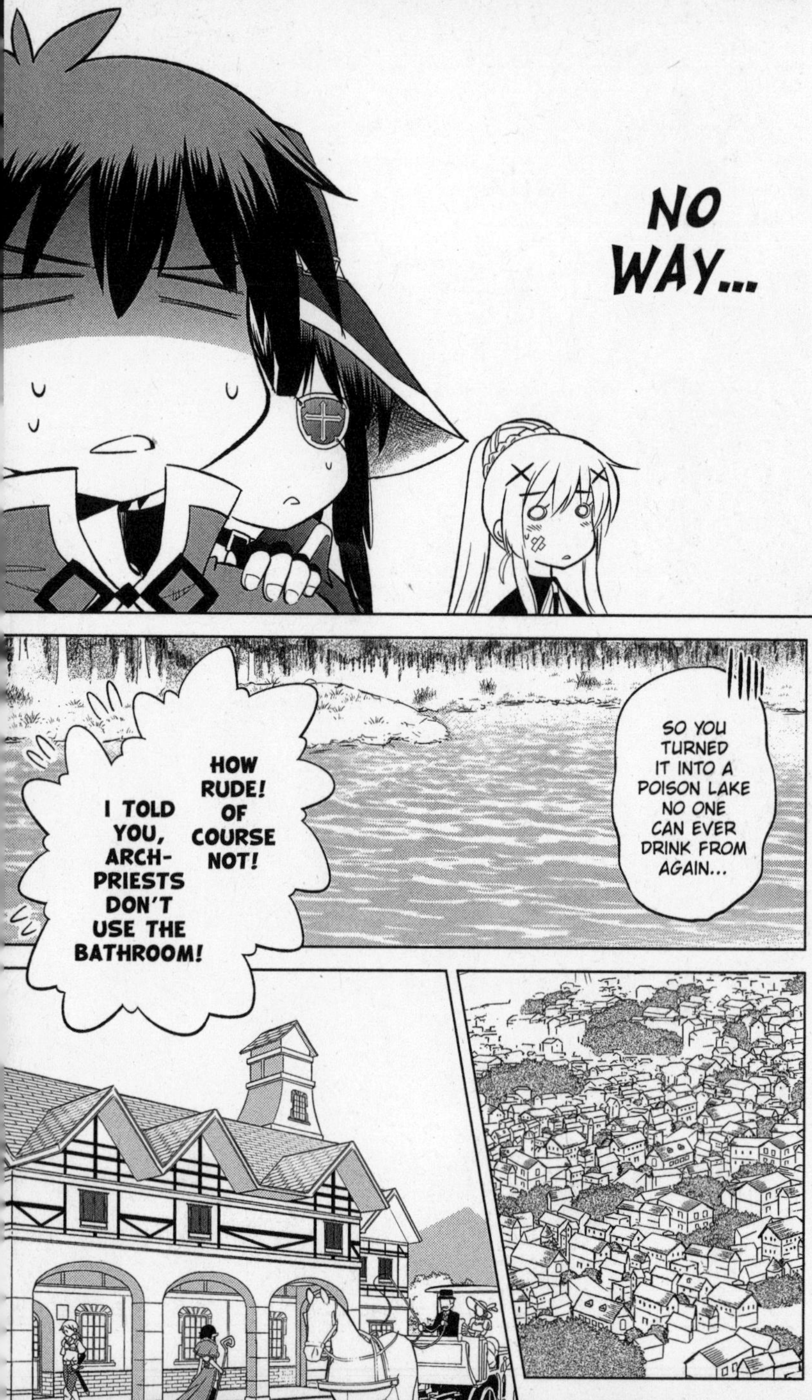
NO WAY...
SO YOU TURNED IT INTO A POISON LAKE NO ONE CAN EVER DRINK FROM AGAIN...
HOW RUDE! OF COURSE NOT!
I TOLD YOU, ARCH-PRIESTS DON'T USE THE BATHROOM!

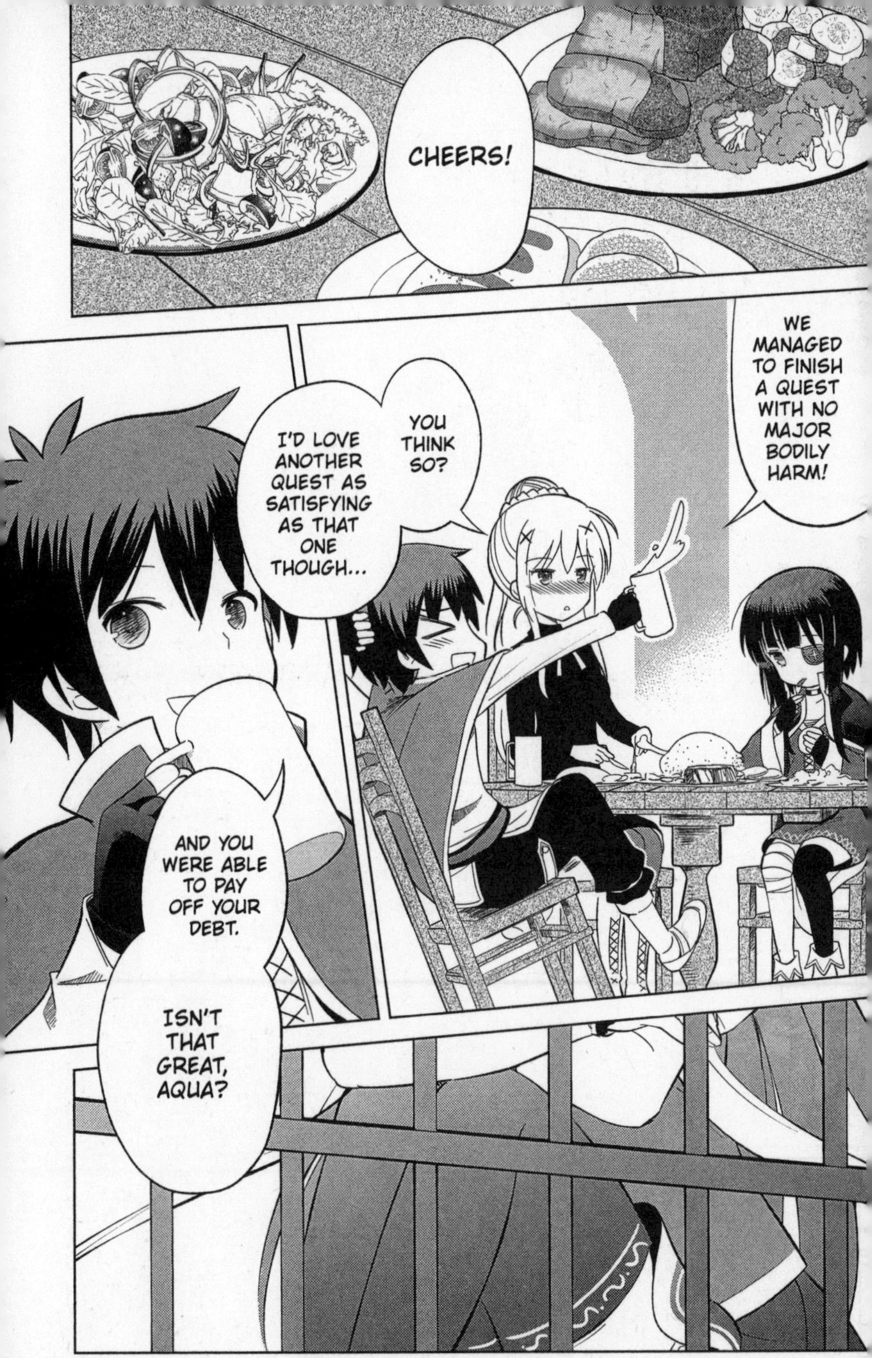
CHEERS!
WE MANAGED TO FINISH A QUEST WITH NO MAJOR BODILY HARM!
YOU THINK SO?
I'D LOVE ANOTHER QUEST AS SATISFYING AS THAT ONE THOUGH...
AND YOU WERE ABLE TO PAY OFF YOUR DEBT.
ISN'T THAT GREAT, AQUA?

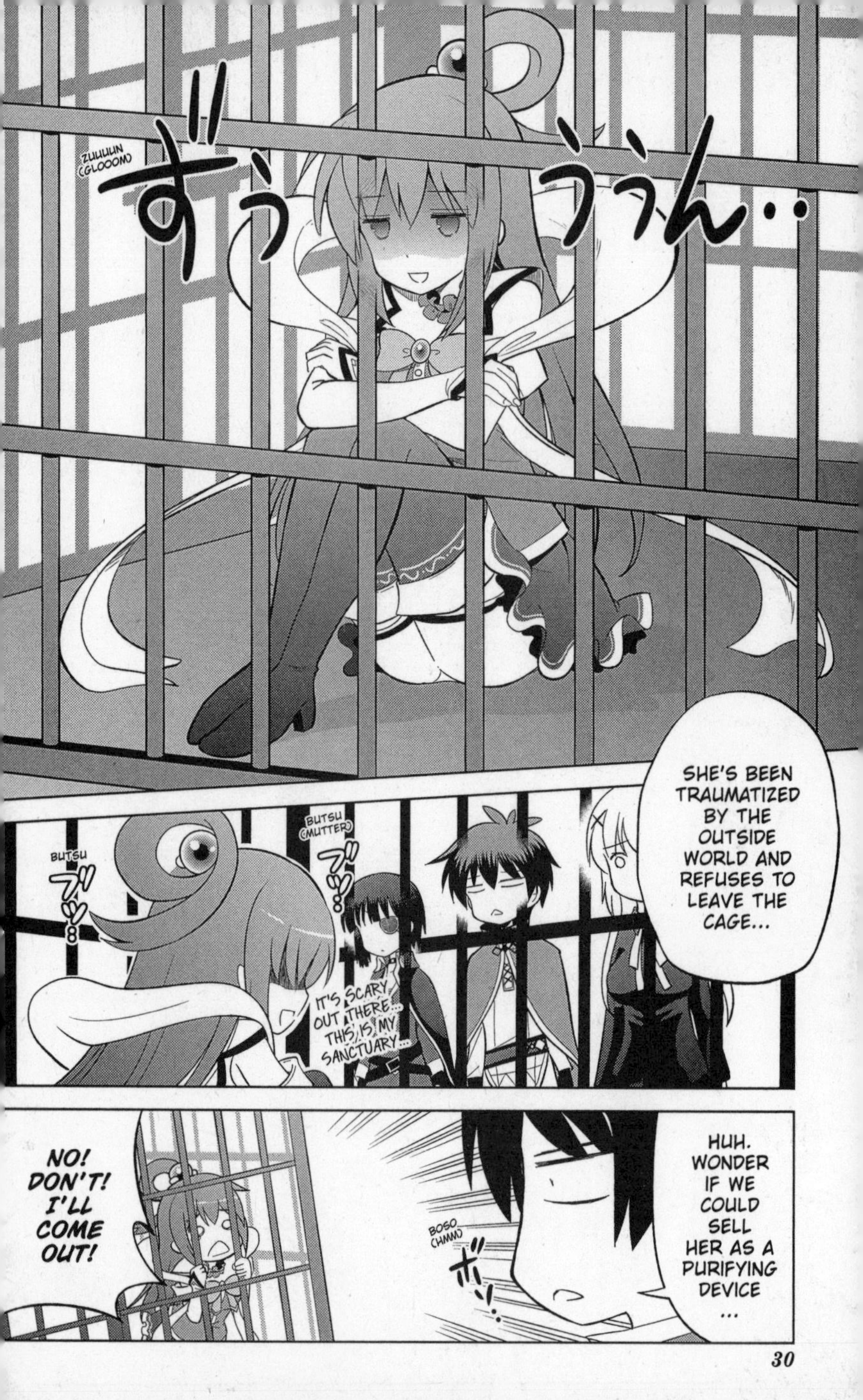

ZUUUUN (GLOOOM)
ずううん‥
SHE'S BEEN TRAUMATIZED BY THE OUTSIDE WORLD AND REFUSES TO LEAVE THE CAGE...
BUTSU (MUTTER)
BUTSU
IT'S SCARY OUT THERE... THIS IS MY SANCTUARY...
HUH. WONDER IF WE COULD SELL HER AS A PURIFYING DEVICE...
BOSO (HMM)
NO! DON'T! I'LL COME OUT!

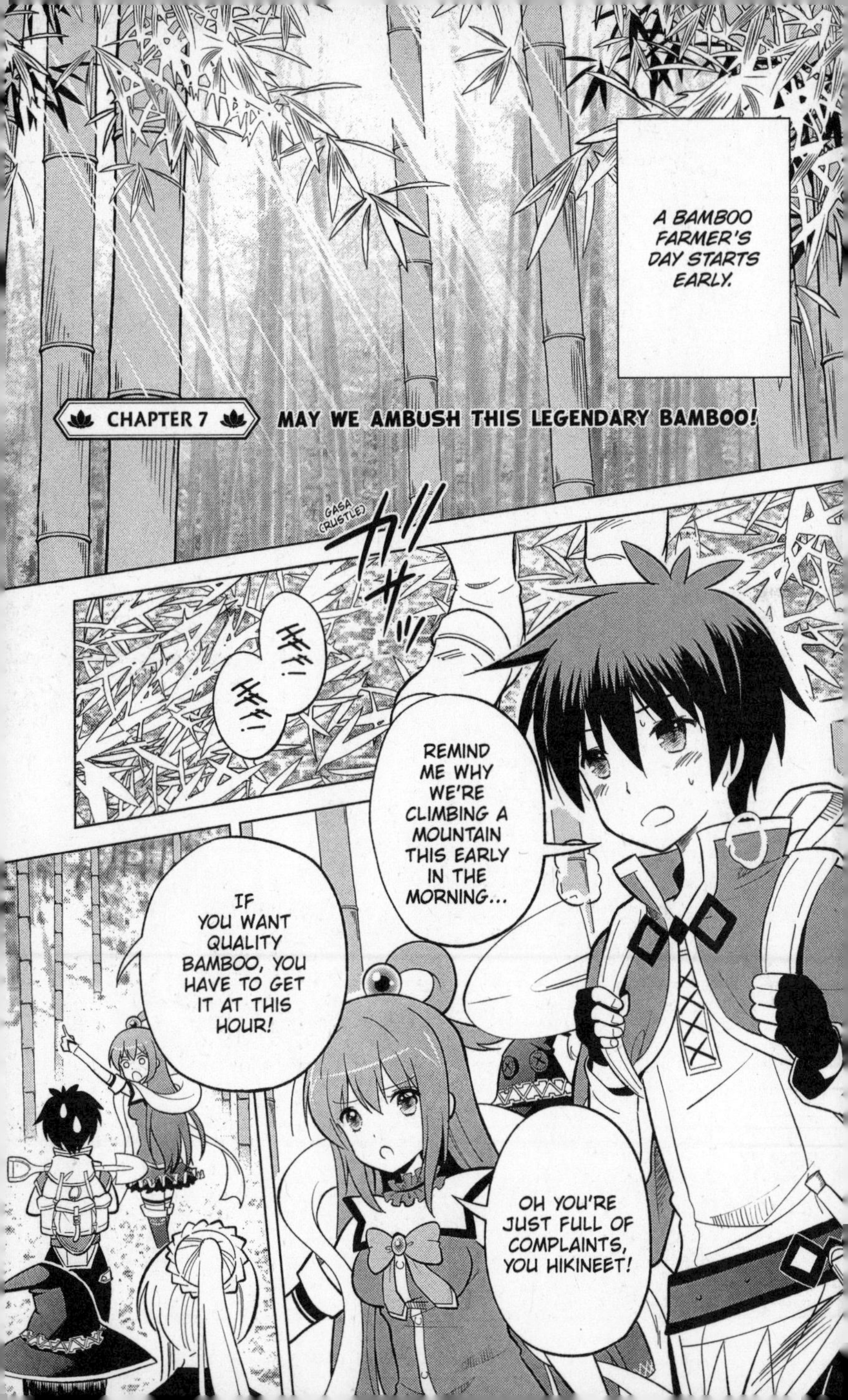
A BAMBOO FARMER'S DAY STARTS EARLY.
CHAPTER 7
MAY WE AMBUSH THIS LEGENDARY BAMBOO!
ガサッ
GASA (RUSTLE)
REMIND ME WHY WE'RE CLIMBING A MOUNTAIN THIS EARLY IN THE MORNING...
IF YOU WANT QUALITY BAMBOO, YOU HAVE TO GET IT AT THIS HOUR!
OH YOU'RE JUST FULL OF COMPLAINTS, YOU HIKINEET!

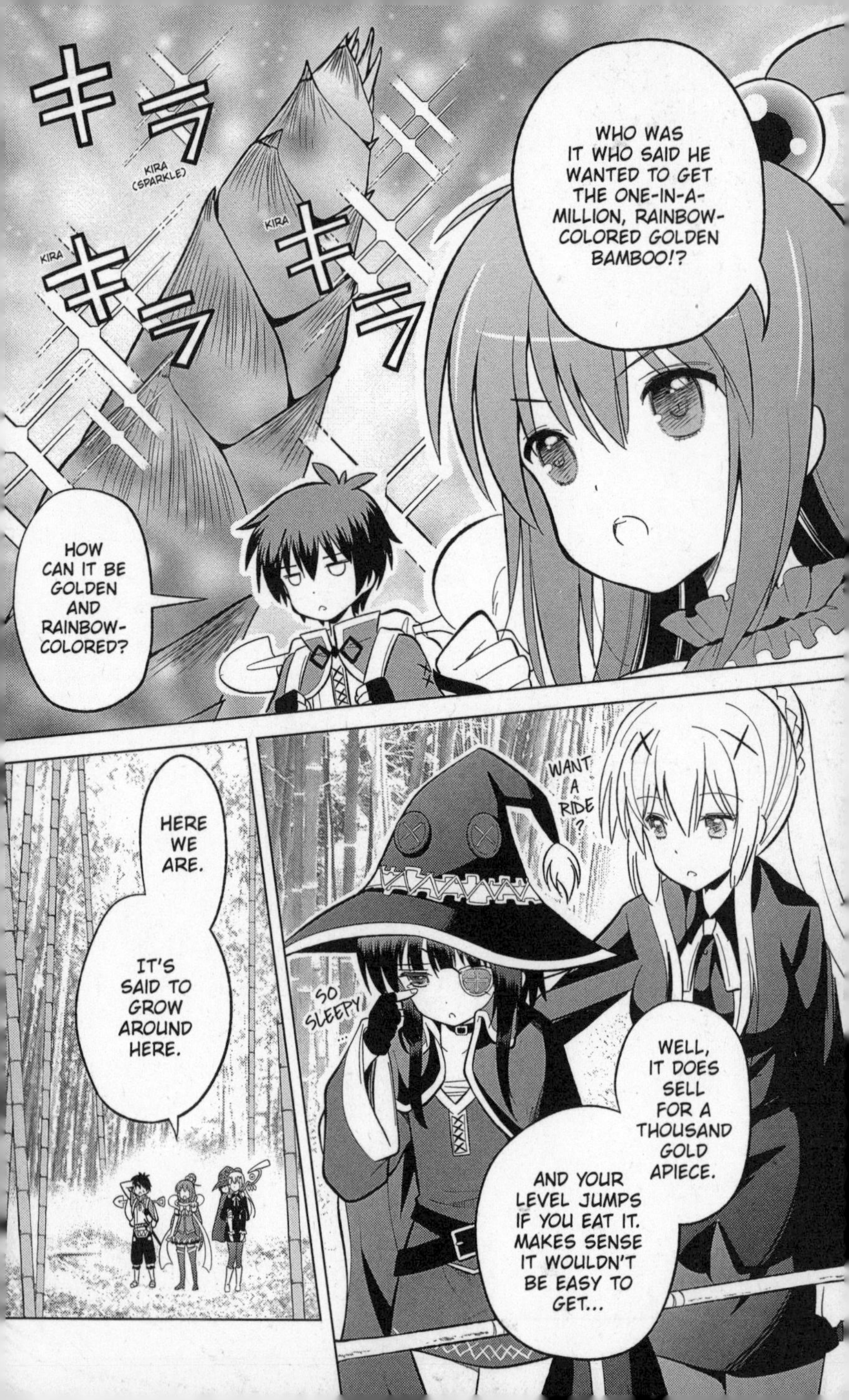
WHO WAS IT WHO SAID HE WANTED TO GET THE ONE-IN-A-MILLION, RAINBOW-COLORED GOLDEN BAMBOO!?
KIRA (SPARKLE)
KIRA
KIRA
HOW CAN IT BE GOLDEN AND RAINBOW-COLORED?
WANT A RIDE?
SO SLEEPY...
WELL, IT DOES SELL FOR A THOUSAND GOLD APIECE.
AND YOUR LEVEL JUMPS IF YOU EAT IT. MAKES SENSE IT WOULDN'T BE EASY TO GET...
HERE WE ARE.
IT'S SAID TO GROW AROUND HERE.

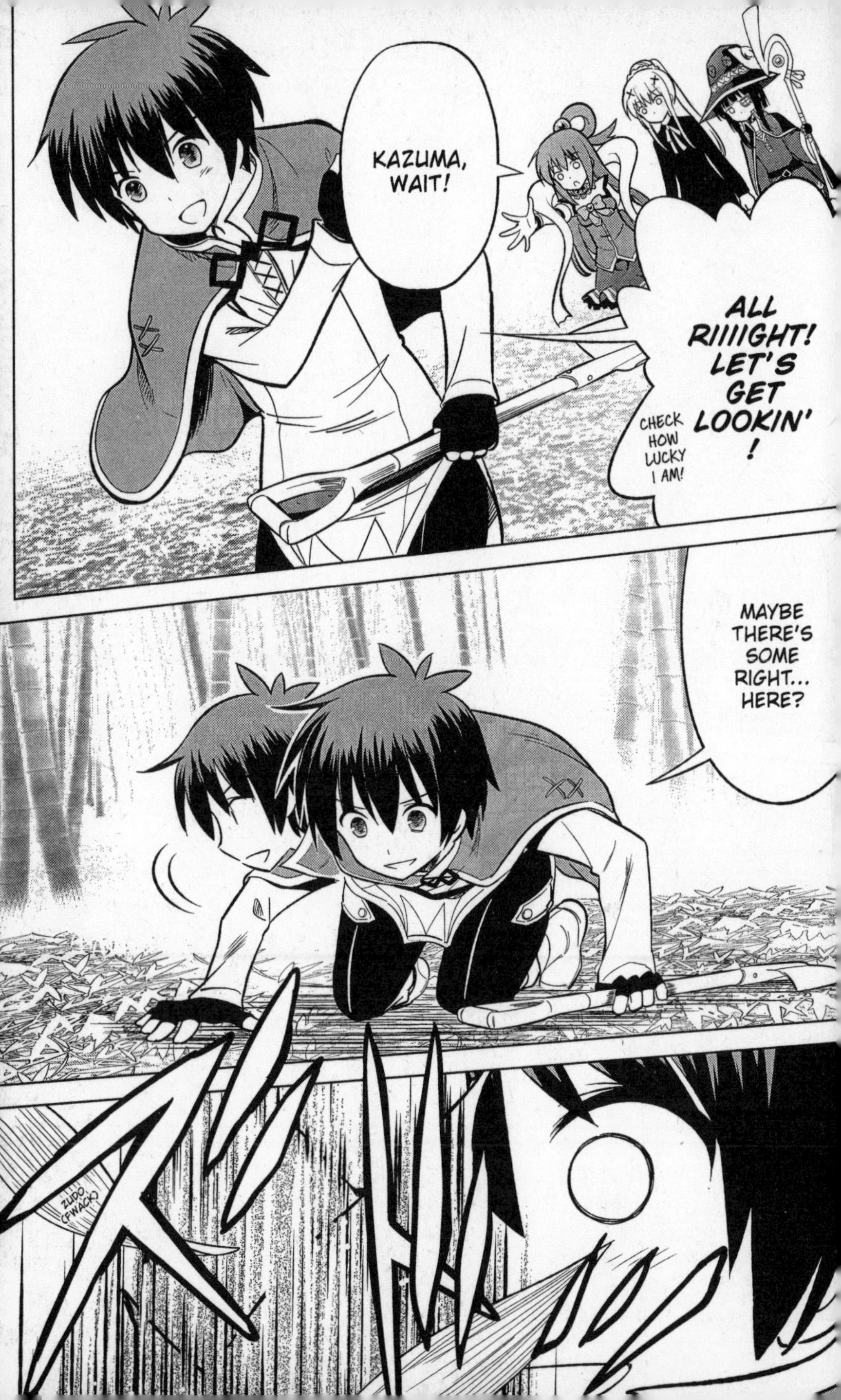
ALL RIIIIGHT! LET'S GET LOOKIN'!
CHECK HOW LUCKY I AM!
KAZUMA, WAIT!
MAYBE THERE'S SOME RIGHT... HERE?
ZUDO (FWACK)

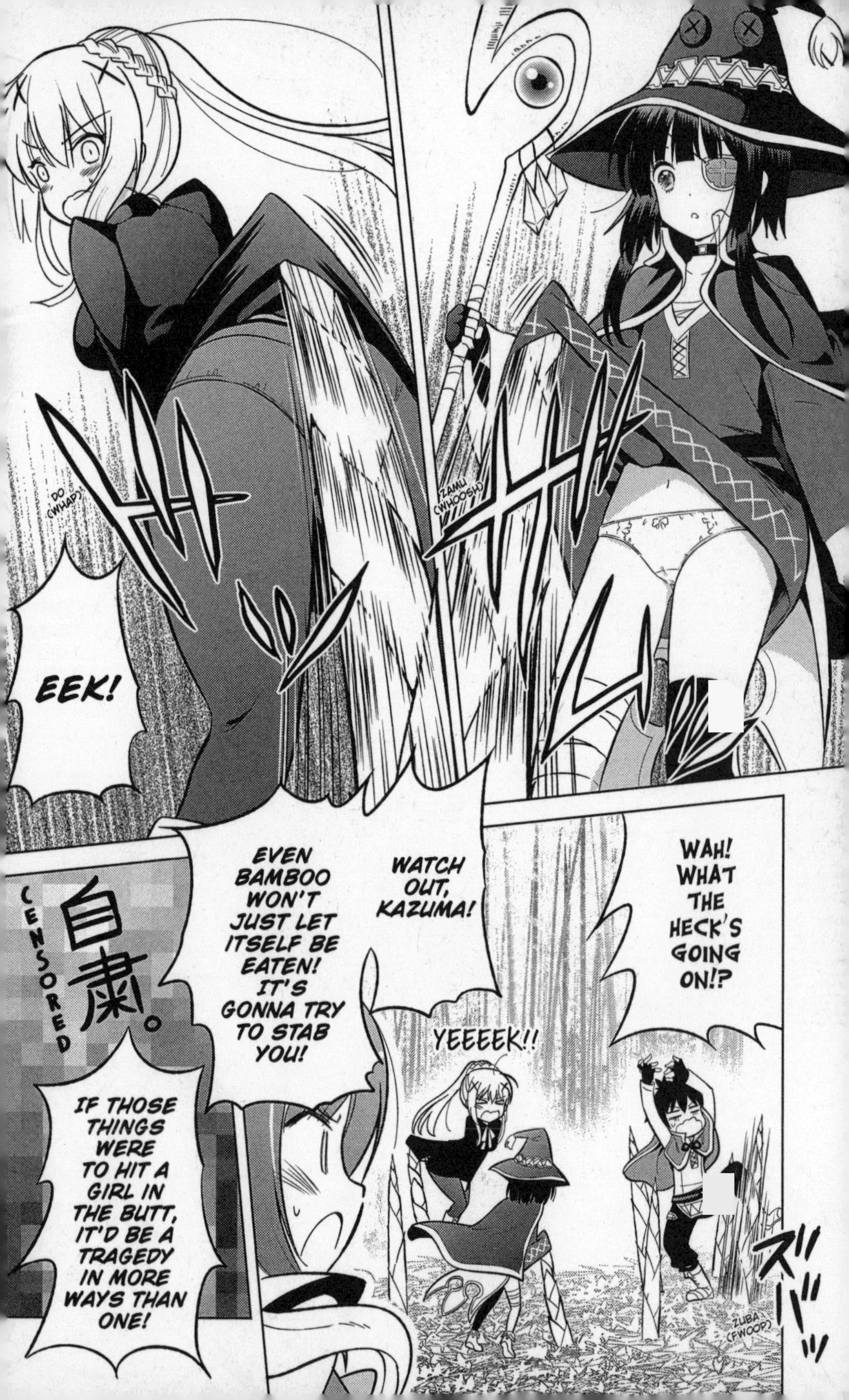
ZAMU (WHOOSH)
DO (WHAP)
EEK!
WAH! WHAT THE HECK'S GOING ON!?
WATCH OUT, KAZUMA!
EVEN BAMBOO WON'T JUST LET ITSELF BE EATEN! IT'S GONNA TRY TO STAB YOU!
YEEEEK!!
ズバッ
ZUBA (FWOOP)
自粛。
CENSORED
IF THOSE THINGS WERE TO HIT A GIRL IN THE BUTT, IT'D BE A TRAGEDY IN MORE WAYS THAN ONE!

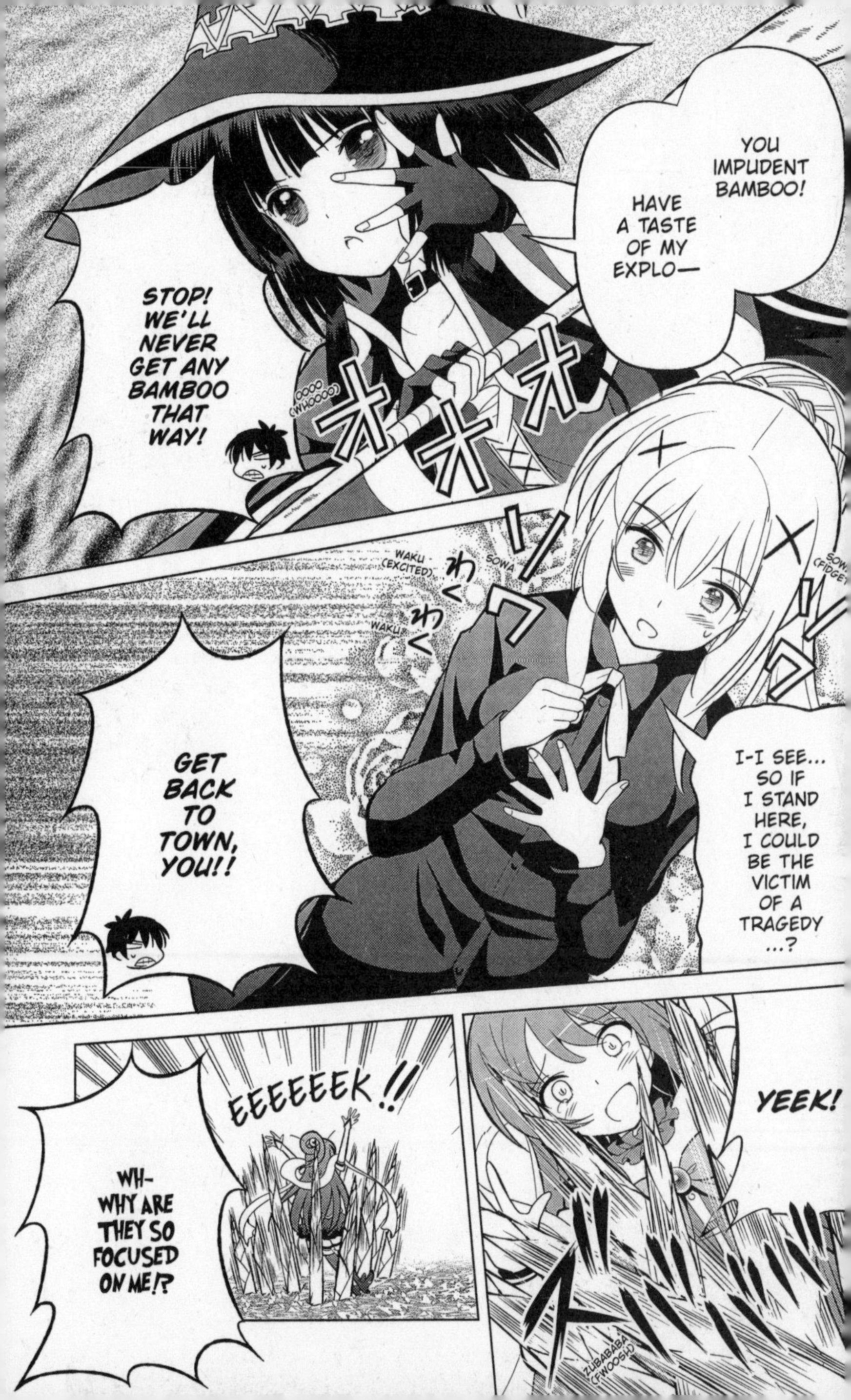
YOU IMPUDENT BAMBOO!
HAVE A TASTE OF MY EXPLO—
OOOO (WHOOOO)
STOP! WE'LL NEVER GET ANY BAMBOO THAT WAY!
SOWA
I-I SEE... SO IF I STAND HERE, I COULD BE THE VICTIM OF A TRAGEDY ...?
SOWA
WAKU (EXCITED)
WAKU
GET BACK TO TOWN, YOU!!
YEEK!
ZUBABABA (FWOOSH)
EEEEEEK!!
WH-WHY ARE THEY SO FOCUSED ON ME!?

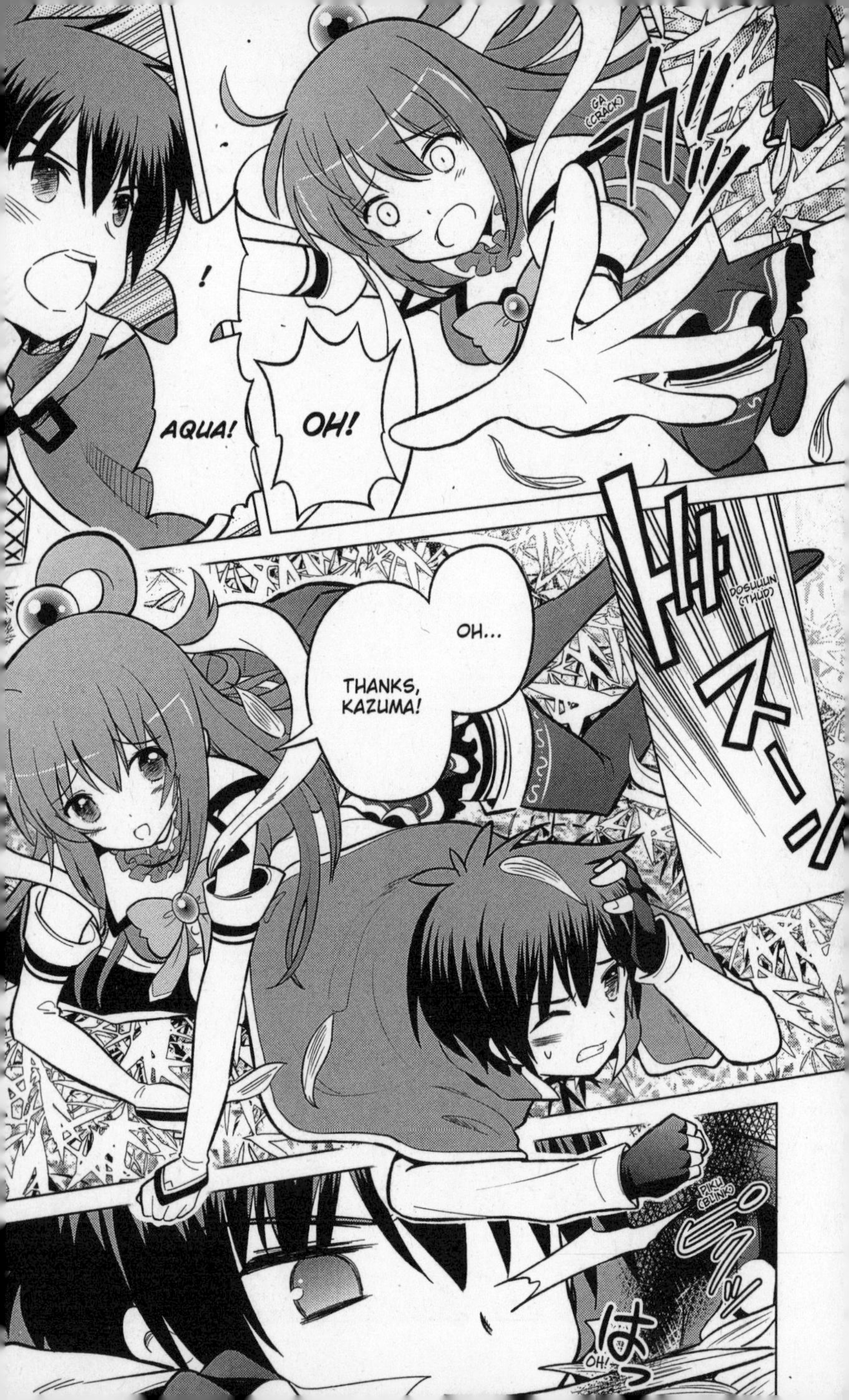
GA (CRACK)
OH!
AQUA!
DOSUUUN (THUD)
OH...
THANKS, KAZUMA!
PIKU (BLINK)
OH!

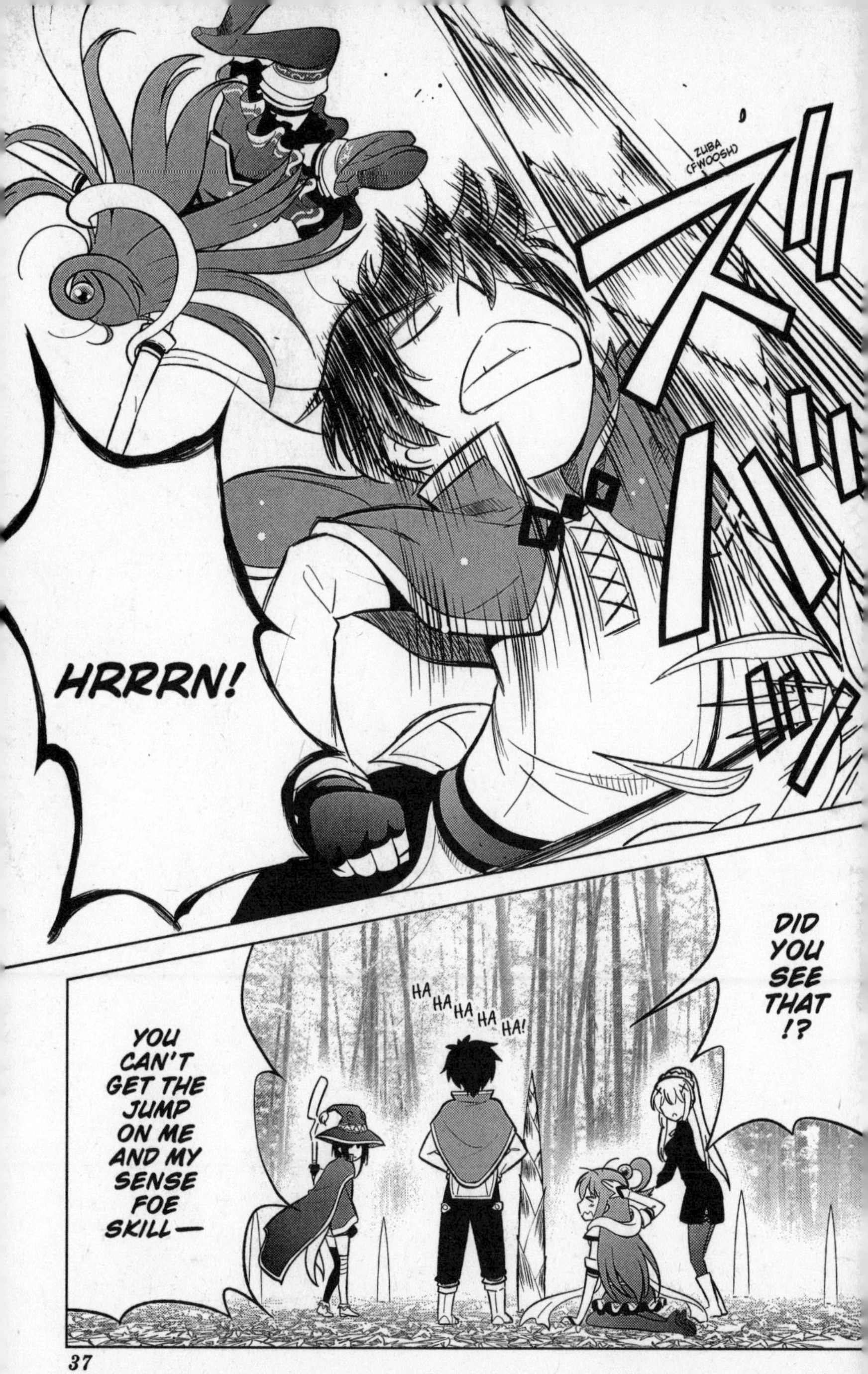
ZUBA (FWOOSH)
HRRRN!
DID YOU SEE THAT!?
HA HA HA HA HA!
YOU CAN'T GET THE JUMP ON ME AND MY SENSE FOE SKILL—

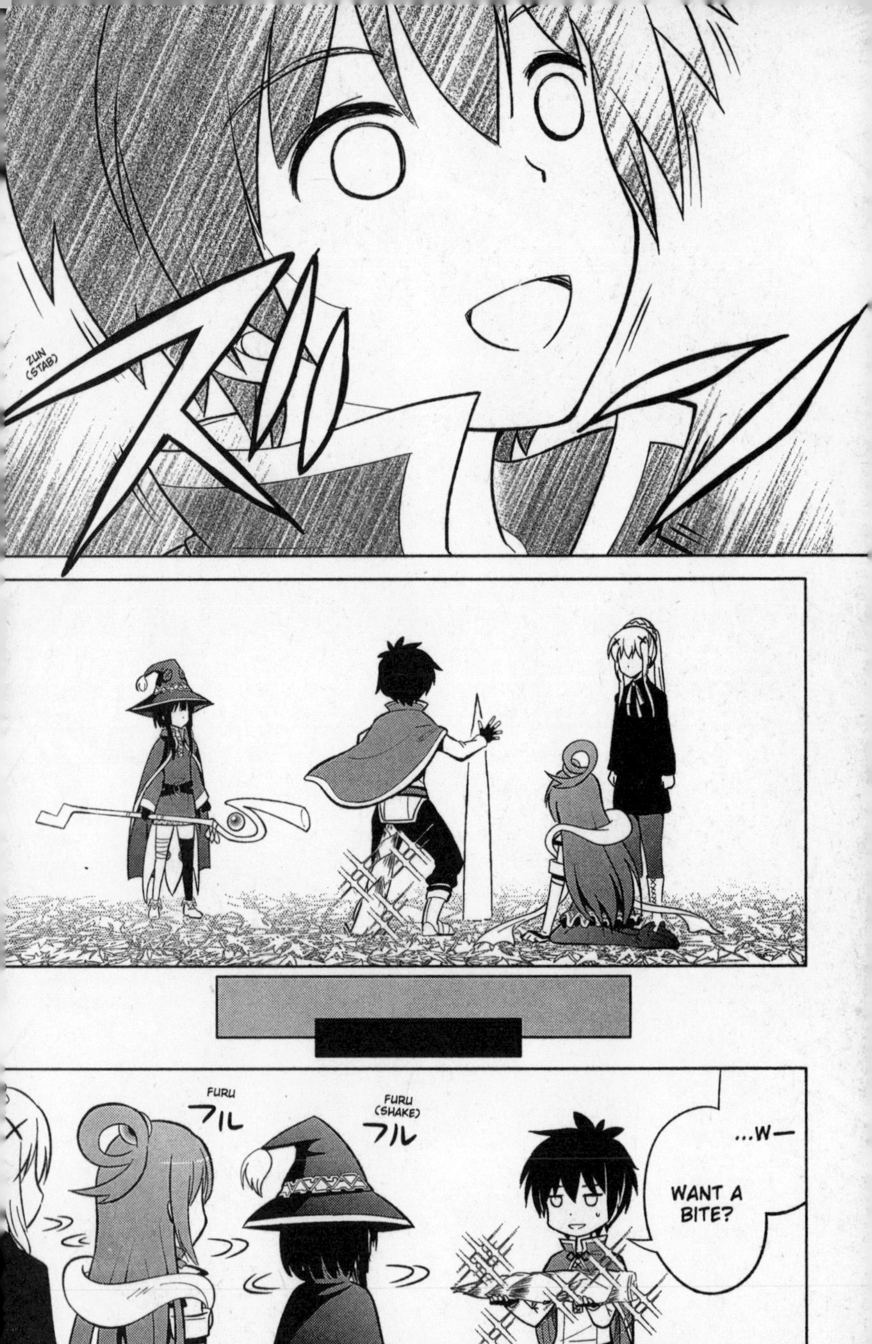
ZUN
(STAB)
...W—
WANT A BITE?
FURU
(SHAKE)
フル
FURU
フル

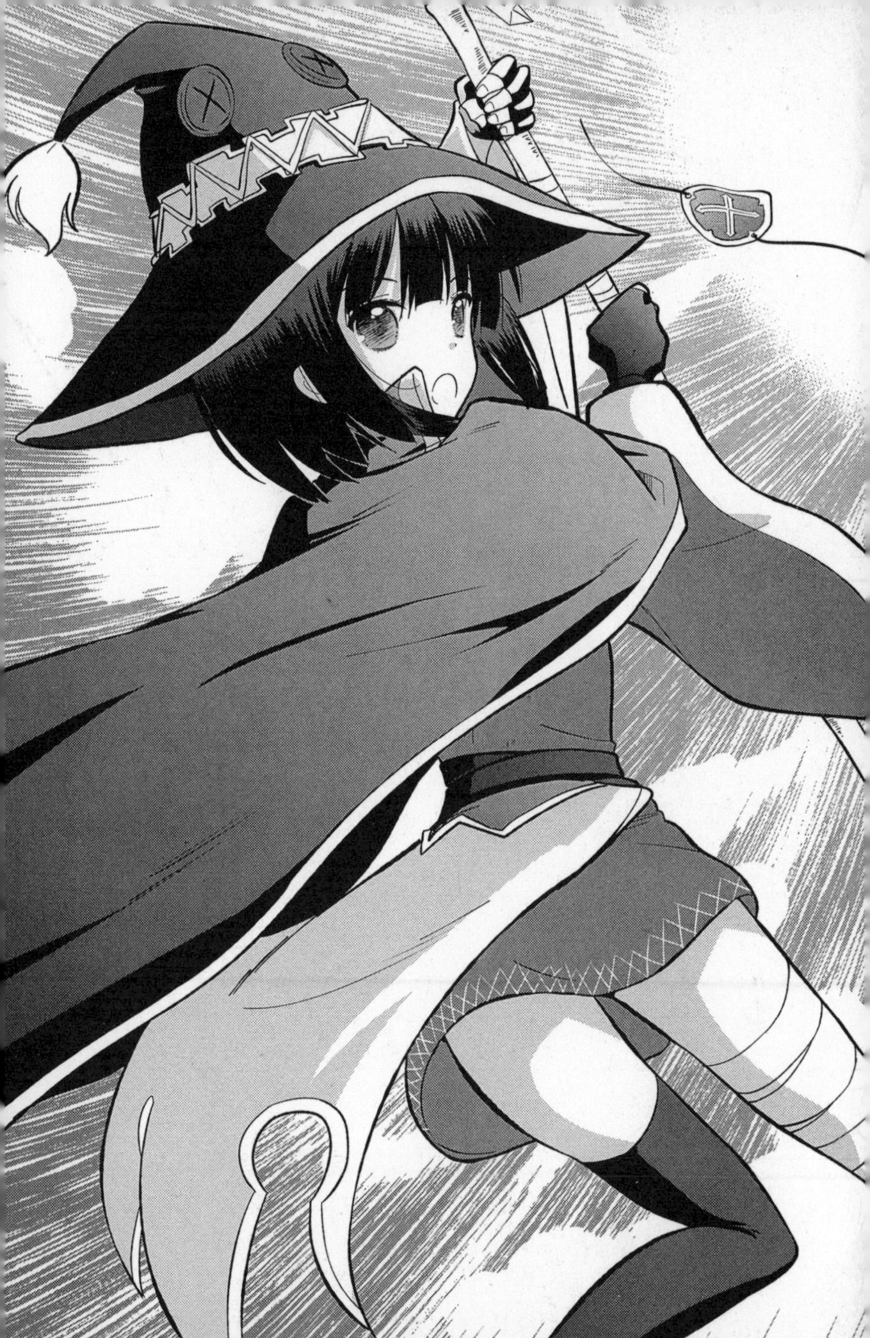

CHAPTER 8 MAY I GET A RESTRAINING ORDER AGAINST THIS ARROGANT ADVENTURER!

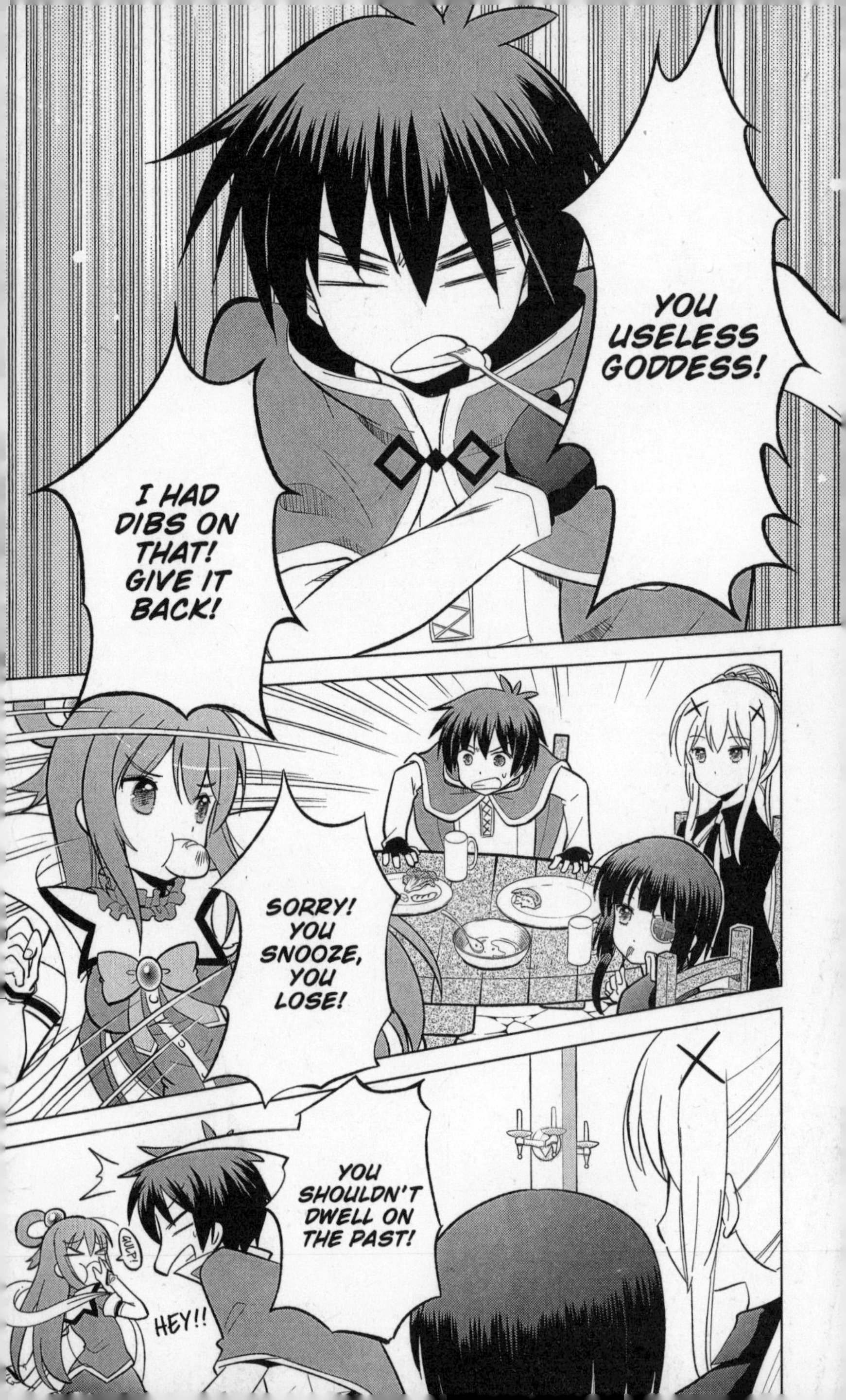
YOU USELESS GODDESS!
I HAD DIBS ON THAT! GIVE IT BACK!
SORRY! YOU SNOOZE, YOU LOSE!
YOU SHOULDN'T DWELL ON THE PAST!
GULP!
HEY!!

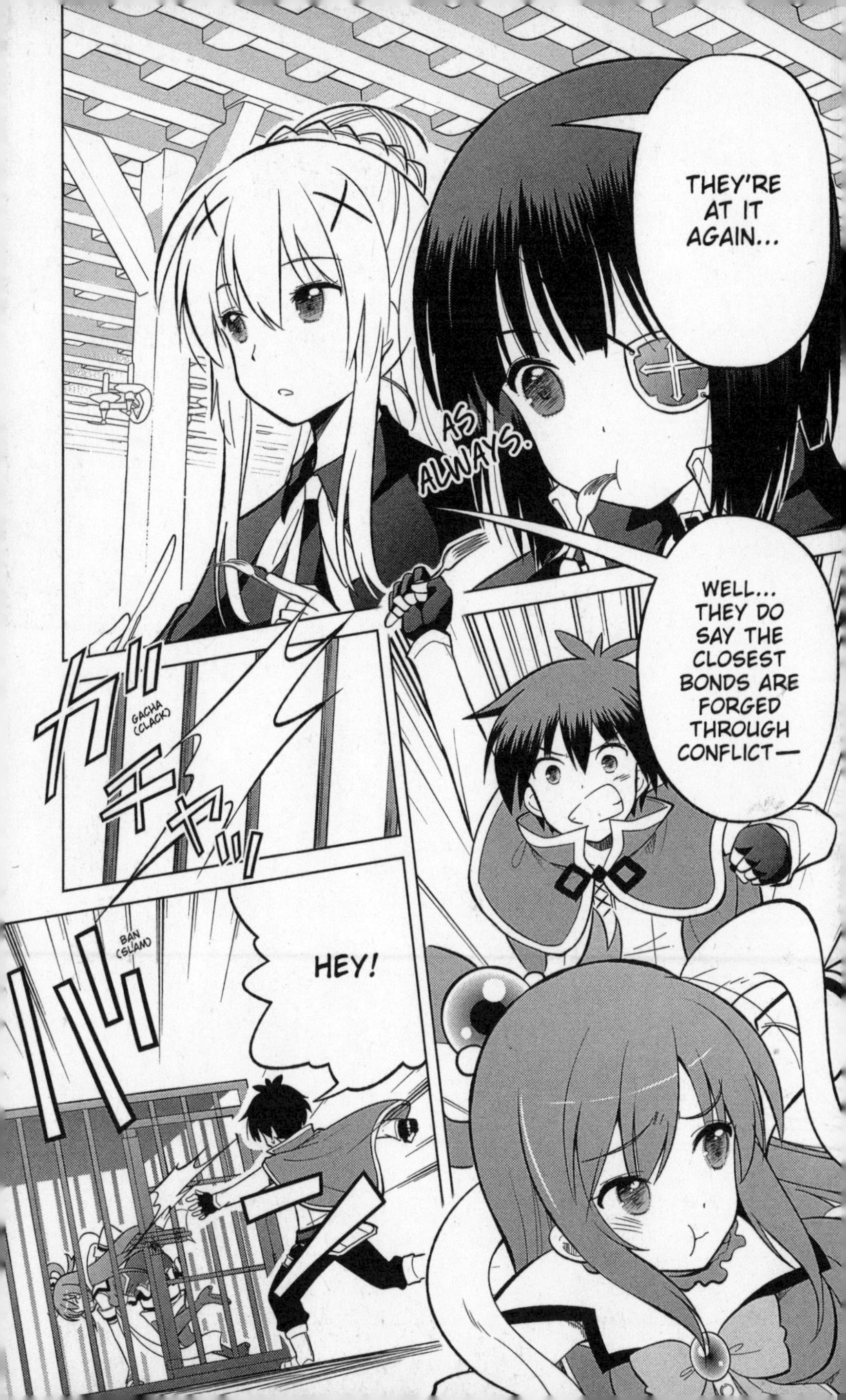
THEY'RE AT IT AGAIN...
AS ALWAYS.
WELL... THEY DO SAY THE CLOSEST BONDS ARE FORGED THROUGH CONFLICT—
GACHA (CLACK)
BAN (SLAM)
HEY!

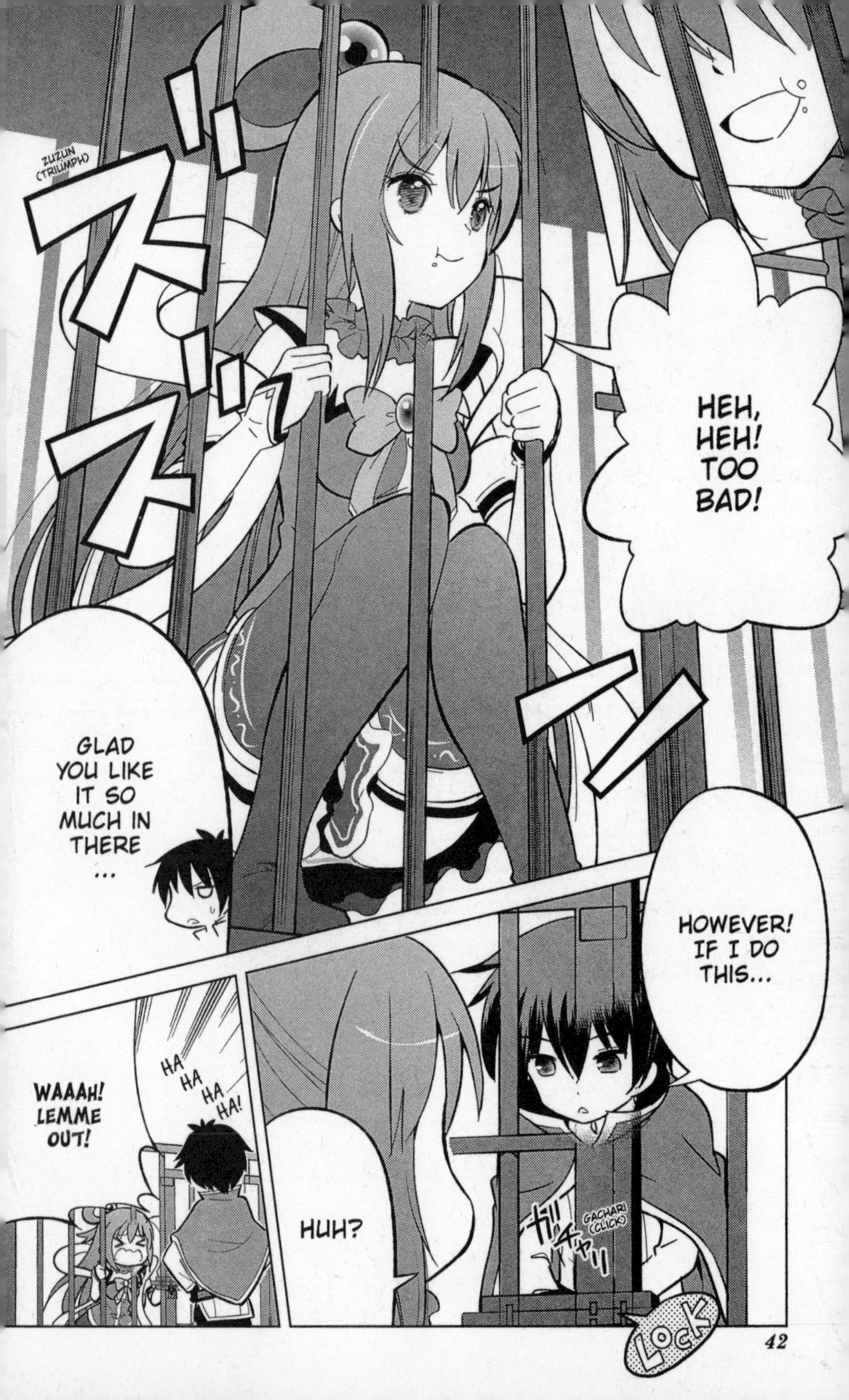
ZUZUN (TRIUMPH)
HEH, HEH! TOO BAD!
GLAD YOU LIKE IT SO MUCH IN THERE ...
HOWEVER! IF I DO THIS...
GACHARI (CLICK)
LOCK
HUH?
HA HA HA HA!
WAAAH! LEMME OUT!

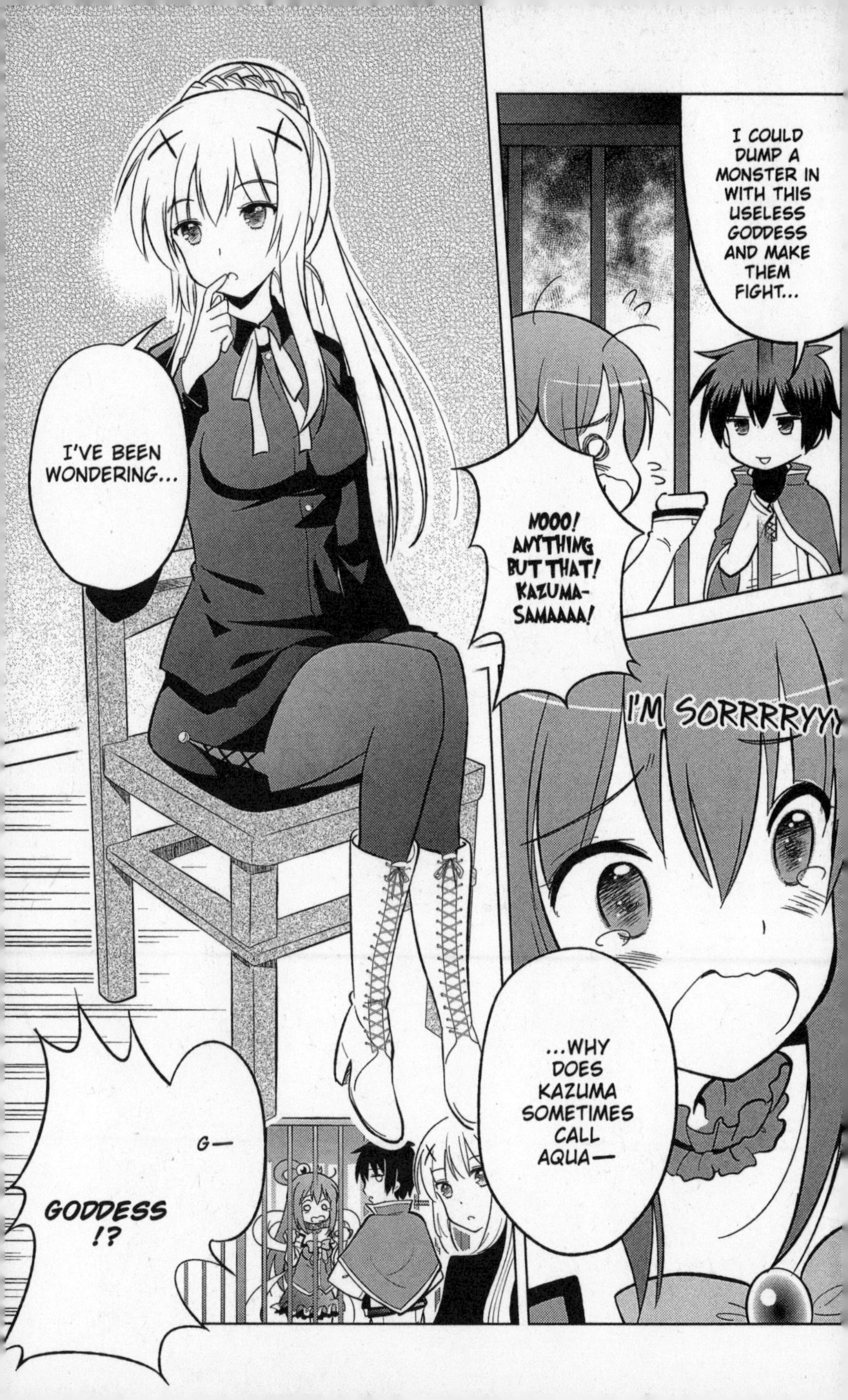
I COULD DUMP A MONSTER IN WITH THIS USELESS GODDESS AND MAKE THEM FIGHT...
NOOO! ANYTHING BUT THAT! KAZUMA-SAMAAAA!
I'M SORRRRYYY
I'VE BEEN WONDERING...
...WHY DOES KAZUMA SOMETIMES CALL AQUA—
G—
GODDESS!?

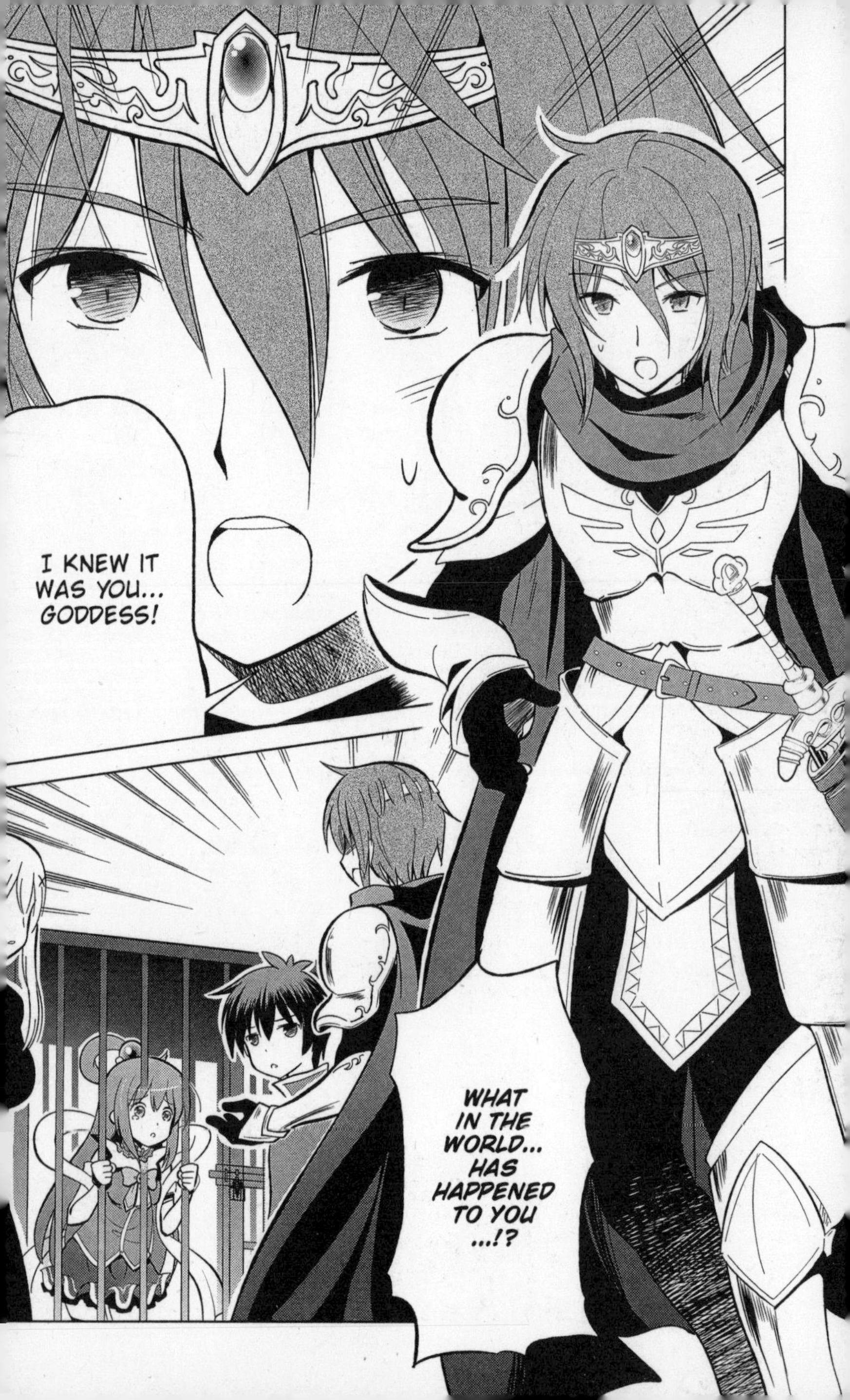
I KNEW IT WAS YOU... GODDESS!
WHAT IN THE WORLD... HAS HAPPENED TO YOU ...!?

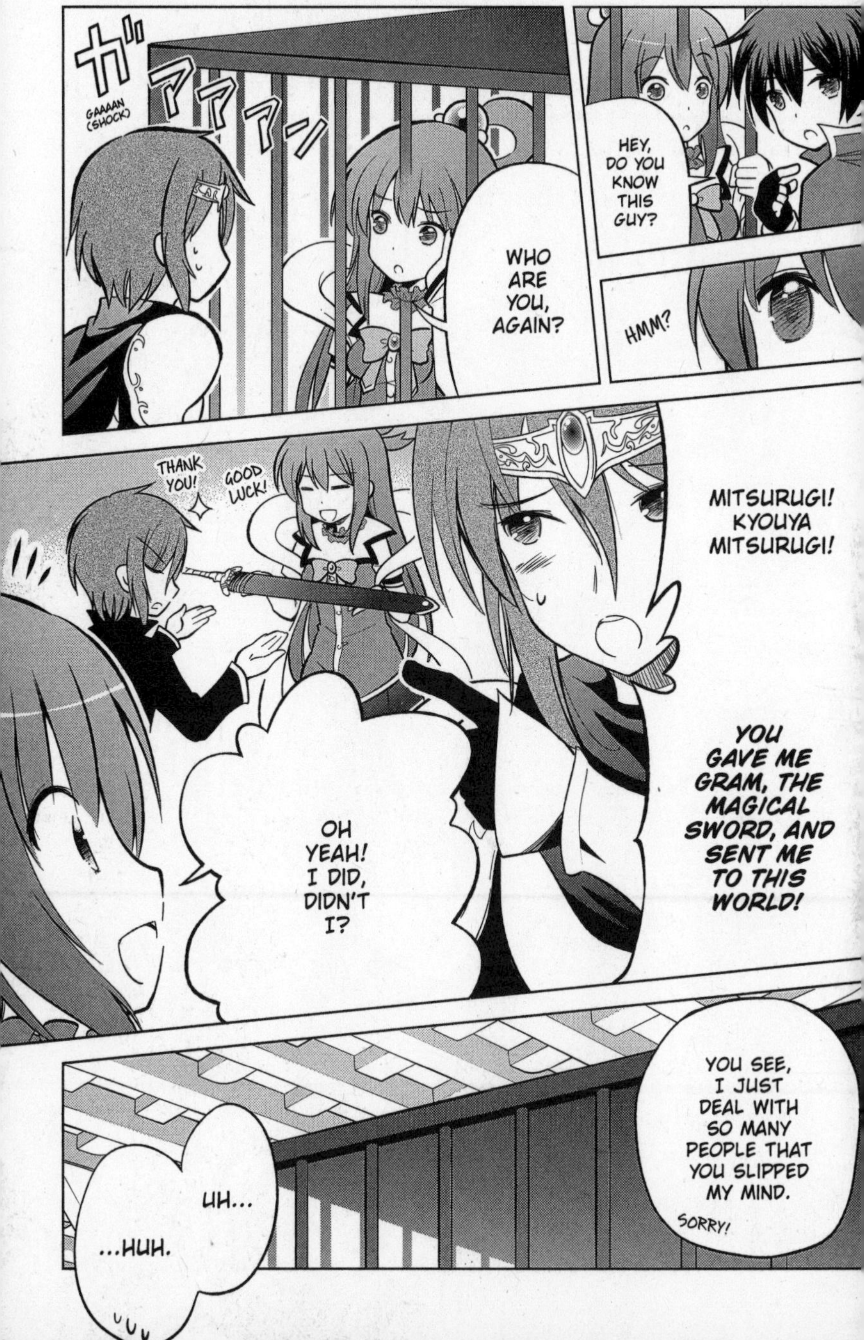
HEY, DO YOU KNOW THIS GUY?
HMM?
WHO ARE YOU, AGAIN?
ガァァン
GAAAAN (SHOCK)
MITSURUGI! KYOUYA MITSURUGI!
YOU GAVE ME GRAM, THE MAGICAL SWORD, AND SENT ME TO THIS WORLD!
GOOD LUCK!
THANK YOU!
OH YEAH! I DID, DIDN'T I?
YOU SEE, I JUST DEAL WITH SO MANY PEOPLE THAT YOU SLIPPED MY MIND.
SORRY!
UH...
...HUH.

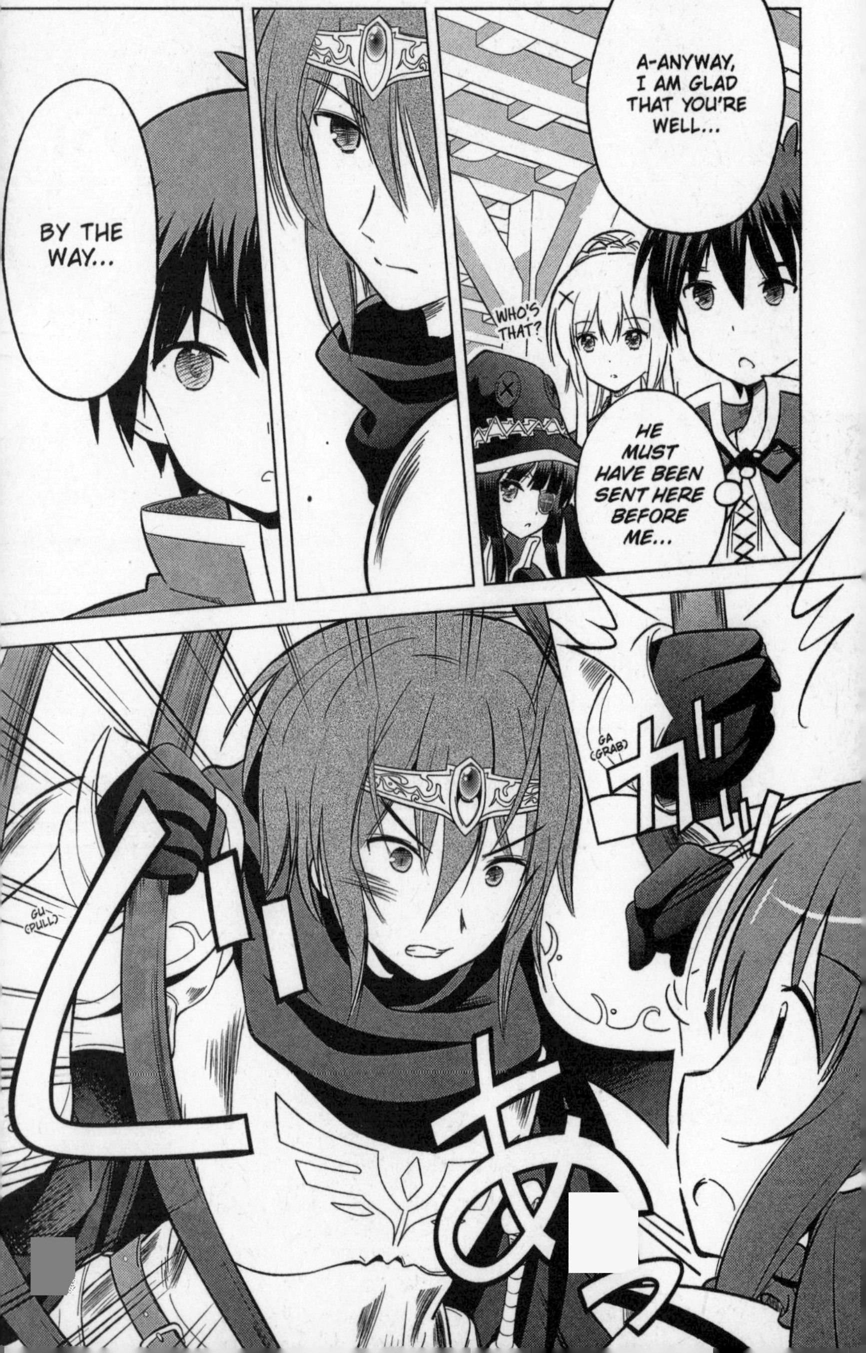
A-ANYWAY, I AM GLAD THAT YOU'RE WELL...
WHO'S THAT?
HE MUST HAVE BEEN SENT HERE BEFORE ME...
BY THE WAY...
GA (GRAB)
GU (PULL)

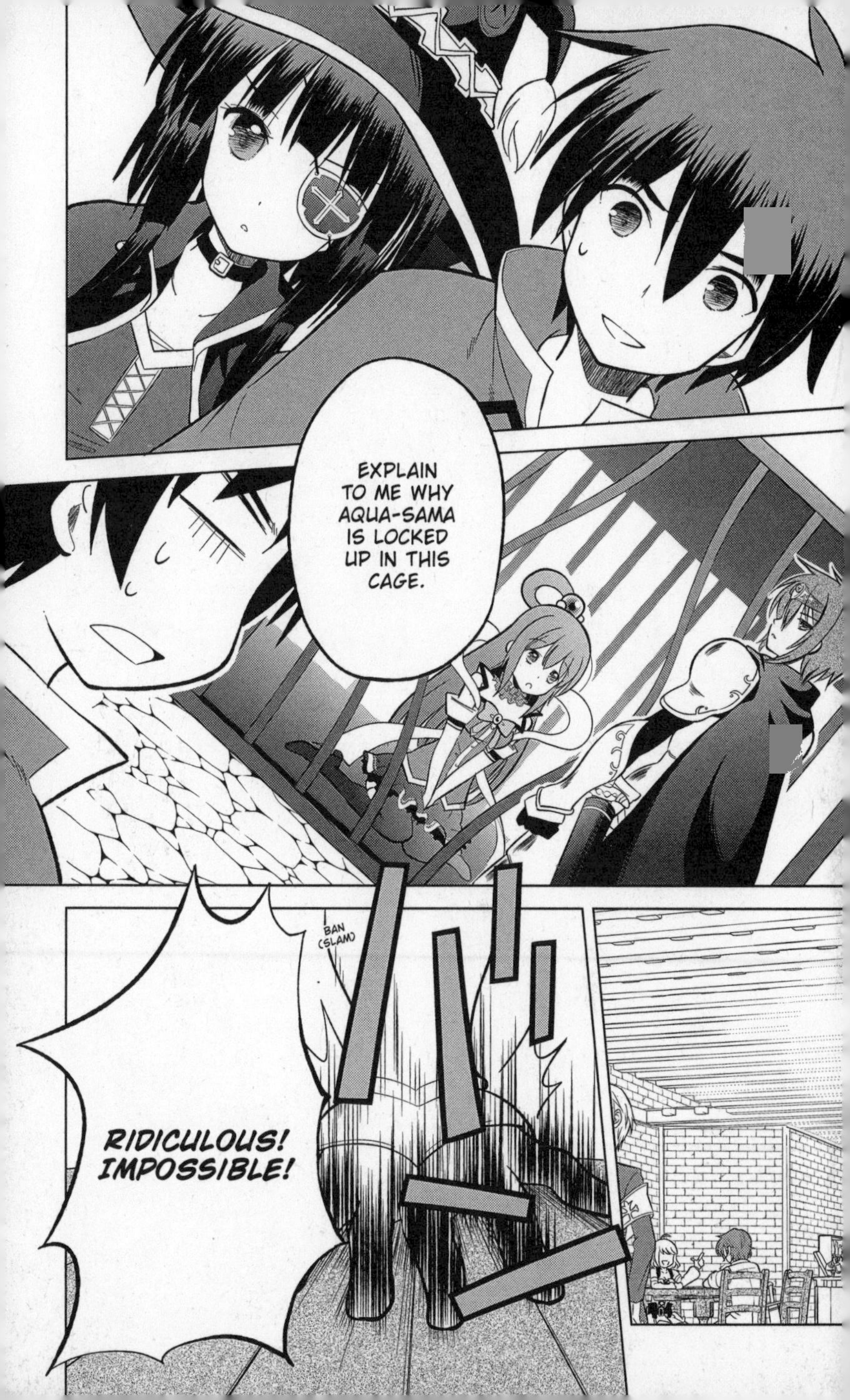
EXPLAIN TO ME WHY AQUA-SAMA IS LOCKED UP IN THIS CAGE.
BAN (SLAM)
RIDICULOUS! IMPOSSIBLE!

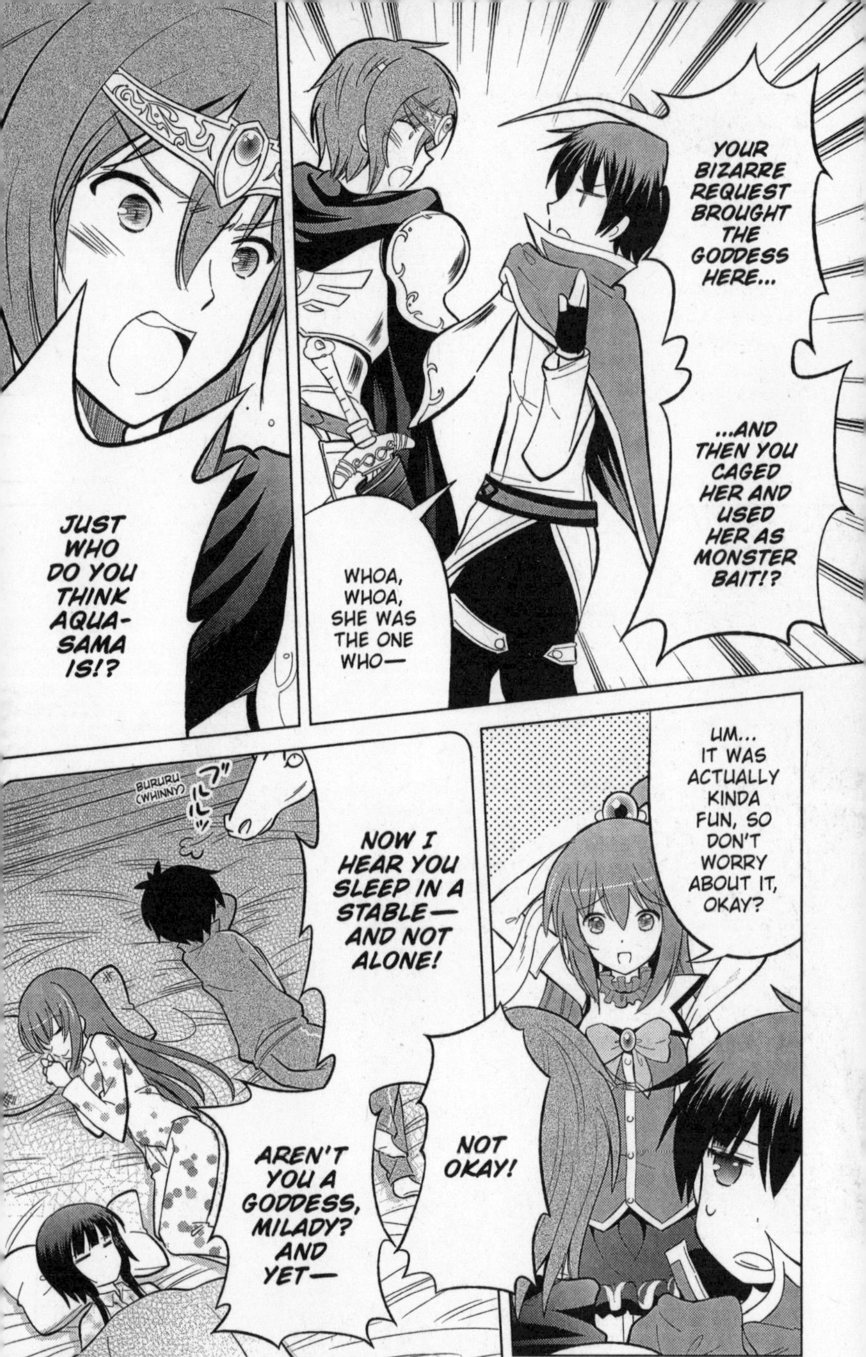
YOUR BIZARRE REQUEST BROUGHT THE GODDESS HERE...
...AND THEN YOU CAGED HER AND USED HER AS MONSTER BAIT!?
WHOA, WHOA, SHE WAS THE ONE WHO—
JUST WHO DO YOU THINK AQUA-SAMA IS!?
UM... IT WAS ACTUALLY KINDA FUN, SO DON'T WORRY ABOUT IT, OKAY?
NOT OKAY!
AREN'T YOU A GODDESS, MILADY? AND YET—
NOW I HEAR YOU SLEEP IN A STABLE—AND NOT ALONE!
BURURU (WHINNY)

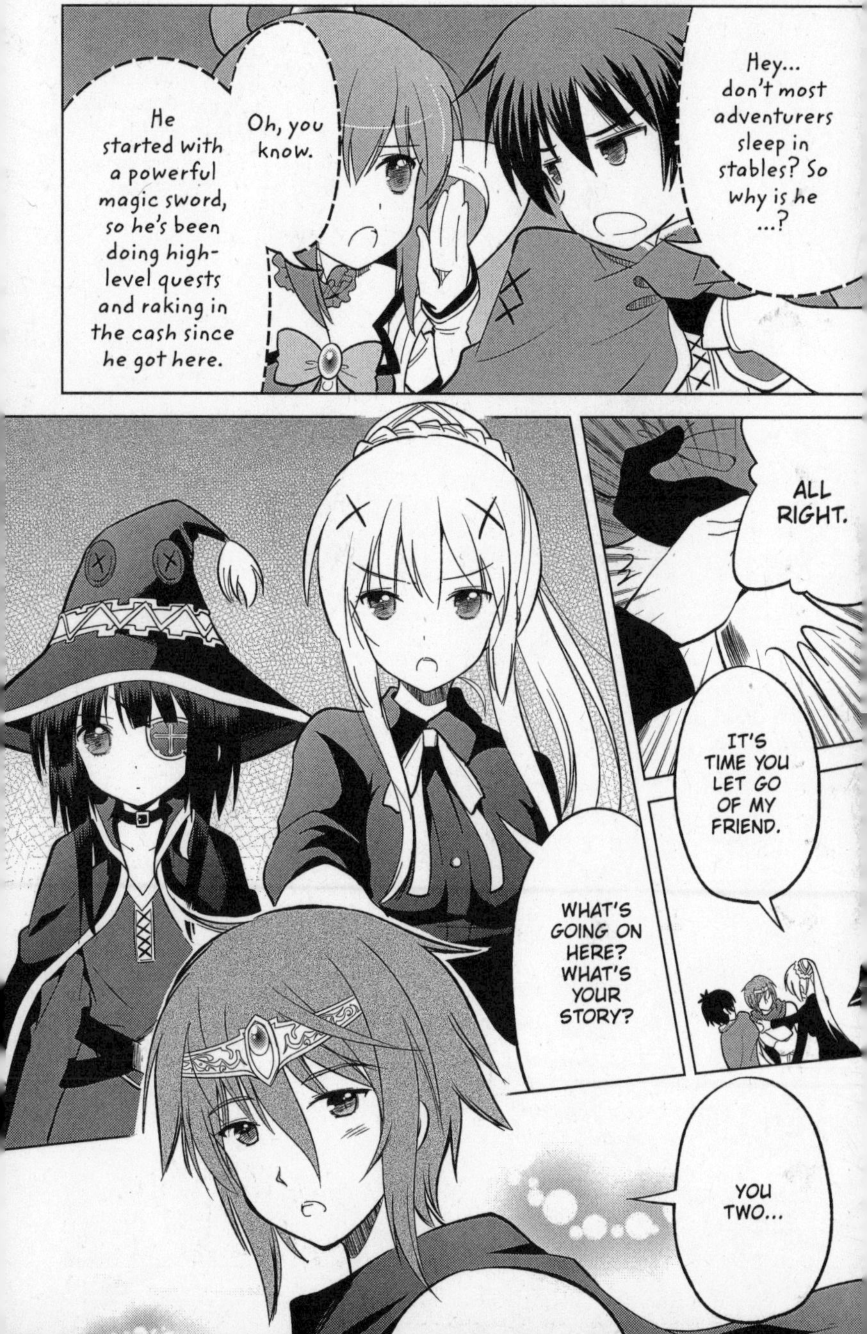
Hey... don't most adventurers sleep in stables? So why is he ...?
Oh, you know.
He started with a powerful magic sword, so he's been doing high-level quests and raking in the cash since he got here.
ALL RIGHT.
IT'S TIME YOU LET GO OF MY FRIEND.
WHAT'S GOING ON HERE? WHAT'S YOUR STORY?
YOU TWO...

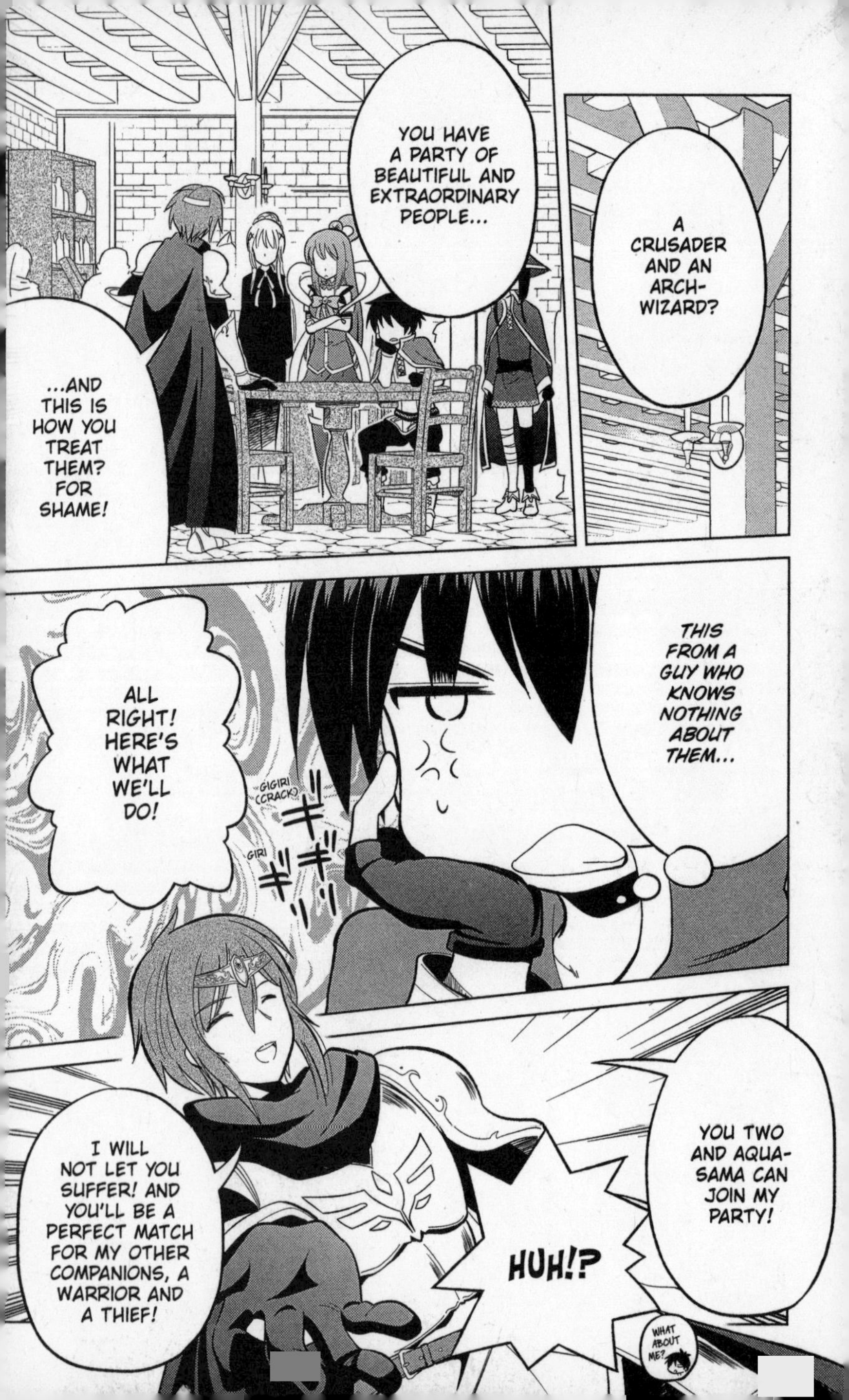
YOU HAVE A PARTY OF BEAUTIFUL AND EXTRAORDINARY PEOPLE...
A CRUSADER AND AN ARCH-WIZARD?
...AND THIS IS HOW YOU TREAT THEM? FOR SHAME!
THIS FROM A GUY WHO KNOWS NOTHING ABOUT THEM...
GIGIRI (CRACK)
GIRI
ALL RIGHT! HERE'S WHAT WE'LL DO!
YOU TWO AND AQUA-SAMA CAN JOIN MY PARTY!
HUH!?
WHAT ABOUT ME?
I WILL NOT LET YOU SUFFER! AND YOU'LL BE A PERFECT MATCH FOR MY OTHER COMPANIONS, A WARRIOR AND A THIEF!

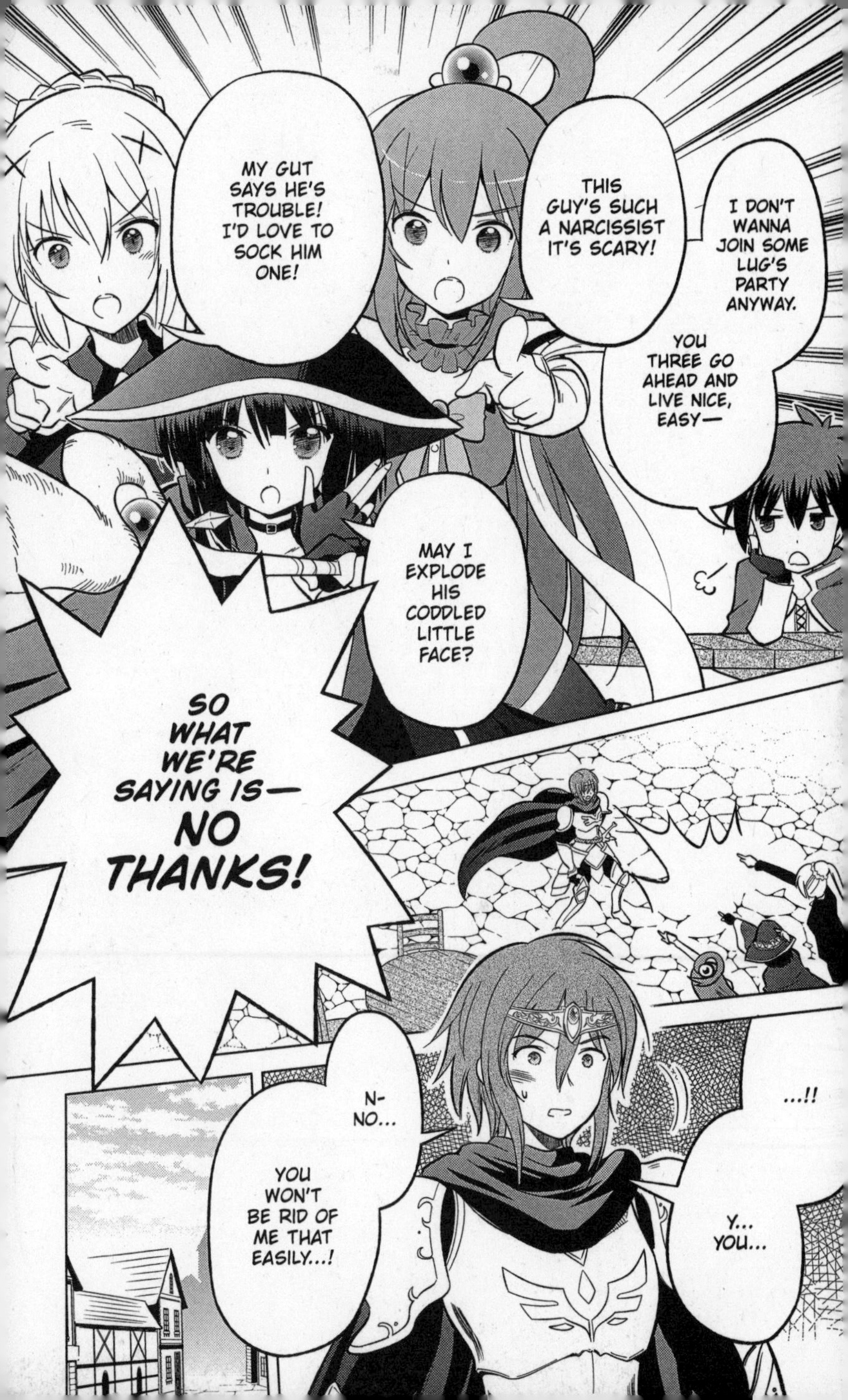
I DON'T WANNA JOIN SOME LUG'S PARTY ANYWAY.
YOU THREE GO AHEAD AND LIVE NICE, EASY—
THIS GUY'S SUCH A NARCISSIST IT'S SCARY!
MY GUT SAYS HE'S TROUBLE! I'D LOVE TO SOCK HIM ONE!
MAY I EXPLODE HIS CODDLED LITTLE FACE?
SO WHAT WE'RE SAYING IS— NO THANKS!
...!!
Y... YOU...
N- NO...
YOU WON'T BE RID OF ME THAT EASILY...!

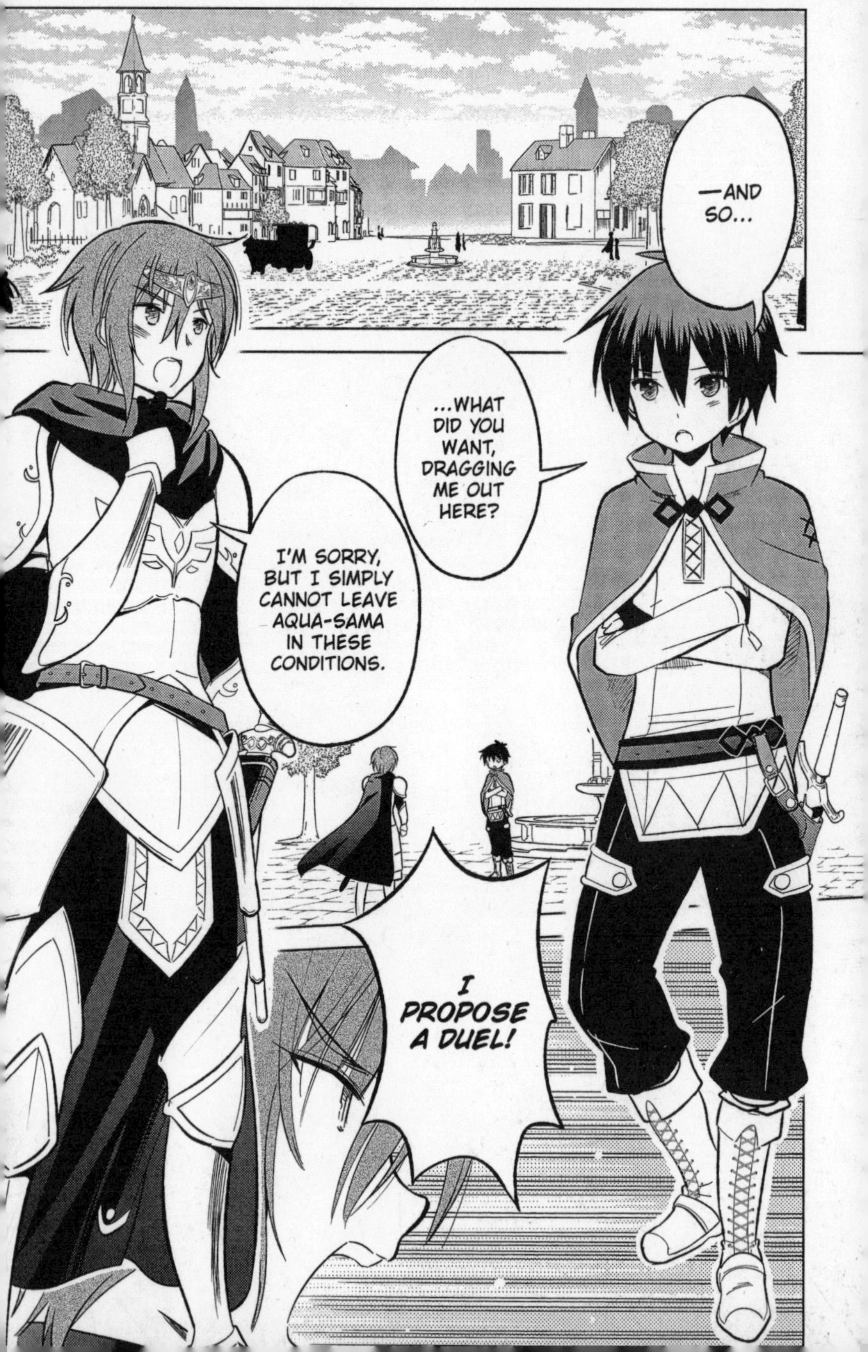
—AND SO...
...WHAT DID YOU WANT, DRAGGING ME OUT HERE?
I'M SORRY, BUT I SIMPLY CANNOT LEAVE AQUA-SAMA IN THESE CONDITIONS.
I PROPOSE A DUEL!

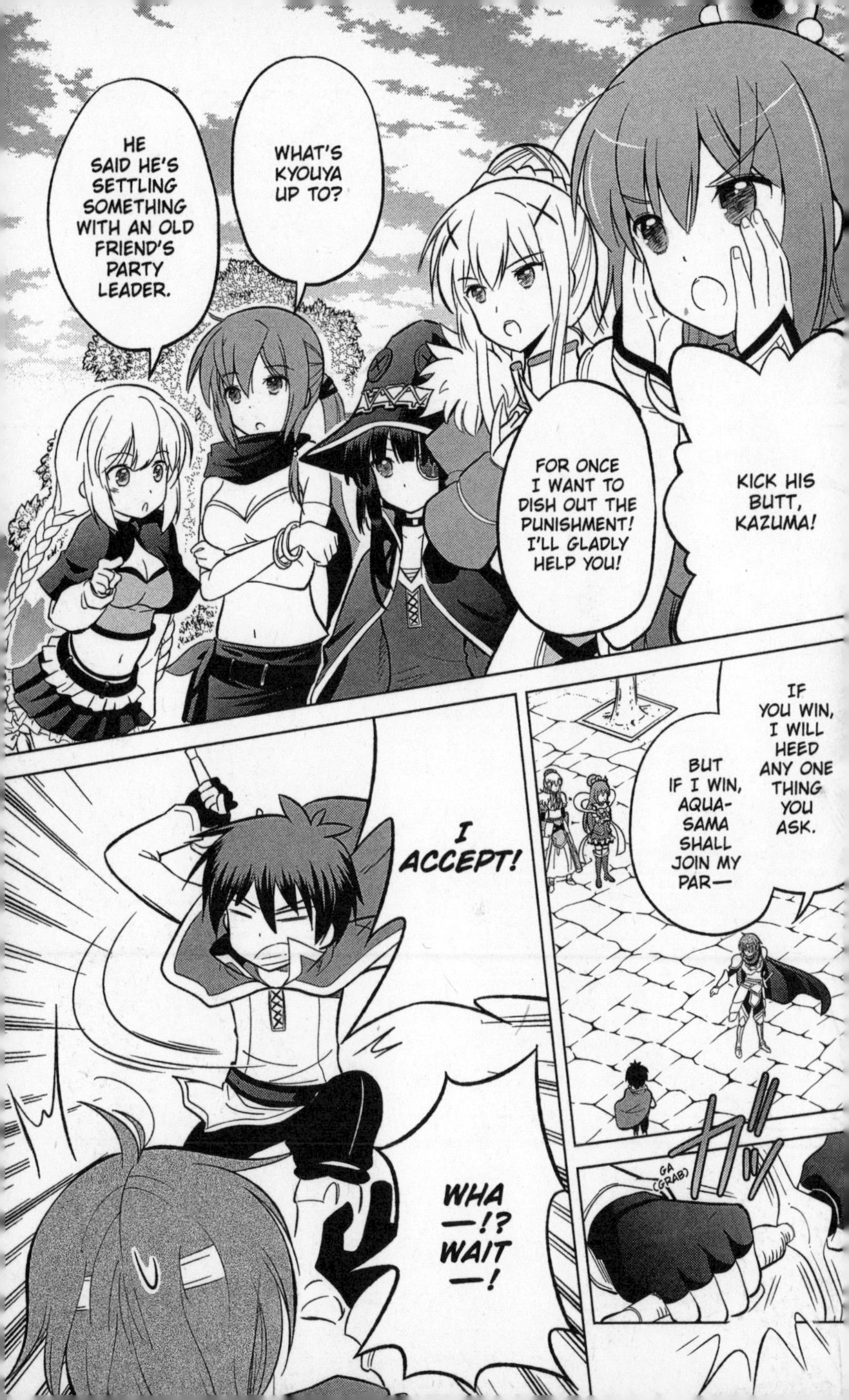

KICK HIS BUTT, KAZUMA!
FOR ONCE I WANT TO DISH OUT THE PUNISHMENT! I'LL GLADLY HELP YOU!
WHAT'S KYOUYA UP TO?
HE SAID HE'S SETTLING SOMETHING WITH AN OLD FRIEND'S PARTY LEADER.
IF YOU WIN, I WILL HEED ANY ONE THING YOU ASK.
BUT IF I WIN, AQUA-SAMA SHALL JOIN MY PAR—
GA (GRAB)
I ACCEPT!
WHA—!? WAIT—!

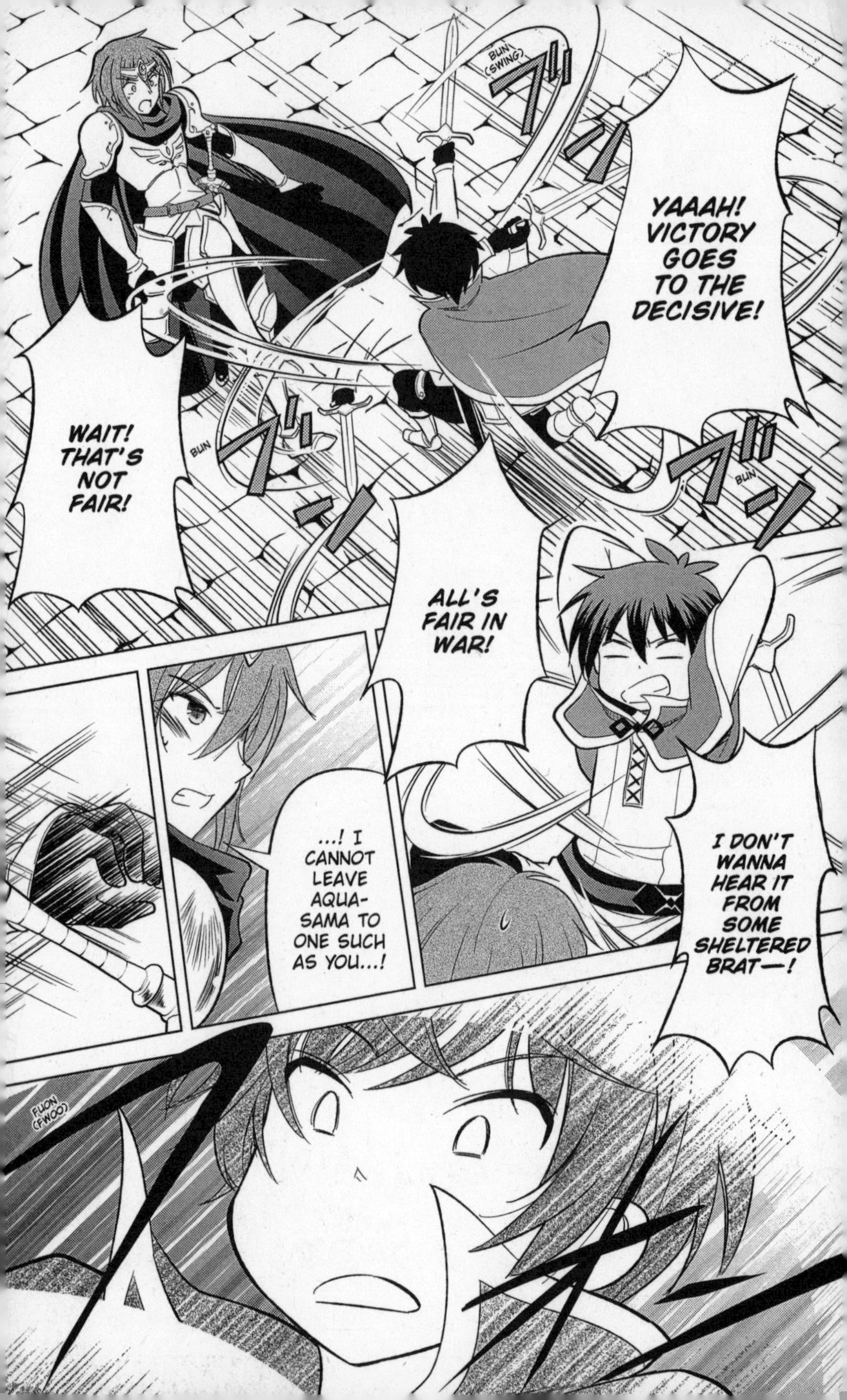
BUN (SWING)
YAAAH! VICTORY GOES TO THE DECISIVE!
BUN
WAIT! THAT'S NOT FAIR!
BUN
ALL'S FAIR IN WAR!
I DON'T WANNA HEAR IT FROM SOME SHELTERED BRAT—!
...! I CANNOT LEAVE AQUA-SAMA TO ONE SUCH AS YOU...!
FUON (FWOO)

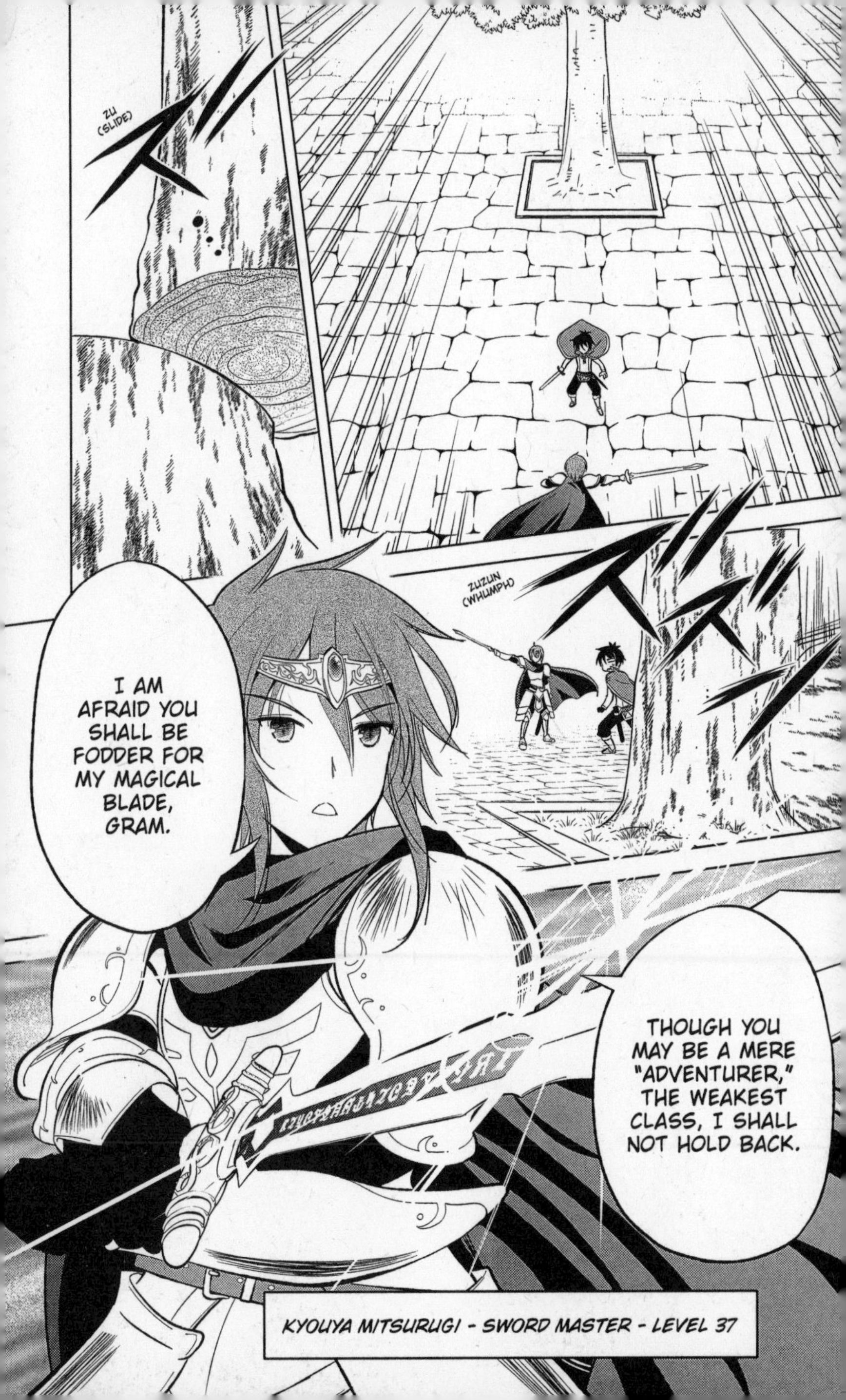
ZU (SLIDE)
ZUZUN (WHUMPH)
I AM AFRAID YOU SHALL BE FODDER FOR MY MAGICAL BLADE, GRAM.
THOUGH YOU MAY BE A MERE "ADVENTURER," THE WEAKEST CLASS, I SHALL NOT HOLD BACK.
KYOUYA MITSURUGI - SWORD MASTER - LEVEL 37

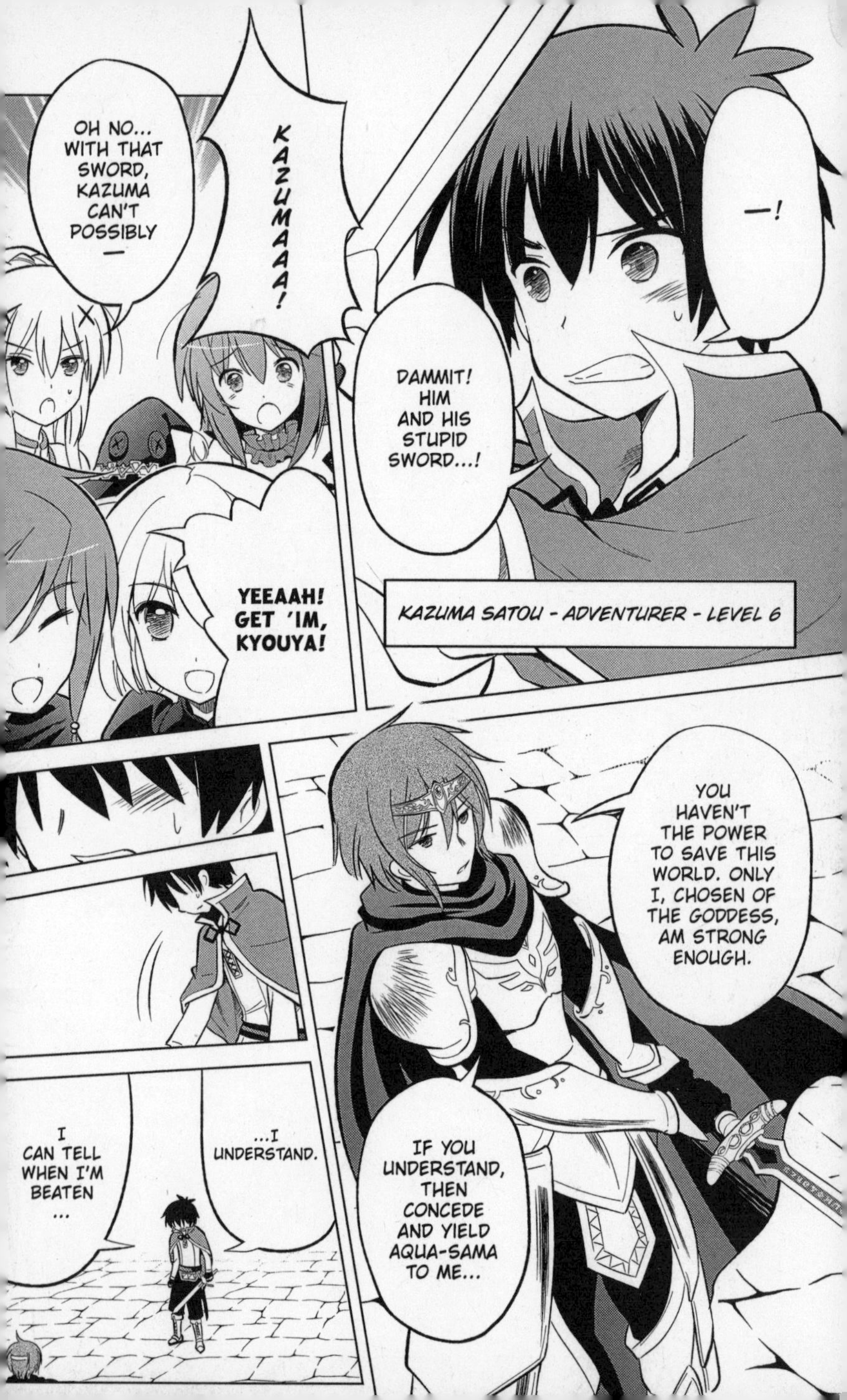
—!
DAMMIT! HIM AND HIS STUPID SWORD...!
KAZUMA SATOU - ADVENTURER - LEVEL 6
KAZUMAAAA!
OH NO... WITH THAT SWORD, KAZUMA CAN'T POSSIBLY —
YEEAAH! GET 'IM, KYOUYA!
YOU HAVEN'T THE POWER TO SAVE THIS WORLD. ONLY I, CHOSEN OF THE GODDESS, AM STRONG ENOUGH.
IF YOU UNDERSTAND, THEN CONCEDE AND YIELD AQUA-SAMA TO ME...
...I UNDERSTAND.
I CAN TELL WHEN I'M BEATEN ...

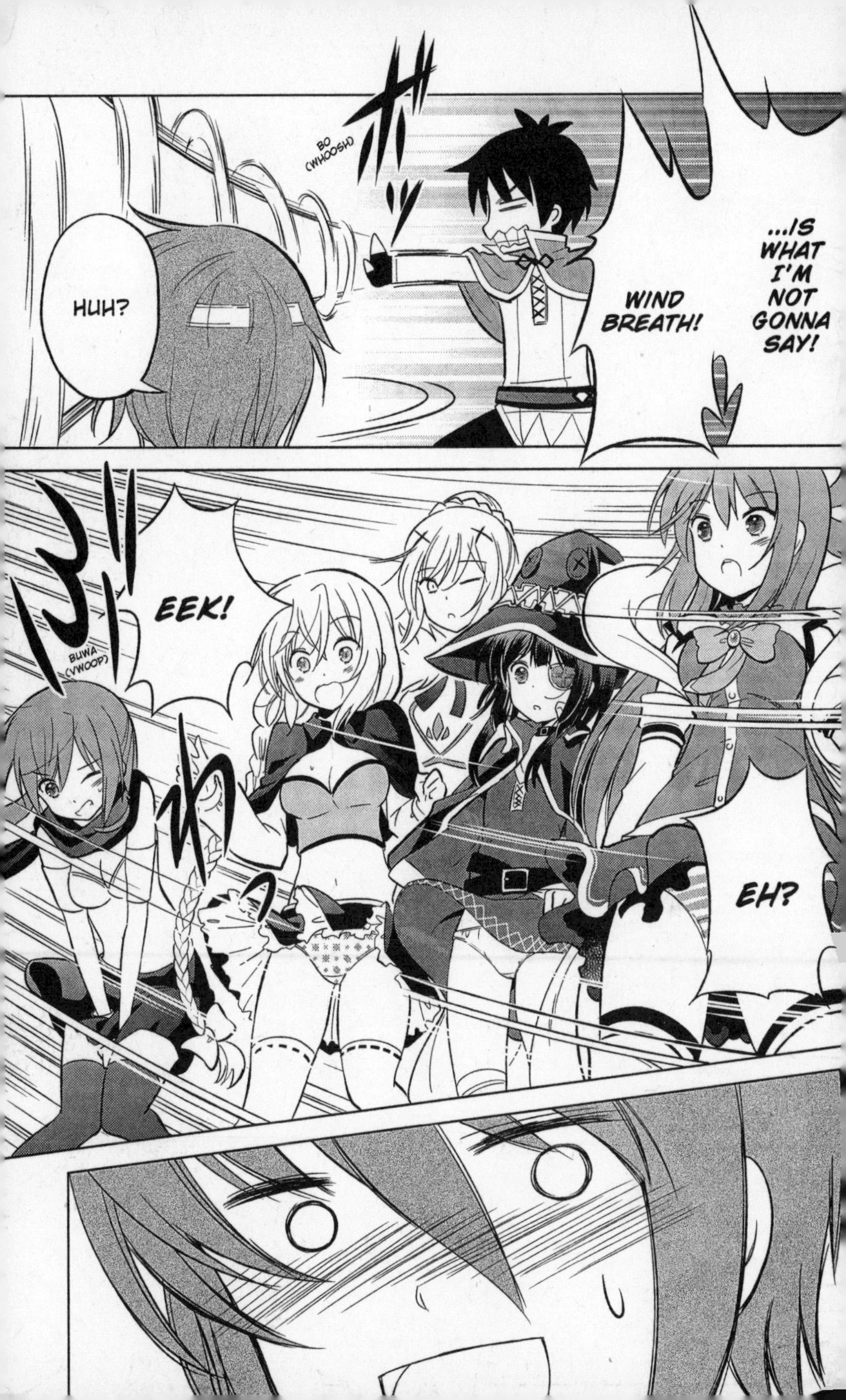
...IS WHAT I'M NOT GONNA SAY!
WIND BREATH!
BO (WHOOSH)
HUH?
EH?
EEK!
BUWA (VWOOP)

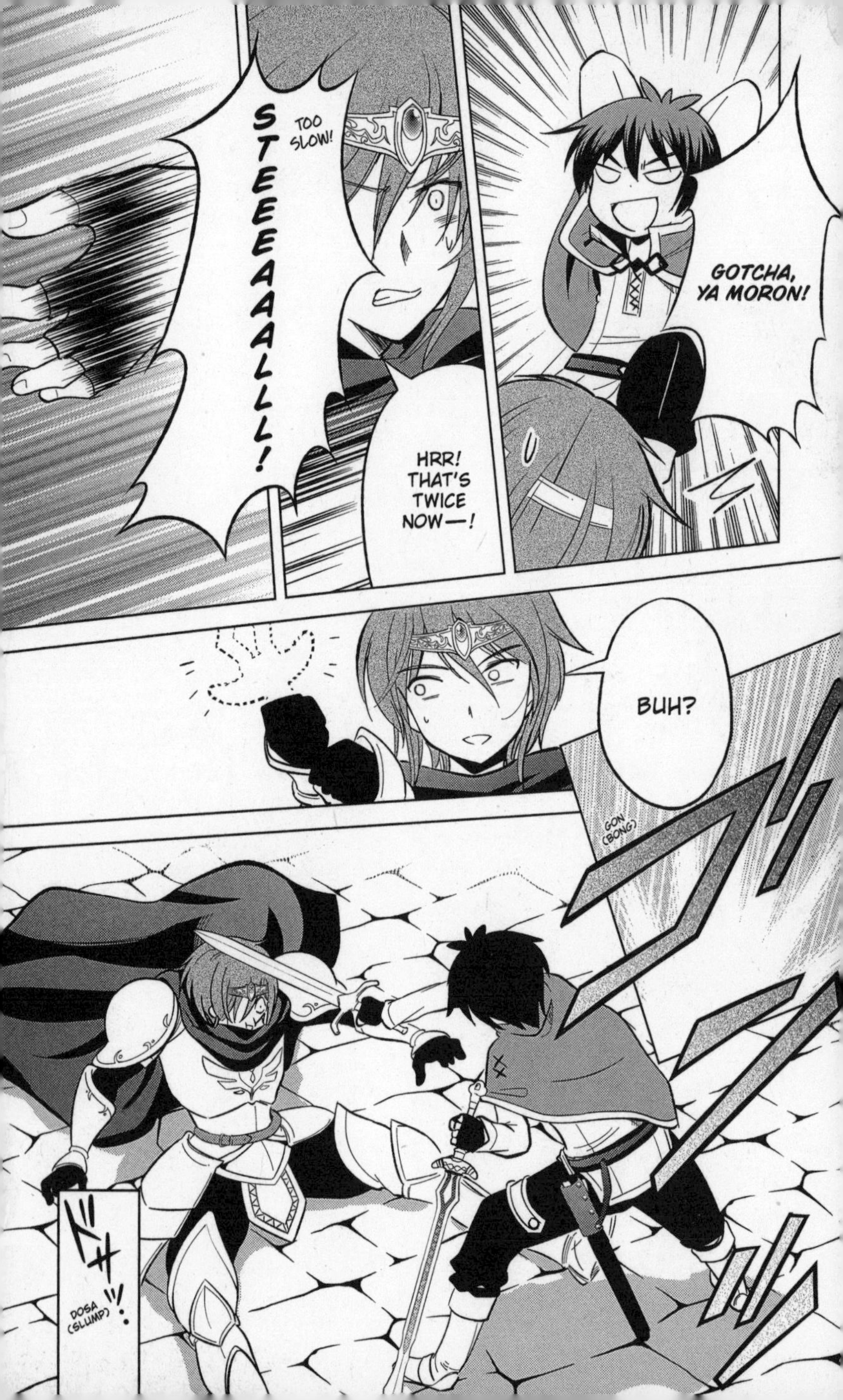
GOTCHA, YA MORON!
TOO SLOW!
HRR! THAT'S TWICE NOW—!
STEEEAAALLL!
BUH?
GON (BONG)
DOSA (SLUMP)

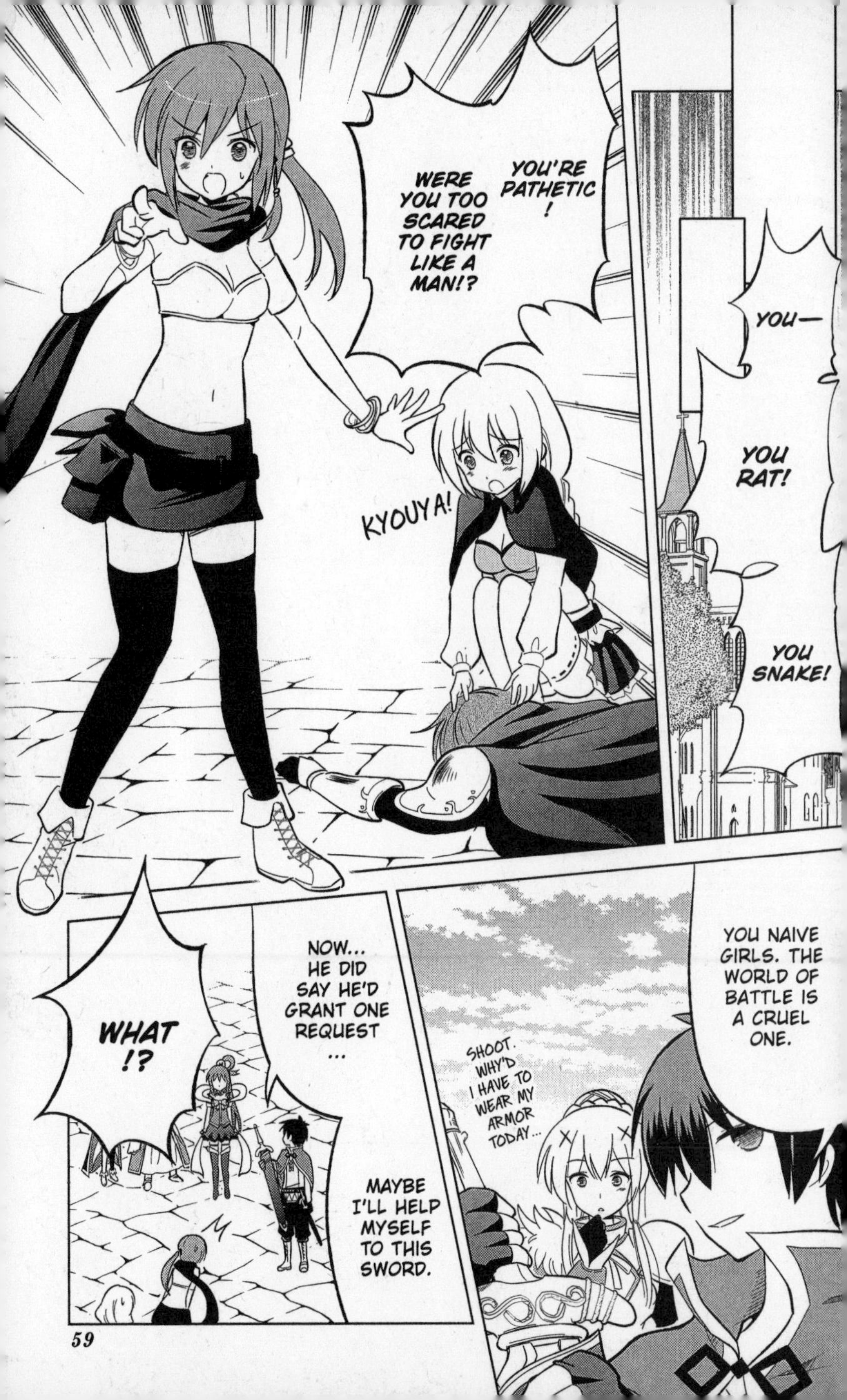
YOU—
YOU RAT!
YOU SNAKE!
YOU'RE PATHETIC!
WERE YOU TOO SCARED TO FIGHT LIKE A MAN!?
KYOUYA!
YOU NAIVE GIRLS. THE WORLD OF BATTLE IS A CRUEL ONE.
SHOOT. WHY'D I HAVE TO WEAR MY ARMOR TODAY...
NOW... HE DID SAY HE'D GRANT ONE REQUEST...
MAYBE I'LL HELP MYSELF TO THIS SWORD.
WHAT!?

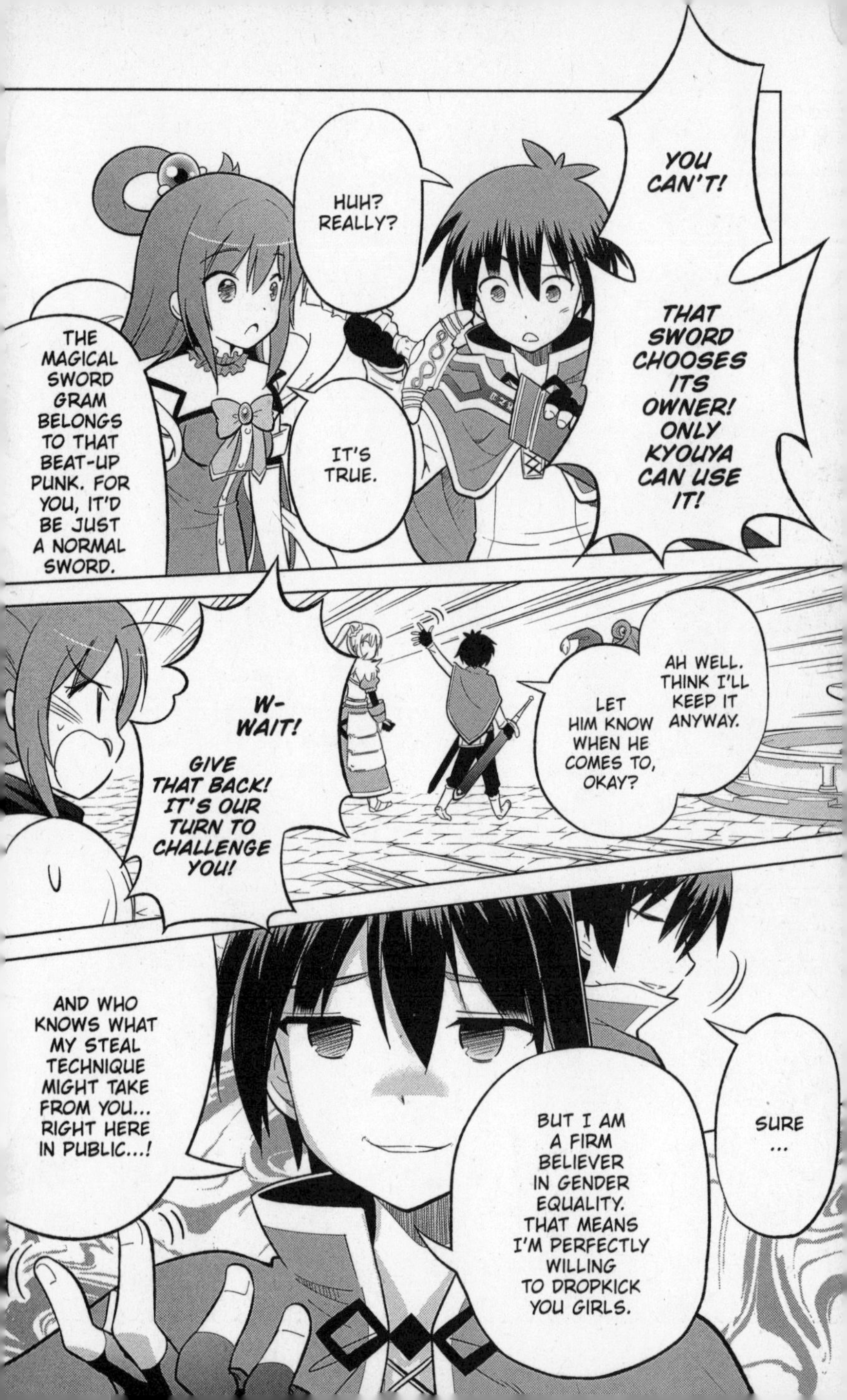
YOU CAN'T!
THAT SWORD CHOOSES ITS OWNER! ONLY KYOUYA CAN USE IT!
HUH? REALLY?
IT'S TRUE.
THE MAGICAL SWORD GRAM BELONGS TO THAT BEAT-UP PUNK. FOR YOU, IT'D BE JUST A NORMAL SWORD.
AH WELL. THINK I'LL KEEP IT ANYWAY.
LET HIM KNOW WHEN HE COMES TO, OKAY?
W-WAIT!
GIVE THAT BACK! IT'S OUR TURN TO CHALLENGE YOU!
SURE...
BUT I AM A FIRM BELIEVER IN GENDER EQUALITY. THAT MEANS I'M PERFECTLY WILLING TO DROPKICK YOU GIRLS.
AND WHO KNOWS WHAT MY STEAL TECHNIQUE MIGHT TAKE FROM YOU... RIGHT HERE IN PUBLIC...!

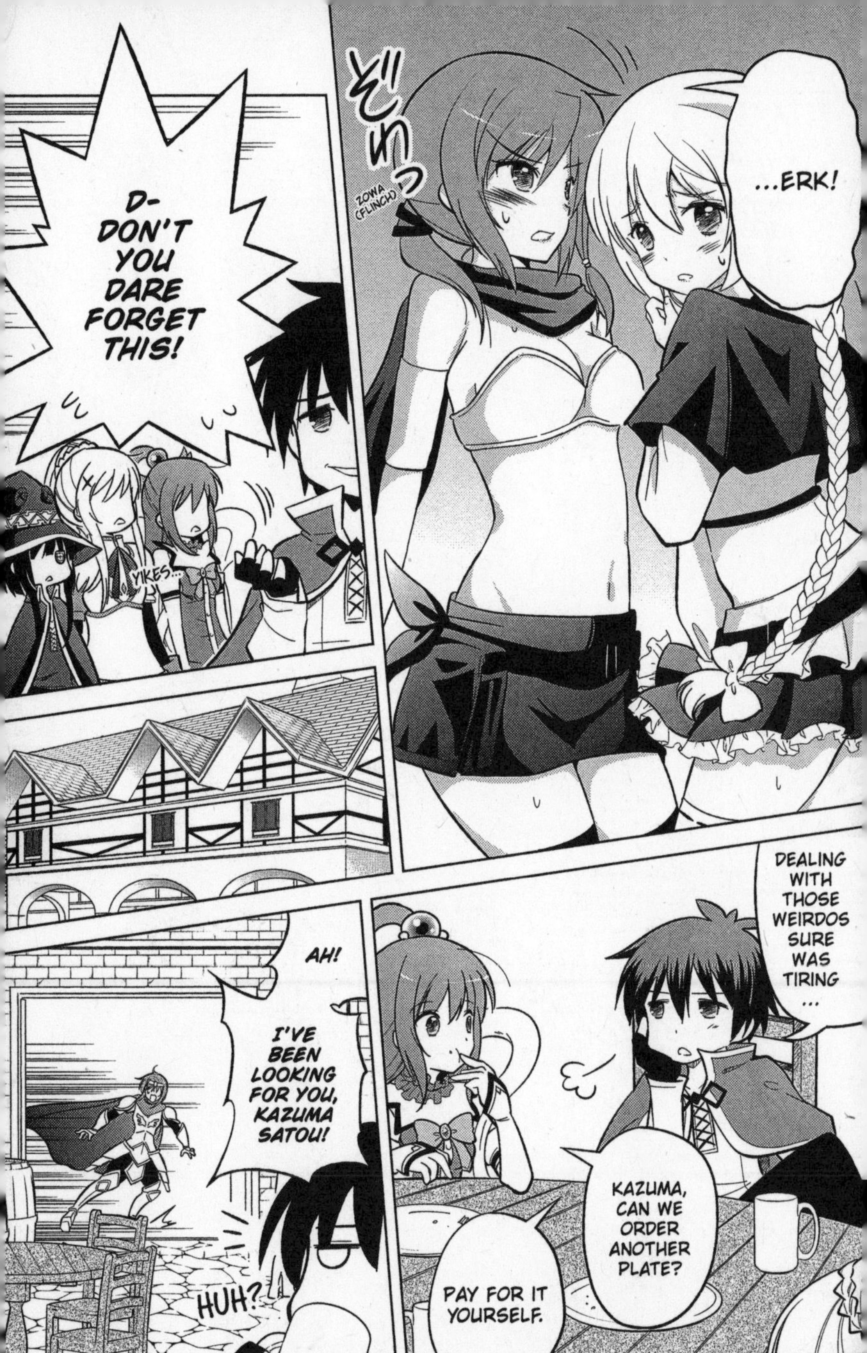
ぞわっ
ZOWA (FLINCH)
...ERK!
D-DON'T YOU DARE FORGET THIS!
YIKES...
DEALING WITH THOSE WEIRDOS SURE WAS TIRING...
KAZUMA, CAN WE ORDER ANOTHER PLATE?
PAY FOR IT YOURSELF.
AH!
I'VE BEEN LOOKING FOR YOU, KAZUMA SATOU!
HUH?

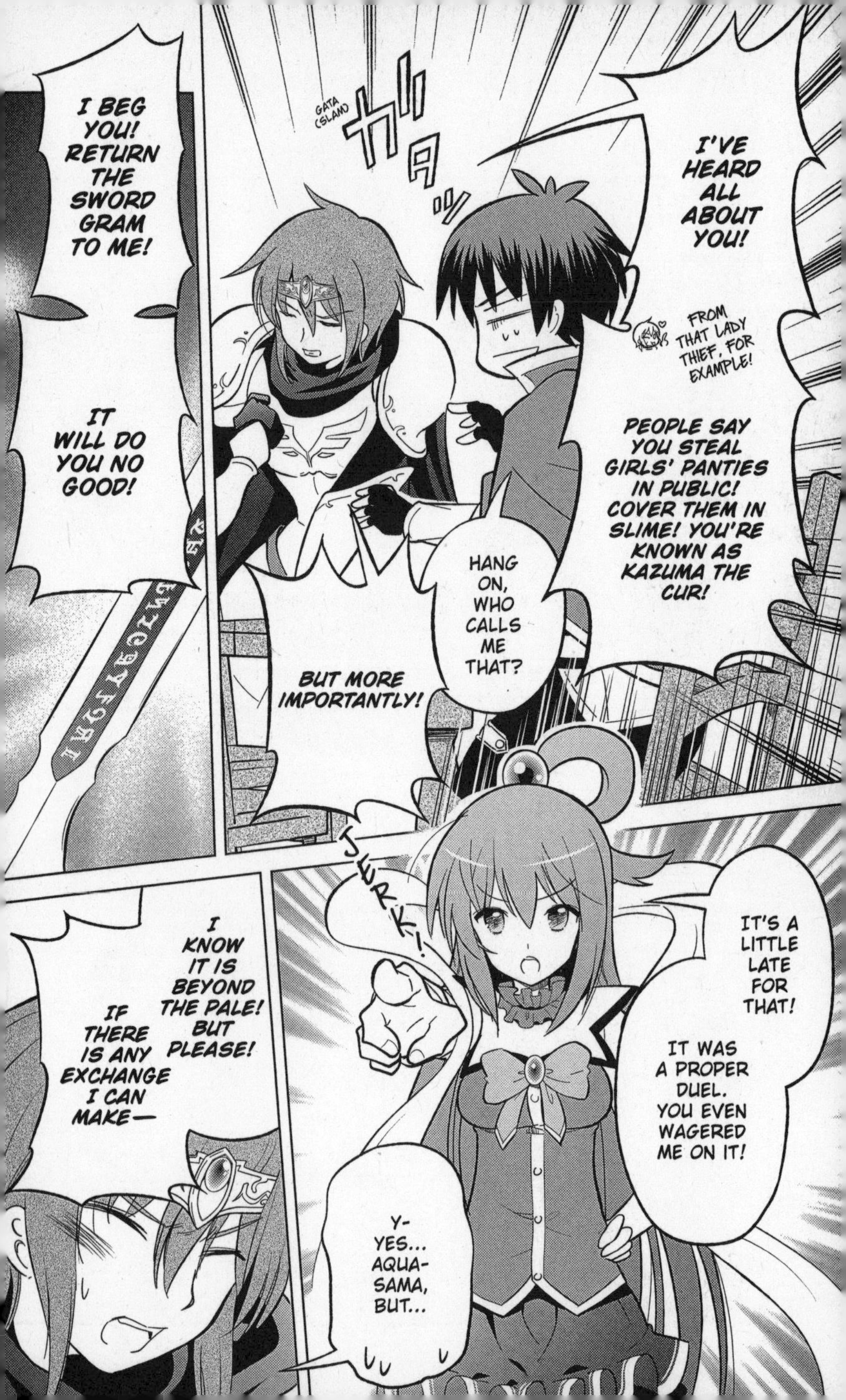

GATA (SLAM)
I'VE HEARD ALL ABOUT YOU!
FROM THAT LADY THIEF, FOR EXAMPLE!
PEOPLE SAY YOU STEAL GIRLS' PANTIES IN PUBLIC! COVER THEM IN SLIME! YOU'RE KNOWN AS KAZUMA THE CUR!
HANG ON, WHO CALLS ME THAT?
BUT MORE IMPORTANTLY!
I BEG YOU! RETURN THE SWORD GRAM TO ME!
IT WILL DO YOU NO GOOD!
JERK!
IT'S A LITTLE LATE FOR THAT!
IT WAS A PROPER DUEL. YOU EVEN WAGERED ME ON IT!
Y-YES... AQUA-SAMA, BUT...
I KNOW IT IS BEYOND THE PALE! BUT PLEASE!
IF THERE IS ANY EXCHANGE I CAN MAKE—

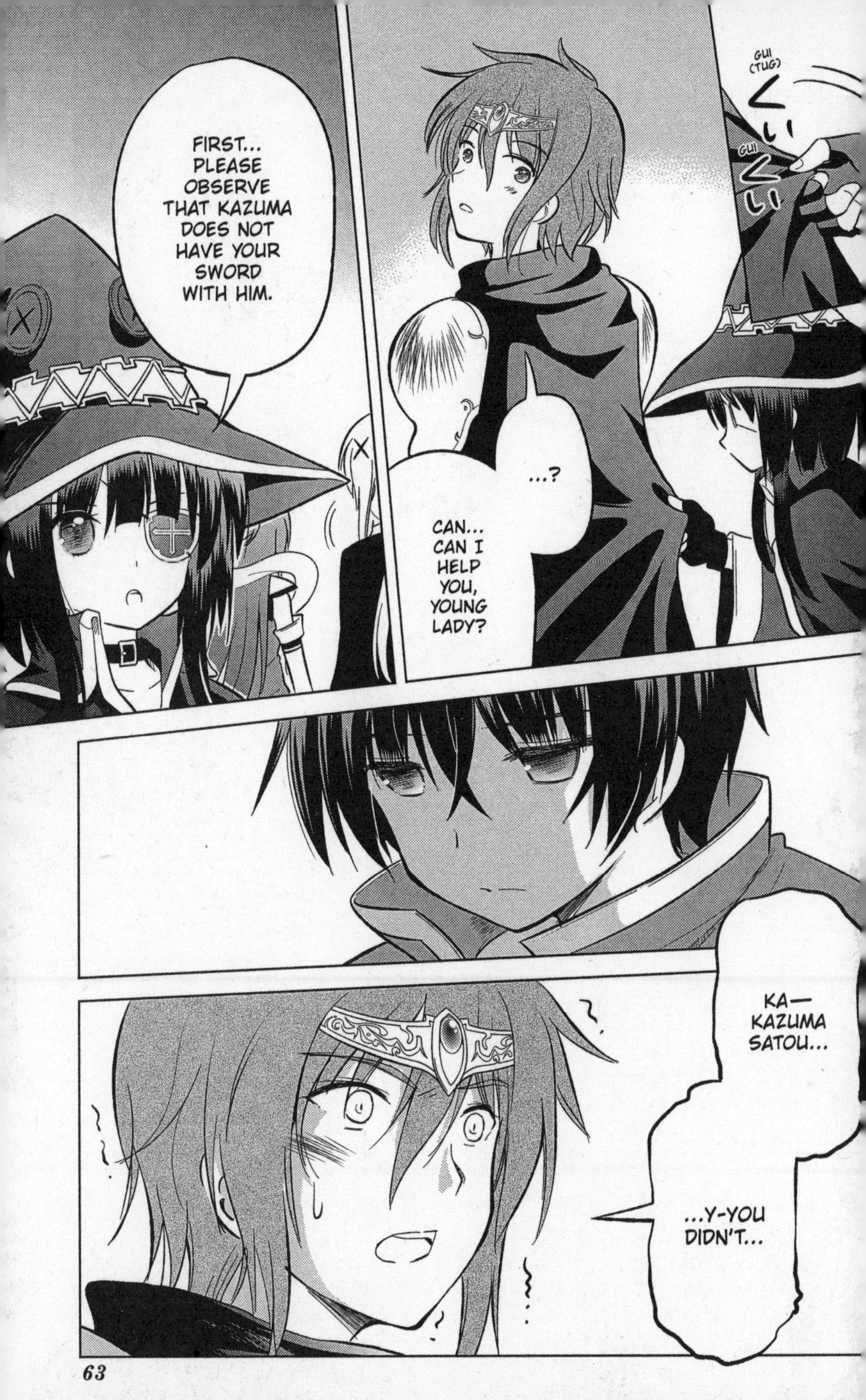
GUI (TUG)
くい
GUI
くい
...?
CAN... CAN I HELP YOU, YOUNG LADY?
FIRST... PLEASE OBSERVE THAT KAZUMA DOES NOT HAVE YOUR SWORD WITH HIM.
KA— KAZUMA SATOU...
...Y-YOU DIDN'T...

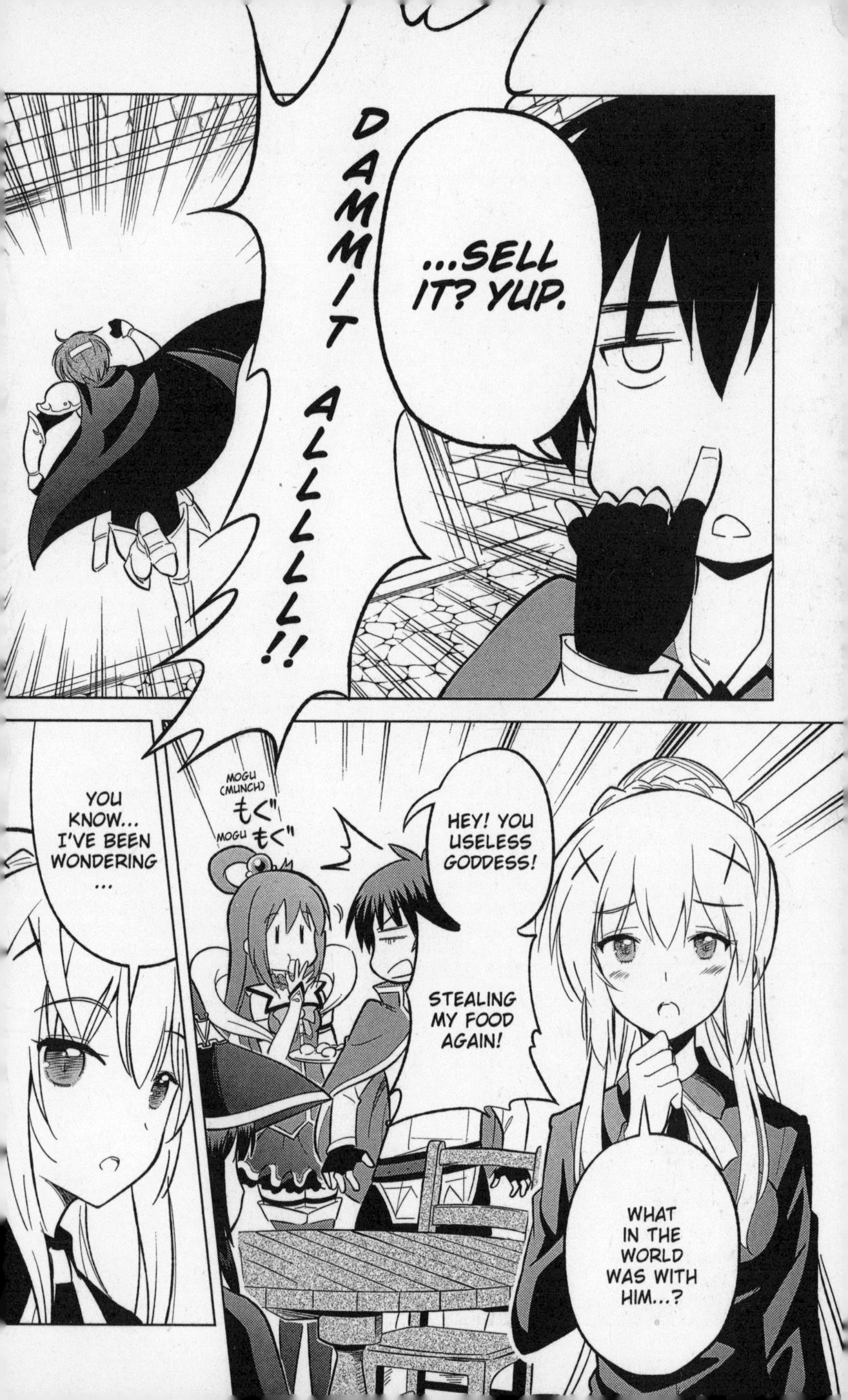
...SELL IT? YUP.
DAMMIT ALLLLLLL!!
HEY! YOU USELESS GODDESS!
STEALING MY FOOD AGAIN!
MOGU (MUNCH) もぐ
MOGU もぐ
WHAT IN THE WORLD WAS WITH HIM...?
YOU KNOW... I'VE BEEN WONDERING...

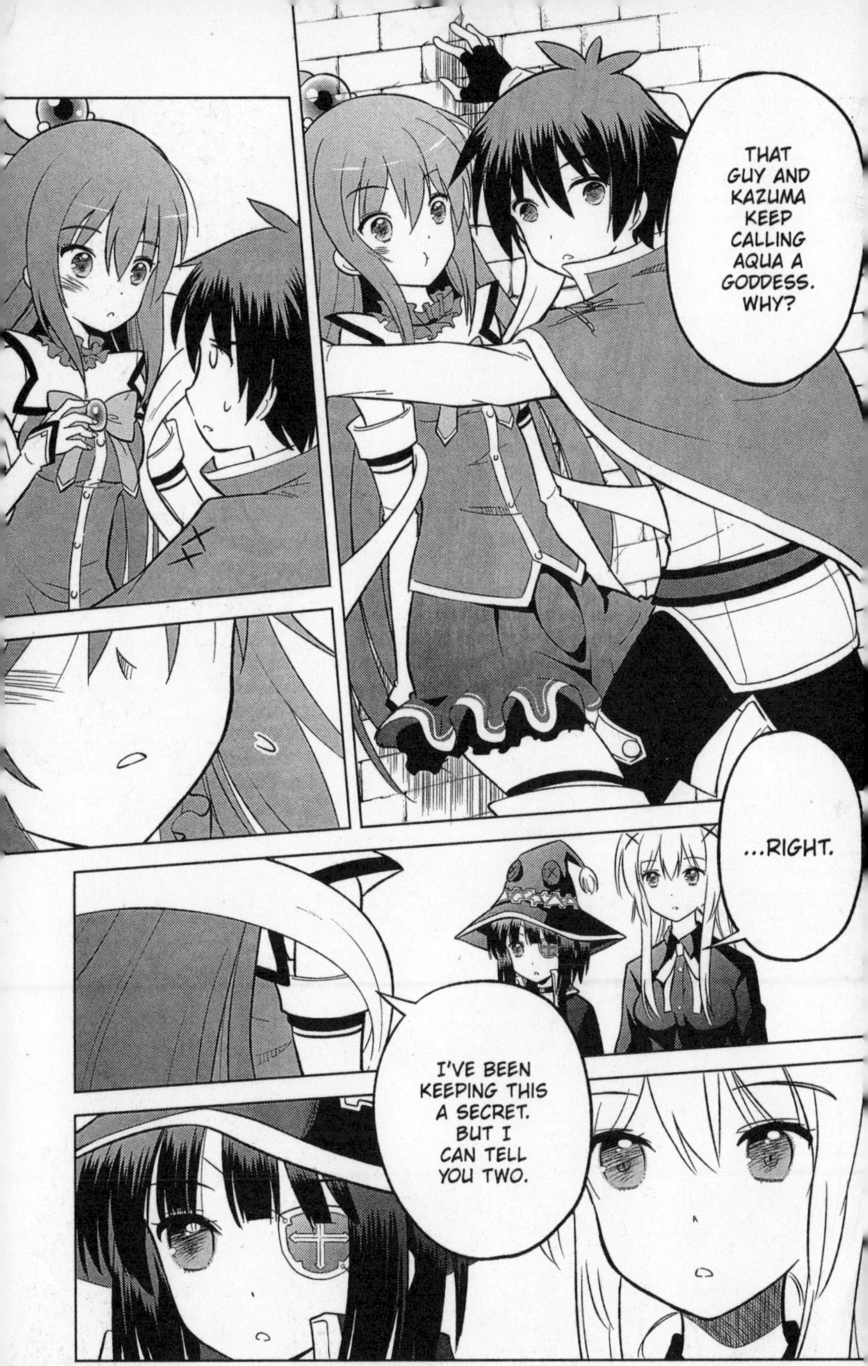
THAT GUY AND KAZUMA KEEP CALLING AQUA A GODDESS. WHY?
...RIGHT.
I'VE BEEN KEEPING THIS A SECRET. BUT I CAN TELL YOU TWO.

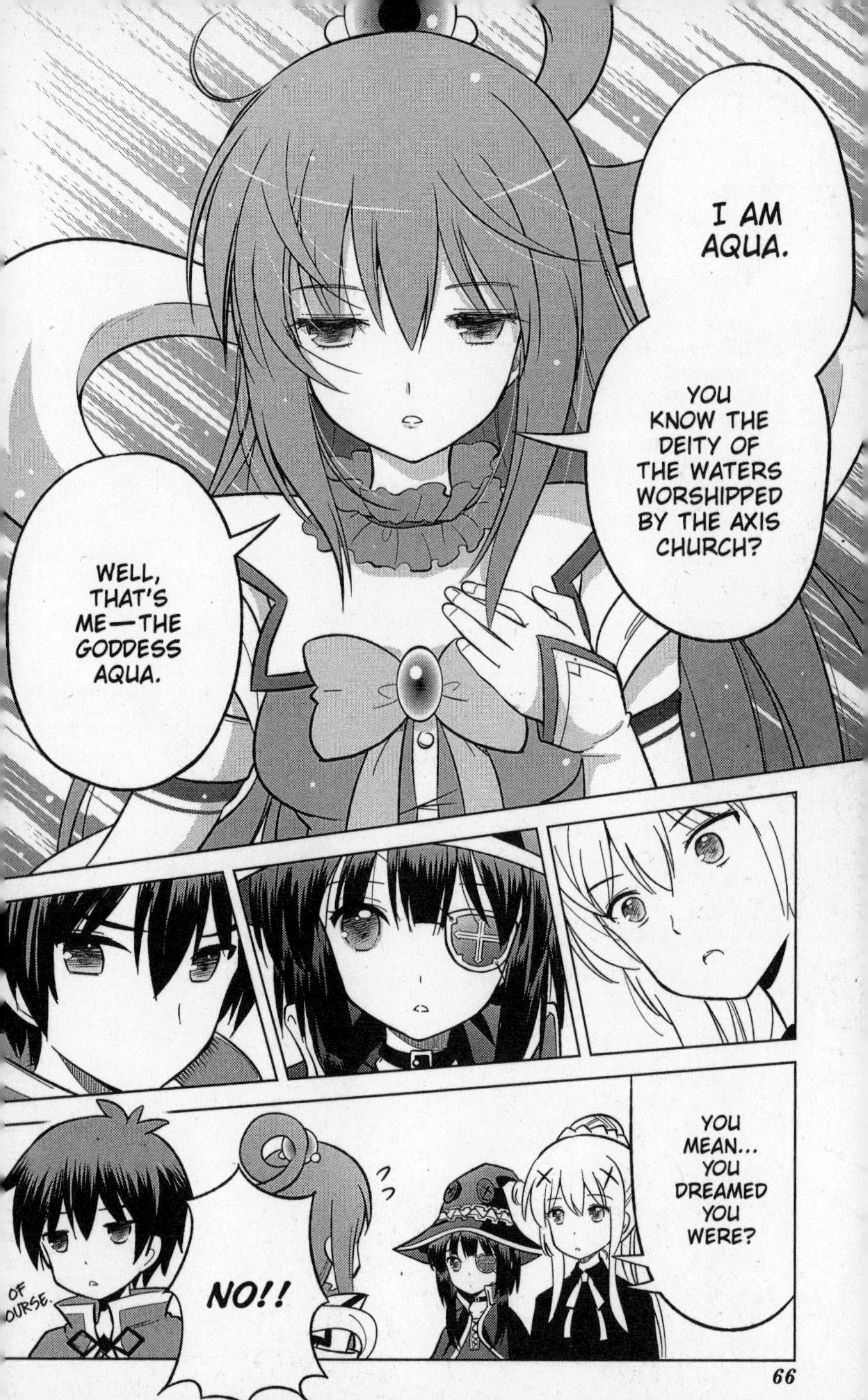
I AM AQUA.
YOU KNOW THE DEITY OF THE WATERS WORSHIPPED BY THE AXIS CHURCH?
WELL, THAT'S ME—THE GODDESS AQUA.
YOU MEAN... YOU DREAMED YOU WERE?
NO!!
OF OURSE.

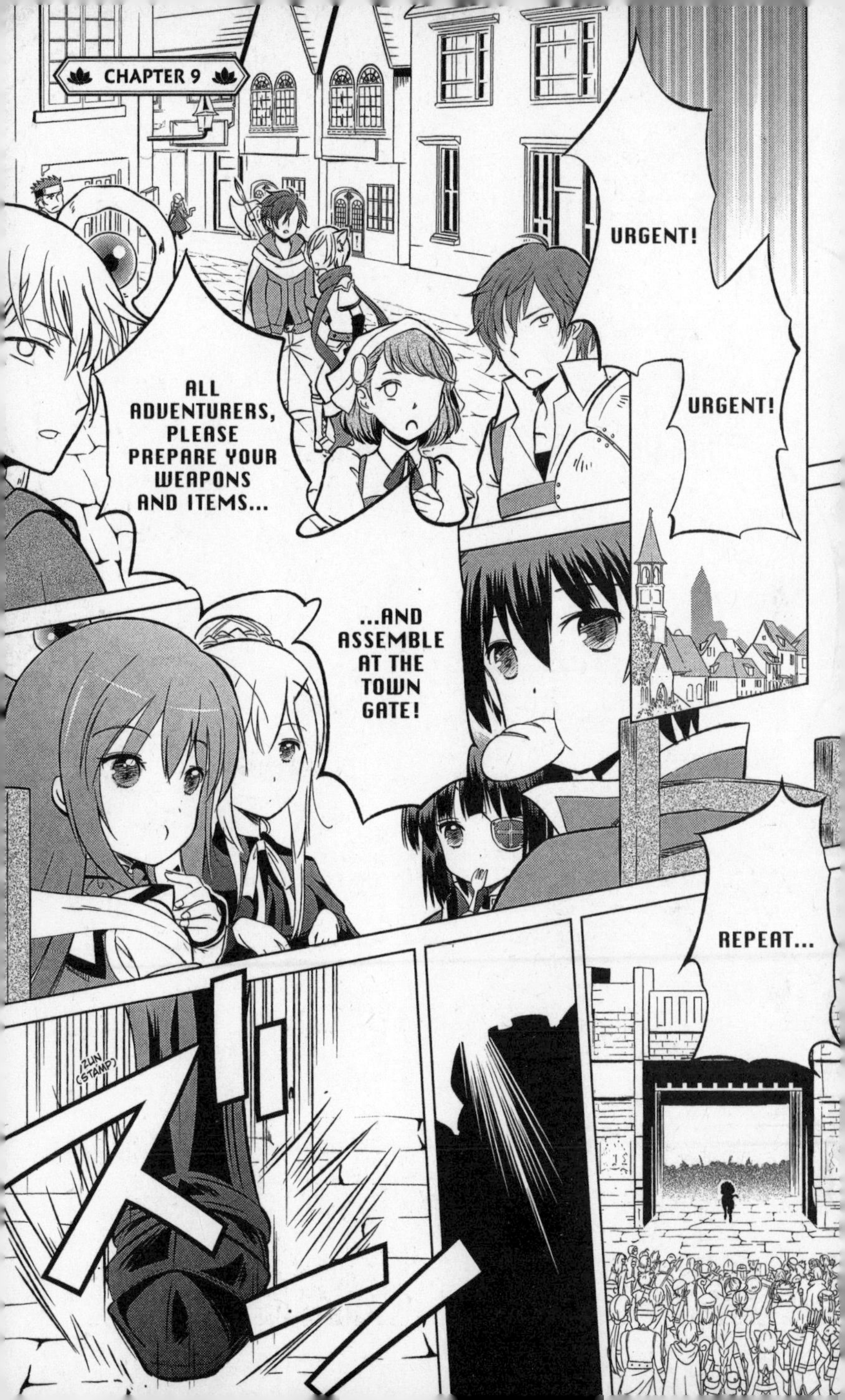
CHAPTER 9
URGENT!
URGENT!
ALL ADVENTURERS, PLEASE PREPARE YOUR WEAPONS AND ITEMS...
...AND ASSEMBLE AT THE TOWN GATE!
REPEAT...
ZUN (STAMP)

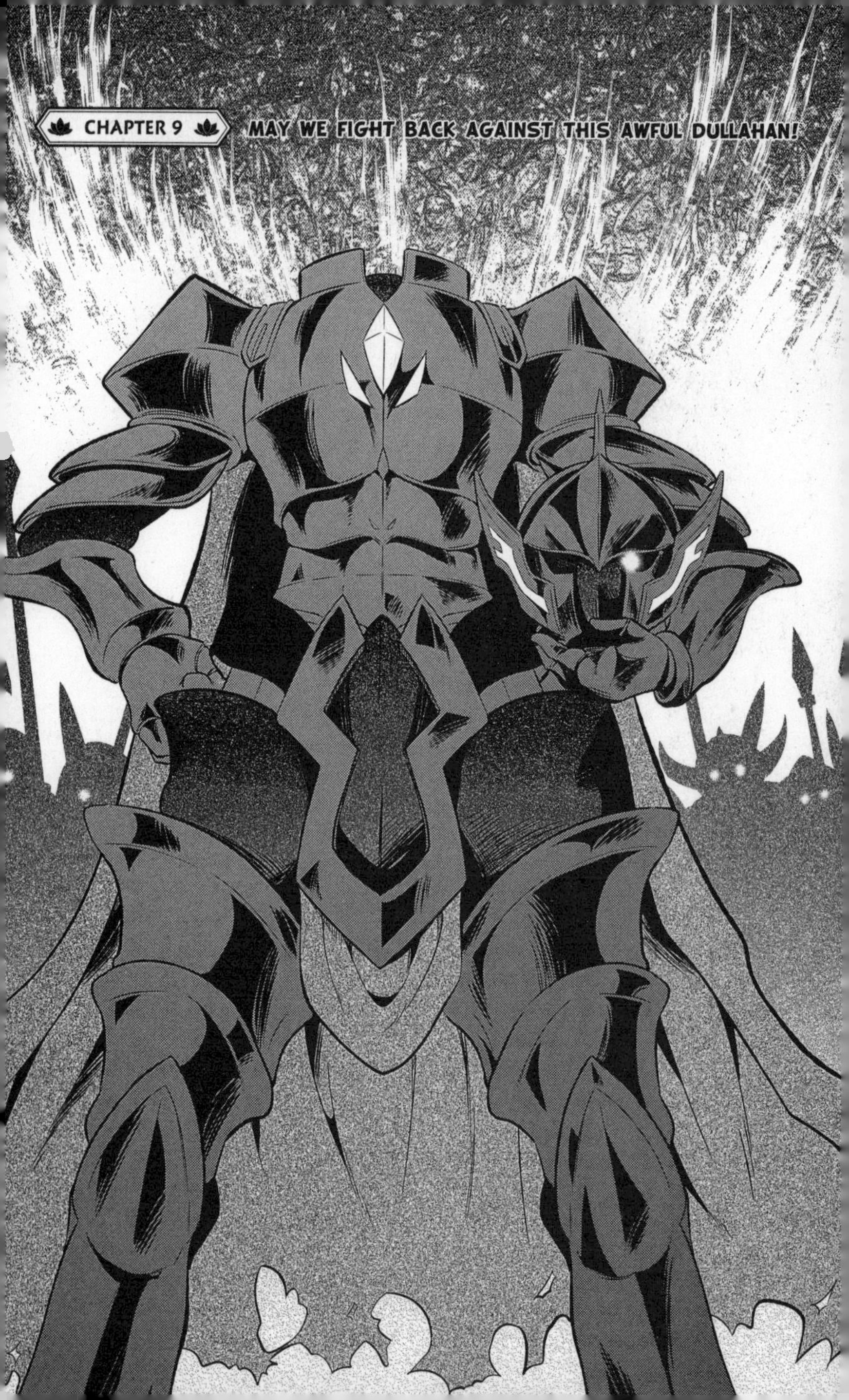
CHAPTER 9
MAY WE FIGHT BACK AGAINST THIS AWFUL DULLAHAN!

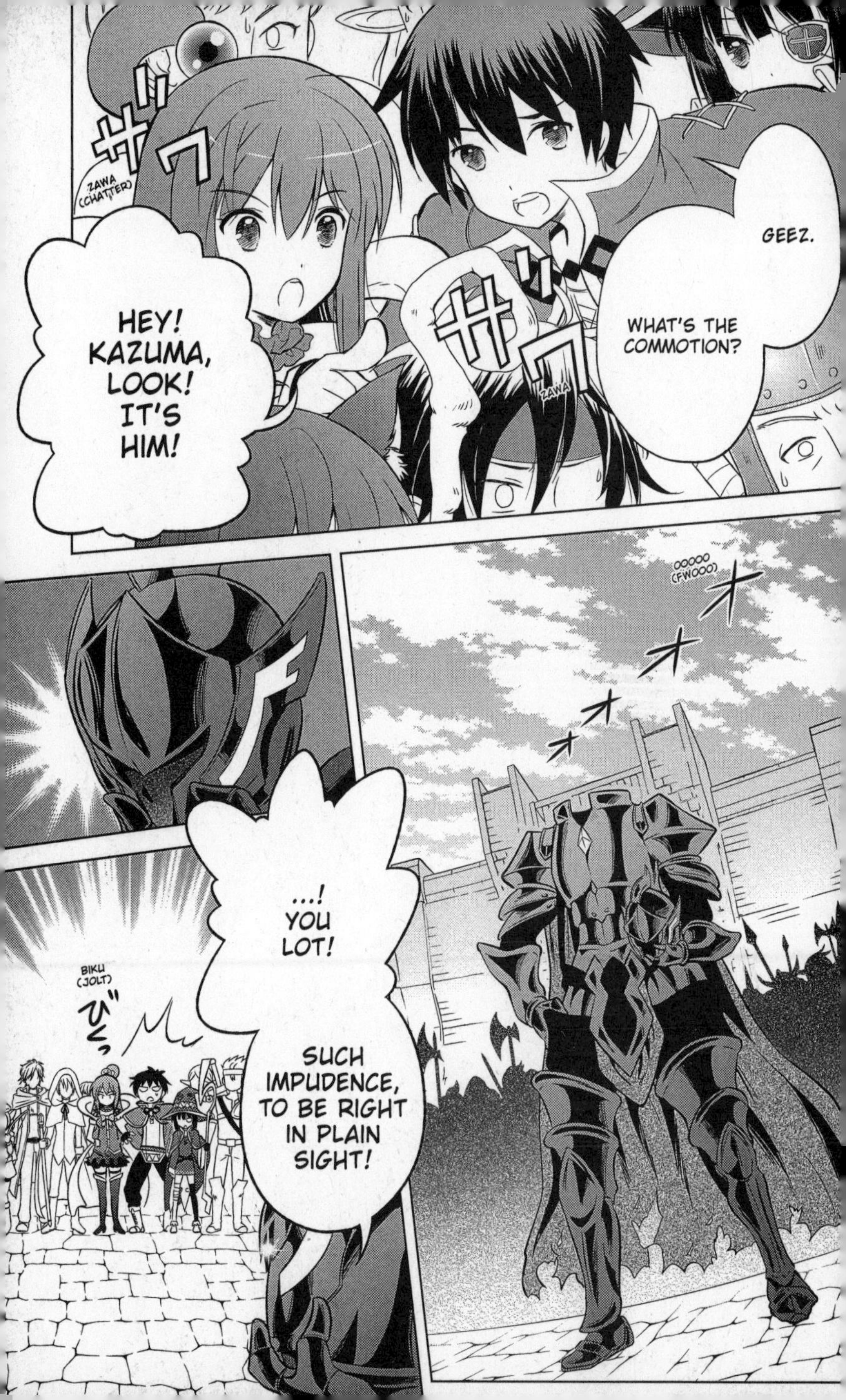
GEEZ.
WHAT'S THE COMMOTION?
ZAWA
ZAWA (CHATTER)
HEY! KAZUMA, LOOK! IT'S HIM!
OOOOO (FWOOO)
...! YOU LOT!
SUCH IMPUDENCE, TO BE RIGHT IN PLAIN SIGHT!
BIKU (JOLT)

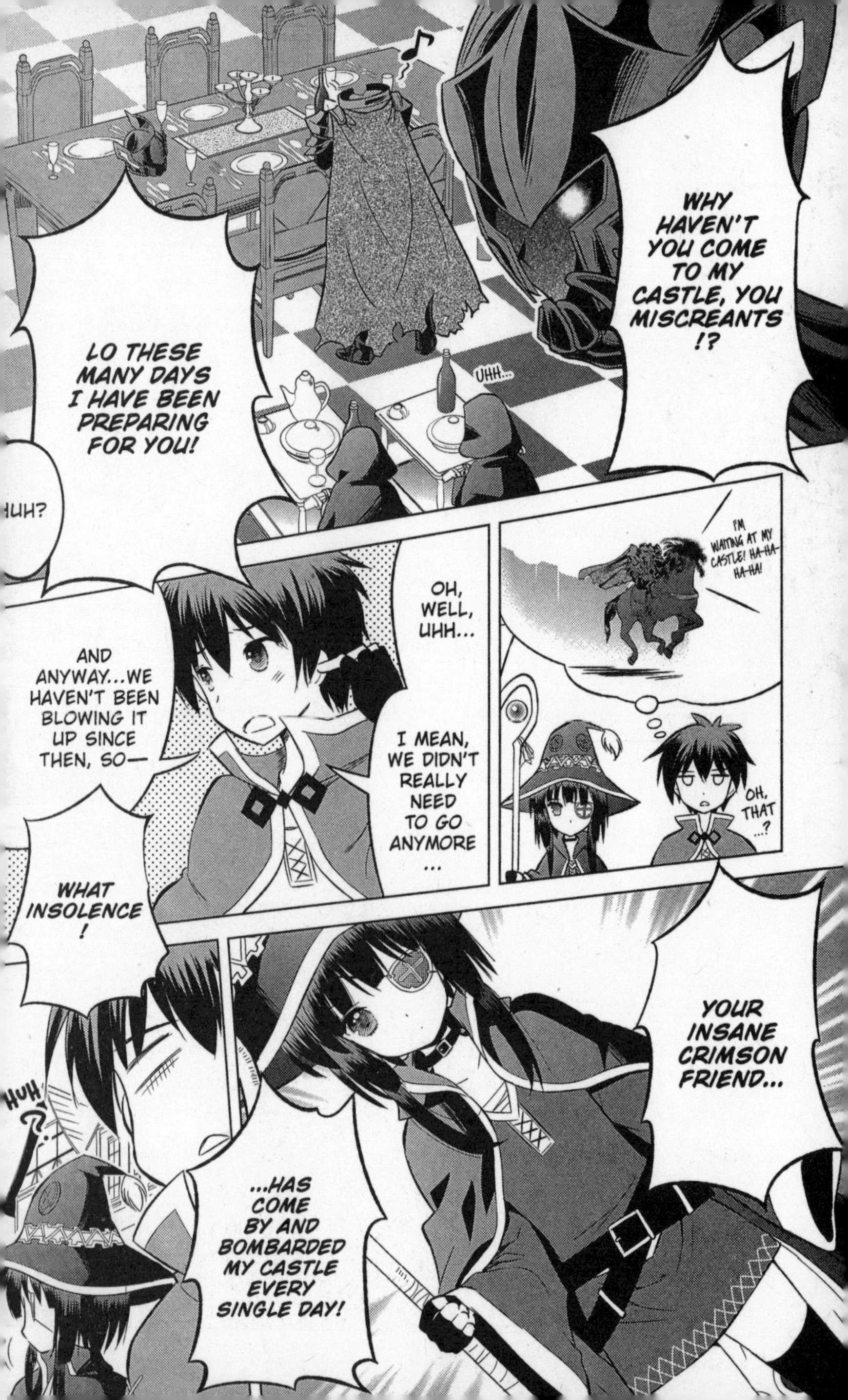
WHY HAVEN'T YOU COME TO MY CASTLE, YOU MISCREANTS!?
UHH...
LO THESE MANY DAYS I HAVE BEEN PREPARING FOR YOU!
HUH?
I'M WAITING AT MY CASTLE! HA-HA-HA-HA!
OH, THAT...?
OH, WELL, UHH...
I MEAN, WE DIDN'T REALLY NEED TO GO ANYMORE...
AND ANYWAY...WE HAVEN'T BEEN BLOWING IT UP SINCE THEN, SO—
WHAT INSOLENCE!
YOUR INSANE CRIMSON FRIEND...
...HAS COME BY AND BOMBARDED MY CASTLE EVERY SINGLE DAY!
HUH?

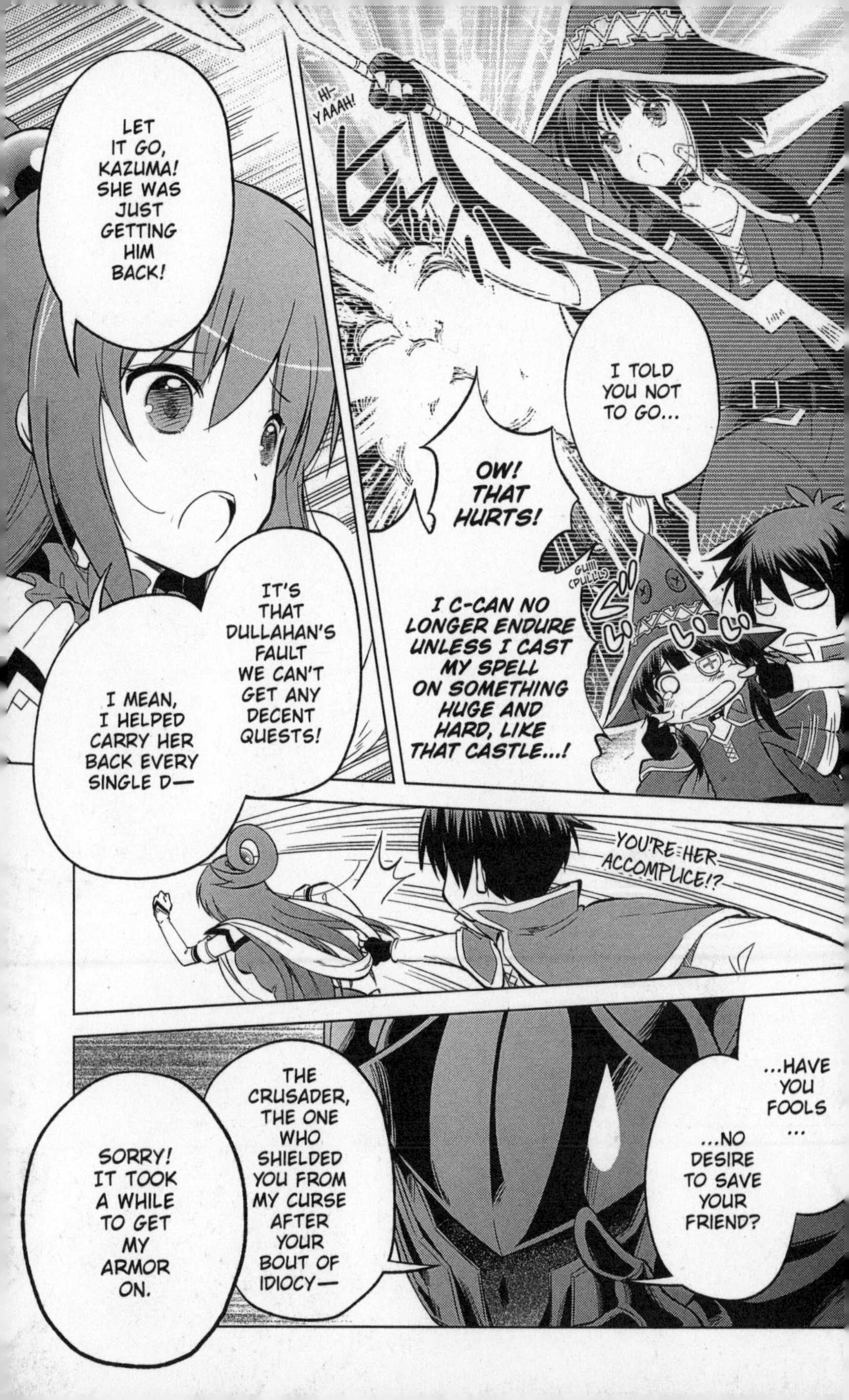
HI-YAAAH!
I TOLD YOU NOT TO GO...
OW! THAT HURTS!
GUIII (PULLL)
I C-CAN NO LONGER ENDURE UNLESS I CAST MY SPELL ON SOMETHING HUGE AND HARD, LIKE THAT CASTLE...!
LET IT GO, KAZUMA! SHE WAS JUST GETTING HIM BACK!
IT'S THAT DULLAHAN'S FAULT WE CAN'T GET ANY DECENT QUESTS!
I MEAN, I HELPED CARRY HER BACK EVERY SINGLE D—
YOU'RE HER ACCOMPLICE!?
...HAVE YOU FOOLS...
...NO DESIRE TO SAVE YOUR FRIEND?
THE CRUSADER, THE ONE WHO SHIELDED YOU FROM MY CURSE AFTER YOUR BOUT OF IDIOCY—
SORRY! IT TOOK A WHILE TO GET MY ARMOR ON.

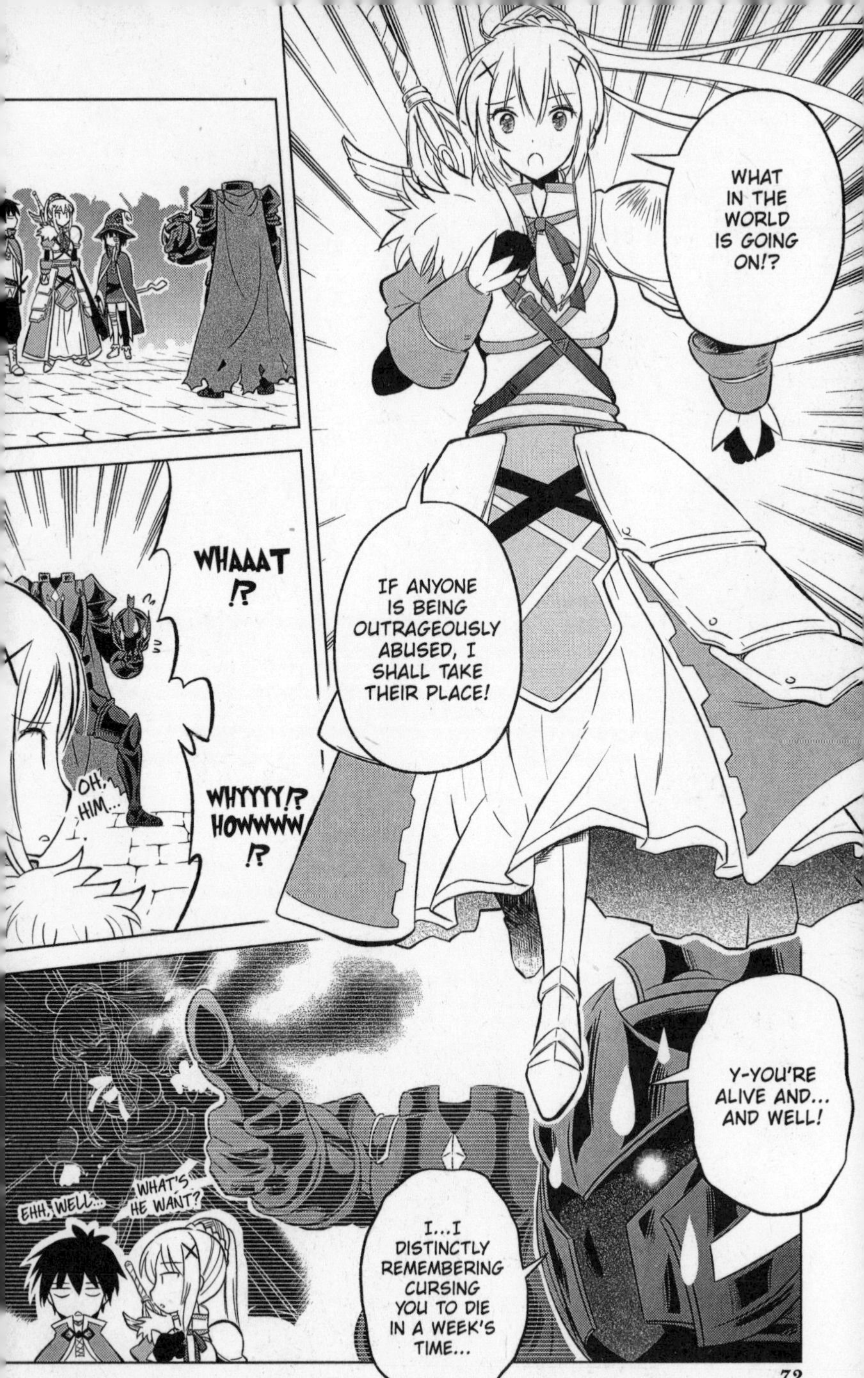
WHAT IN THE WORLD IS GOING ON!?
IF ANYONE IS BEING OUTRAGEOUSLY ABUSED, I SHALL TAKE THEIR PLACE!
WHAAAT!?
WHYYYY!? HOWWWW!?
OH, HIM...
Y-YOU'RE ALIVE AND... AND WELL!
I...I DISTINCTLY REMEMBERING CURSING YOU TO DIE IN A WEEK'S TIME...
WHAT'S HE WANT?
EHH, WELL...

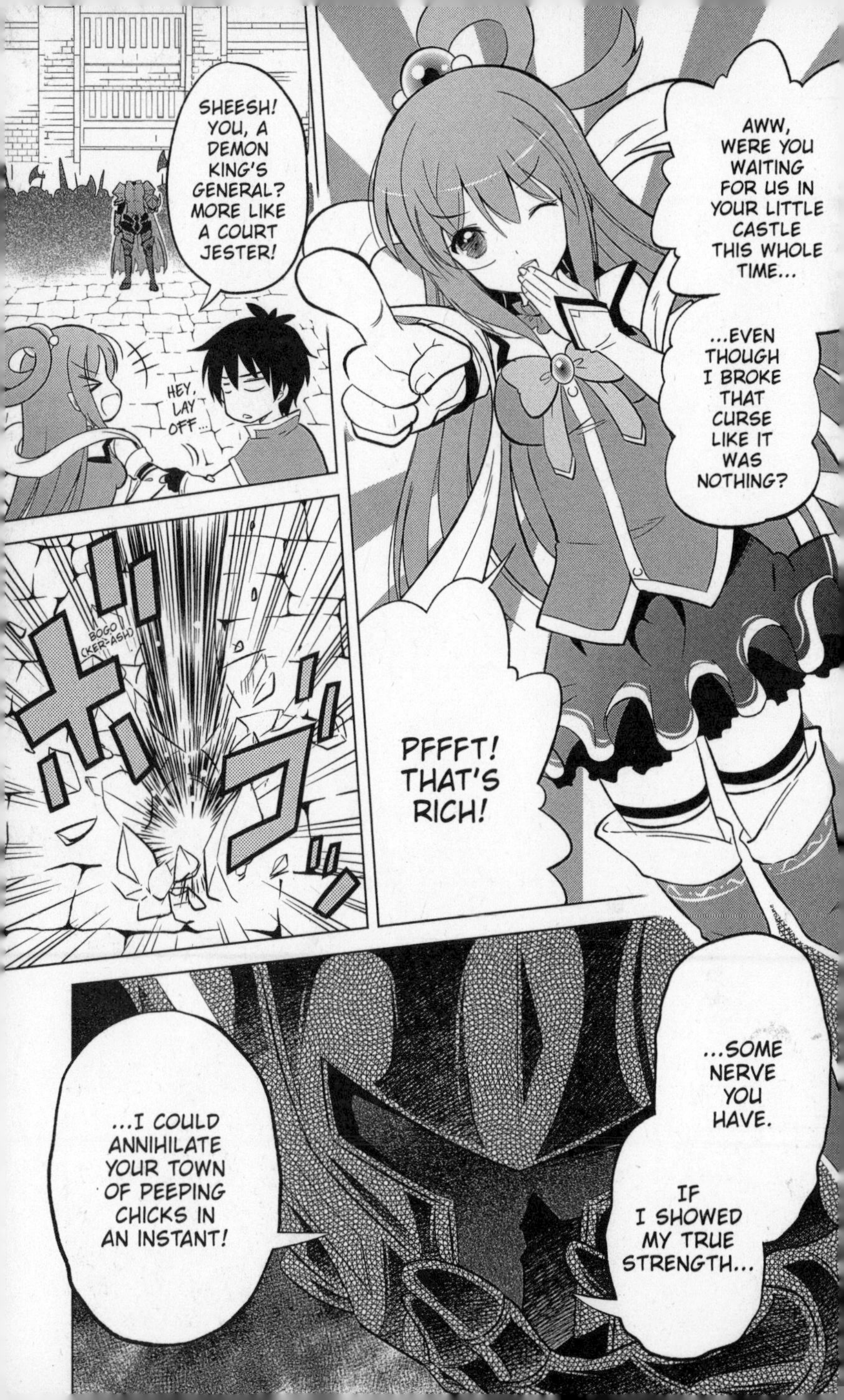
AWW, WERE YOU WAITING FOR US IN YOUR LITTLE CASTLE THIS WHOLE TIME...
...EVEN THOUGH I BROKE THAT CURSE LIKE IT WAS NOTHING?
PFFFT! THAT'S RICH!
SHEESH! YOU, A DEMON KING'S GENERAL? MORE LIKE A COURT JESTER!
HEY, LAY OFF...
BOGO (KER-ASH)
...SOME NERVE YOU HAVE.
IF I SHOWED MY TRUE STRENGTH...
...I COULD ANNIHILATE YOUR TOWN OF PEEPING CHICKS IN AN INSTANT!

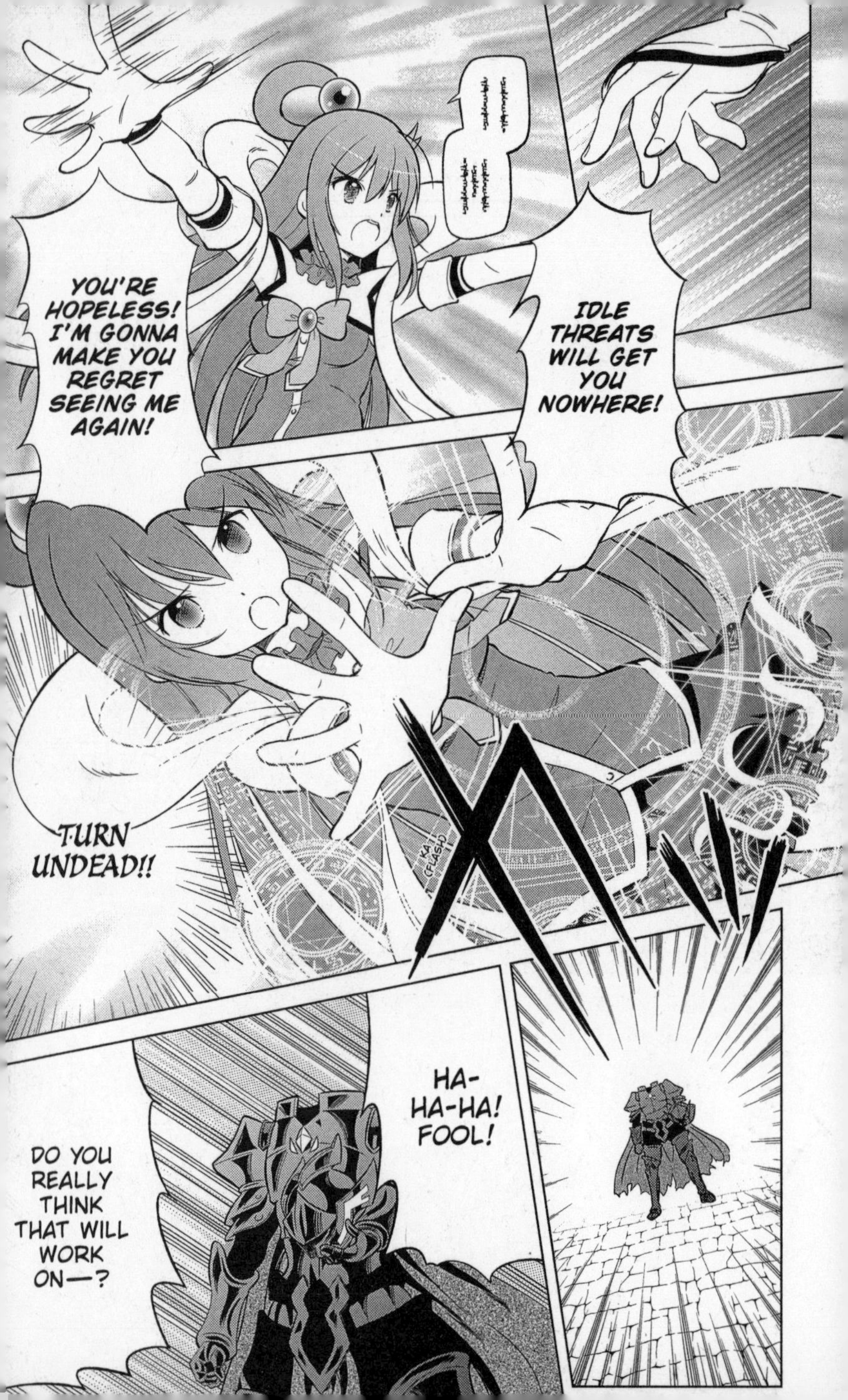
IDLE THREATS WILL GET YOU NOWHERE!
YOU'RE HOPELESS! I'M GONNA MAKE YOU REGRET SEEING ME AGAIN!
TURN UNDEAD!!
KA! (FLASH)
HA-HA-HA! FOOL!
DO YOU REALLY THINK THAT WILL WORK ON—?

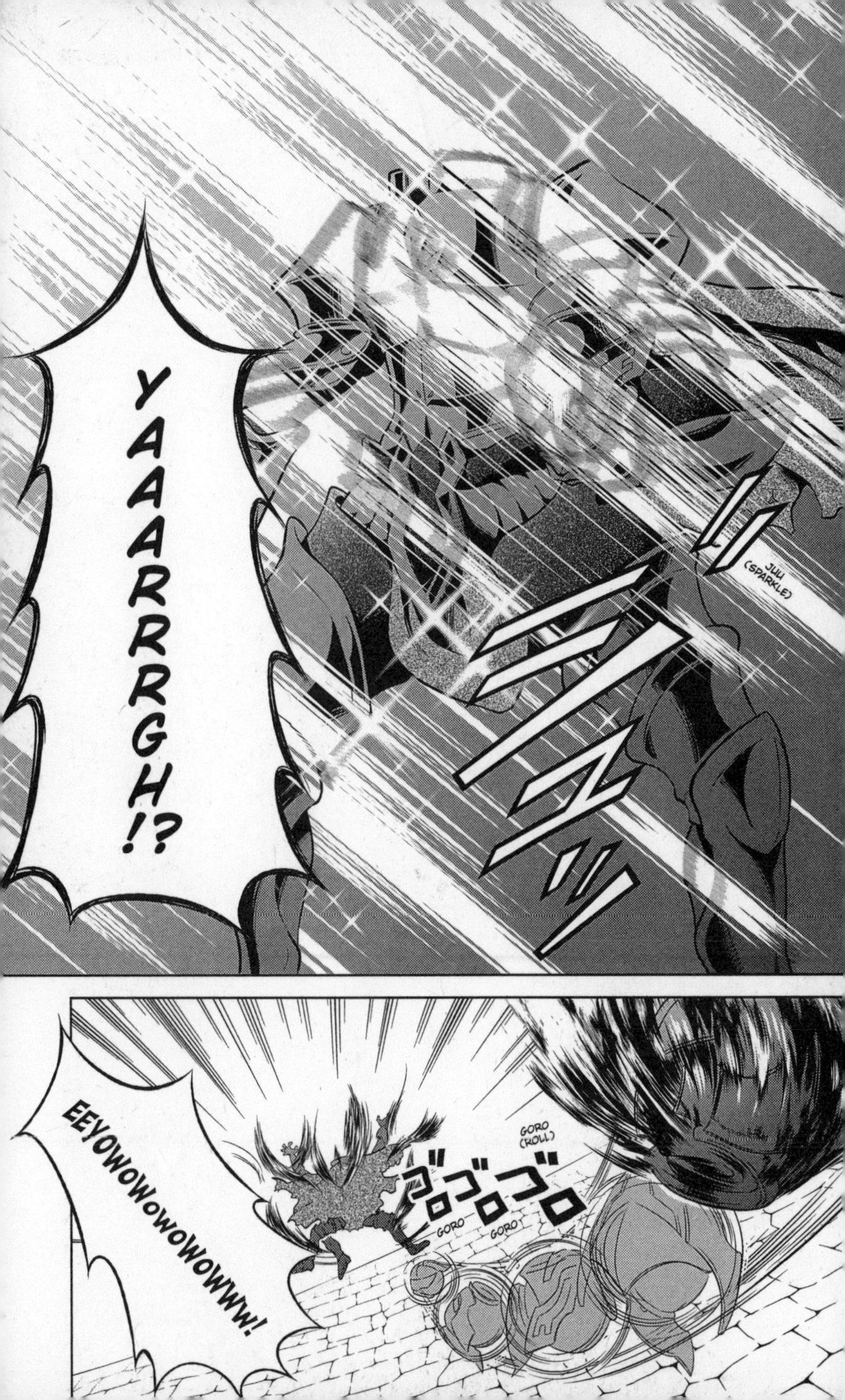
YAAARRRGH!?
JUU (SPARKLE)
ジュ〜ッ
EEYOWOWOWOWOWWW!
GORO (ROLL)
ゴロゴロゴロ
GORO GORO

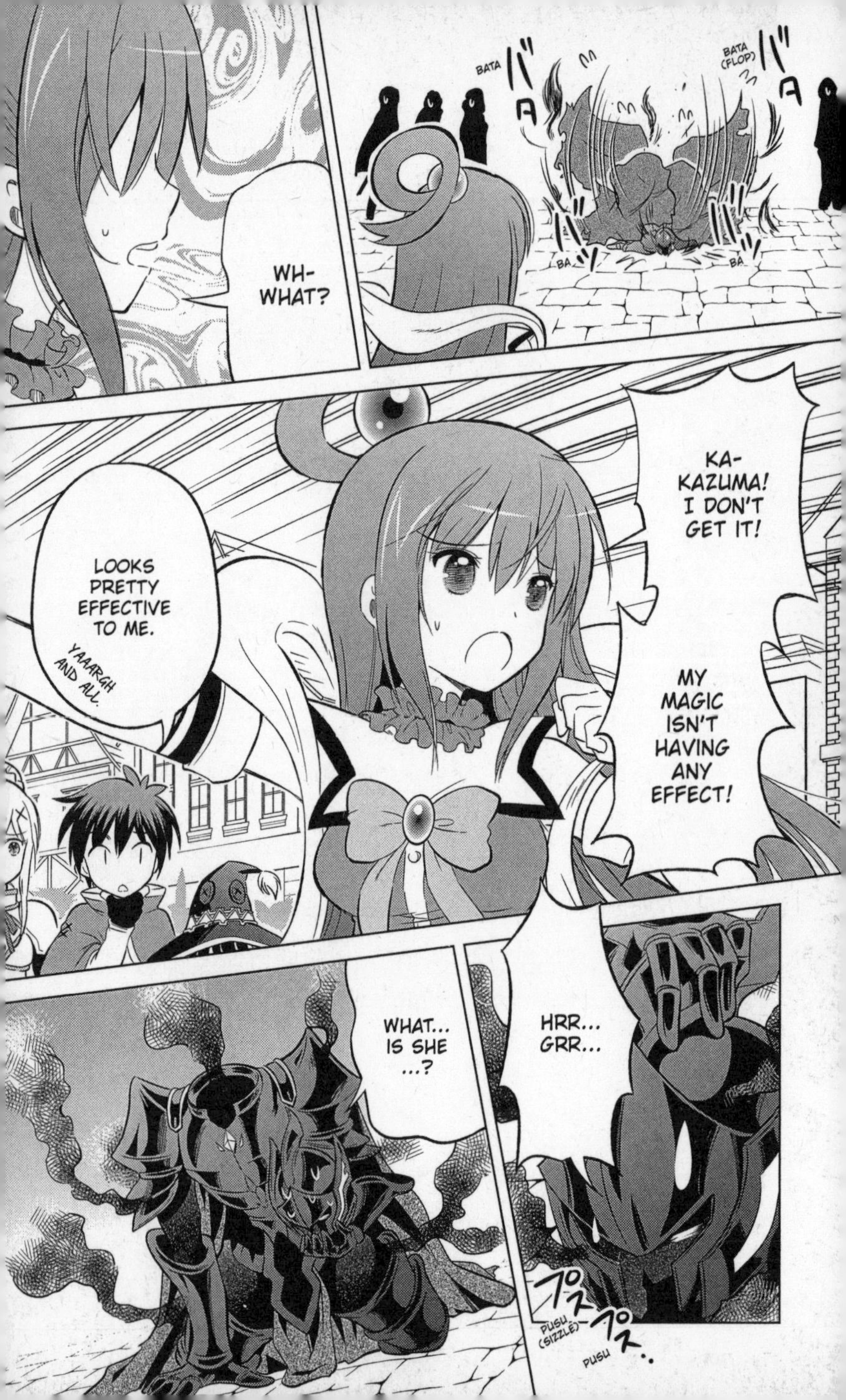
BATA (FLOP)
BATA
BA
BA
WH- WHAT?
KA-KAZUMA! I DON'T GET IT!
MY MAGIC ISN'T HAVING ANY EFFECT!
LOOKS PRETTY EFFECTIVE TO ME.
YAAARGH AND ALL.
HRR... GRR...
PUSU (SIZZLE)
PUSU
WHAT... IS SHE ...?

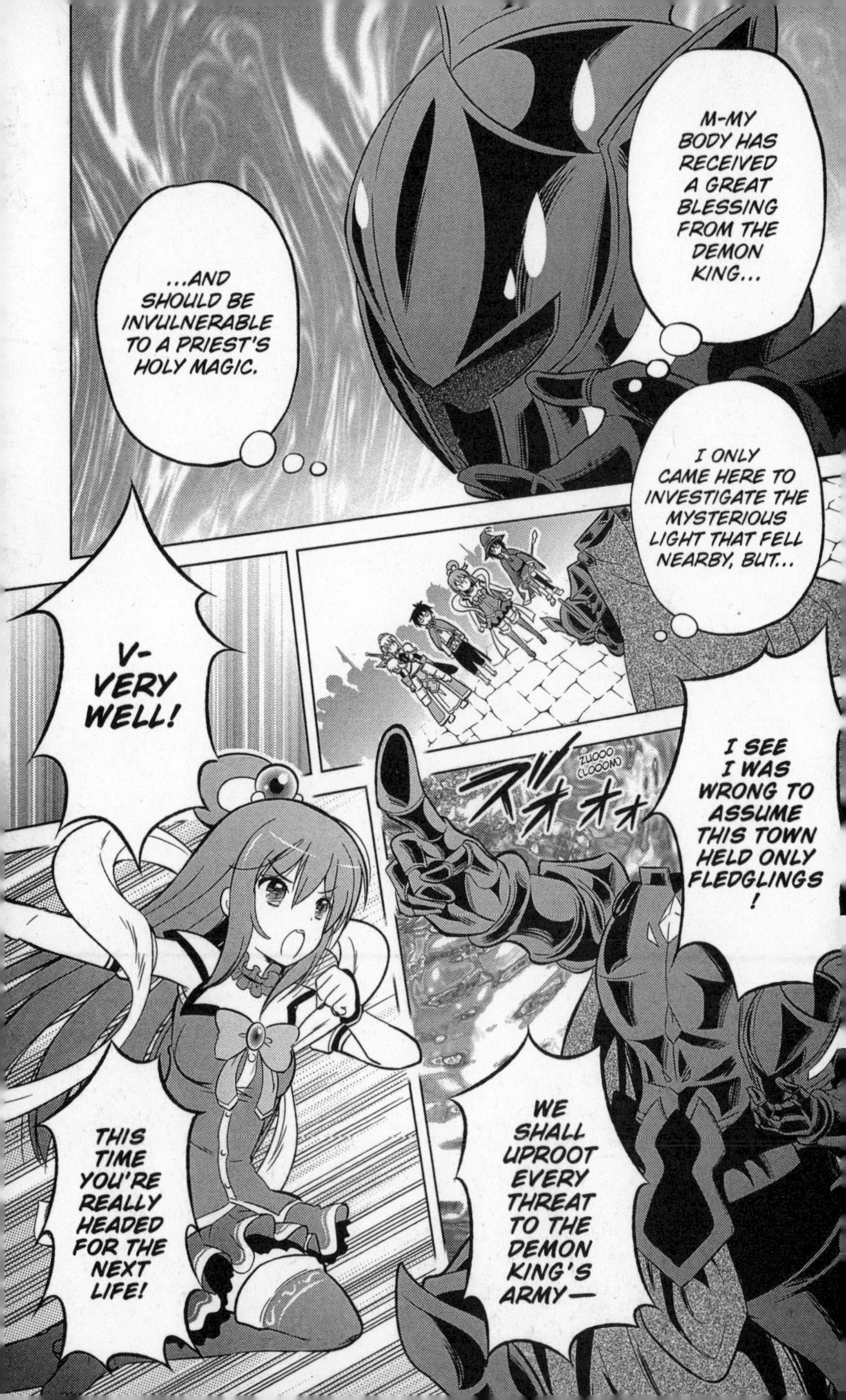
M-MY BODY HAS RECEIVED A GREAT BLESSING FROM THE DEMON KING...
...AND SHOULD BE INVULNERABLE TO A PRIEST'S HOLY MAGIC.
I ONLY CAME HERE TO INVESTIGATE THE MYSTERIOUS LIGHT THAT FELL NEARBY, BUT...
I SEE I WAS WRONG TO ASSUME THIS TOWN HELD ONLY FLEDGLINGS!
ZUOOO (LOOOM)
WE SHALL UPROOT EVERY THREAT TO THE DEMON KING'S ARMY—
V-VERY WELL!
THIS TIME YOU'RE REALLY HEADED FOR THE NEXT LIFE!

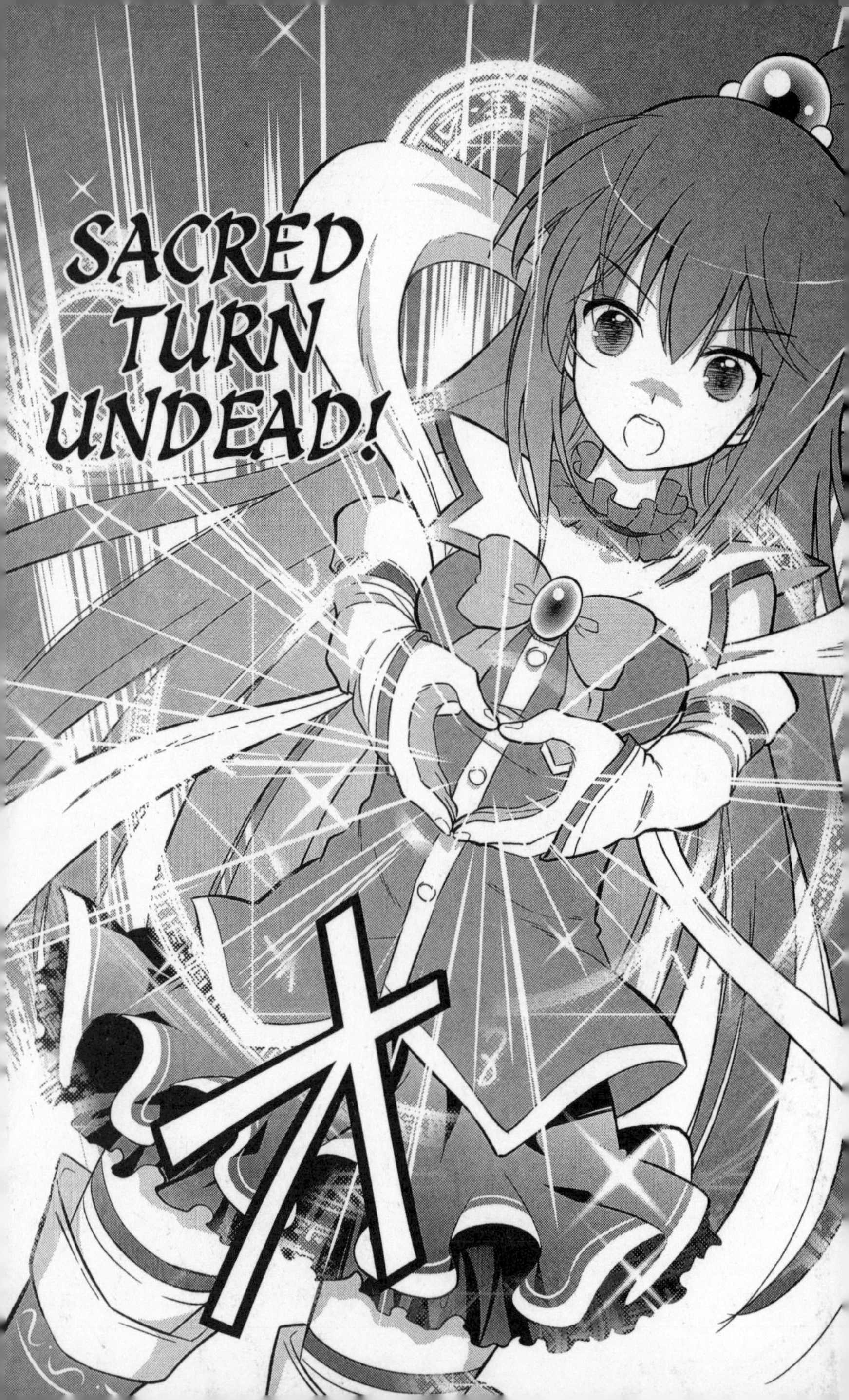
SACRED TURN UNDEAD!

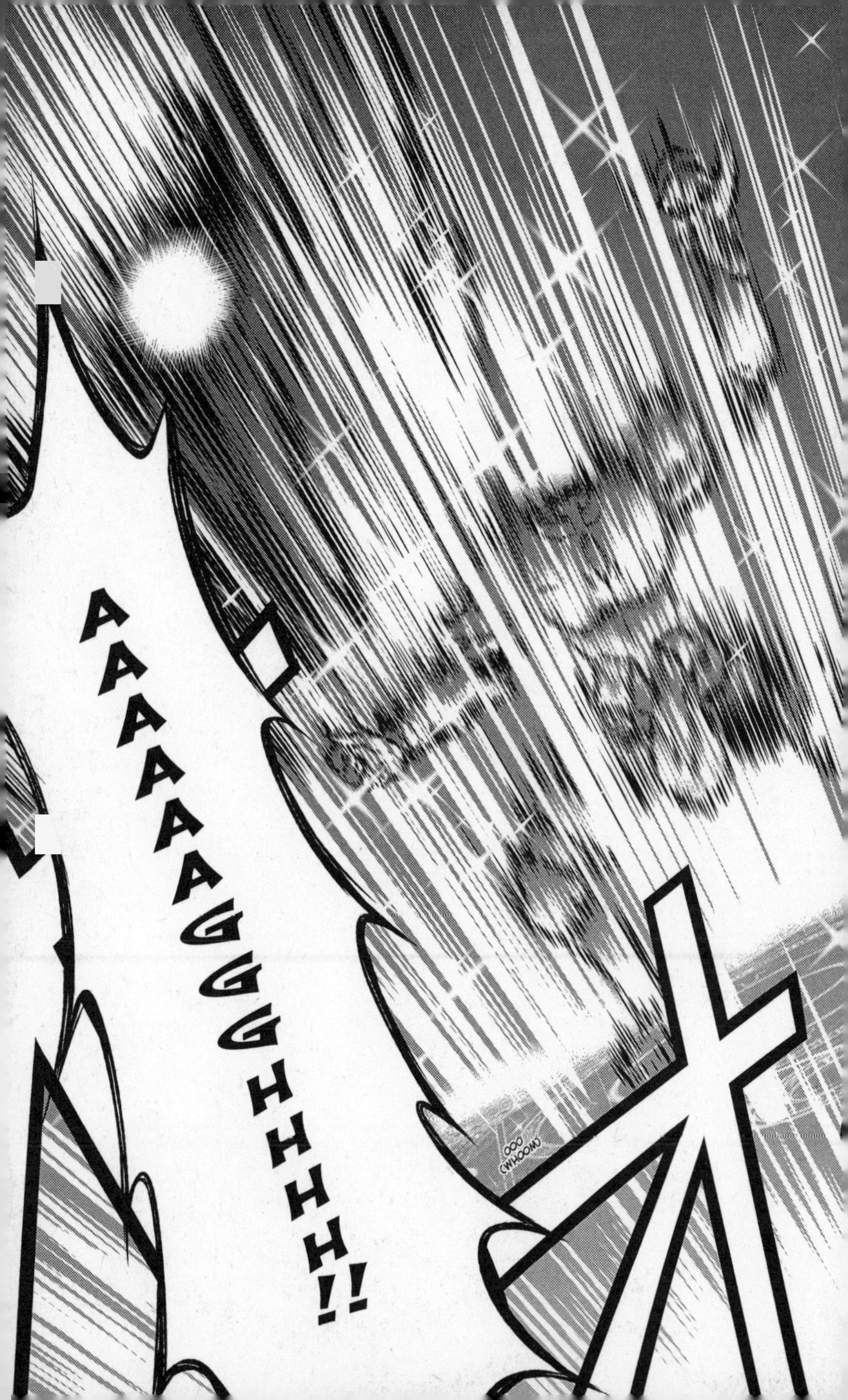
AAAAAAGGGHHHH!!
(WHOOM)
OOO

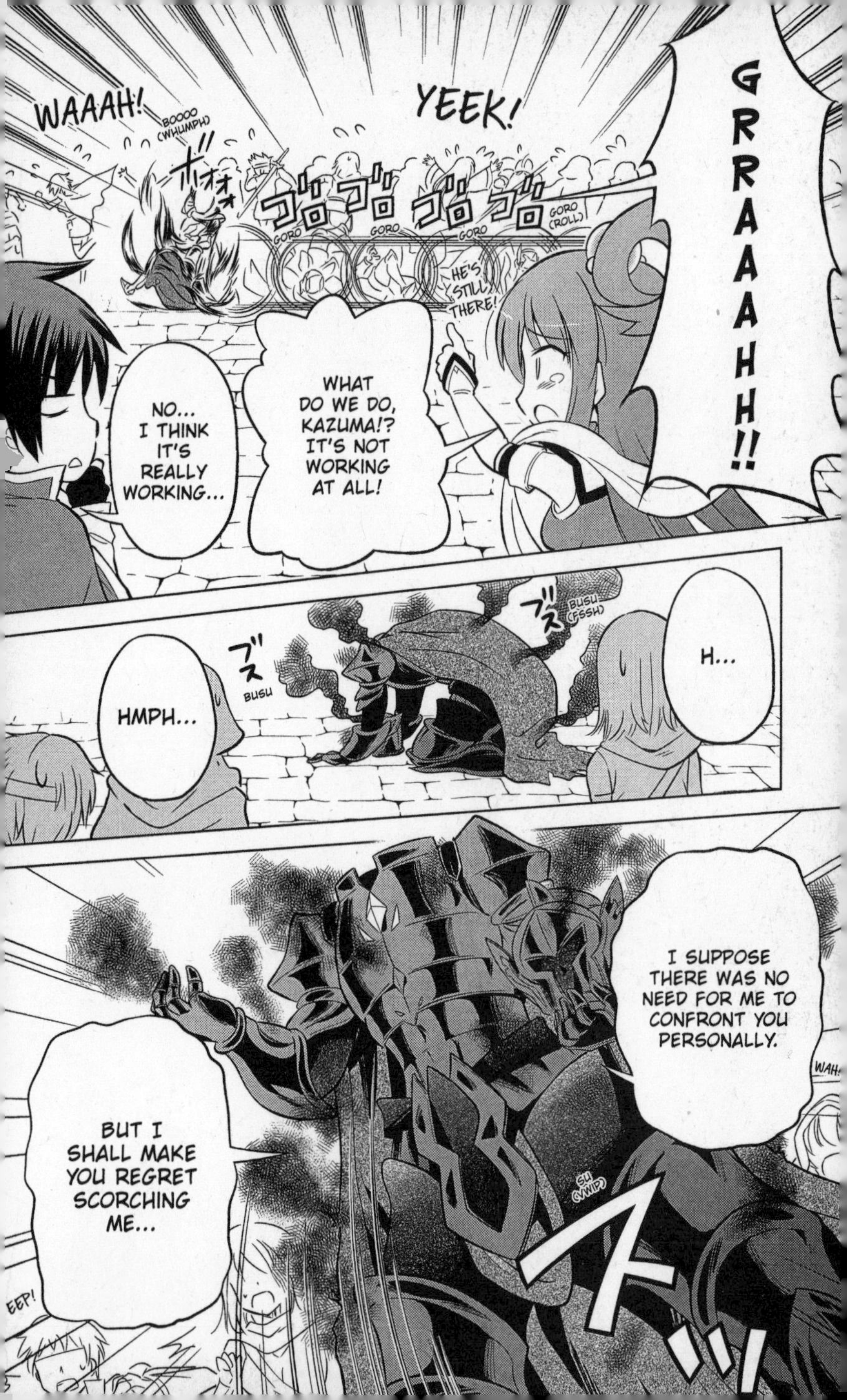
GRRAAAAHH!!
YEEK!
GORO (ROLL)
GORO
GORO
GORO
BOOOO (WHUMPH)
WAAAH!
HE'S STILL THERE!
WHAT DO WE DO, KAZUMA!? IT'S NOT WORKING AT ALL!
NO... I THINK IT'S REALLY WORKING...
H...
BUSU (FSSH)
BUSU
HMPH...
I SUPPOSE THERE WAS NO NEED FOR ME TO CONFRONT YOU PERSONALLY.
WAH!
SU (WHIP)
BUT I SHALL MAKE YOU REGRET SCORCHING ME...
EEP!

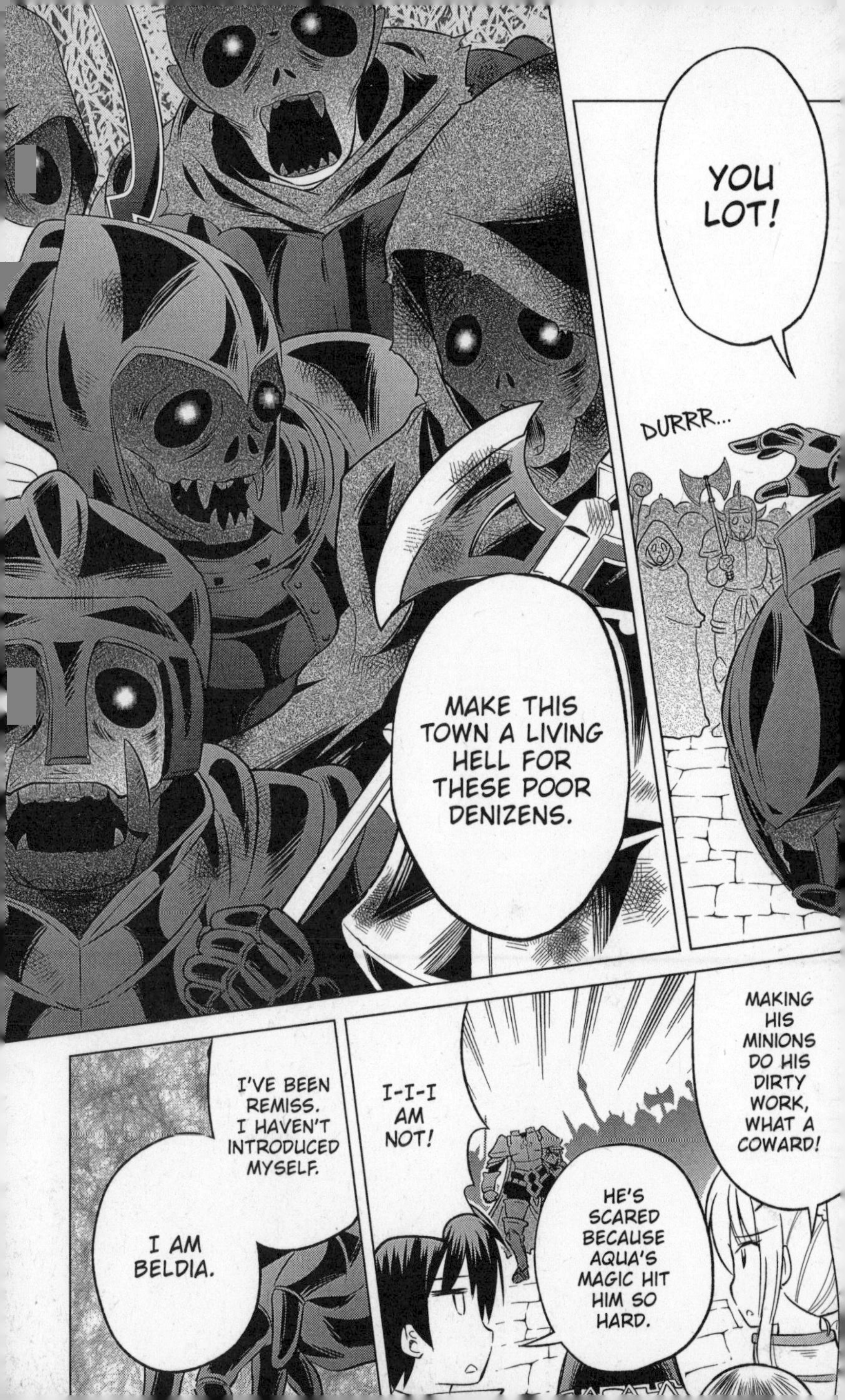
YOU LOT!
DURRR...
MAKE THIS TOWN A LIVING HELL FOR THESE POOR DENIZENS.
MAKING HIS MINIONS DO HIS DIRTY WORK, WHAT A COWARD!
HE'S SCARED BECAUSE AQUA'S MAGIC HIT HIM SO HARD.
I-I-I AM NOT!
I'VE BEEN REMISS. I HAVEN'T INTRODUCED MYSELF.
I AM BELDIA.

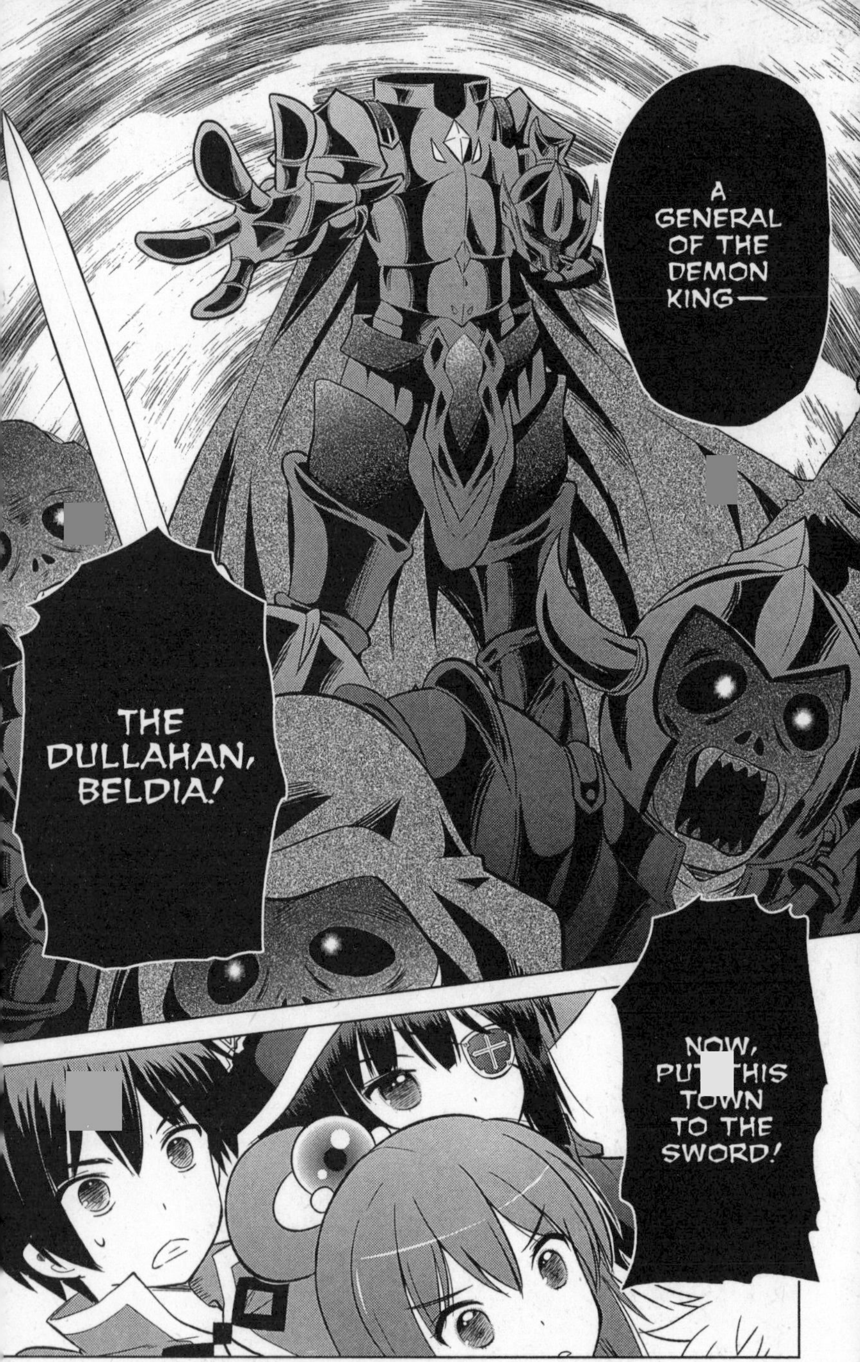
A GENERAL OF THE DEMON KING—
THE DULLAHAN, BELDIA!
NOW, PUT THIS TOWN TO THE SWORD!

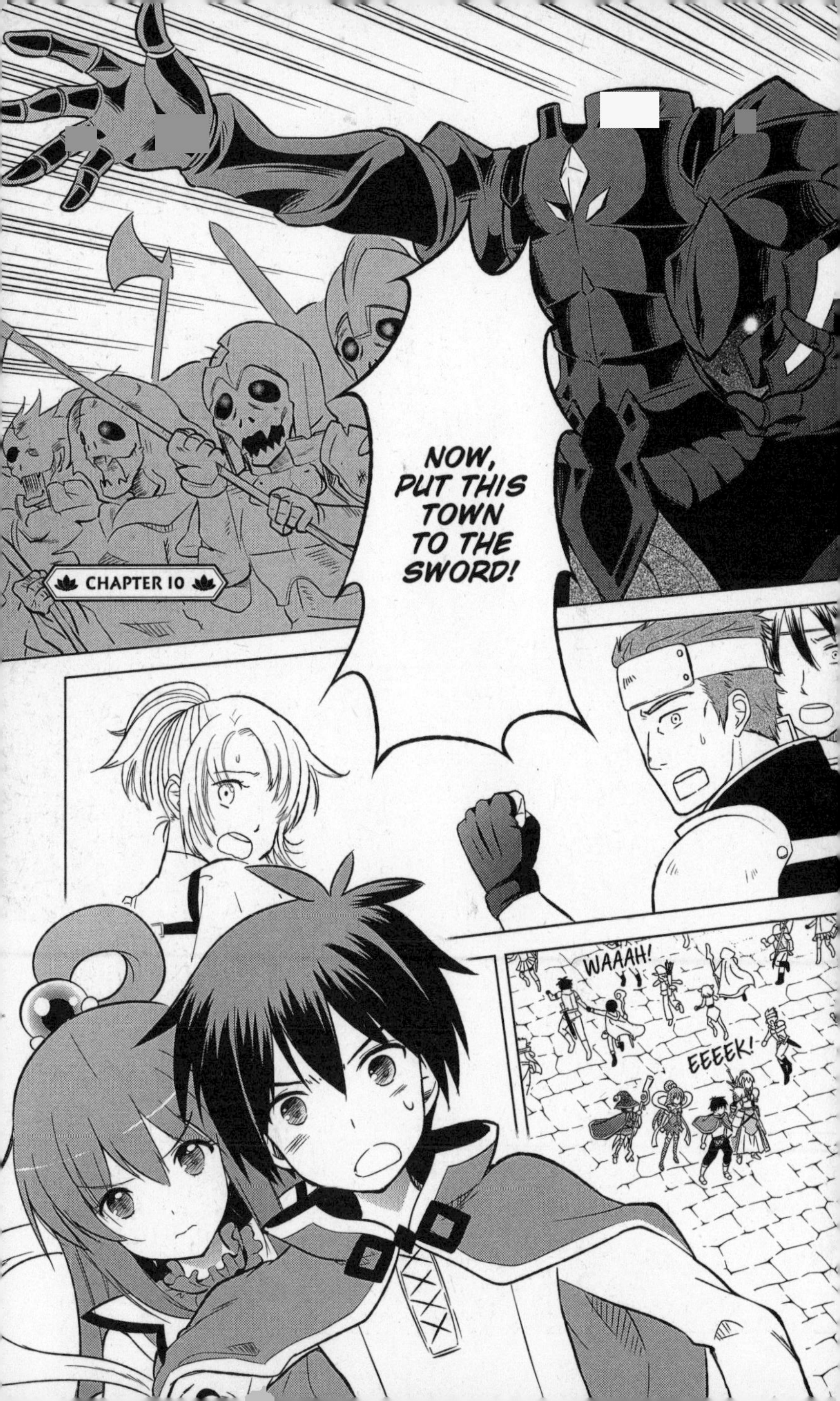
NOW, PUT THIS TOWN TO THE SWORD!
CHAPTER 10
WAAAH!
EEEEK!

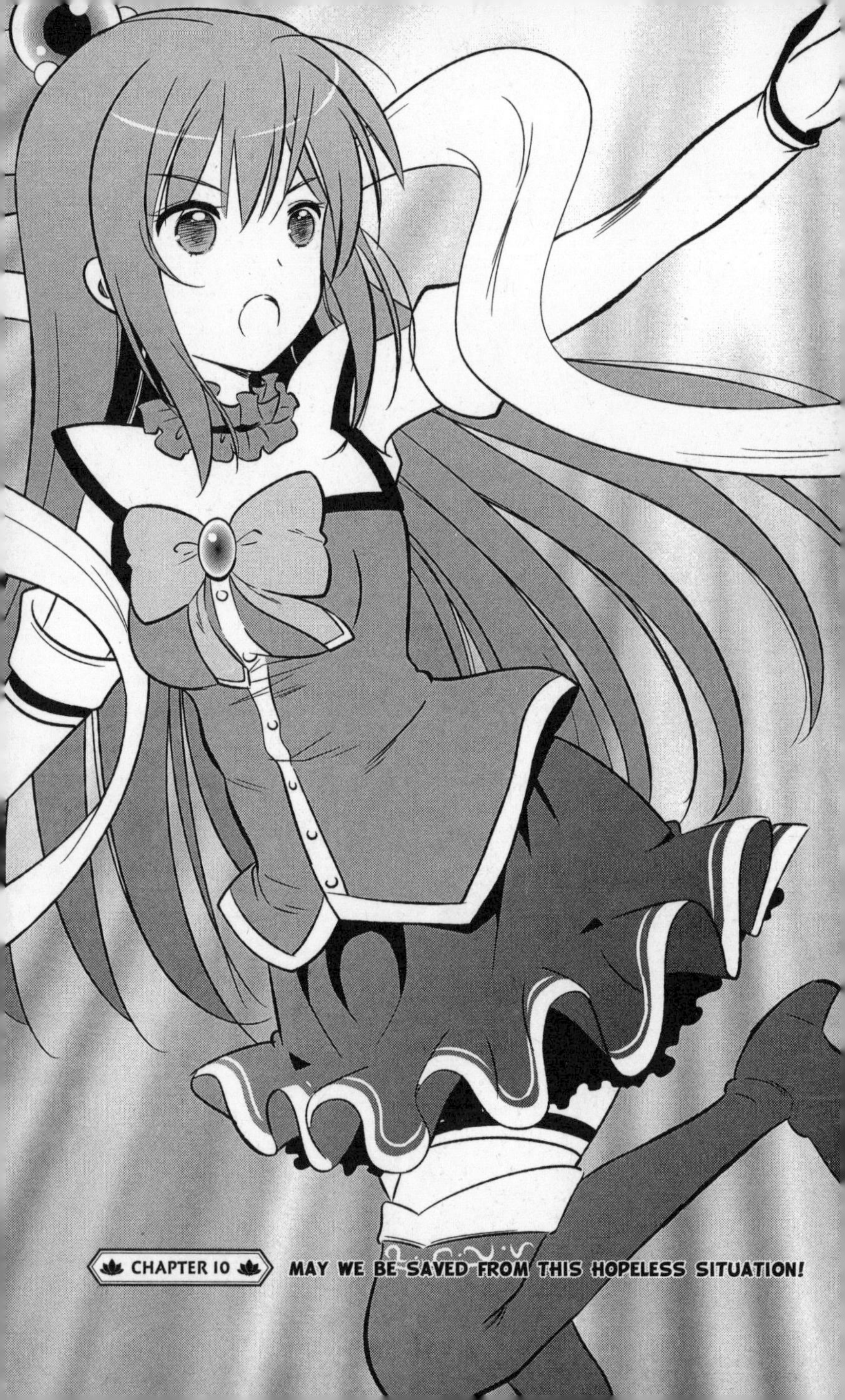
CHAPTER 10
MAY WE BE SAVED FROM THIS HOPELESS SITUATION!

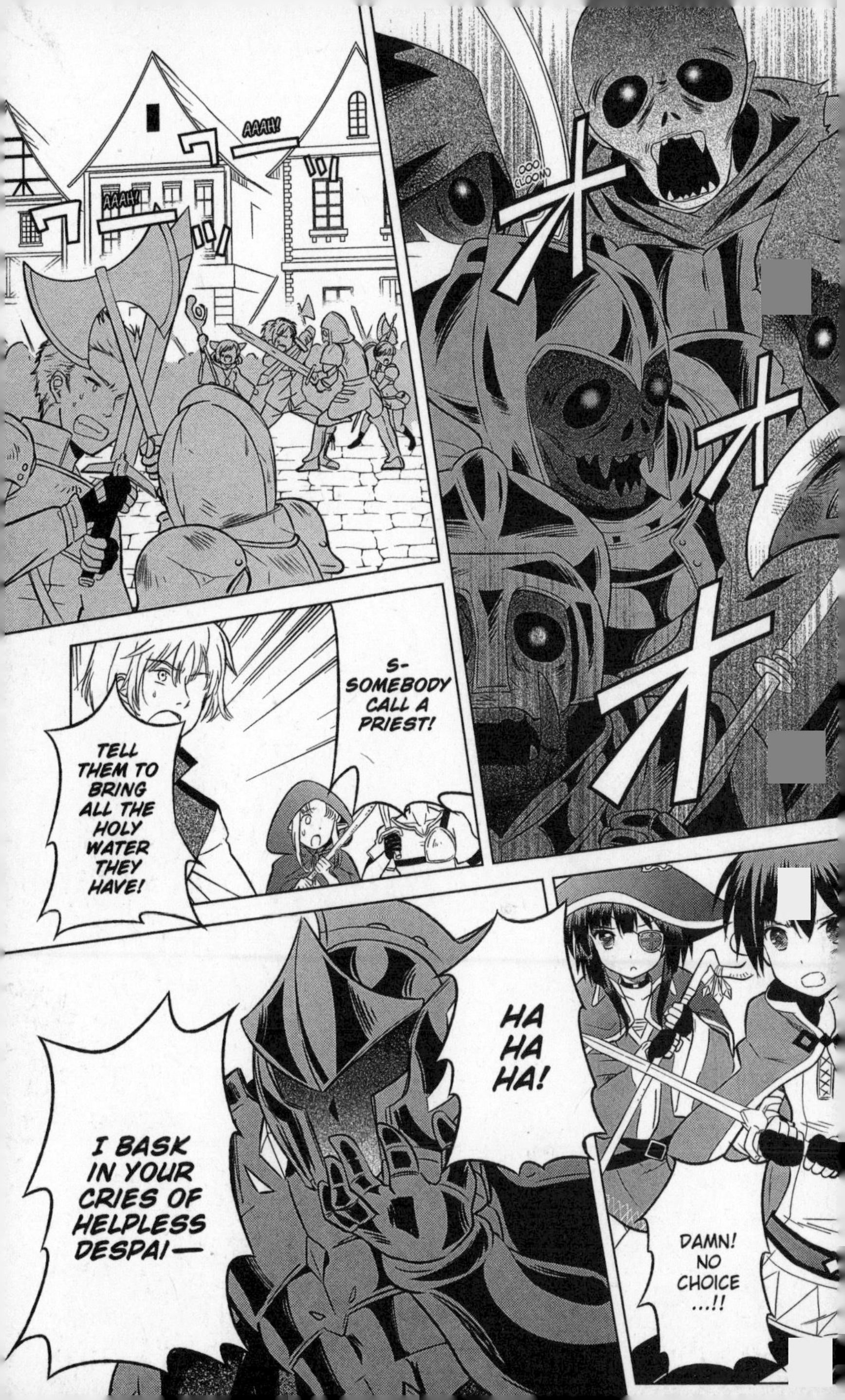
OOO (LOOM)
AAAH!
AAAH!
S-SOMEBODY CALL A PRIEST!
TELL THEM TO BRING ALL THE HOLY WATER THEY HAVE!
HA HA HA!
I BASK IN YOUR CRIES OF HELPLESS DESPAI—
DAMN! NO CHOICE...!!

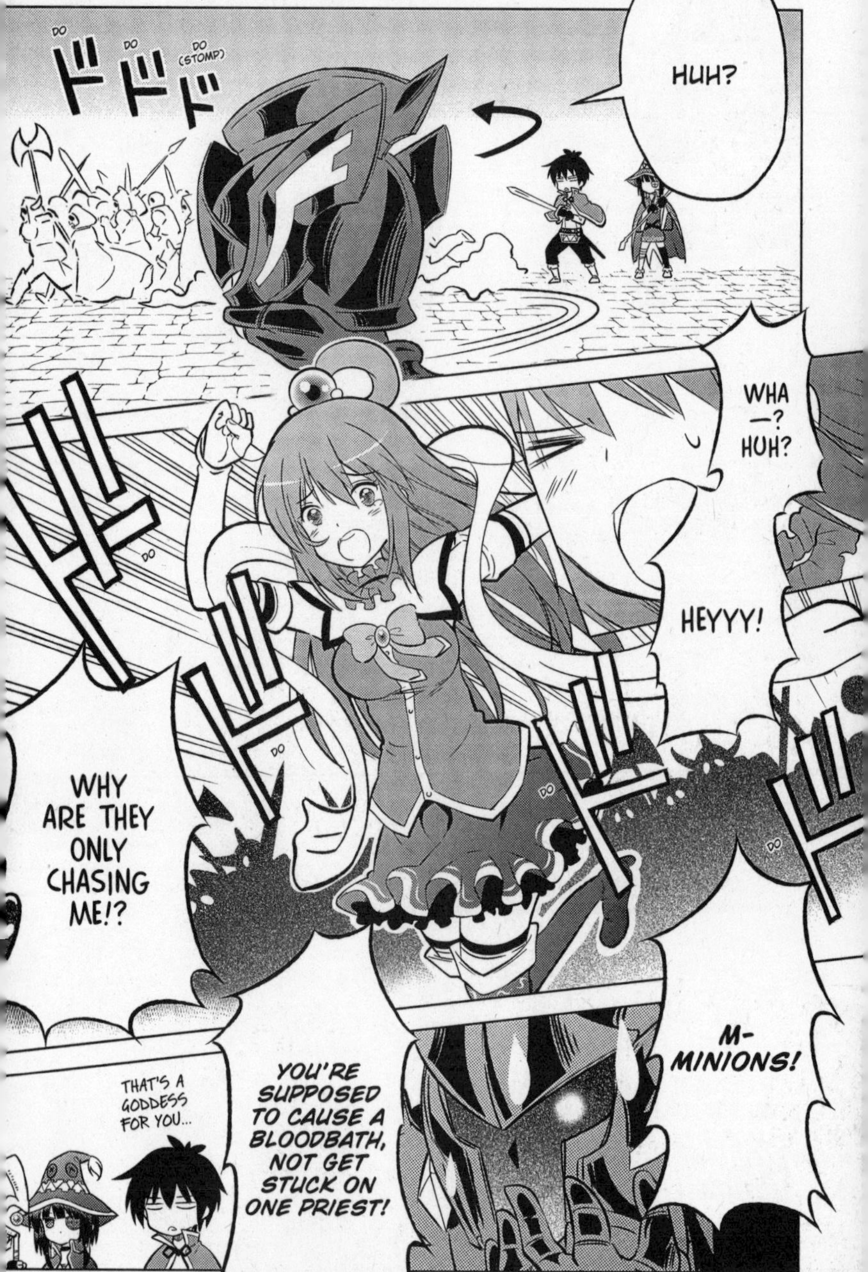
HUH?
ドドド
DO DO DO (STOMP)
WHA—? HUH?
HEYYY!
WHY ARE THEY ONLY CHASING ME!?
DO DO DO DO
M-MINIONS!
YOU'RE SUPPOSED TO CAUSE A BLOODBATH, NOT GET STUCK ON ONE PRIEST!
THAT'S A GODDESS FOR YOU...

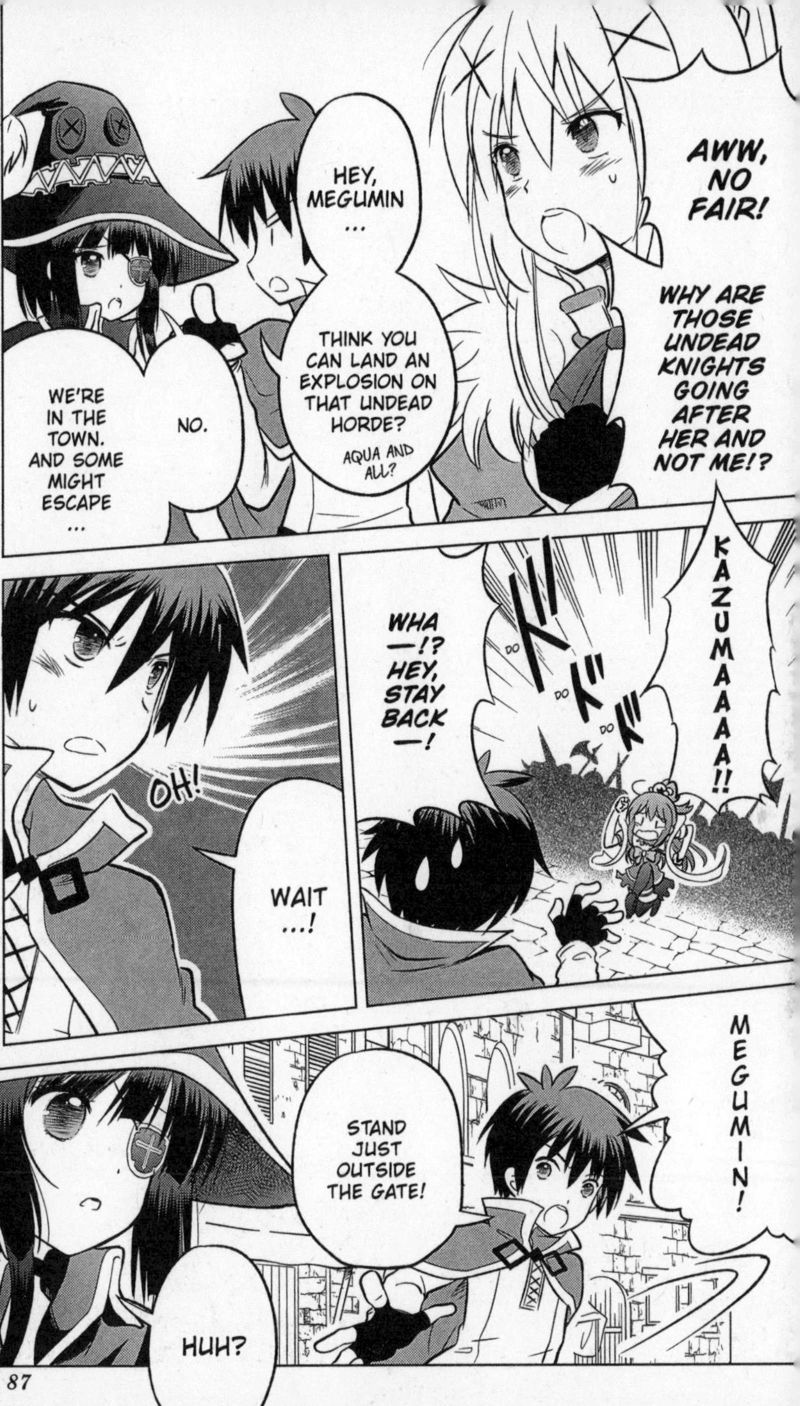
AWW, NO FAIR!
WHY ARE THOSE UNDEAD KNIGHTS GOING AFTER HER AND NOT ME!?
HEY, MEGUMIN ...
THINK YOU CAN LAND AN EXPLOSION ON THAT UNDEAD HORDE?
AQUA AND ALL?
NO.
WE'RE IN THE TOWN. AND SOME MIGHT ESCAPE ...
KAZUMAAAAAA!!
DO
DO
DO
WHA—!? HEY, STAY BACK—!
OH!
WAIT ...!
MEGUMIN!
STAND JUST OUTSIDE THE GATE!
HUH?

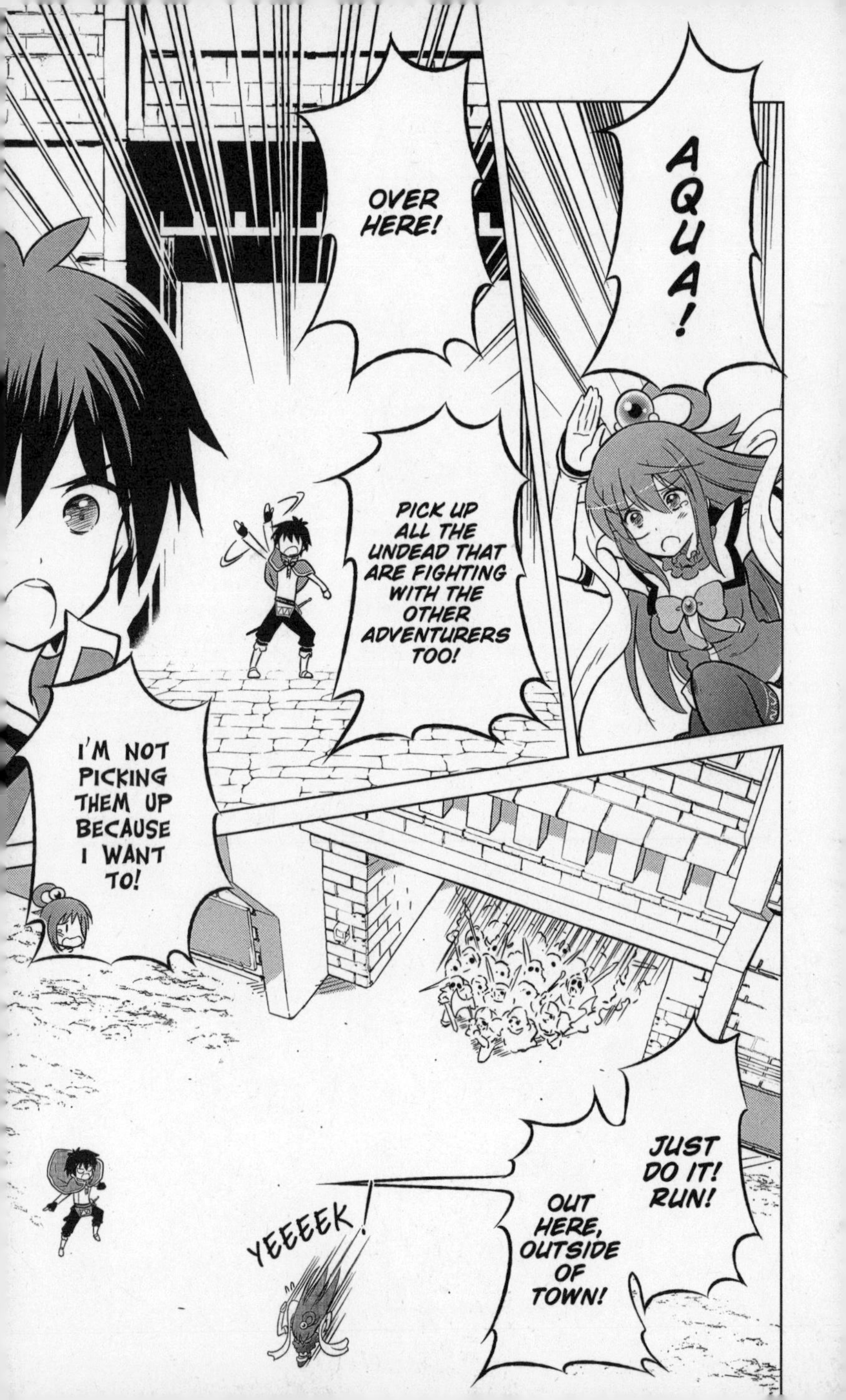
AQUA!
OVER HERE!
PICK UP ALL THE UNDEAD THAT ARE FIGHTING WITH THE OTHER ADVENTURERS TOO!
I'M NOT PICKING THEM UP BECAUSE I WANT TO!
JUST DO IT! RUN!
OUT HERE, OUTSIDE OF TOWN!
YEEEEK!

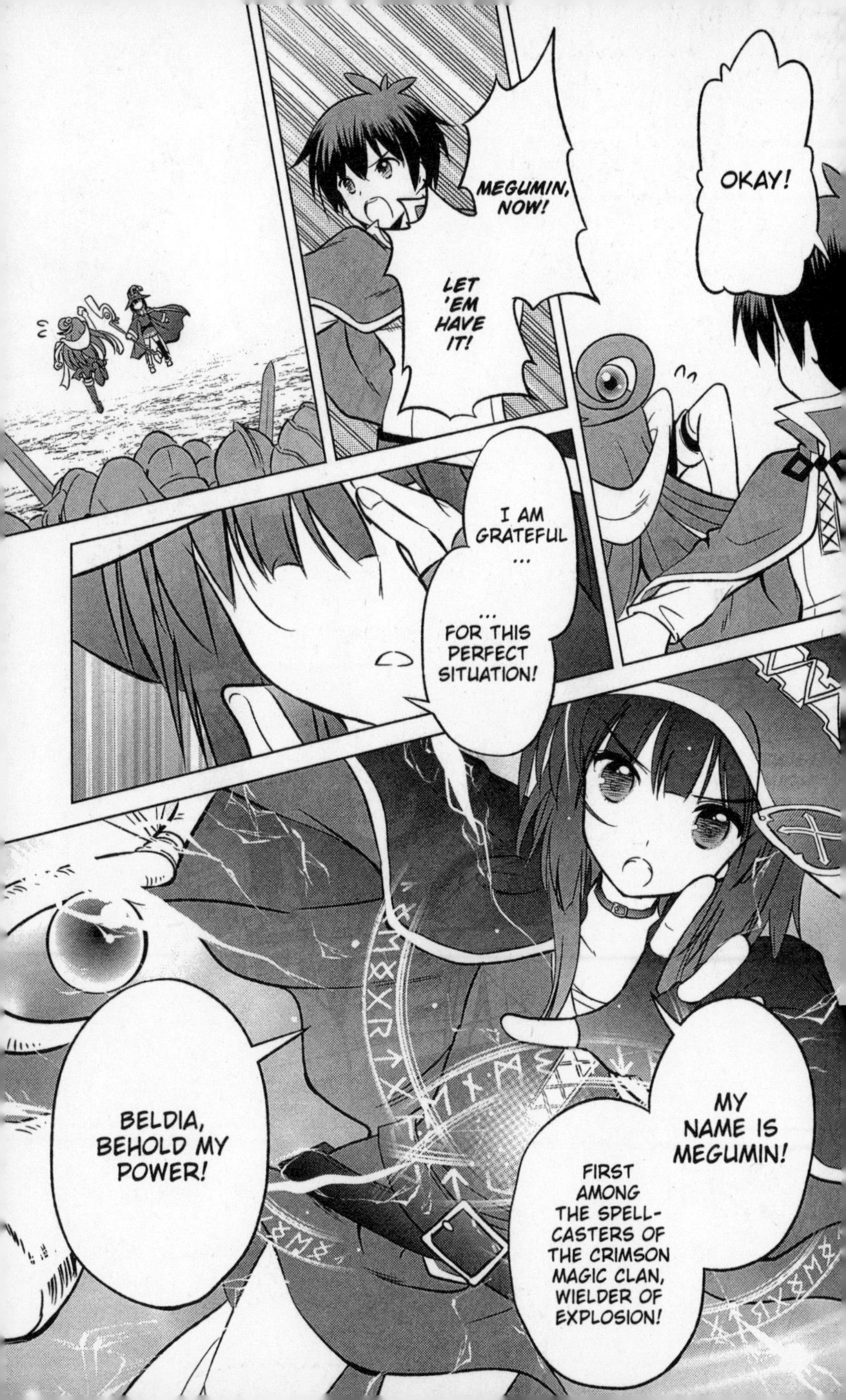
MEGUMIN, NOW!
LET 'EM HAVE IT!
OKAY!
I AM GRATEFUL ...
... FOR THIS PERFECT SITUATION!
MY NAME IS MEGUMIN!
FIRST AMONG THE SPELL-CASTERS OF THE CRIMSON MAGIC CLAN, WIELDER OF EXPLOSION!
BELDIA, BEHOLD MY POWER!

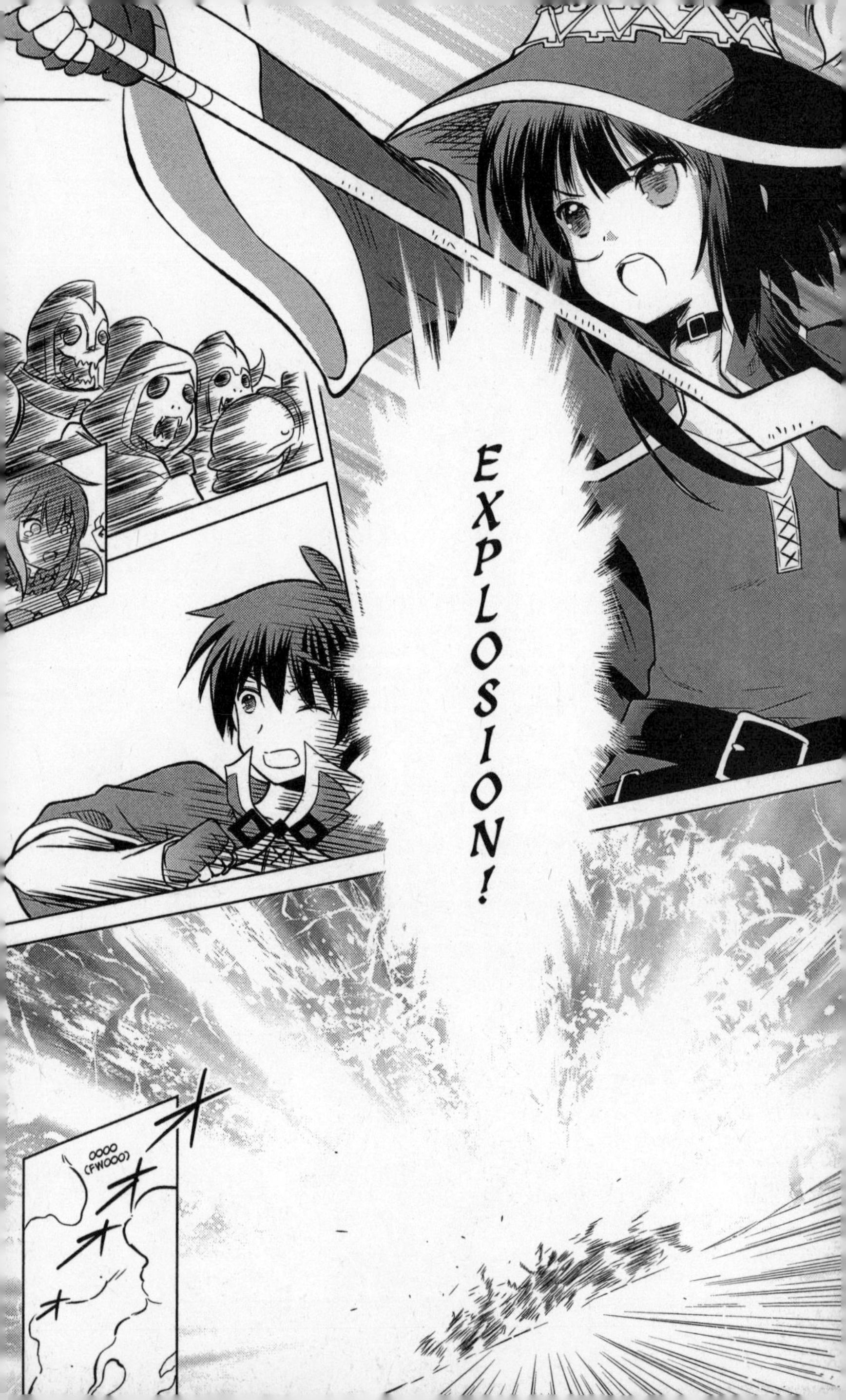
EXPLOSION!
OOOO (FWOOO)

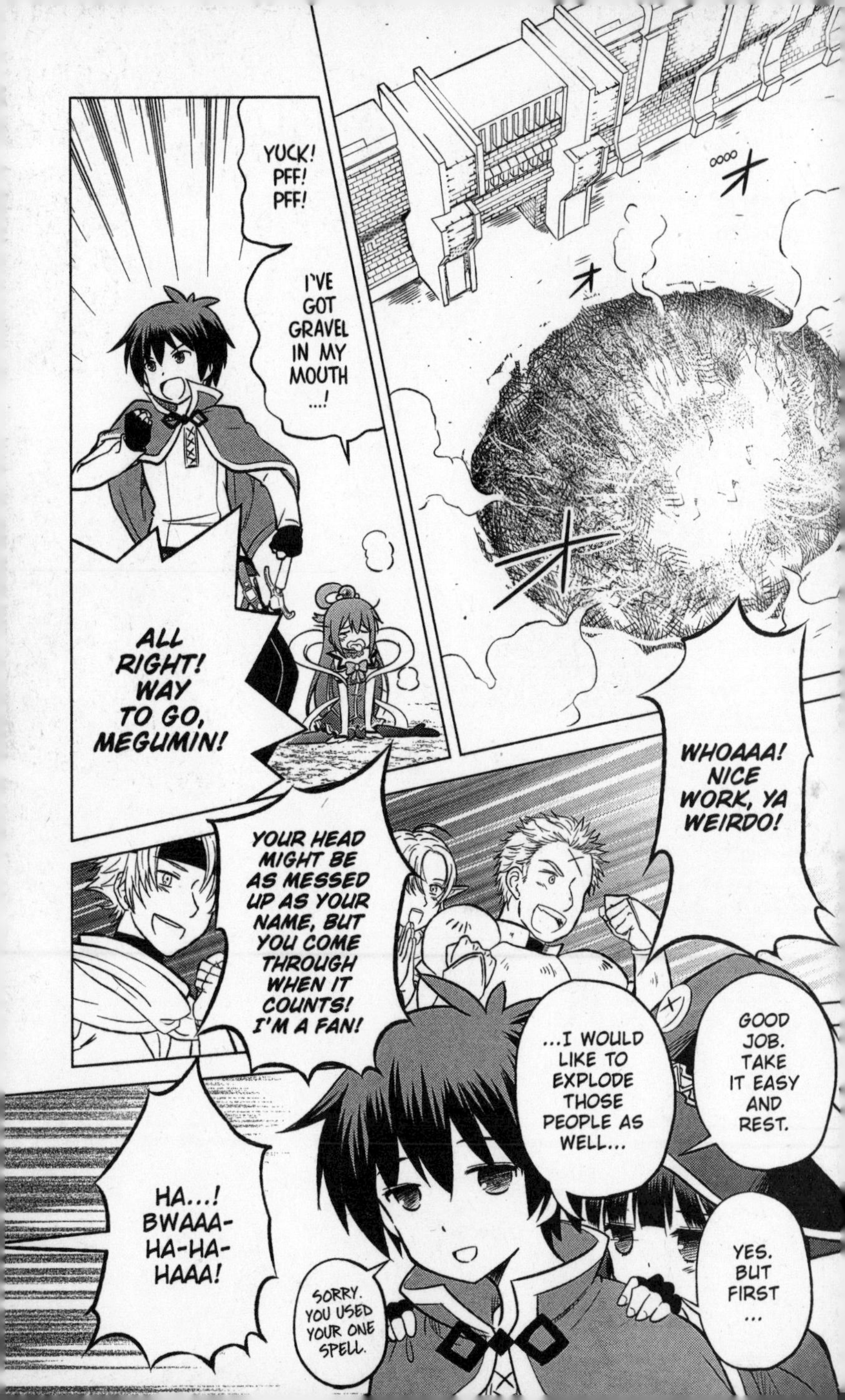
YUCK! PFF! PFF!
I'VE GOT GRAVEL IN MY MOUTH ...!
ALL RIGHT! WAY TO GO, MEGUMIN!
WHOAAA! NICE WORK, YA WEIRDO!
YOUR HEAD MIGHT BE AS MESSED UP AS YOUR NAME, BUT YOU COME THROUGH WHEN IT COUNTS! I'M A FAN!
GOOD JOB. TAKE IT EASY AND REST.
...I WOULD LIKE TO EXPLODE THOSE PEOPLE AS WELL...
YES. BUT FIRST ...
SORRY. YOU USED YOUR ONE SPELL.
HA...! BWAAAA-HA-HA-HAAAA!

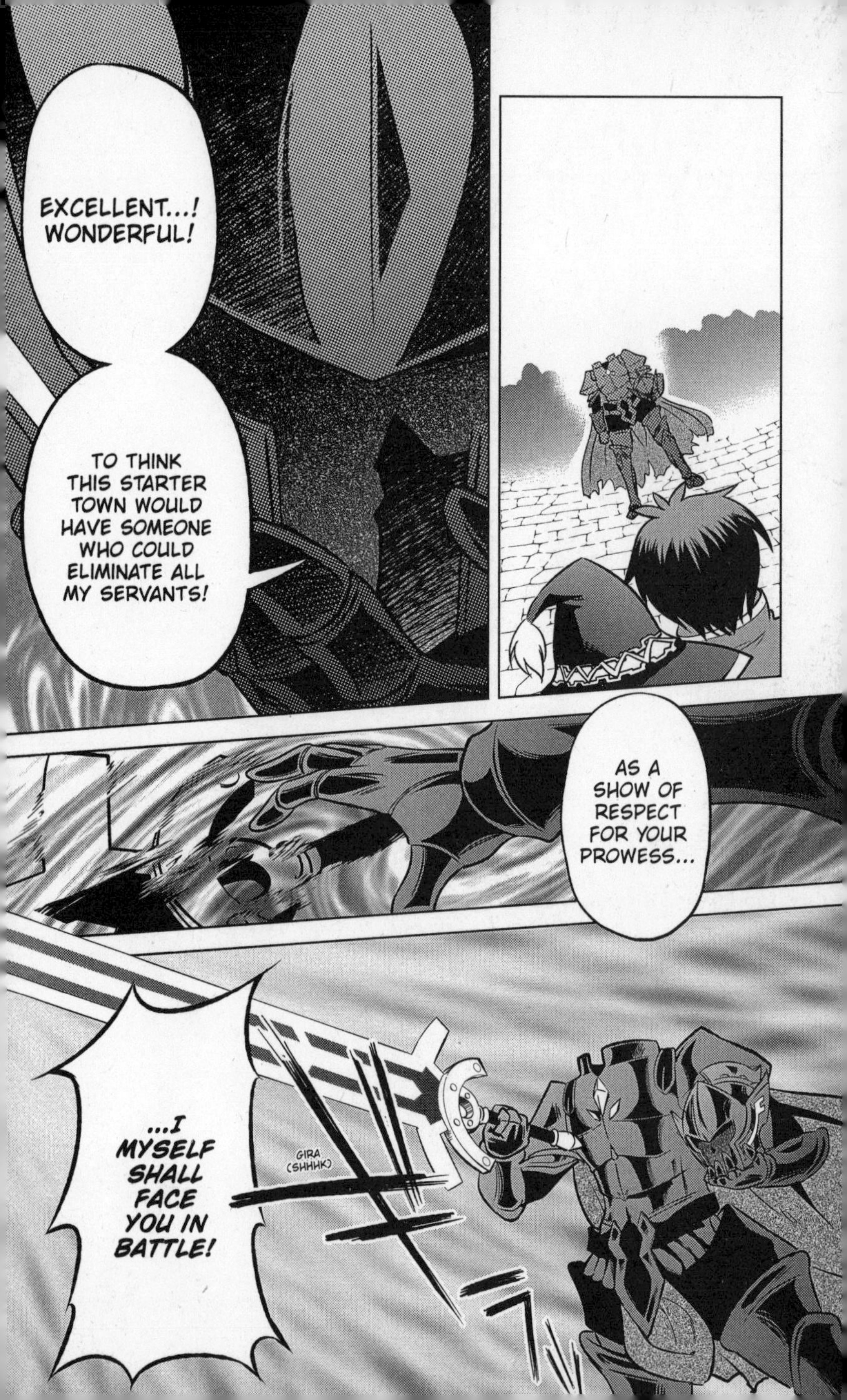
EXCELLENT...! WONDERFUL!
TO THINK THIS STARTER TOWN WOULD HAVE SOMEONE WHO COULD ELIMINATE ALL MY SERVANTS!
AS A SHOW OF RESPECT FOR YOUR PROWESS...
...I MYSELF SHALL FACE YOU IN BATTLE!
GIRA (SHHHK)

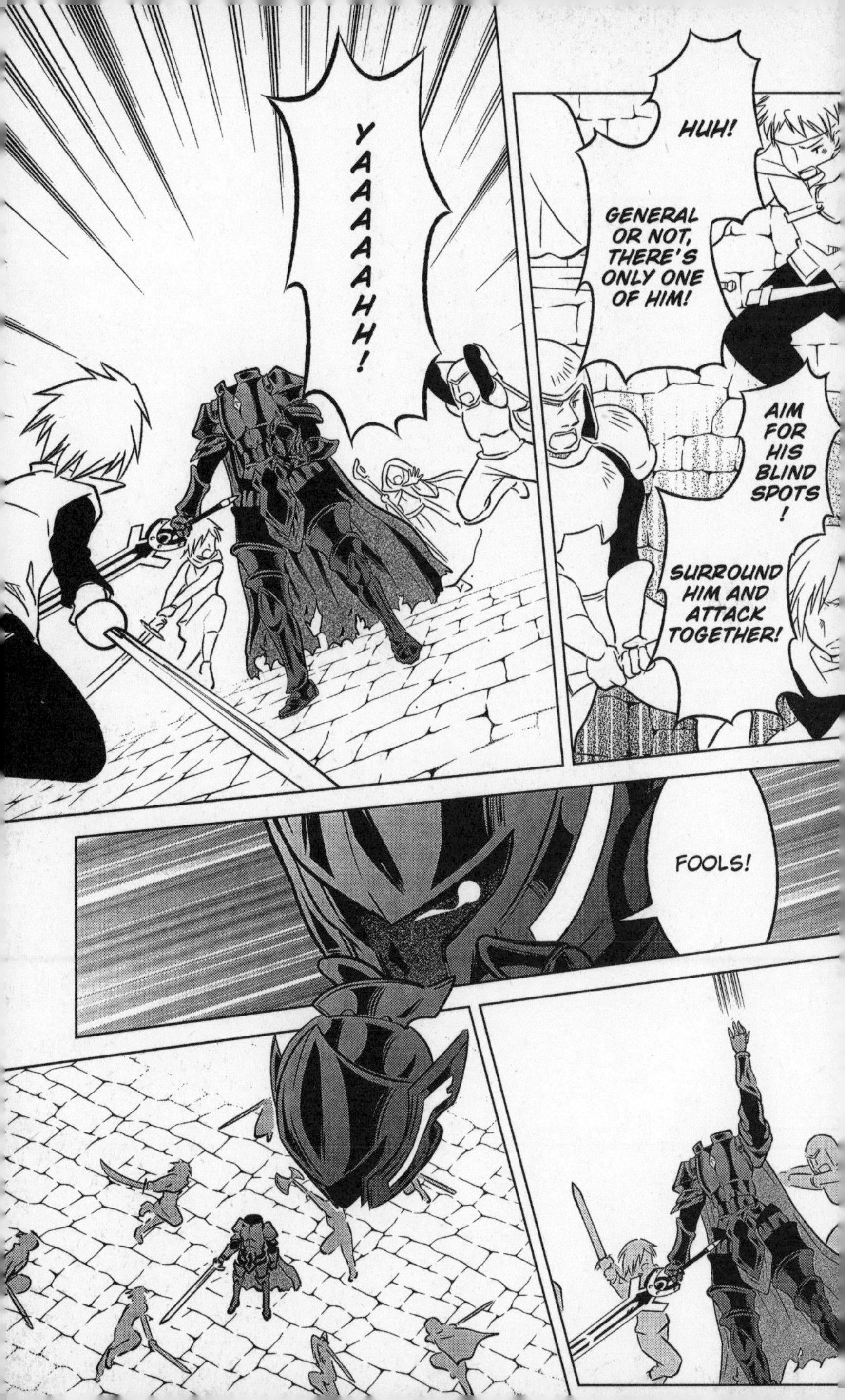
HUH!
GENERAL OR NOT, THERE'S ONLY ONE OF HIM!
AIM FOR HIS BLIND SPOTS!
SURROUND HIM AND ATTACK TOGETHER!
YAAAAAAAHH!
FOOLS!

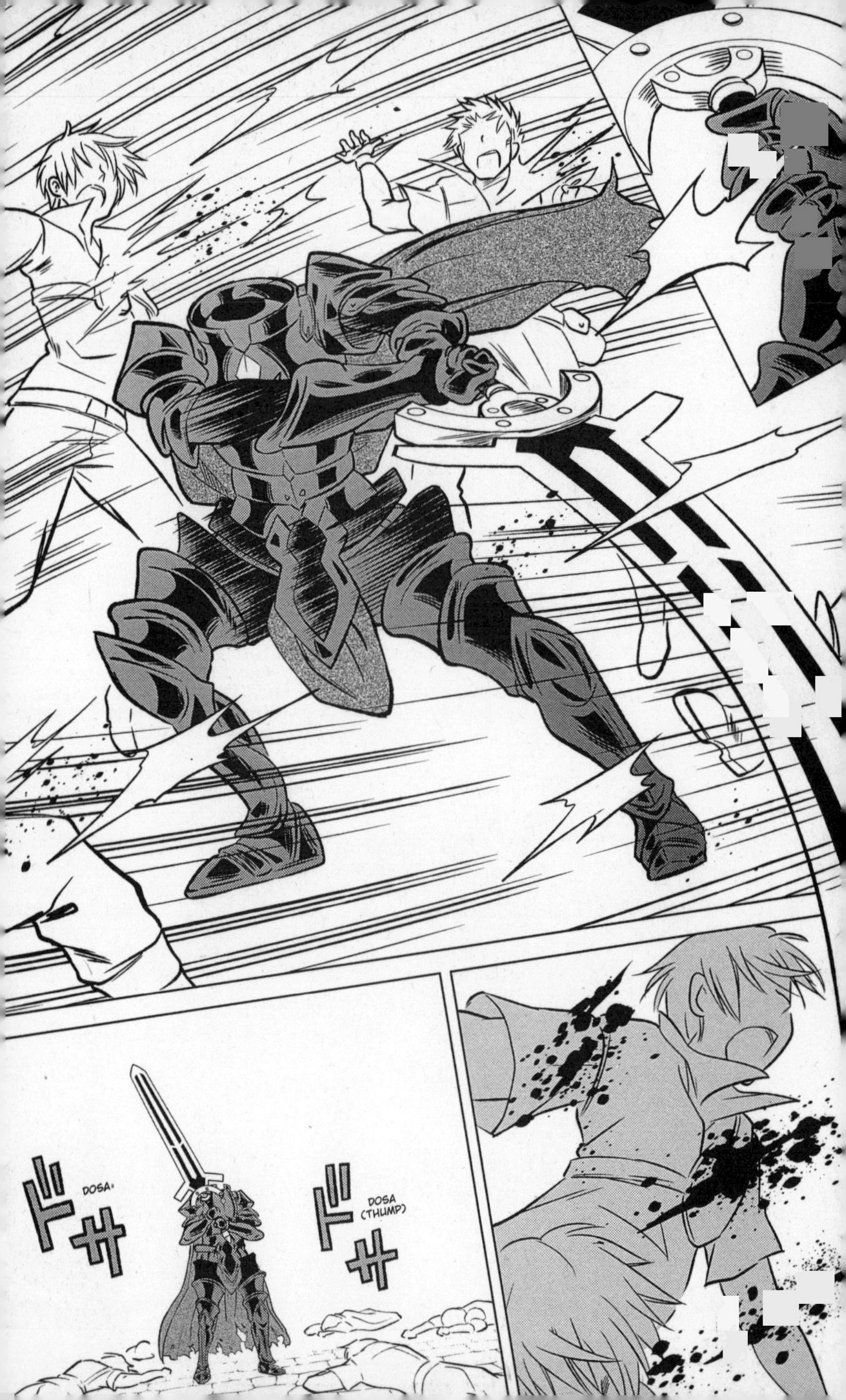

DOSA
(THUMP)
DOSA

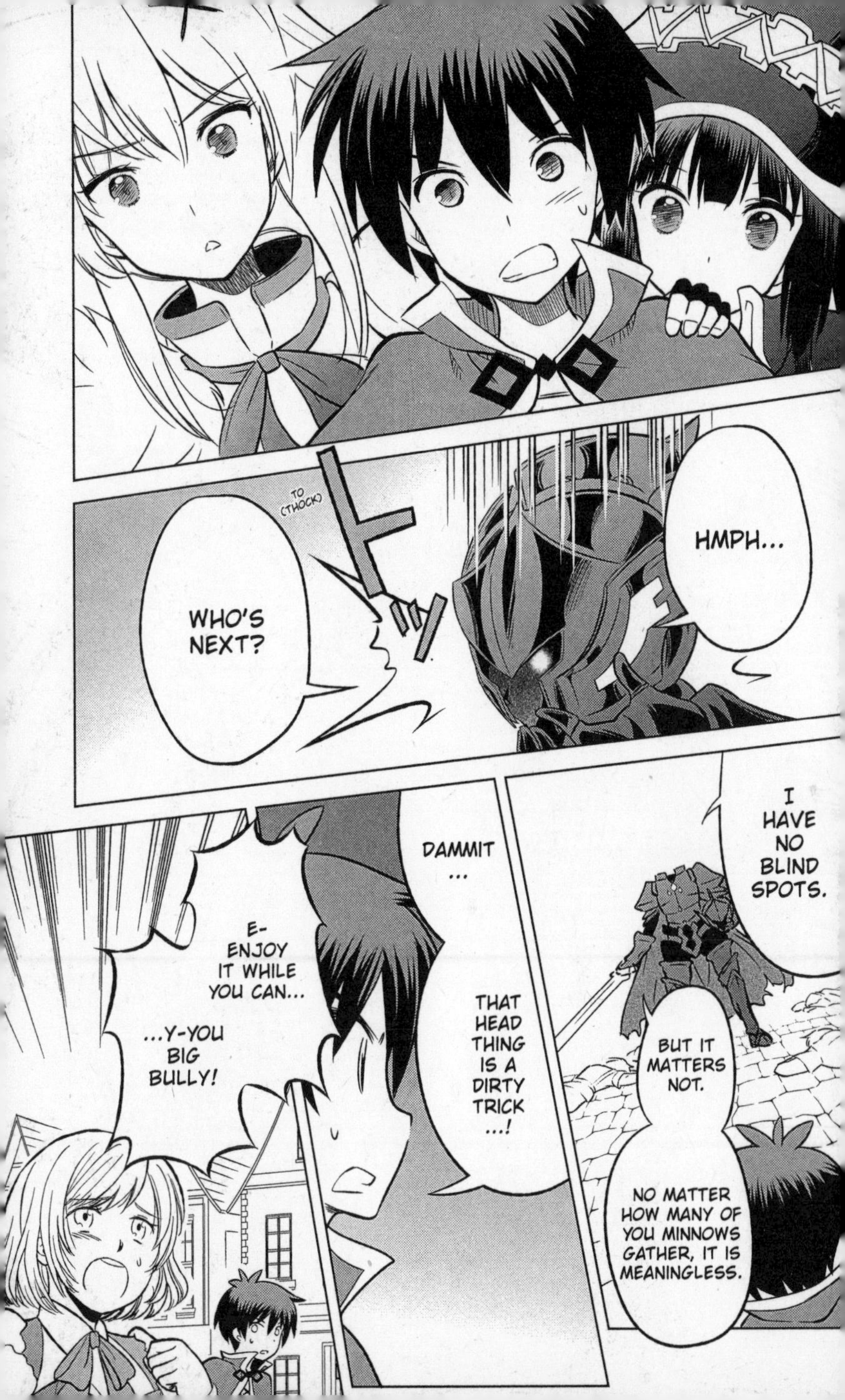
HMPH...
TO (THOCK)
WHO'S NEXT?
I HAVE NO BLIND SPOTS.
BUT IT MATTERS NOT.
NO MATTER HOW MANY OF YOU MINNOWS GATHER, IT IS MEANINGLESS.
DAMMIT...
THAT HEAD THING IS A DIRTY TRICK...!
E-ENJOY IT WHILE YOU CAN...
...Y-YOU BIG BULLY!

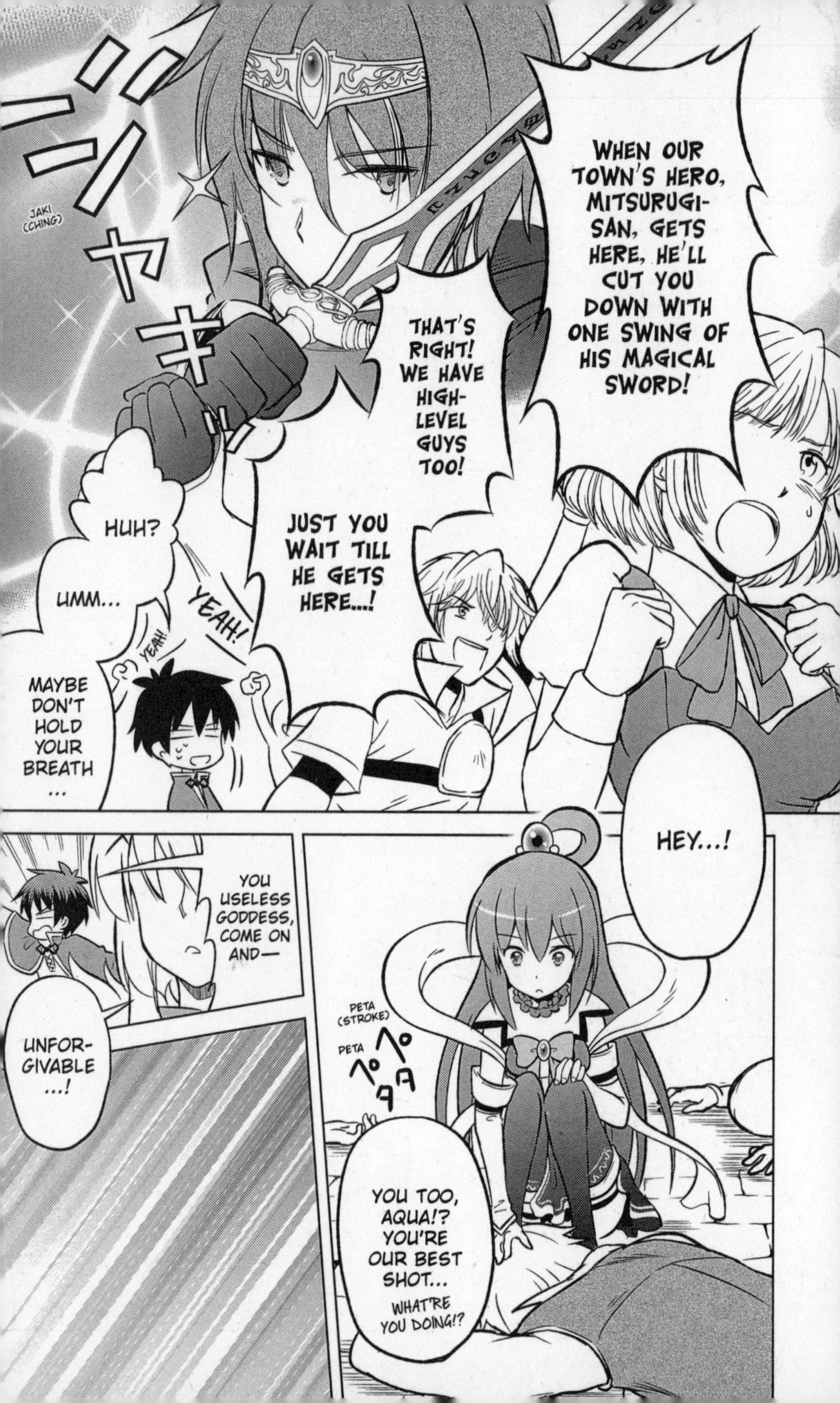
WHEN OUR TOWN'S HERO, MITSURUGI-SAN, GETS HERE, HE'LL CUT YOU DOWN WITH ONE SWING OF HIS MAGICAL SWORD!
THAT'S RIGHT! WE HAVE HIGH-LEVEL GUYS TOO!
JUST YOU WAIT TILL HE GETS HERE...!
ジャキッ
JAKI (CHING)
HUH?
UMM...
YEAH!
YEAH!
MAYBE DON'T HOLD YOUR BREATH ...
HEY...!
PETA (STROKE)
PETA
ペタペタ
YOU TOO, AQUA!? YOU'RE OUR BEST SHOT...
WHAT'RE YOU DOING!?
YOU USELESS GODDESS, COME ON AND—
UNFORGIVABLE ...!

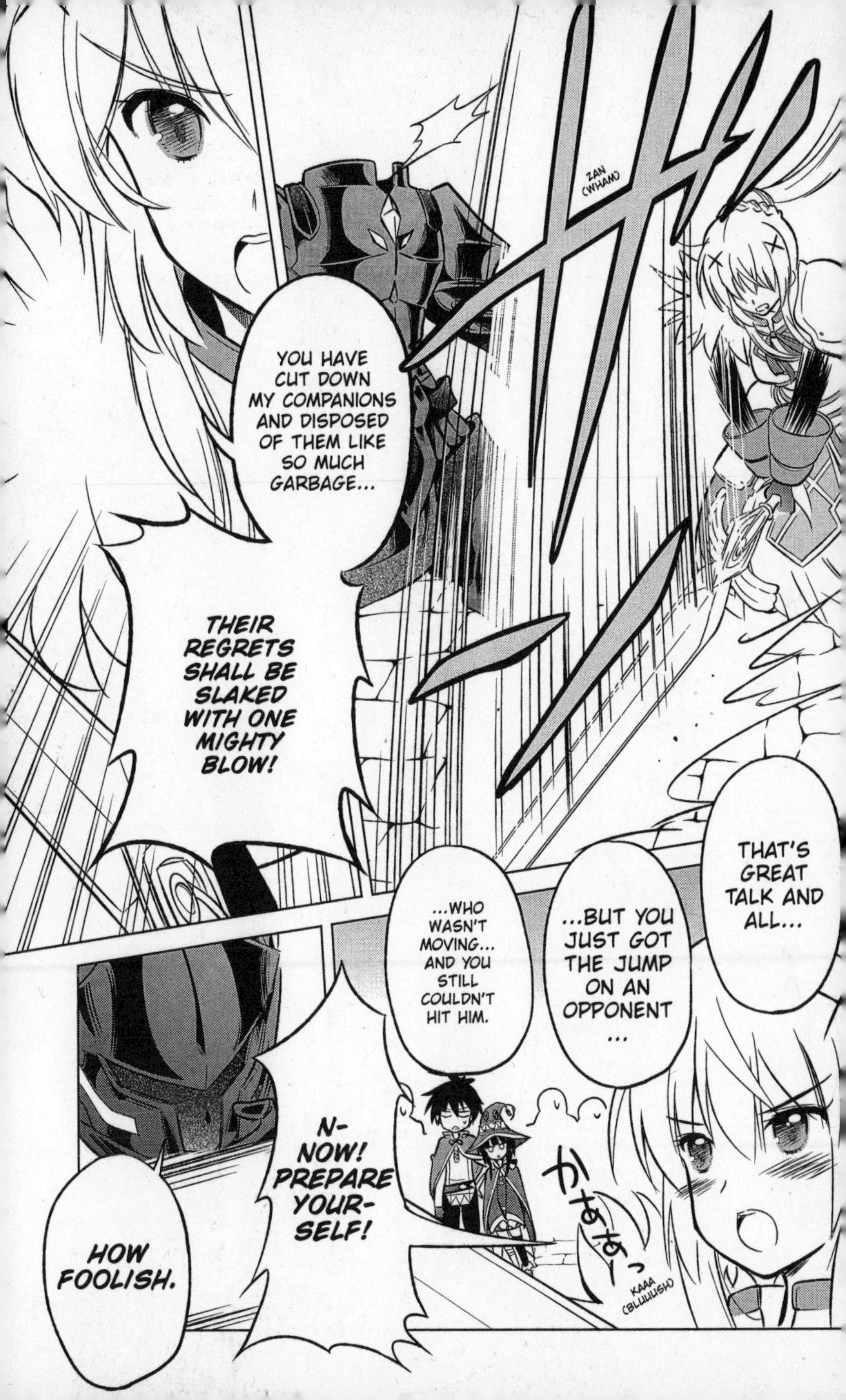
ZAN (WHAM)
YOU HAVE CUT DOWN MY COMPANIONS AND DISPOSED OF THEM LIKE SO MUCH GARBAGE...
THEIR REGRETS SHALL BE SLAKED WITH ONE MIGHTY BLOW!
THAT'S GREAT TALK AND ALL...
...BUT YOU JUST GOT THE JUMP ON AN OPPONENT...
...WHO WASN'T MOVING... AND YOU STILL COULDN'T HIT HIM.
かあぁっ
KAAA (BLUUUSH)
N-NOW! PREPARE YOURSELF!
HOW FOOLISH.

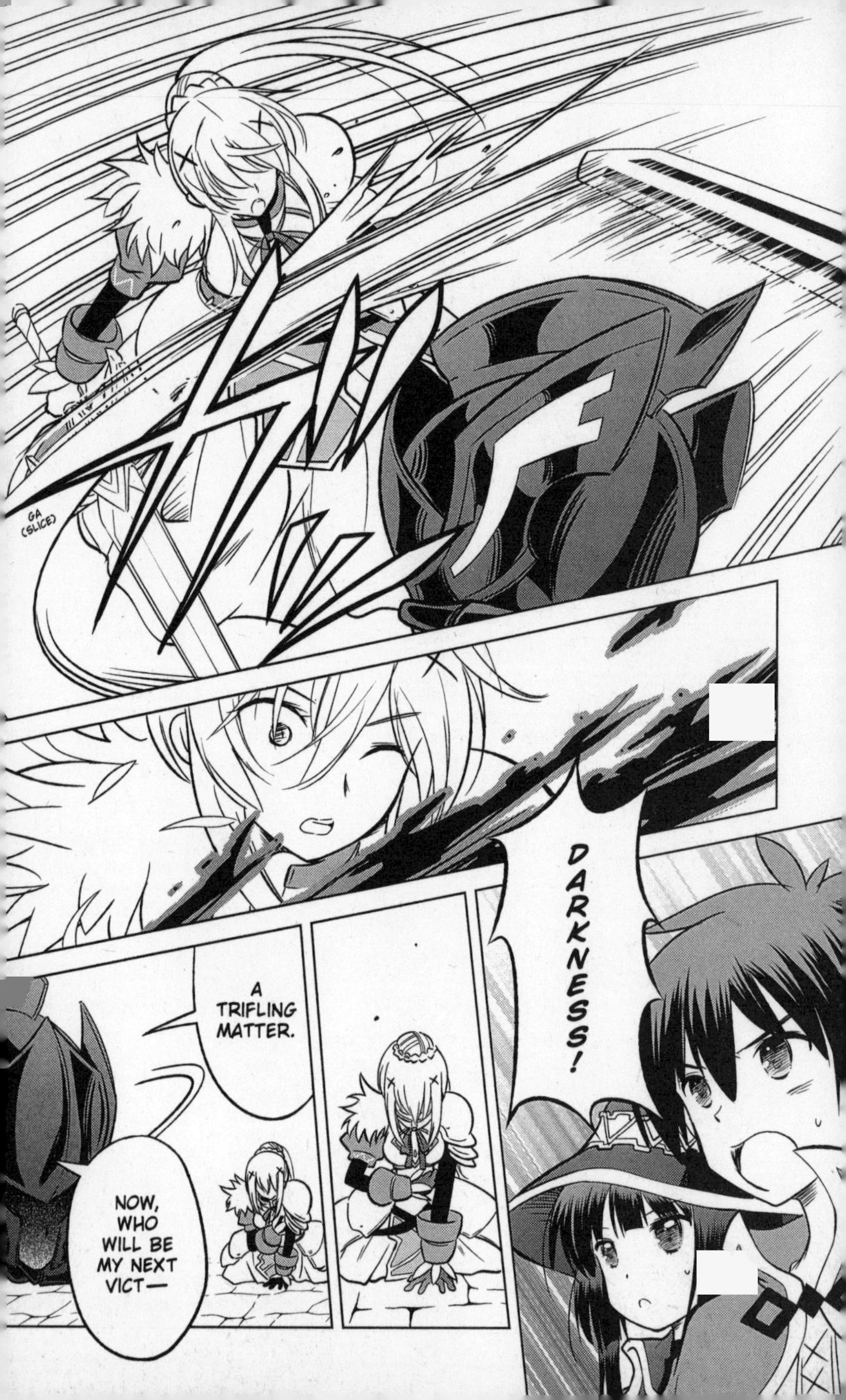
GA (SLICE)
DARKNESS!
A TRIFLING MATTER.
NOW, WHO WILL BE MY NEXT VICT—

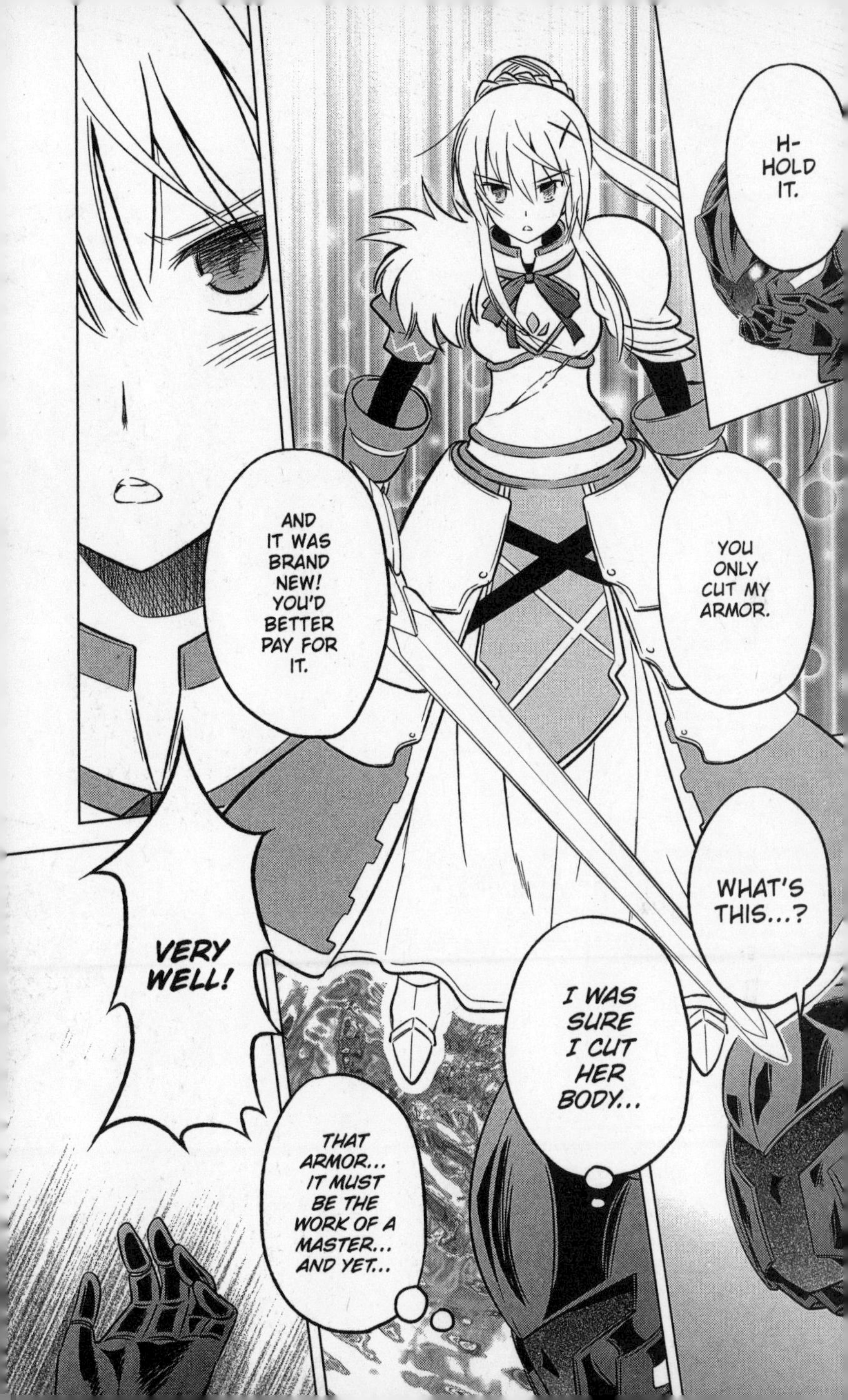
H-HOLD IT.
YOU ONLY CUT MY ARMOR.
AND IT WAS BRAND NEW! YOU'D BETTER PAY FOR IT.
WHAT'S THIS...?
I WAS SURE I CUT HER BODY...
THAT ARMOR... IT MUST BE THE WORK OF A MASTER... AND YET...
VERY WELL!

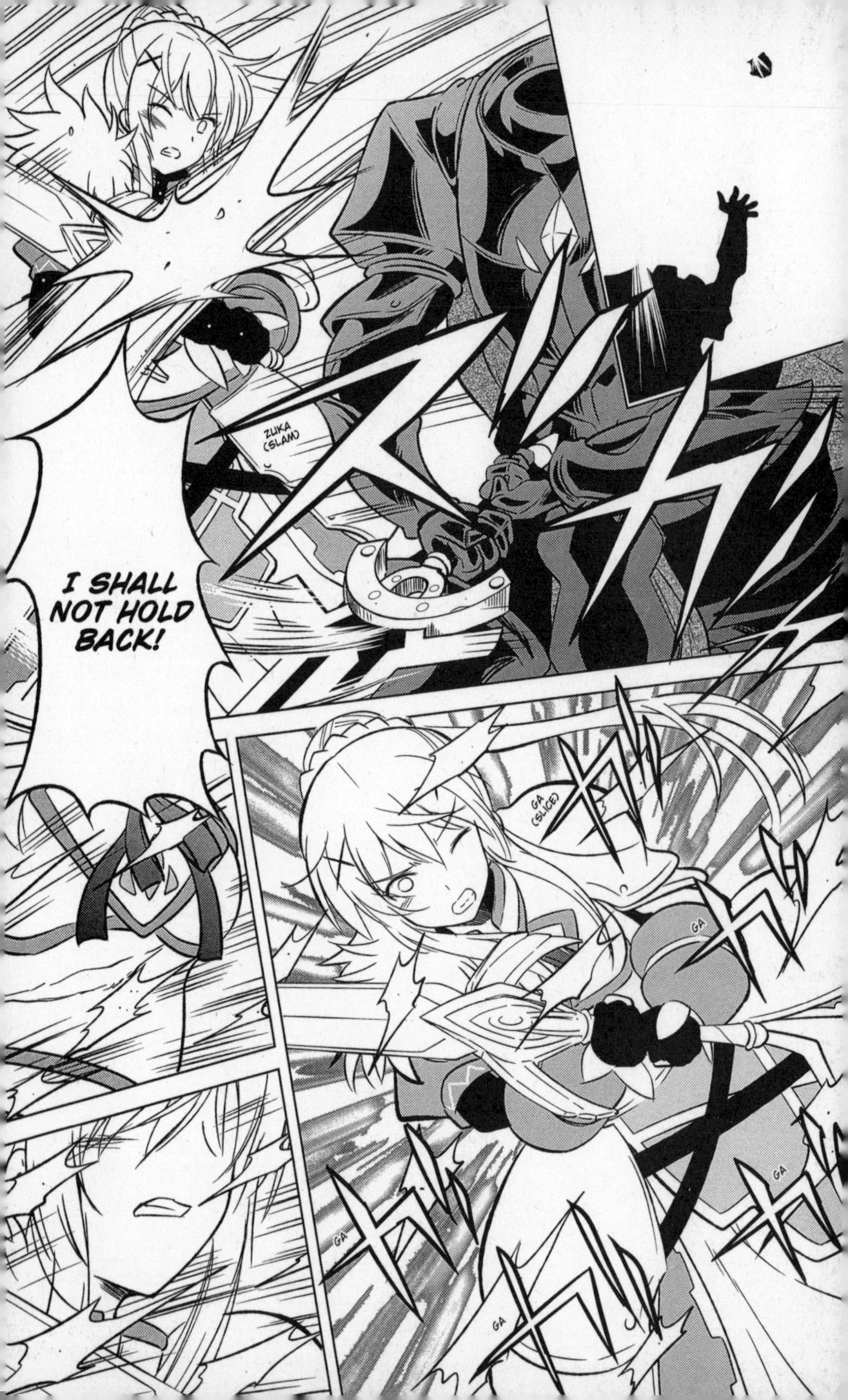
ZUKA (SLAM)
I SHALL NOT HOLD BACK!
GA (SLICE)
GA
GA
GA
GA

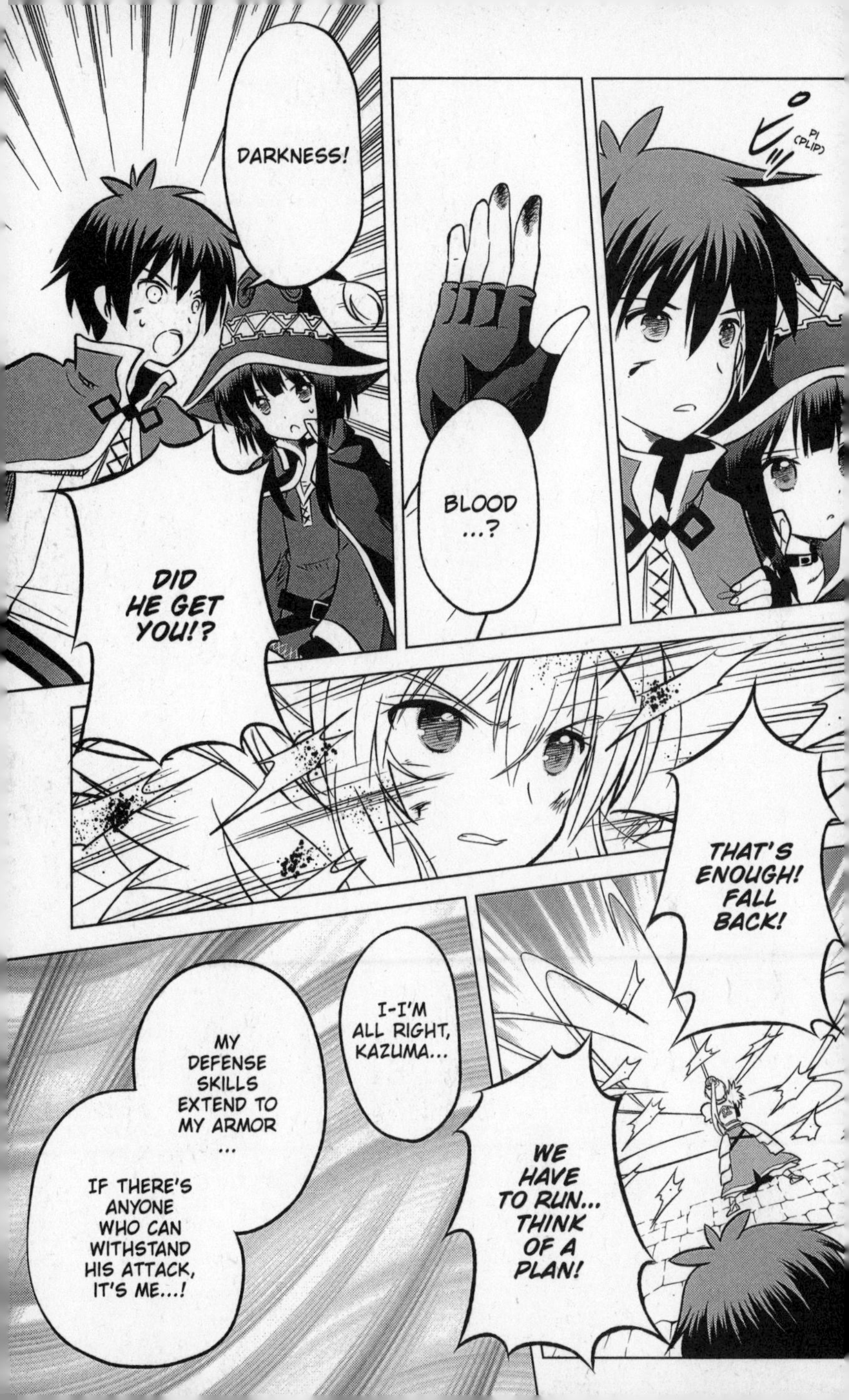
PI (PLIP)
BLOOD ...?
DARKNESS!
DID HE GET YOU!?
THAT'S ENOUGH! FALL BACK!
WE HAVE TO RUN... THINK OF A PLAN!
I-I'M ALL RIGHT, KAZUMA...
MY DEFENSE SKILLS EXTEND TO MY ARMOR ...
IF THERE'S ANYONE WHO CAN WITHSTAND HIS ATTACK, IT'S ME...!

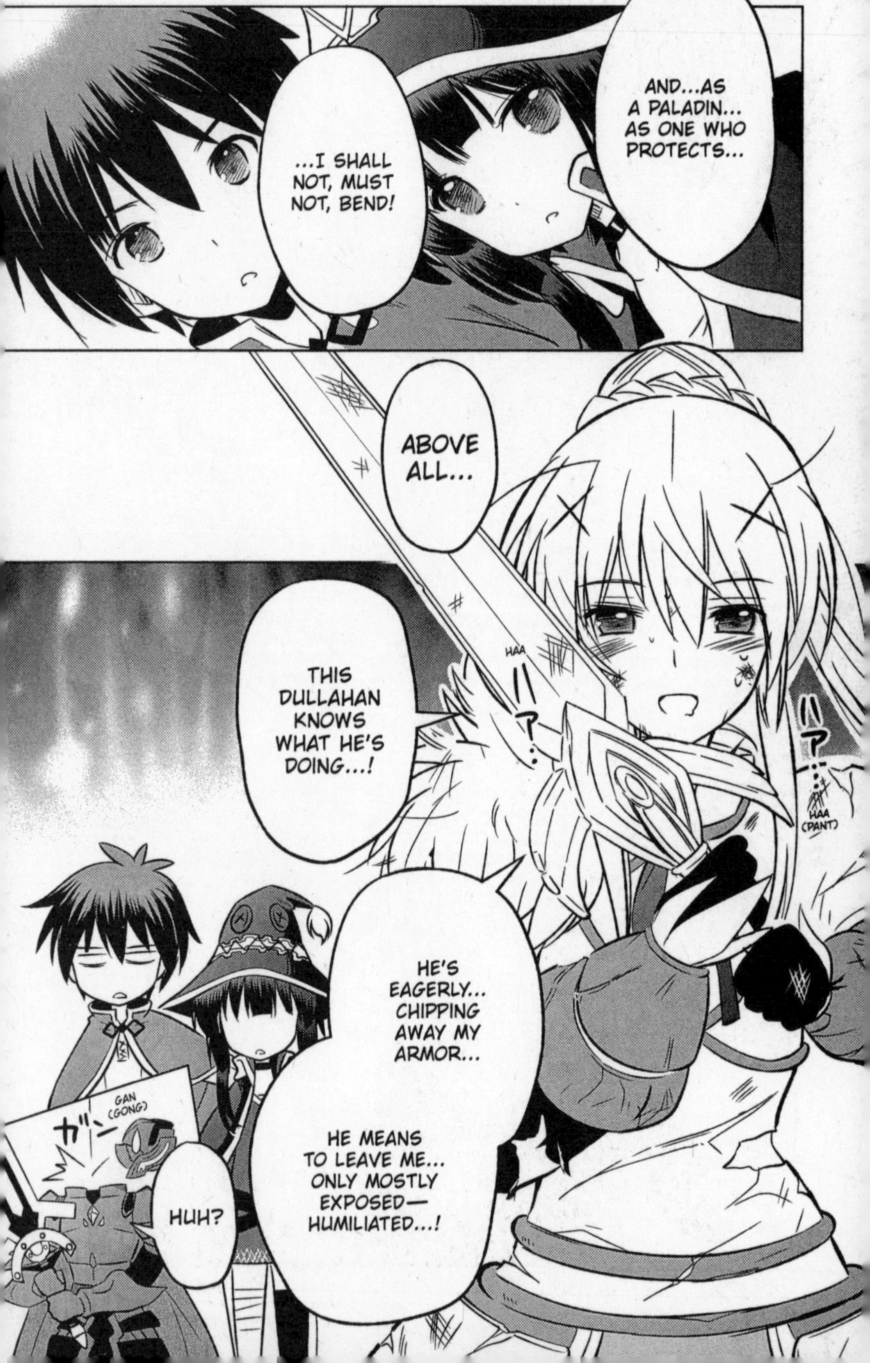
AND...AS A PALADIN... AS ONE WHO PROTECTS...
...I SHALL NOT, MUST NOT, BEND!
ABOVE ALL...
ハア…
HAA (PANT)
ハア…
HAA
THIS DULLAHAN KNOWS WHAT HE'S DOING...!
HE'S EAGERLY... CHIPPING AWAY MY ARMOR...
HE MEANS TO LEAVE ME... ONLY MOSTLY EXPOSED—HUMILIATED...!
HUH?
ガン
GAN (GONG)

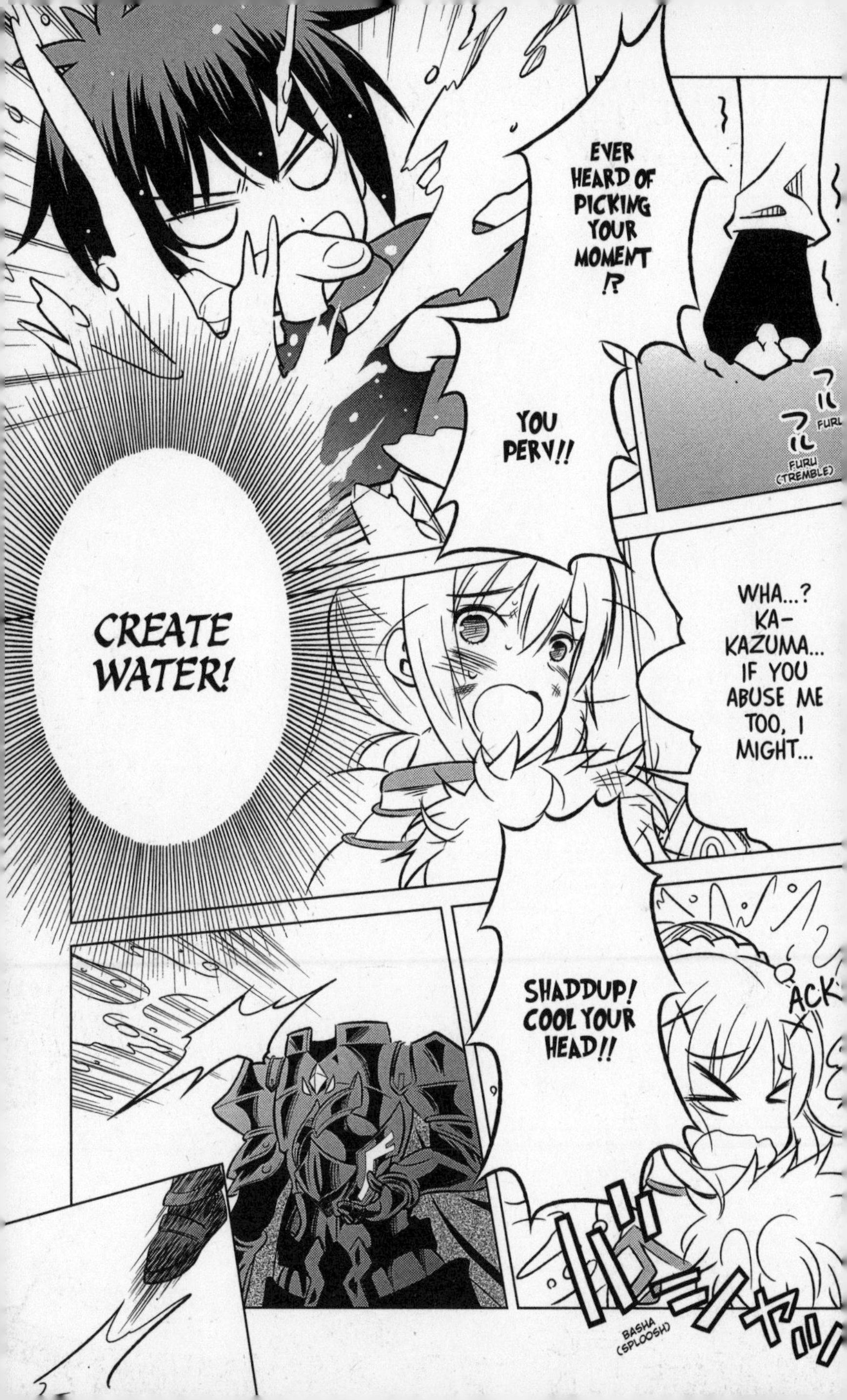
FURU FURU (TREMBLE)
EVER HEARD OF PICKING YOUR MOMENT!?
YOU PERV!!
WHA...? KA-KAZUMA... IF YOU ABUSE ME TOO, I MIGHT...
SHADDUP! COOL YOUR HEAD!!
CREATE WATER!
ACK
BASHA (SPLOOSH)

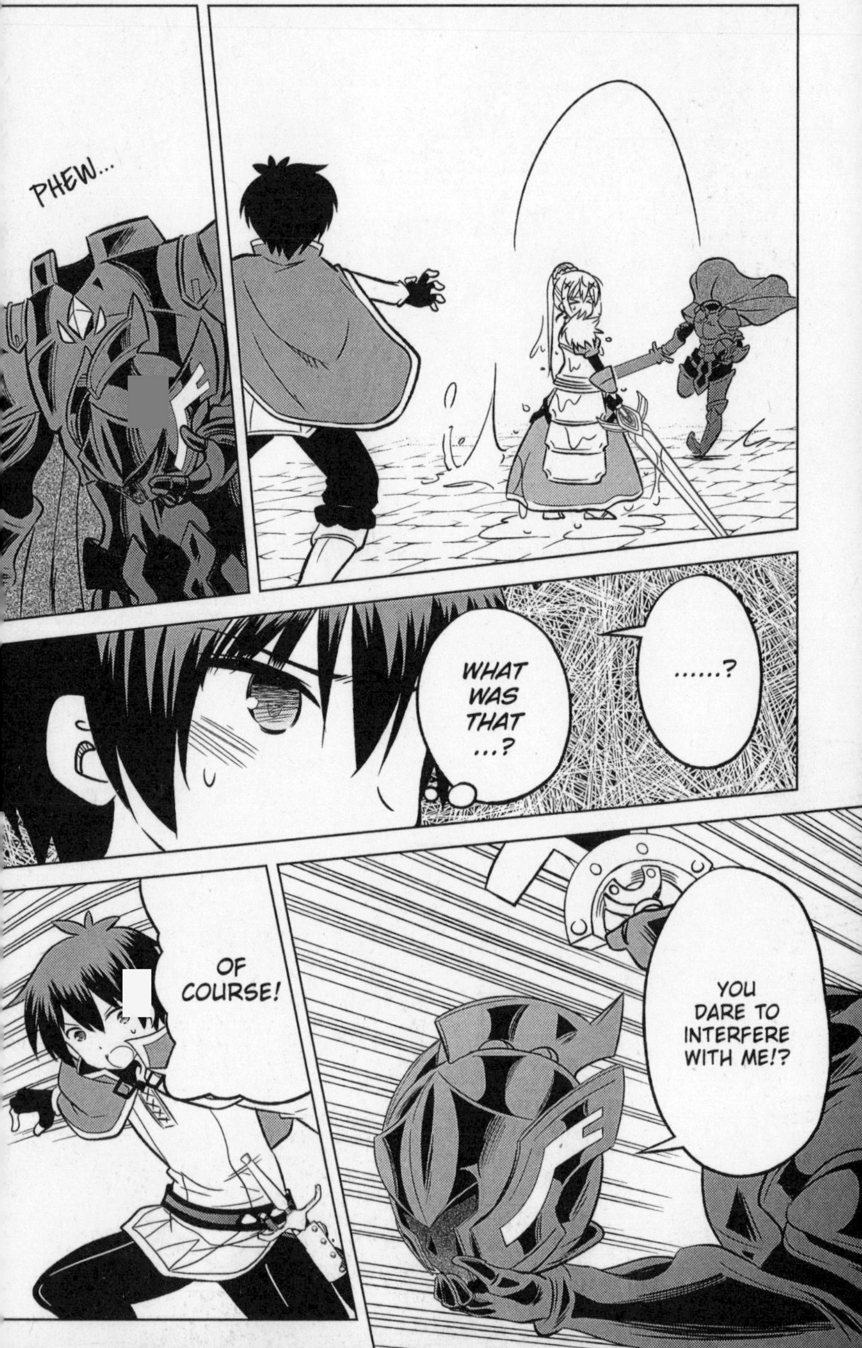
PHEW...
......?
WHAT WAS THAT ...?
YOU DARE TO INTERFERE WITH ME!?
OF COURSE!

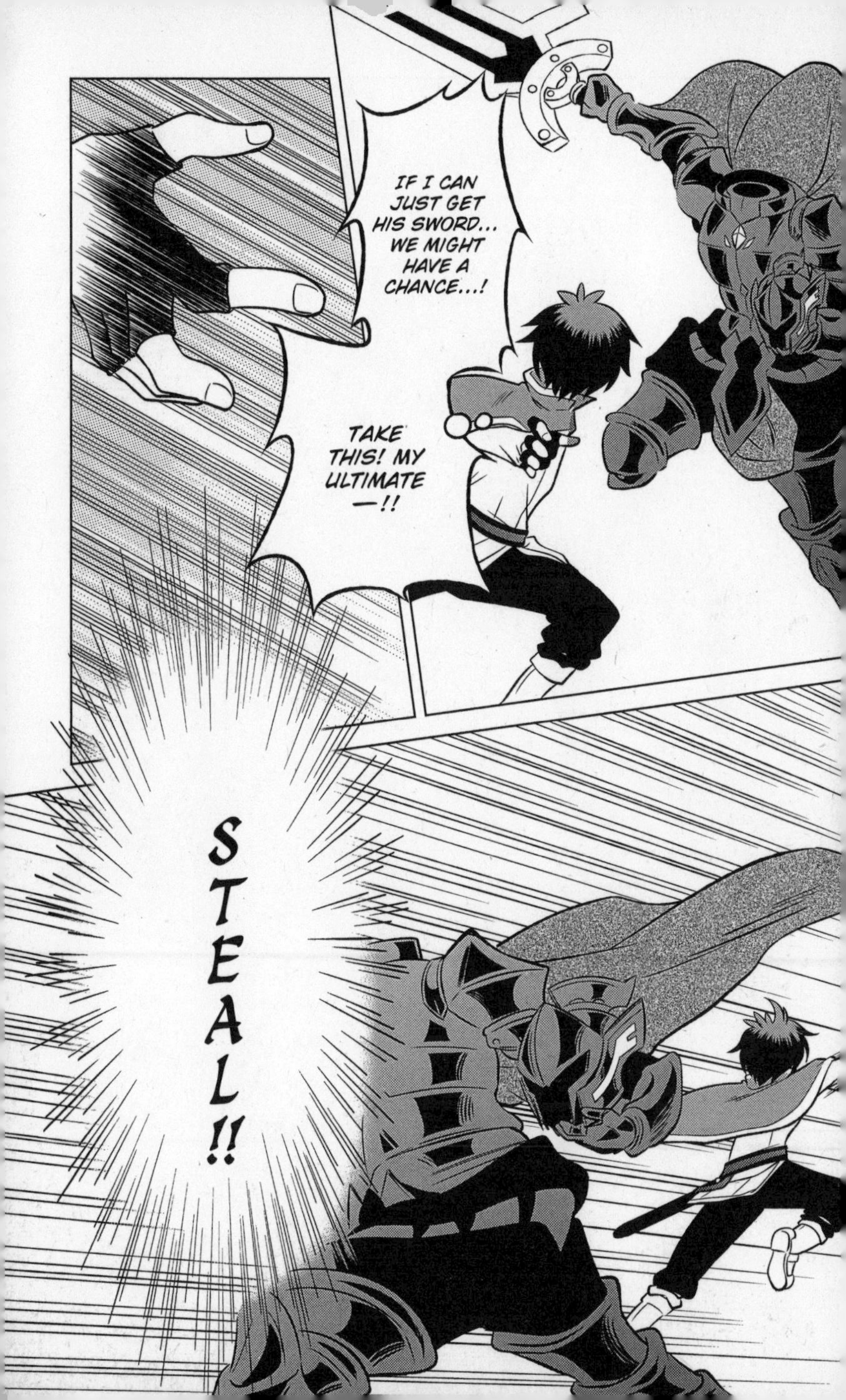
IF I CAN JUST GET HIS SWORD... WE MIGHT HAVE A CHANCE...!
TAKE THIS! MY ULTIMATE —!!
STEAL!!

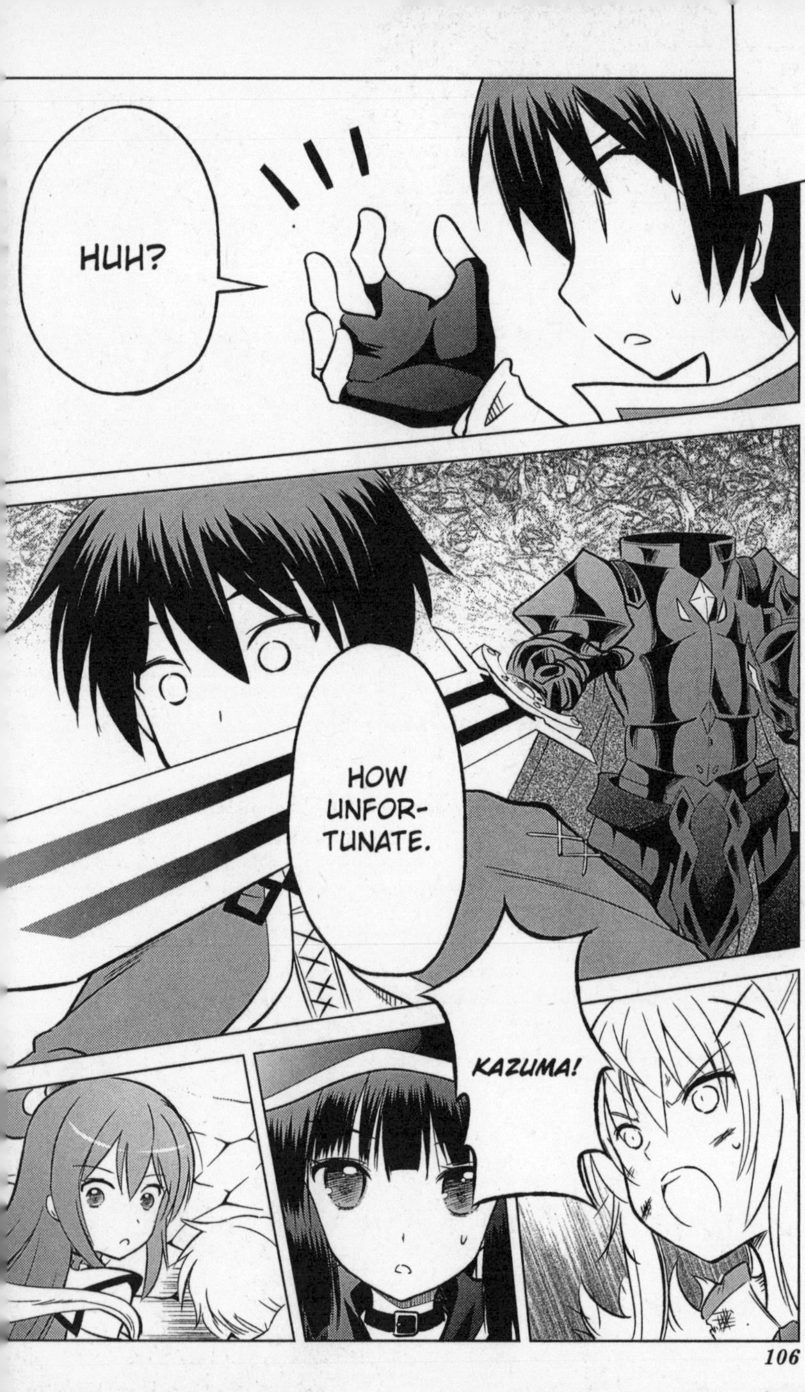
HUH?
HOW UNFOR-TUNATE.
KAZUMA!

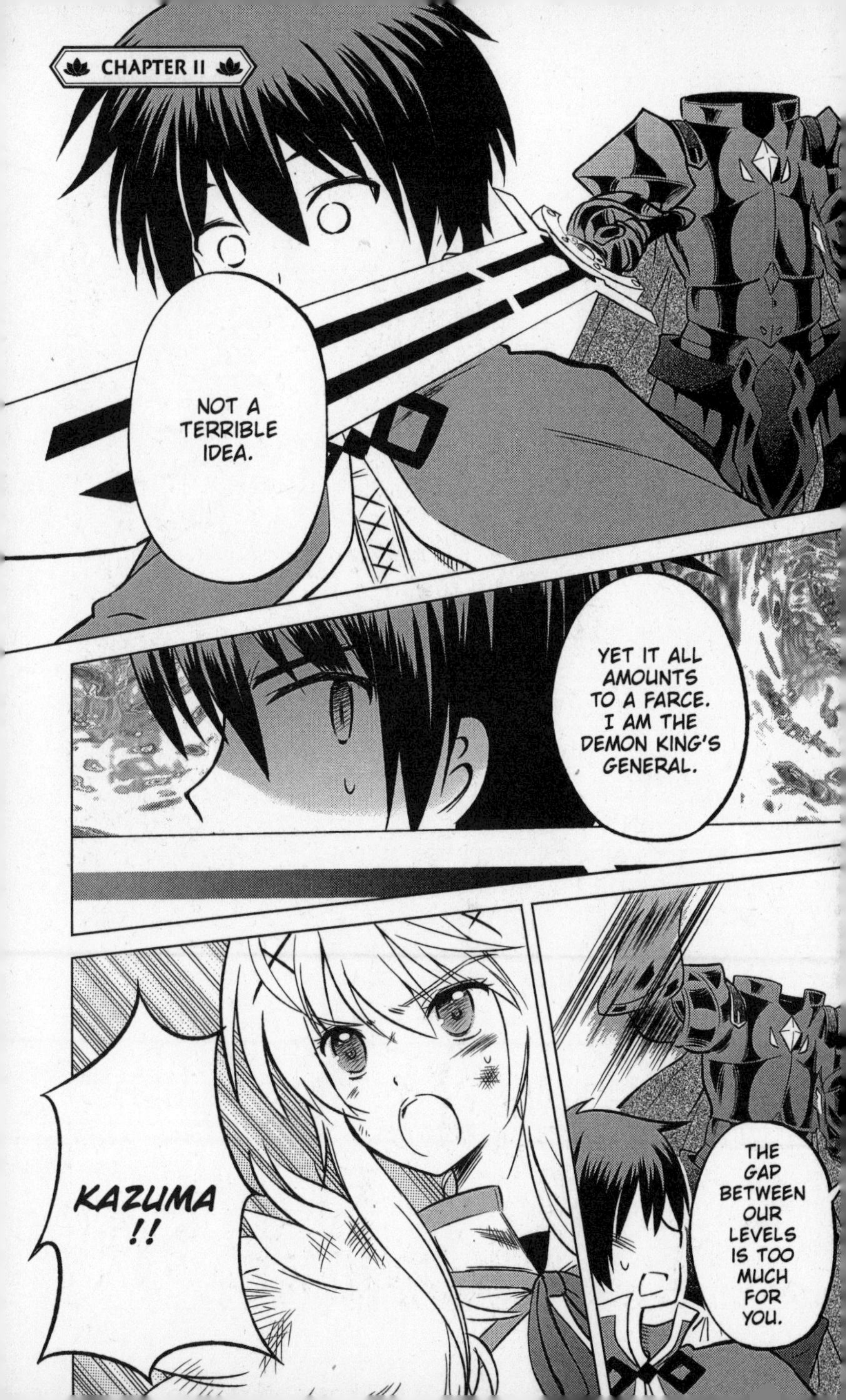
NOT A TERRIBLE IDEA.
YET IT ALL AMOUNTS TO A FARCE. I AM THE DEMON KING'S GENERAL.
THE GAP BETWEEN OUR LEVELS IS TOO MUCH FOR YOU.
KAZUMA!!

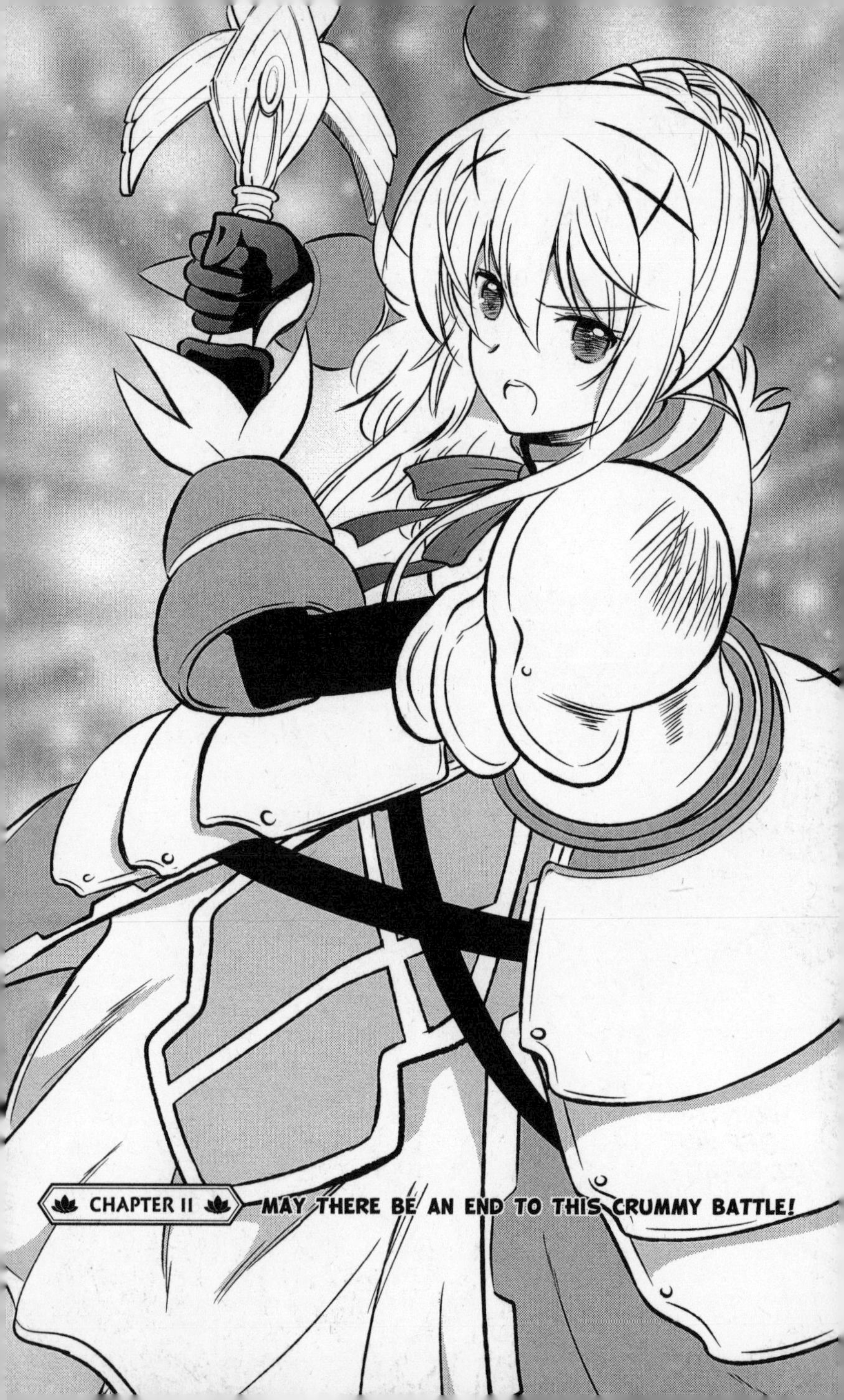
CHAPTER 11
MAY THERE BE AN END TO THIS CRUMMY BATTLE!

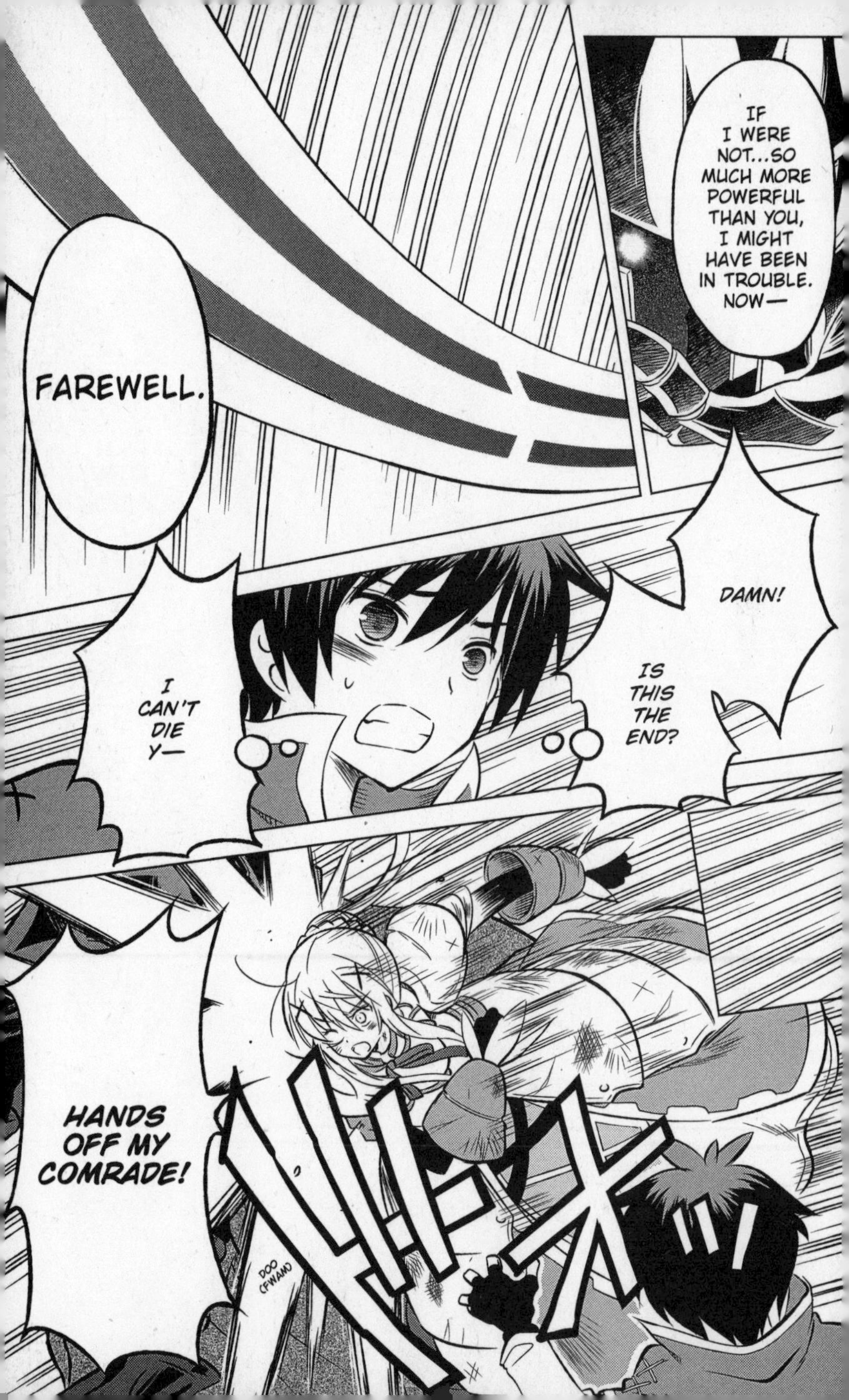
IF I WERE NOT...SO MUCH MORE POWERFUL THAN YOU, I MIGHT HAVE BEEN IN TROUBLE. NOW—
FAREWELL.
DAMN!
IS THIS THE END?
I CAN'T DIE Y—
HANDS OFF MY COMRADE!
DOO (FWAM)

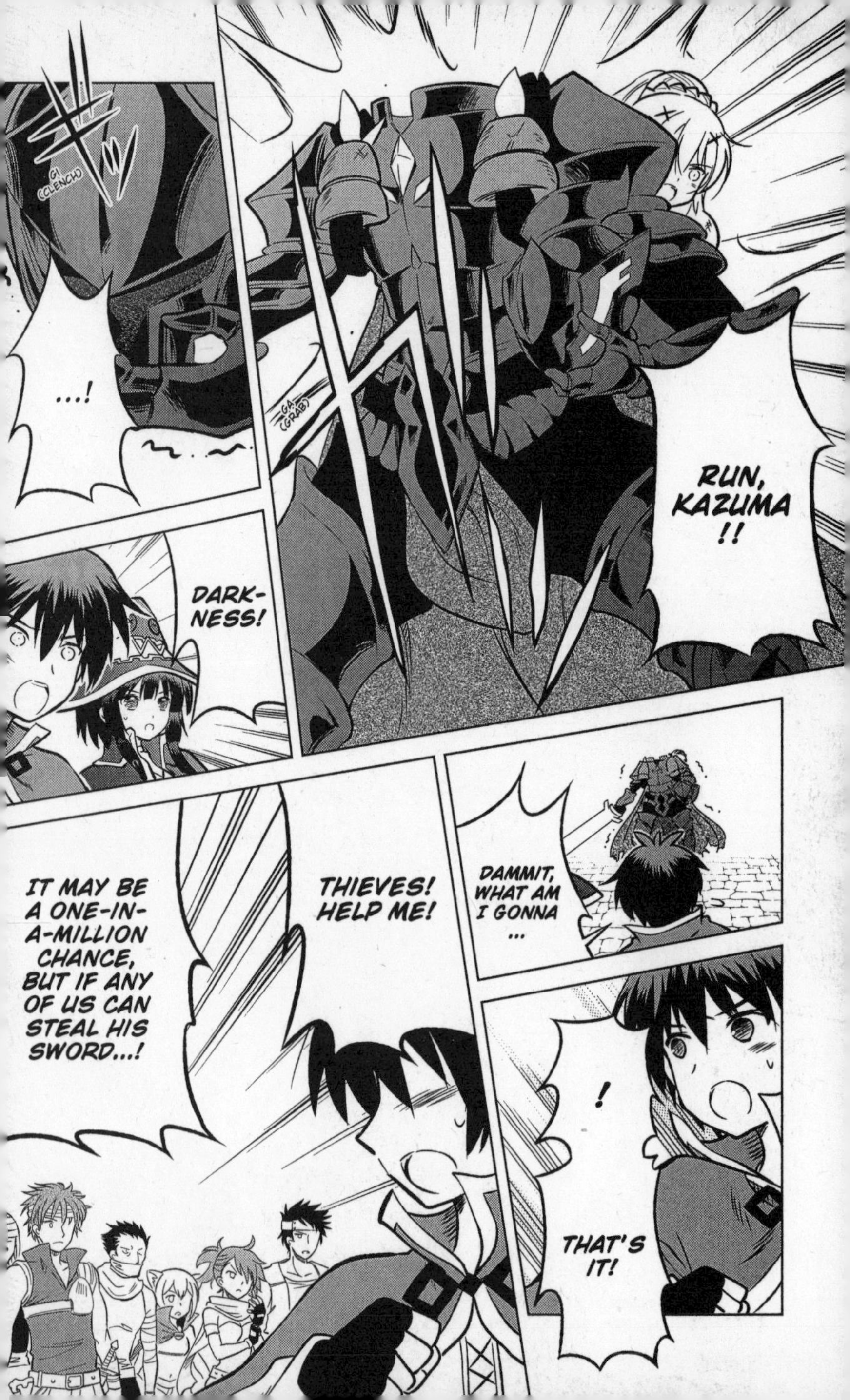
GA (GRAB)
RUN, KAZUMA!!
GI (CLENCH)
...!
DARK-NESS!
DAMMIT, WHAT AM I GONNA ...
!
THAT'S IT!
THIEVES! HELP ME!
IT MAY BE A ONE-IN-A-MILLION CHANCE, BUT IF ANY OF US CAN STEAL HIS SWORD...!

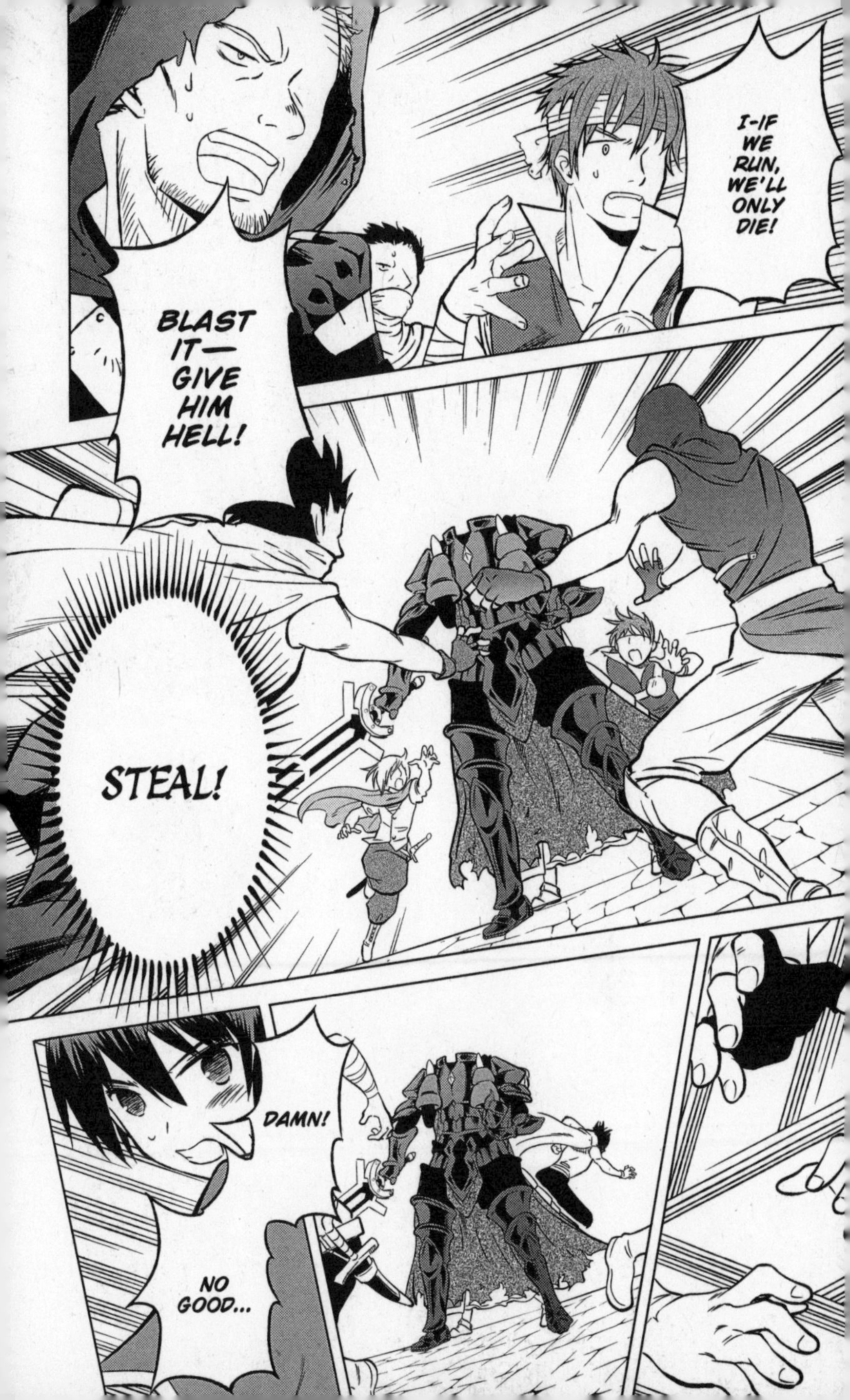
I-IF WE RUN, WE'LL ONLY DIE!
BLAST IT— GIVE HIM HELL!
STEAL!
DAMN!
NO GOOD...

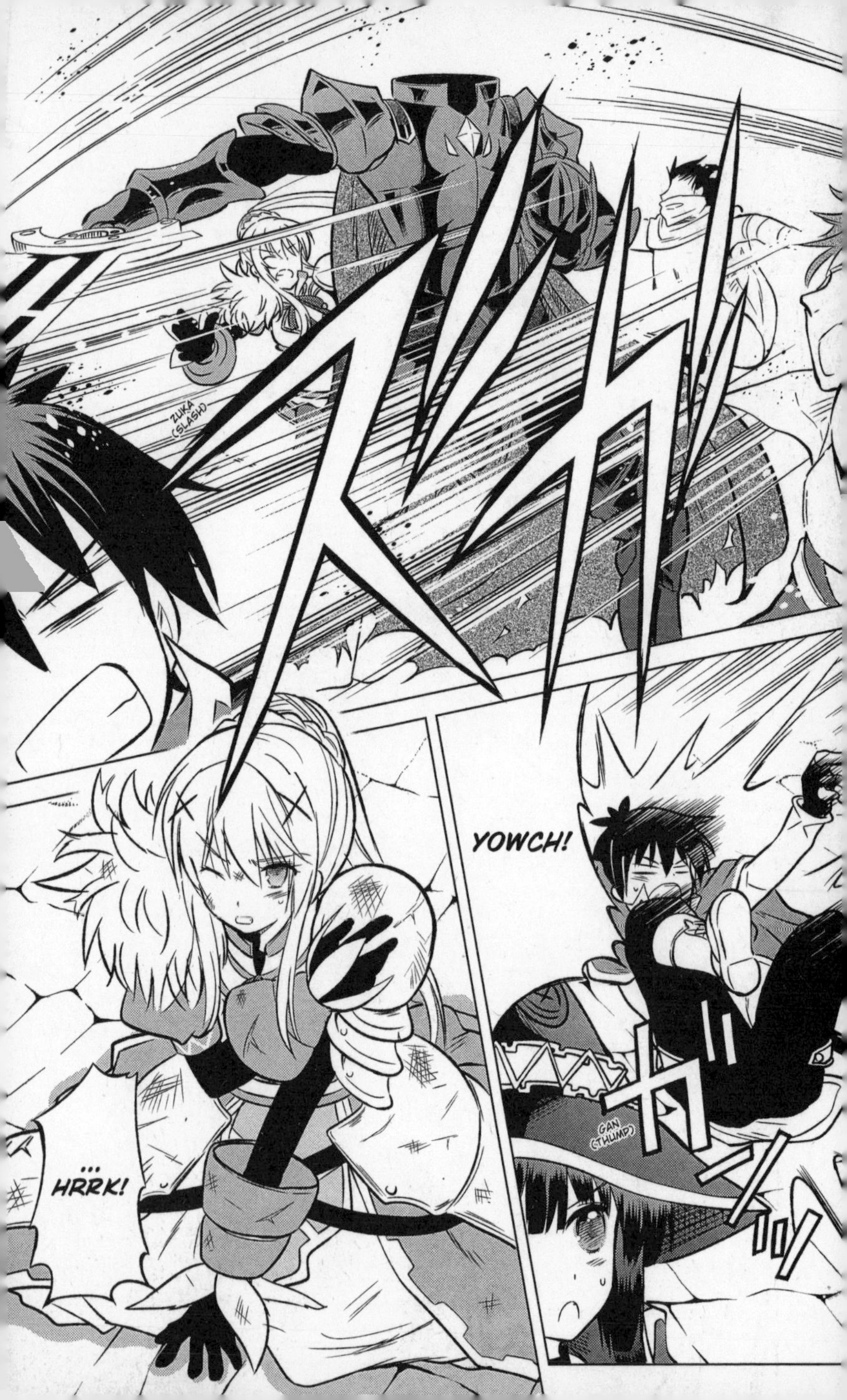
ZUKA (SLASH)
YOWCH!
GAN (THUMP)
... HRRK!

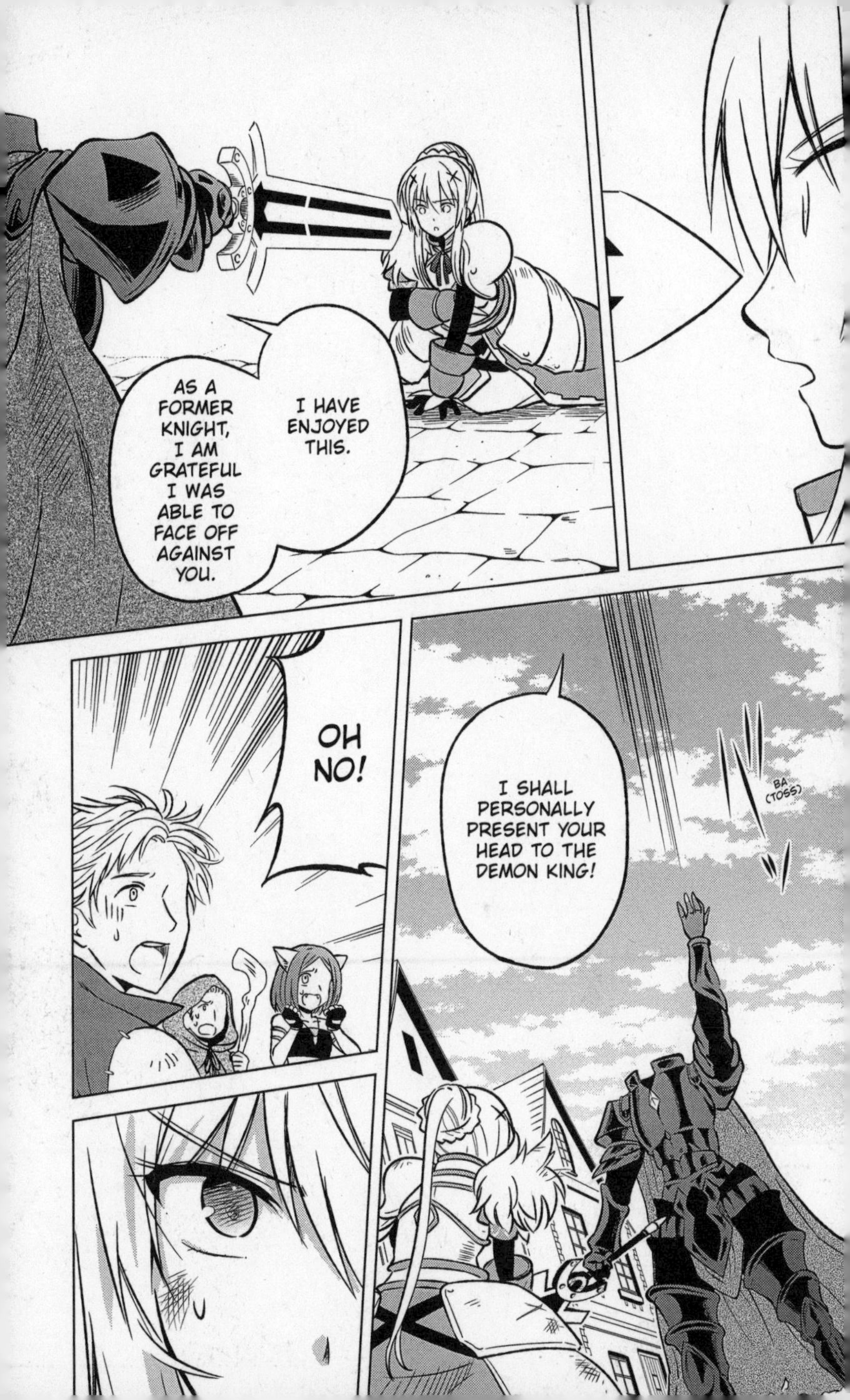
I HAVE ENJOYED THIS.
AS A FORMER KNIGHT, I AM GRATEFUL I WAS ABLE TO FACE OFF AGAINST YOU.
I SHALL PERSONALLY PRESENT YOUR HEAD TO THE DEMON KING!
BA (TOSS)
OH NO!

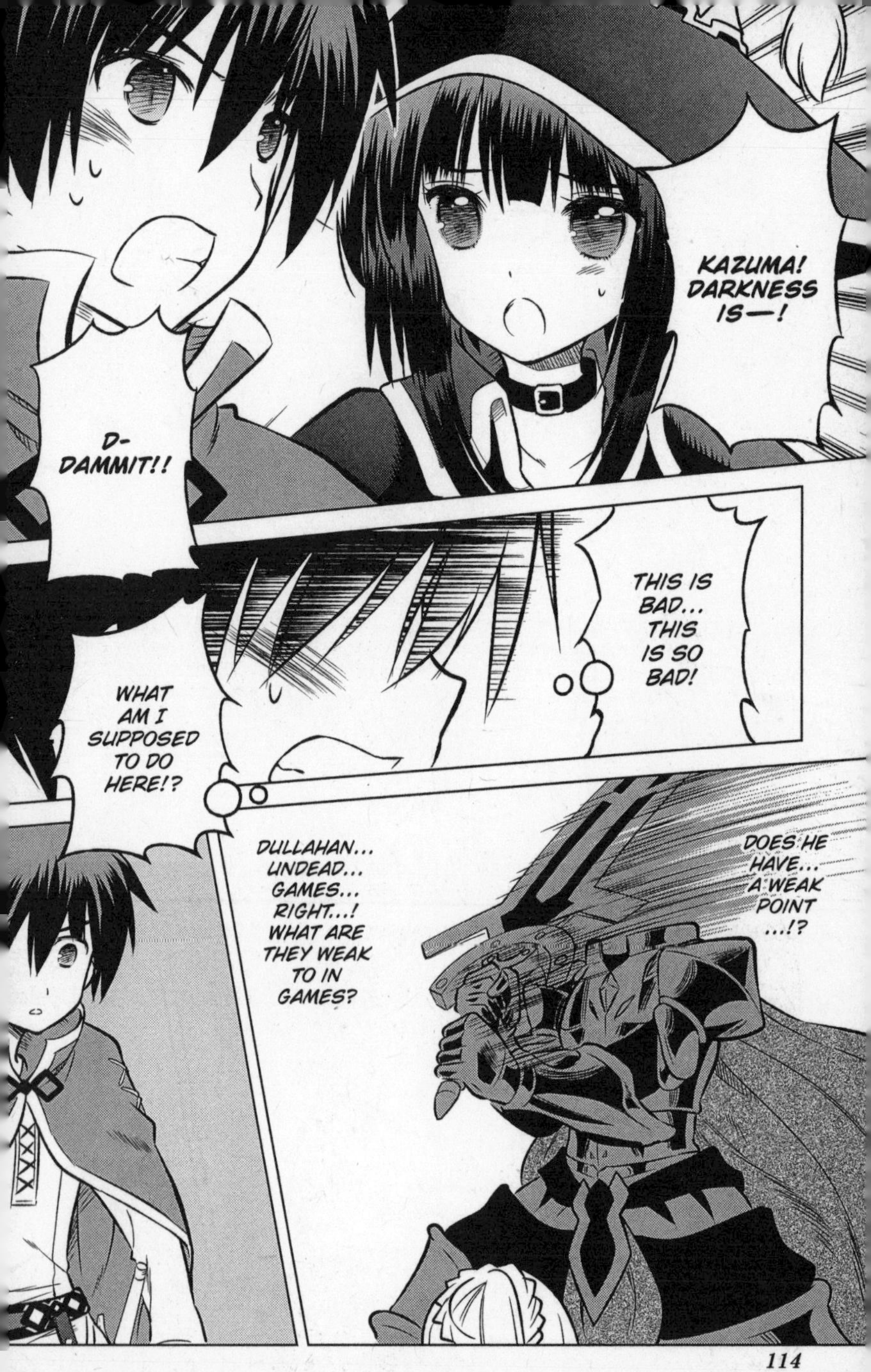
KAZUMA! DARKNESS IS—!
D-DAMMIT!!
THIS IS BAD... THIS IS SO BAD!
WHAT AM I SUPPOSED TO DO HERE!?
DOES HE HAVE... A WEAK POINT ...!?
DULLAHAN... UNDEAD... GAMES... RIGHT...! WHAT ARE THEY WEAK TO IN GAMES?

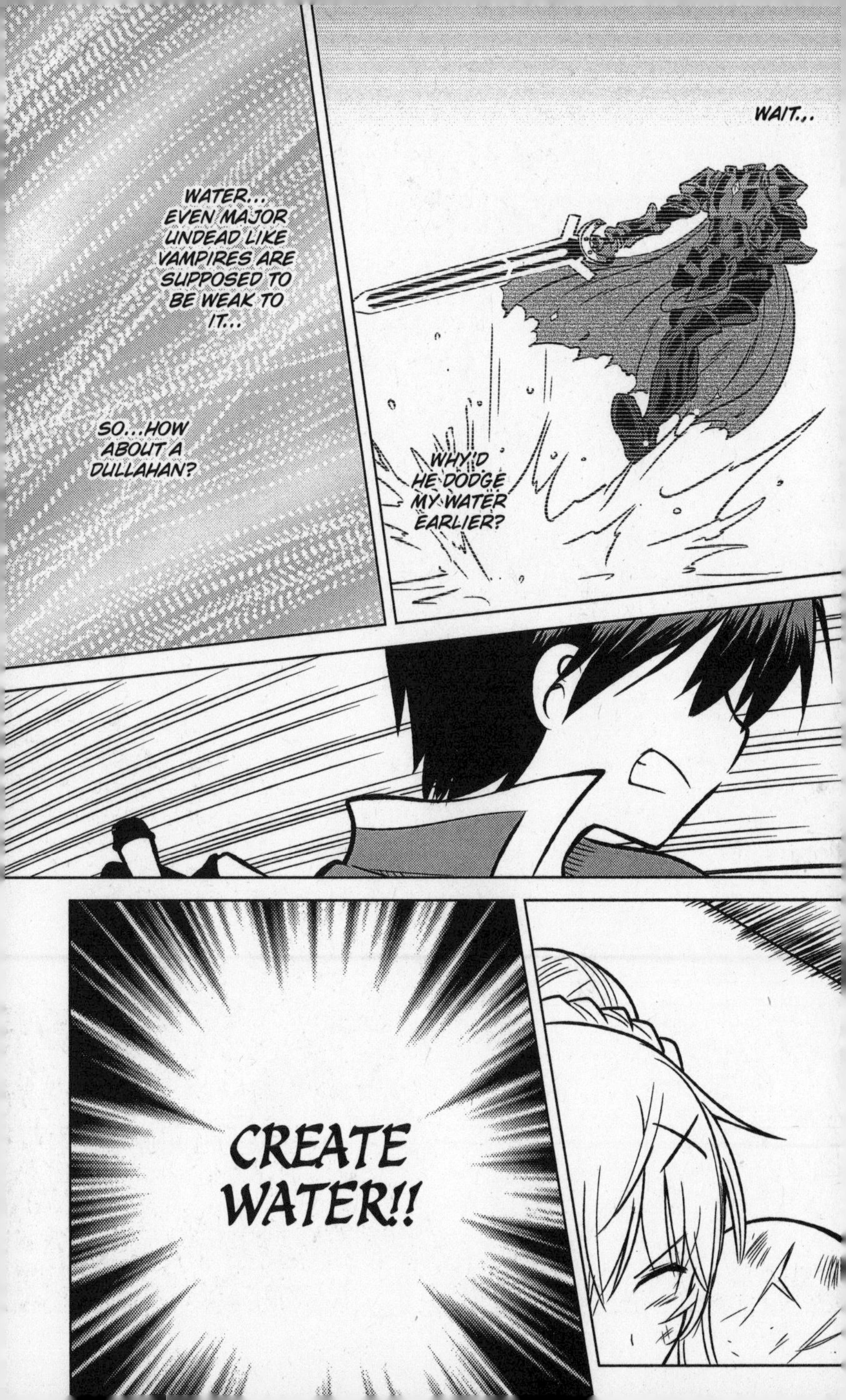
WAIT...
WHY'D HE DODGE MY WATER EARLIER?
WATER... EVEN MAJOR UNDEAD LIKE VAMPIRES ARE SUPPOSED TO BE WEAK TO IT...
SO...HOW ABOUT A DULLAHAN?
CREATE WATER!!

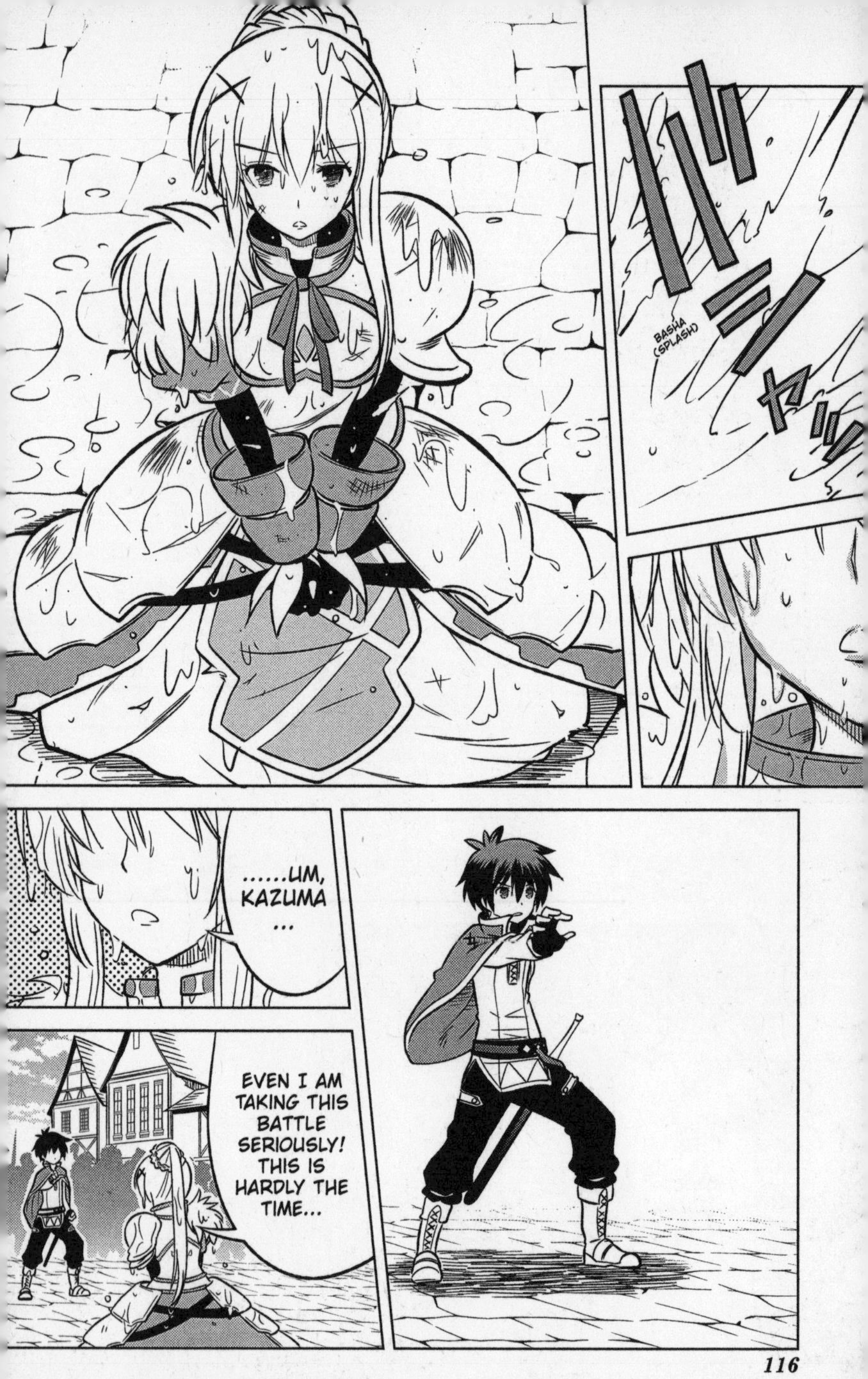
BASHA (SPLASH)
......UM, KAZUMA ...
EVEN I AM TAKING THIS BATTLE SERIOUSLY! THIS IS HARDLY THE TIME...

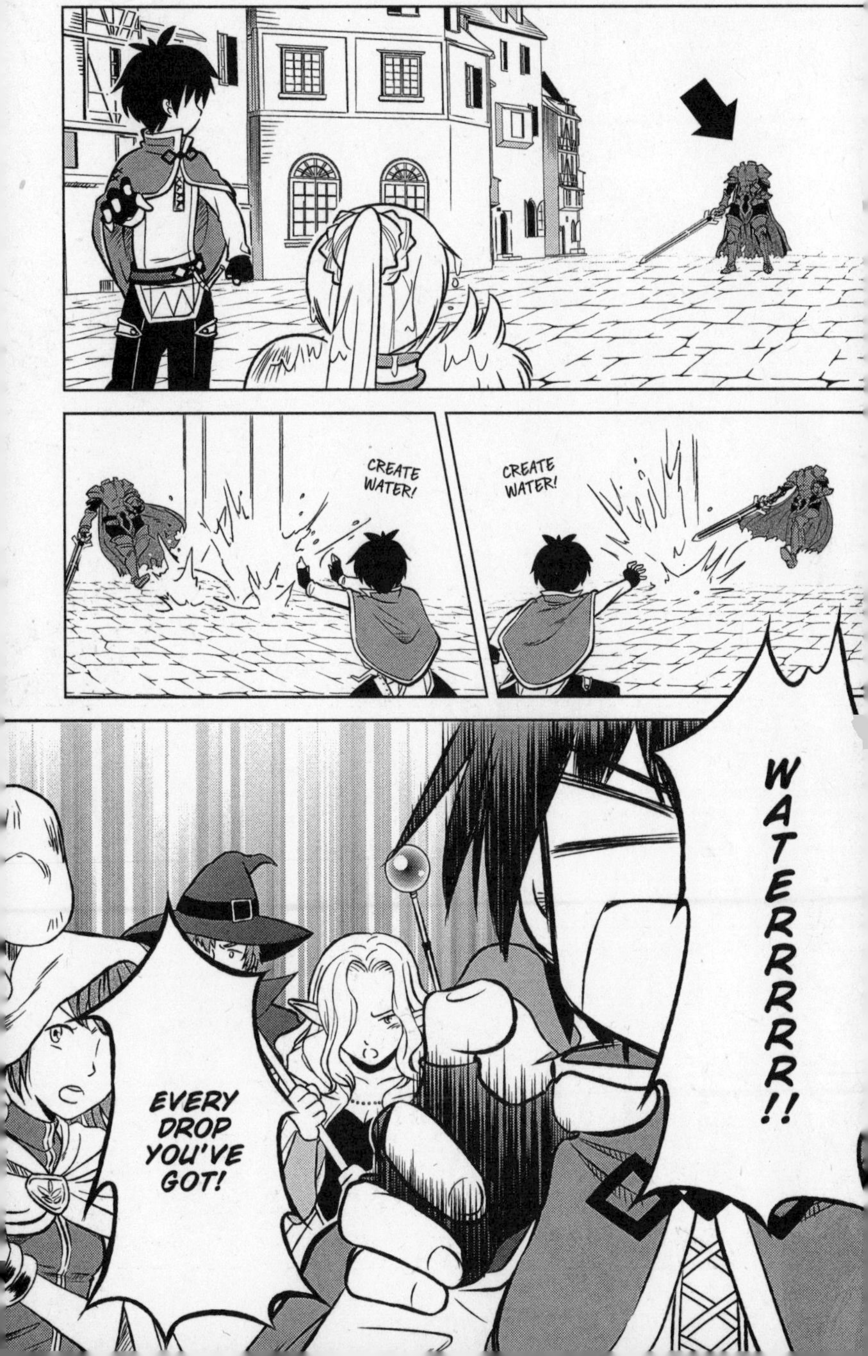
CREATE WATER!
CREATE WATER!
WATERRRRR!!
EVERY DROP YOU'VE GOT!

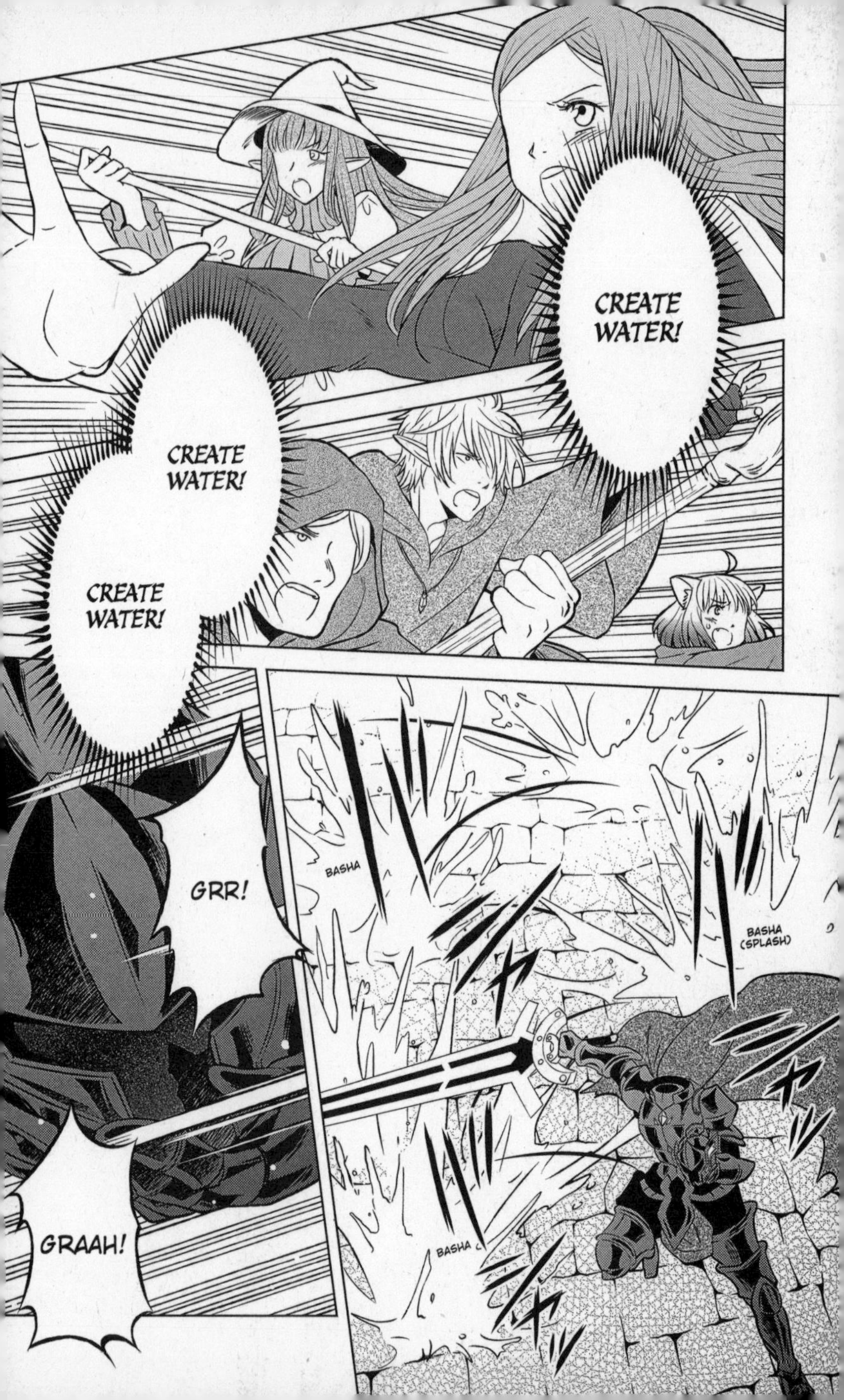
CREATE WATER!
CREATE WATER!
CREATE WATER!
BASHA (SPLASH)
BASHA
BASHA
GRR!
GRAAH!

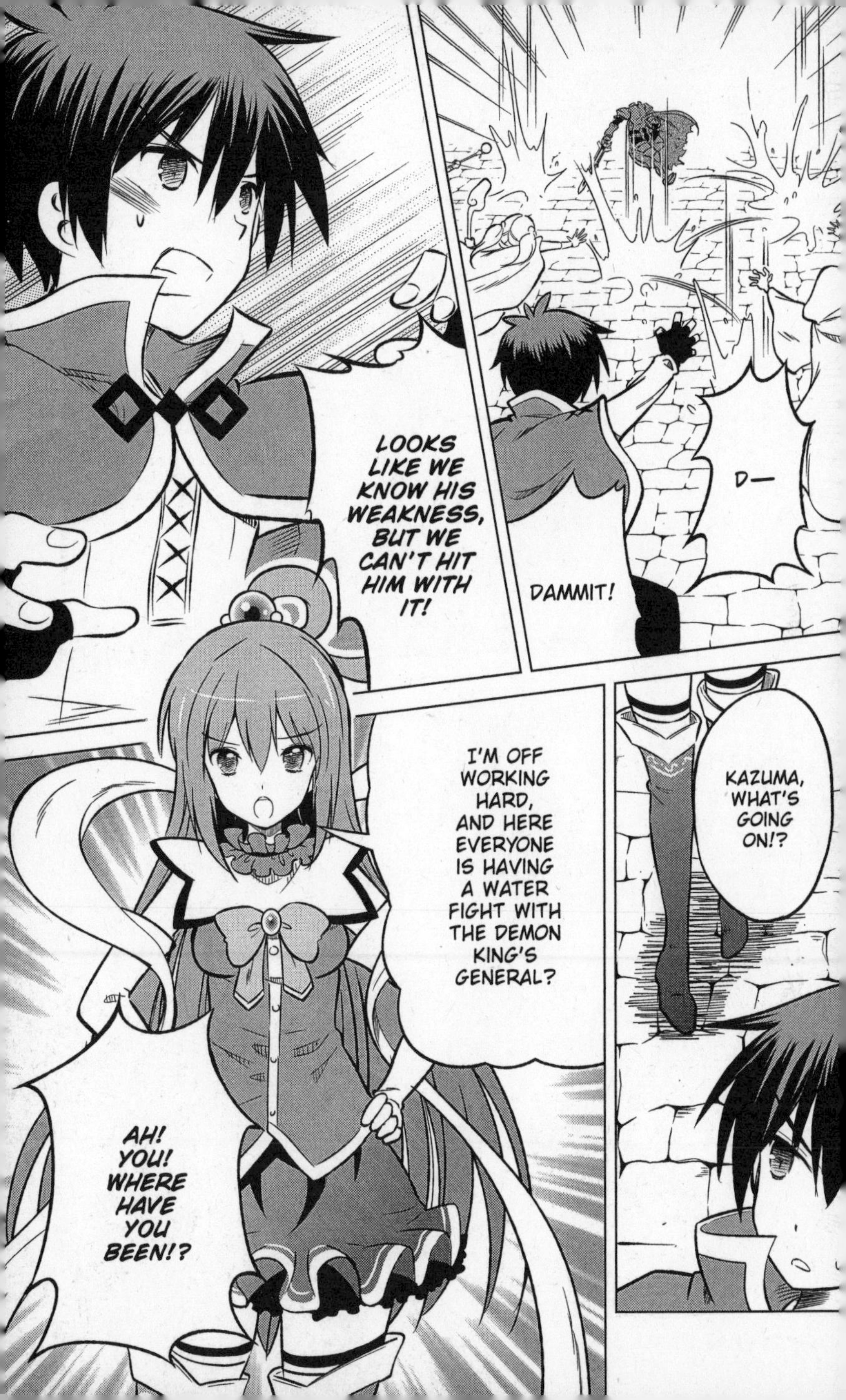
D—
DAMMIT!
LOOKS LIKE WE KNOW HIS WEAKNESS, BUT WE CAN'T HIT HIM WITH IT!
KAZUMA, WHAT'S GOING ON!?
I'M OFF WORKING HARD, AND HERE EVERYONE IS HAVING A WATER FIGHT WITH THE DEMON KING'S GENERAL?
AH! YOU! WHERE HAVE YOU BEEN!?

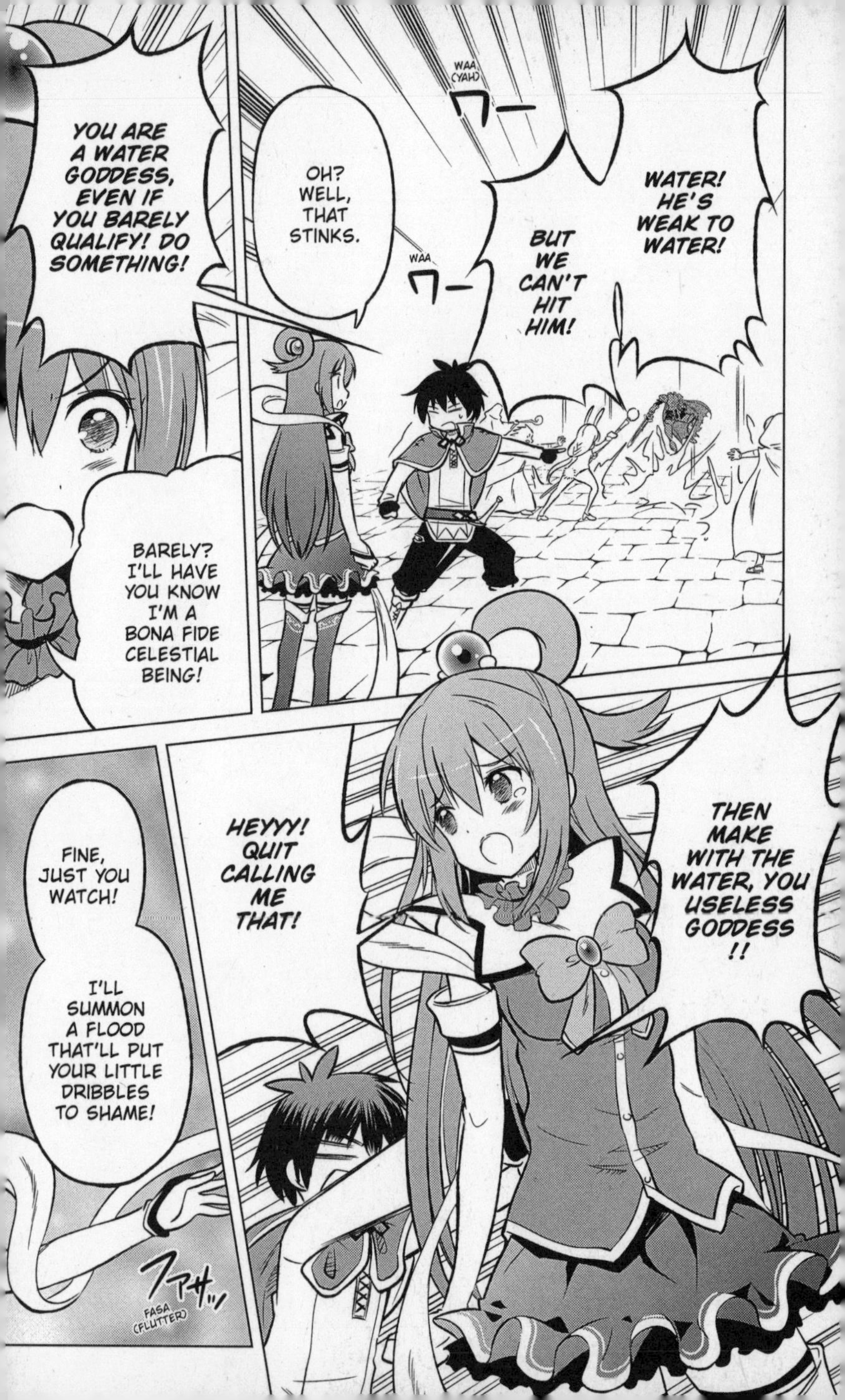

WAA (YAH)
WATER! HE'S WEAK TO WATER!
BUT WE CAN'T HIT HIM!
WAA
OH? WELL, THAT STINKS.
YOU ARE A WATER GODDESS, EVEN IF YOU BARELY QUALIFY! DO SOMETHING!
BARELY? I'LL HAVE YOU KNOW I'M A BONA FIDE CELESTIAL BEING!
THEN MAKE WITH THE WATER, YOU USELESS GODDESS!!
HEYYY! QUIT CALLING ME THAT!
FINE, JUST YOU WATCH!
I'LL SUMMON A FLOOD THAT'LL PUT YOUR LITTLE DRIBBLES TO SHAME!
FASA (FLUTTER)

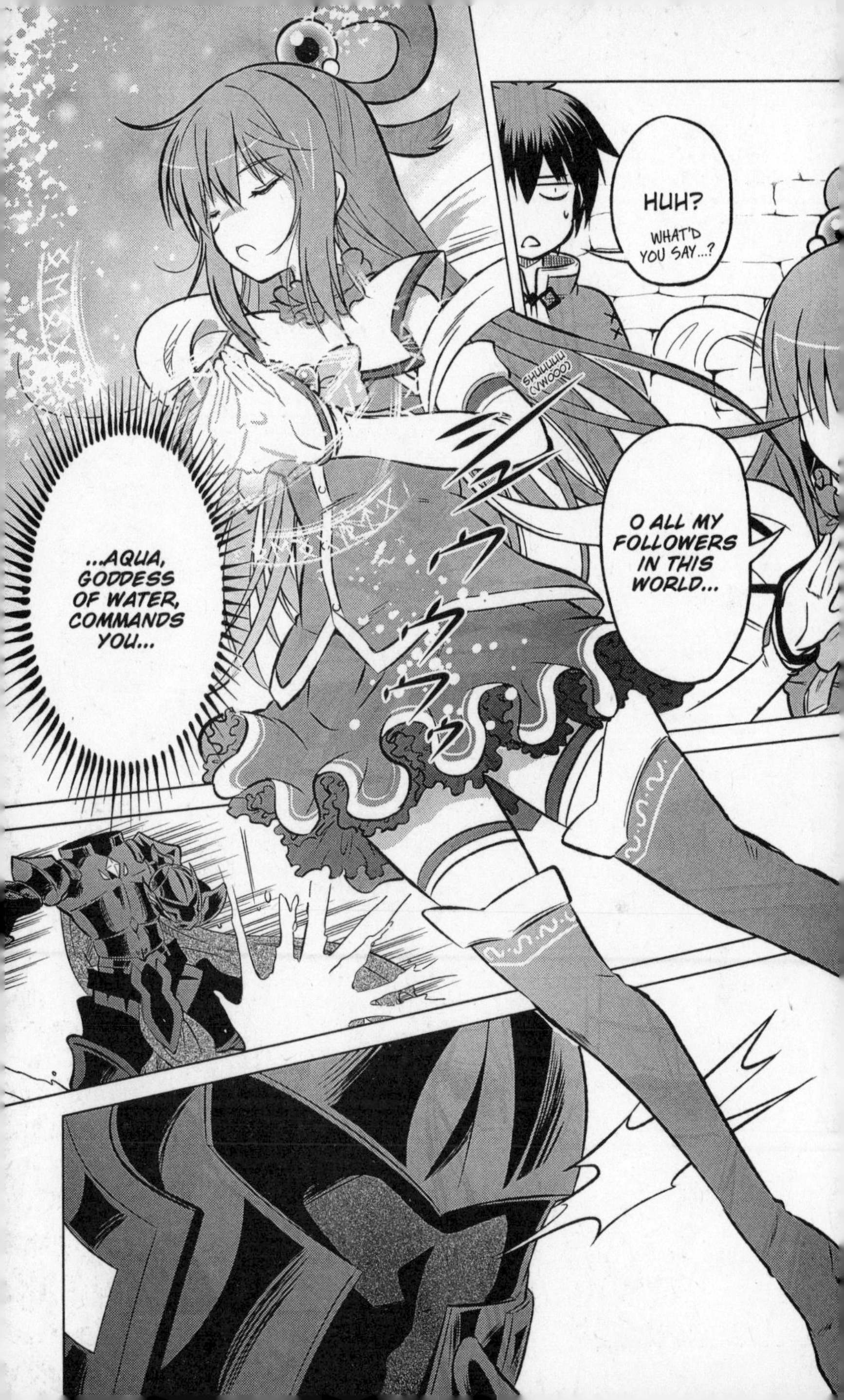
HUH?
WHAT'D YOU SAY...?
O ALL MY FOLLOWERS IN THIS WORLD...
SHUUUUU (VWOOO)
...AQUA, GODDESS OF WATER, COMMANDS YOU...

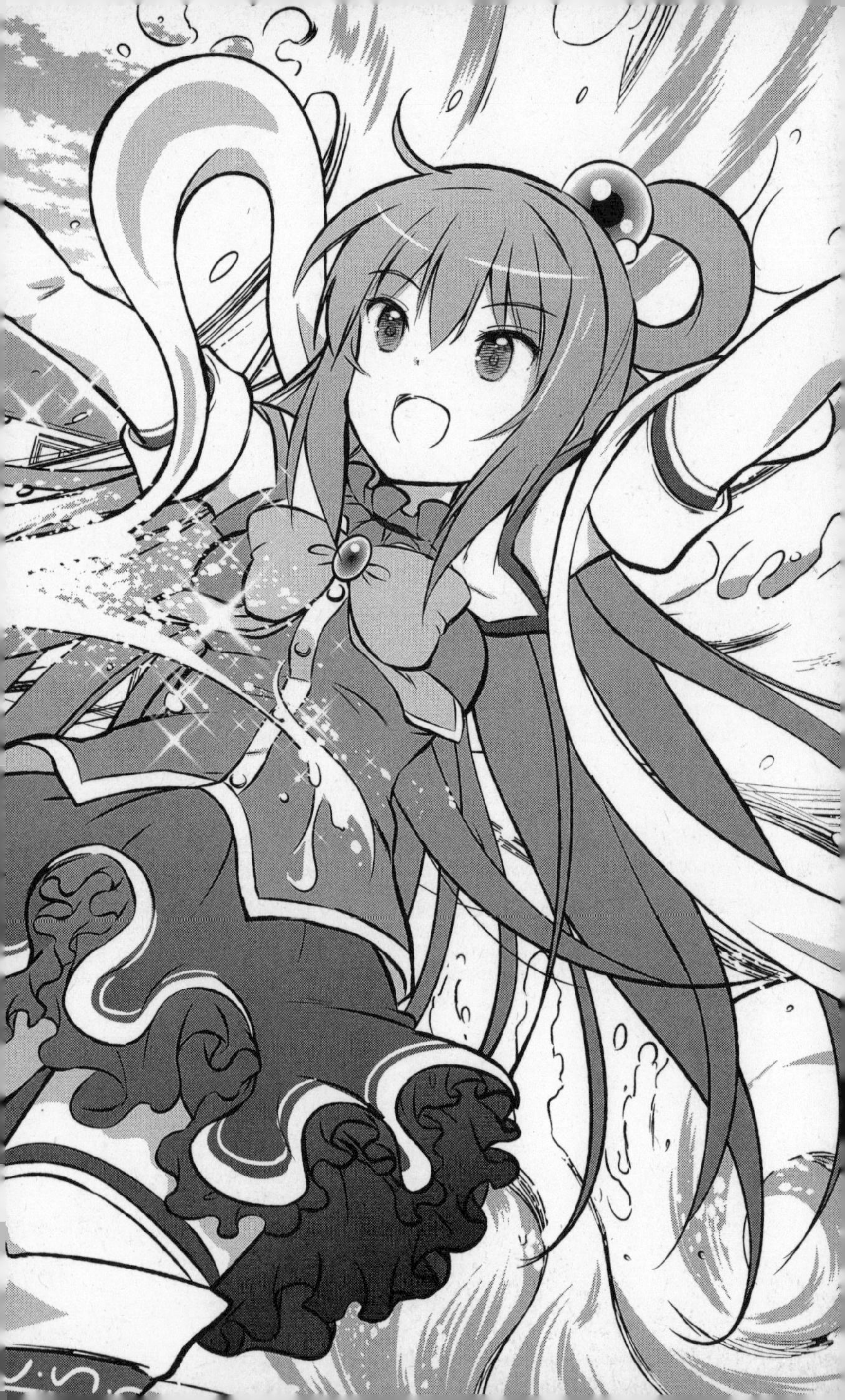

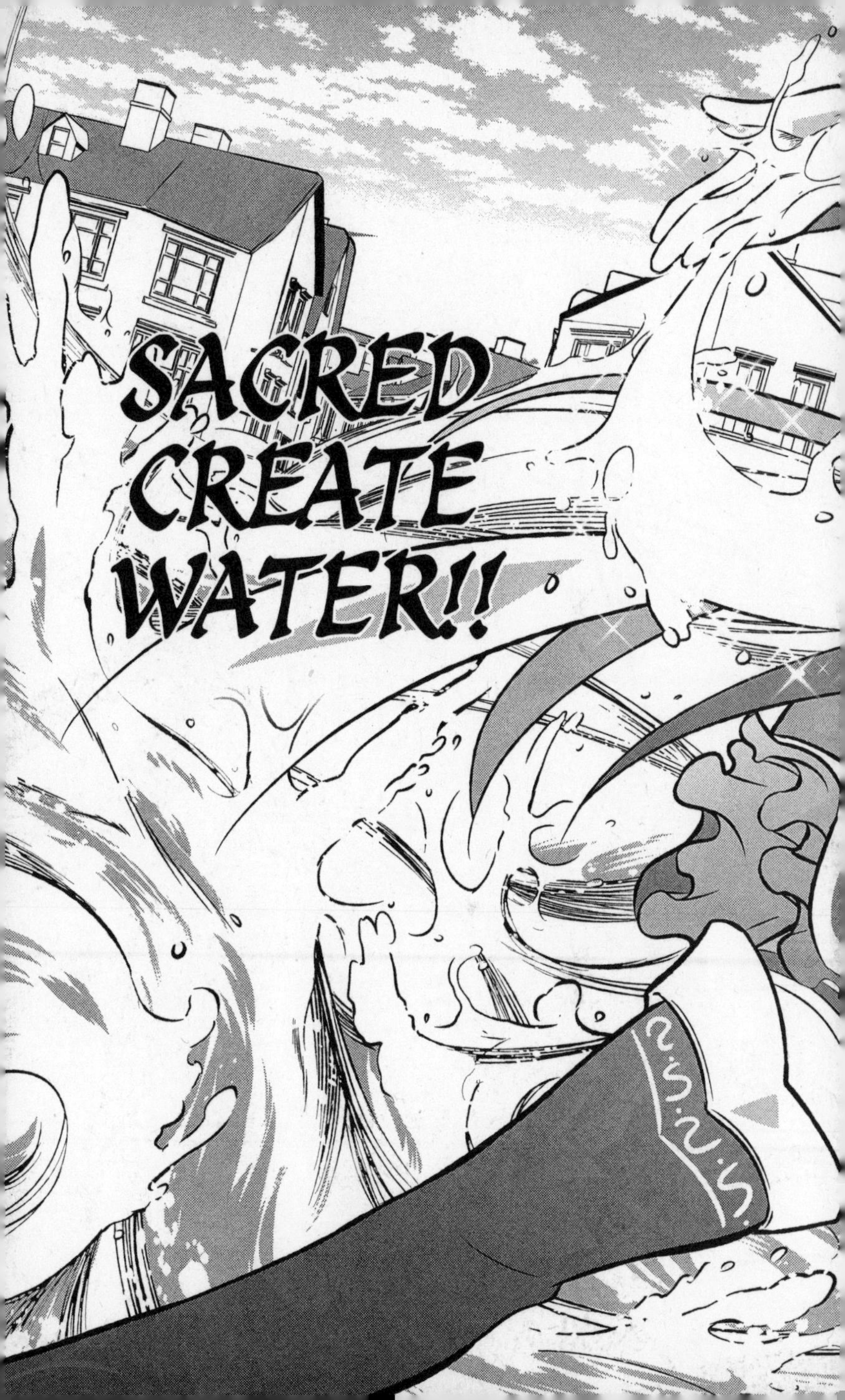
SACRED CREATE WATER!!

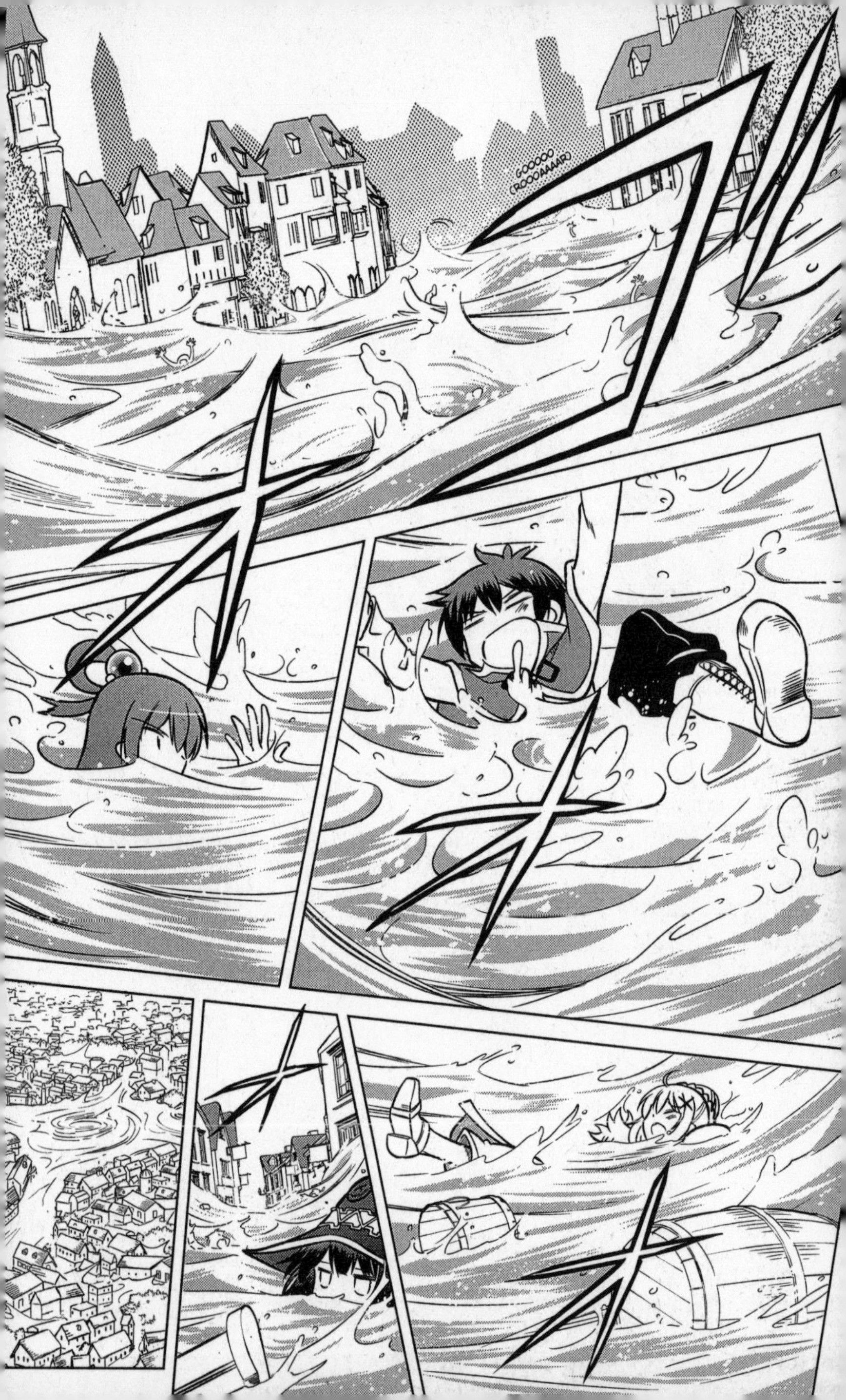
GOOOOO
(ROOOAAAAR)

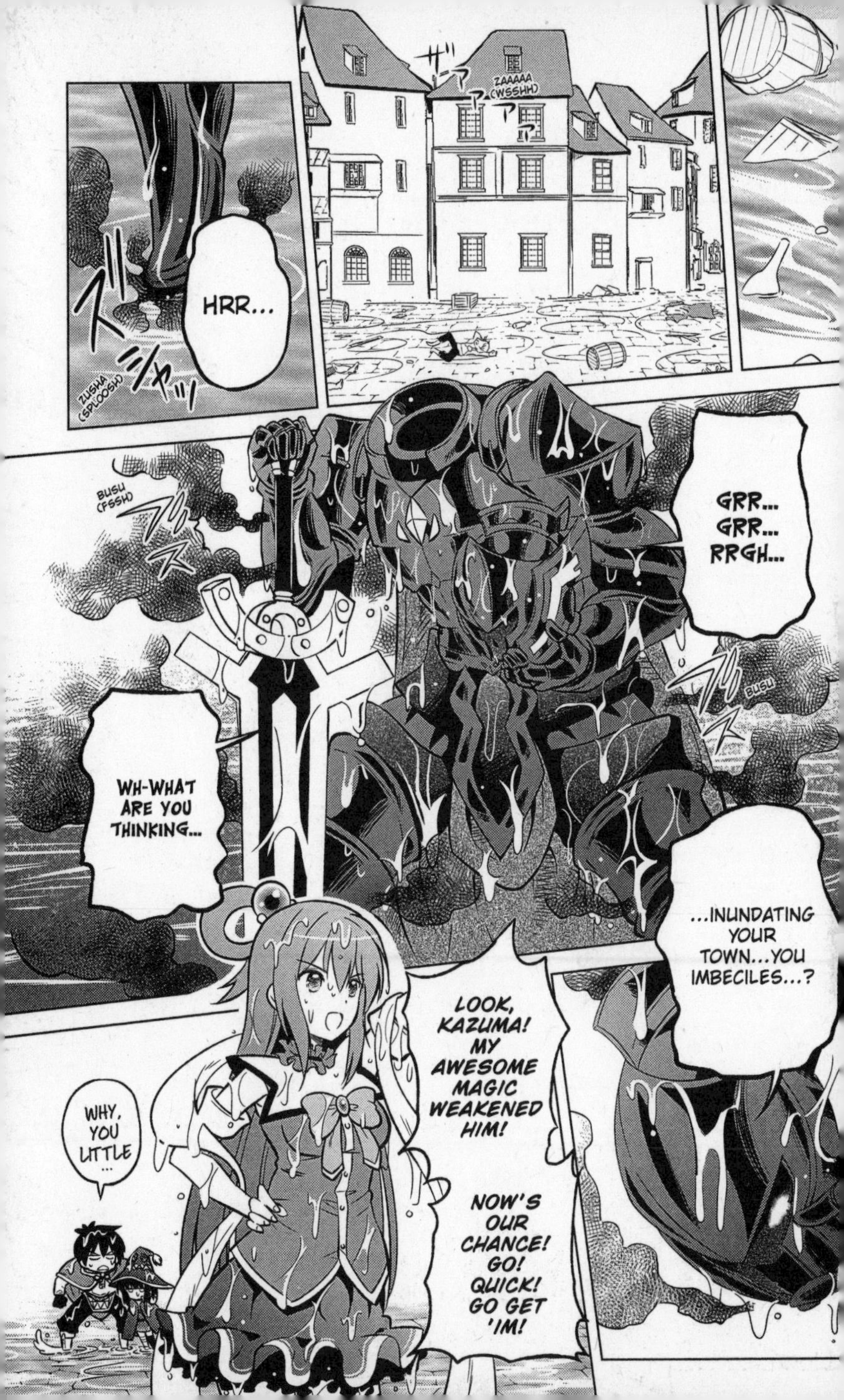
ZAAAAA (WSSHH)
HRR...
ZUSHA (SPLOOSH)
GRR... GRR... RRGH...
BUSU (FSSH)
BUSU
WH-WHAT ARE YOU THINKING...
...INUNDATING YOUR TOWN...YOU IMBECILES...?
LOOK, KAZUMA! MY AWESOME MAGIC WEAKENED HIM!
NOW'S OUR CHANCE! GO! QUICK! GO GET 'IM!
WHY, YOU LITTLE ...

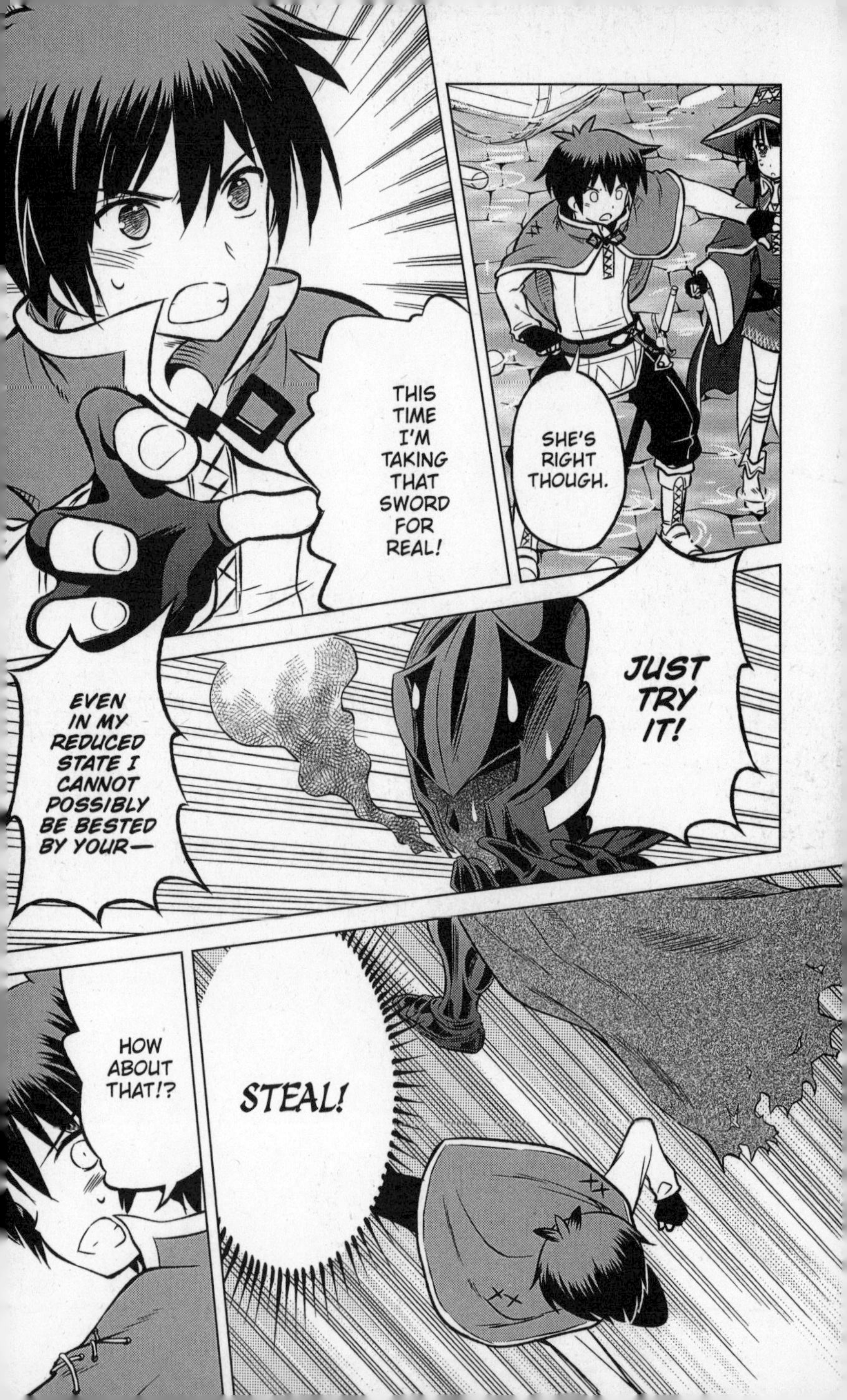

SHE'S RIGHT THOUGH.
THIS TIME I'M TAKING THAT SWORD FOR REAL!
JUST TRY IT!
EVEN IN MY REDUCED STATE I CANNOT POSSIBLY BE BESTED BY YOUR—
STEAL!
HOW ABOUT THAT!?

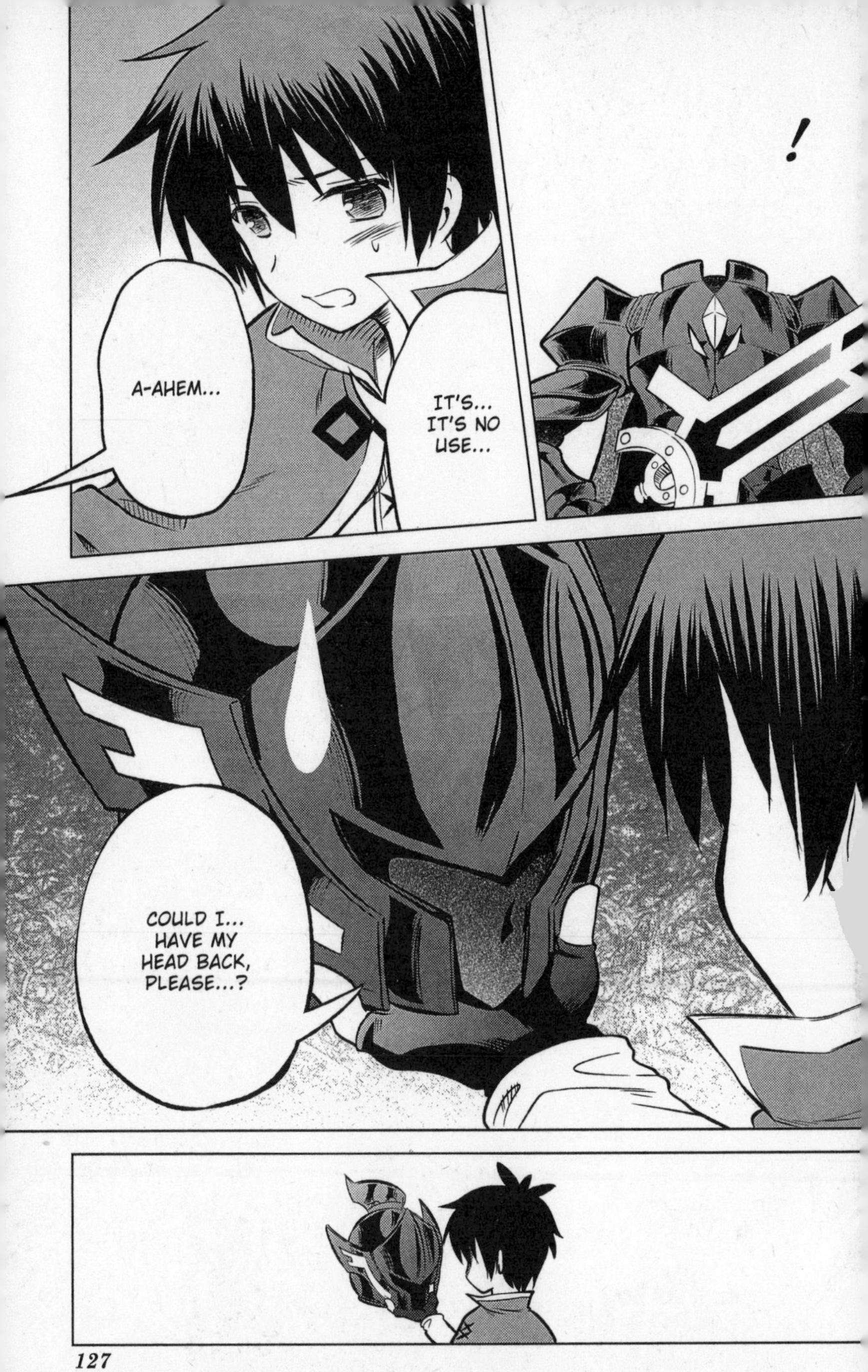
!
IT'S... IT'S NO USE...
A-AHEM...
COULD I... HAVE MY HEAD BACK, PLEASE...?

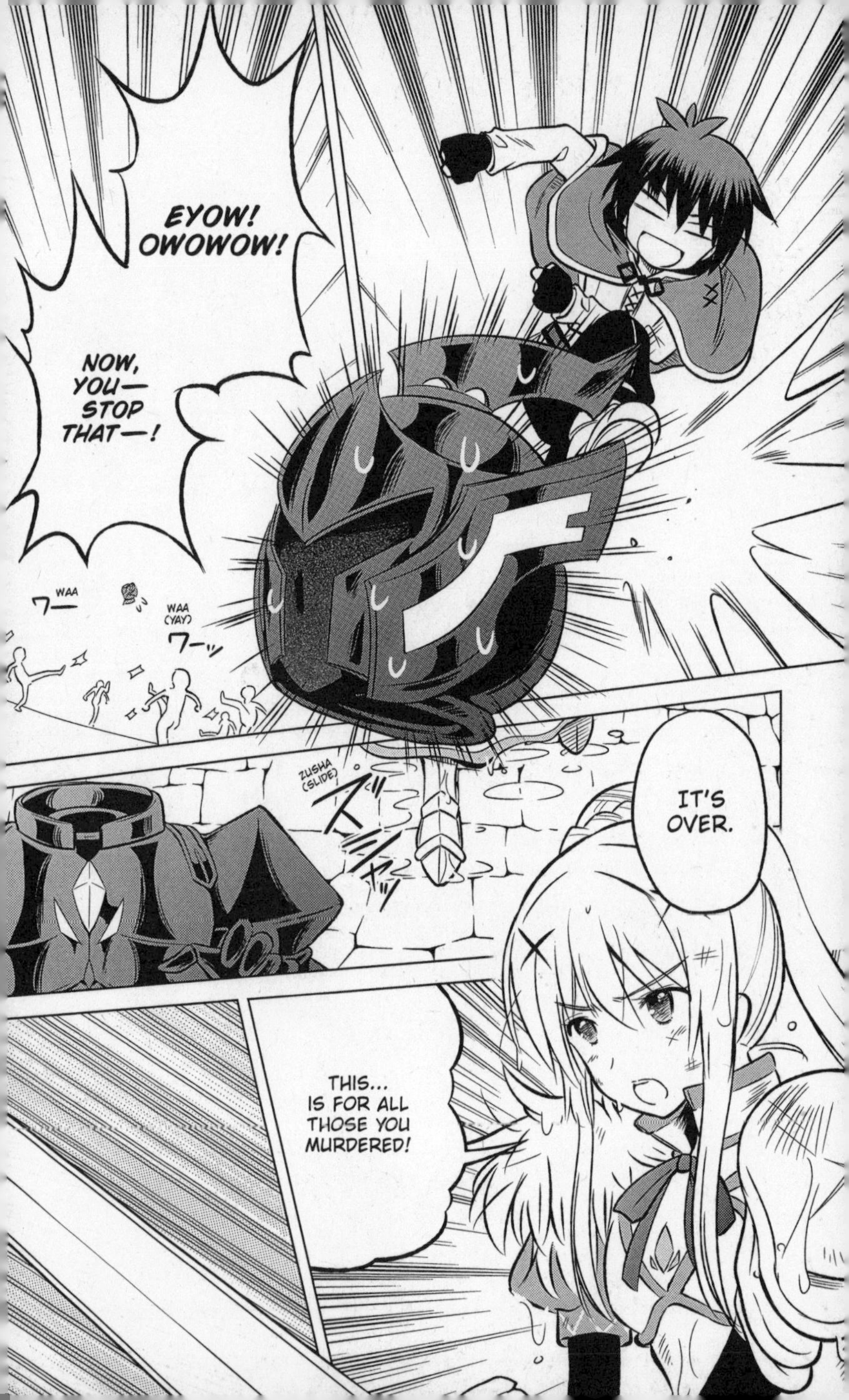
EYOW! OWOWOW!
NOW, YOU— STOP THAT—!
WAA (YAY) ワーッ
WAA ワー
IT'S OVER.
ZUSHA (SLIDE)
THIS... IS FOR ALL THOSE YOU MURDERED!

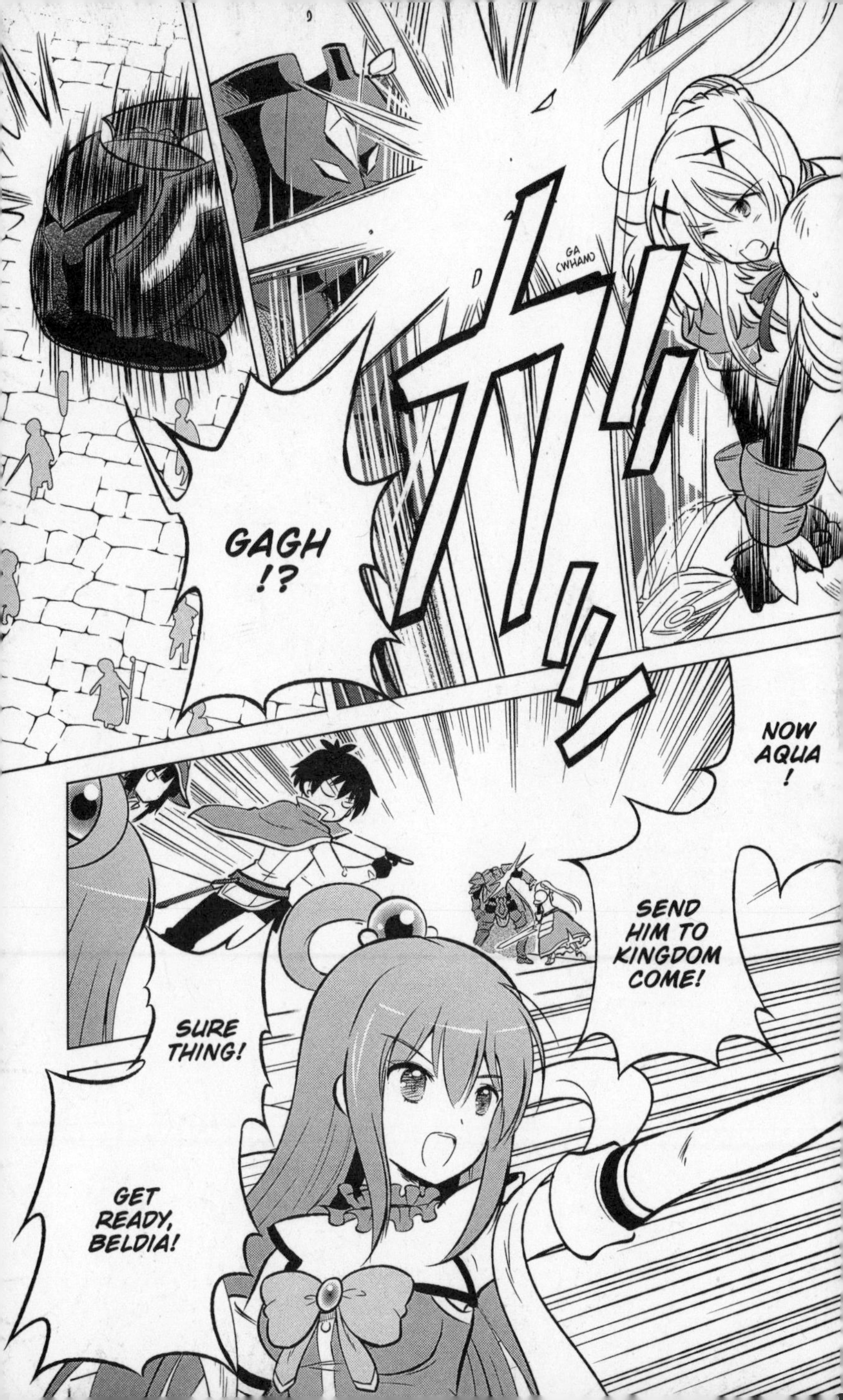
GA (WHAM)
GAGH !?
NOW AQUA !
SEND HIM TO KINGDOM COME!
SURE THING!
GET READY, BELDIA!

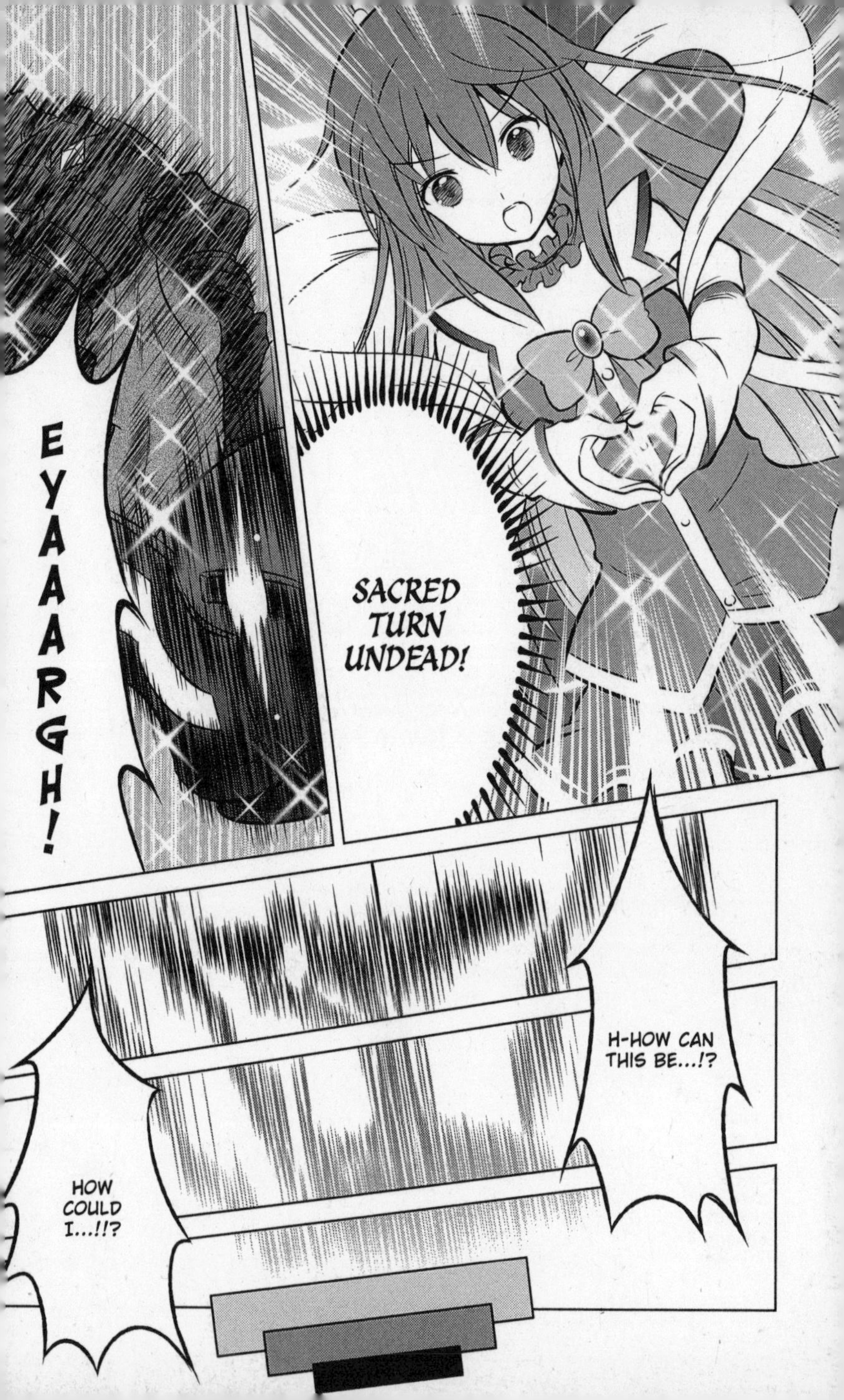
SACRED TURN UNDEAD!
EYAAAARGH!
H-HOW CAN THIS BE...!?
HOW COULD I...!!?

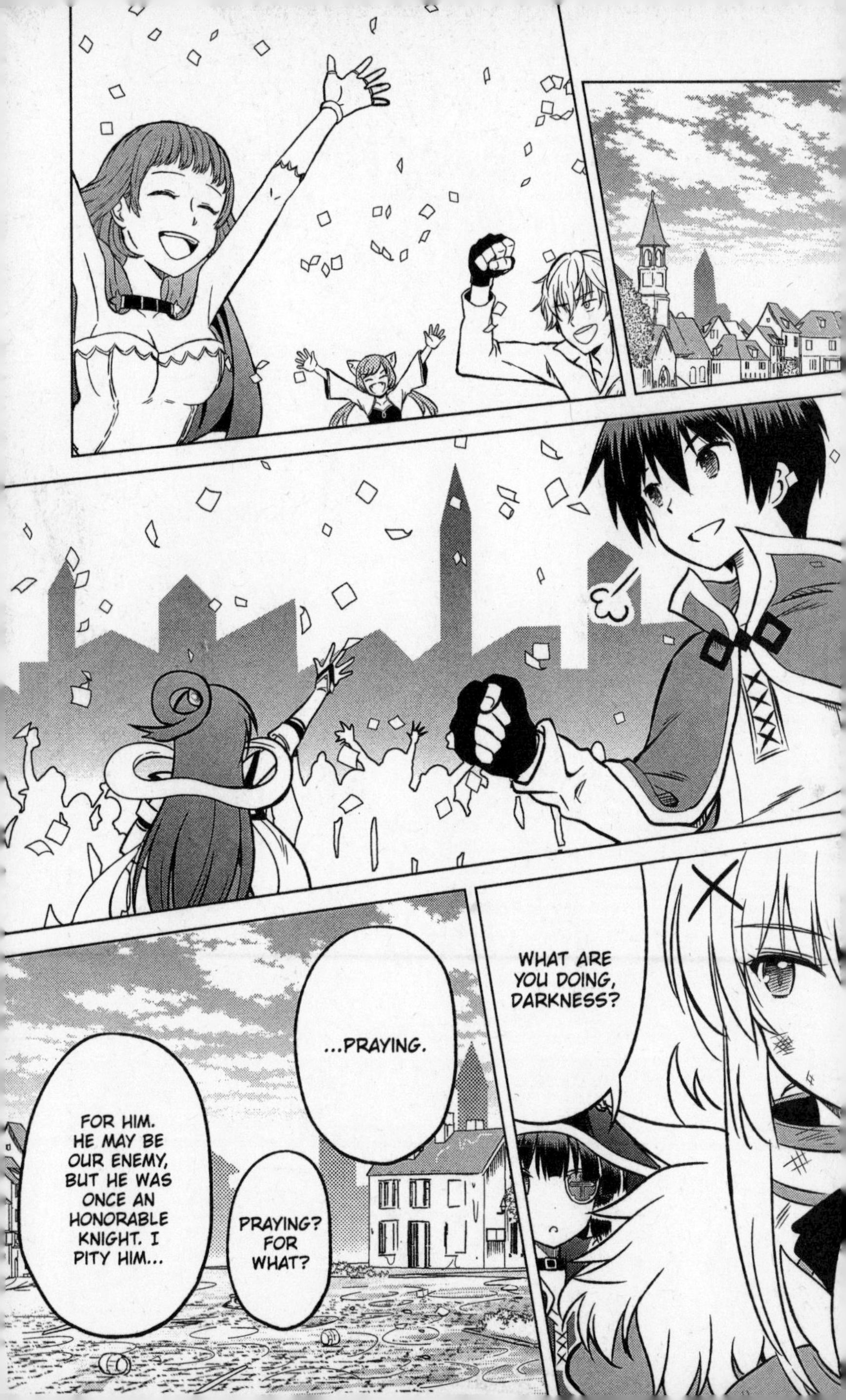
WHAT ARE YOU DOING, DARKNESS?
...PRAYING.
PRAYING? FOR WHAT?
FOR HIM. HE MAY BE OUR ENEMY, BUT HE WAS ONCE AN HONORABLE KNIGHT. I PITY HIM...

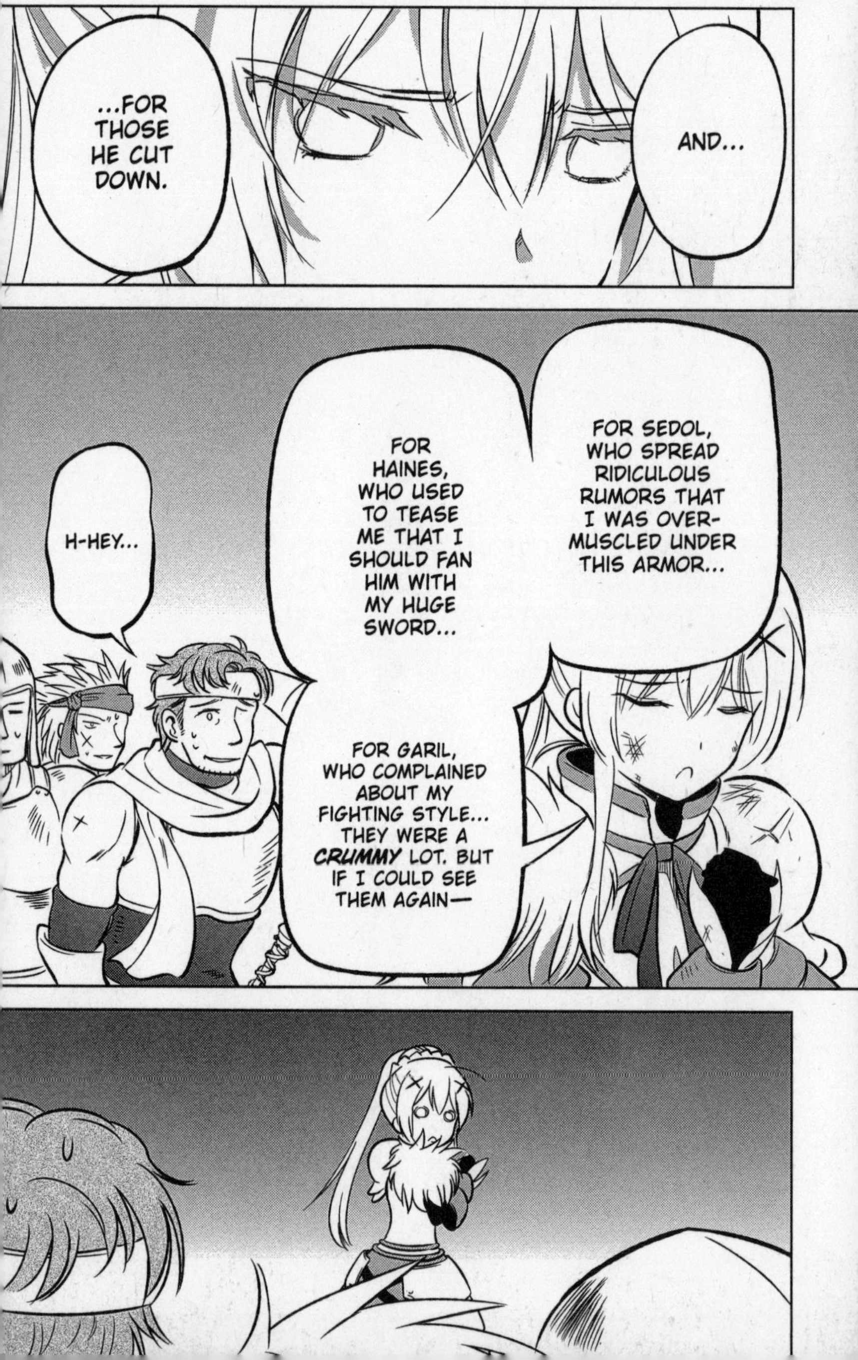
...FOR THOSE HE CUT DOWN.
AND...
FOR SEDOL, WHO SPREAD RIDICULOUS RUMORS THAT I WAS OVER-MUSCLED UNDER THIS ARMOR...
FOR HAINES, WHO USED TO TEASE ME THAT I SHOULD FAN HIM WITH MY HUGE SWORD...
FOR GARIL, WHO COMPLAINED ABOUT MY FIGHTING STYLE... THEY WERE A *CRUMMY* LOT. BUT IF I COULD SEE THEM AGAIN—
H-HEY...

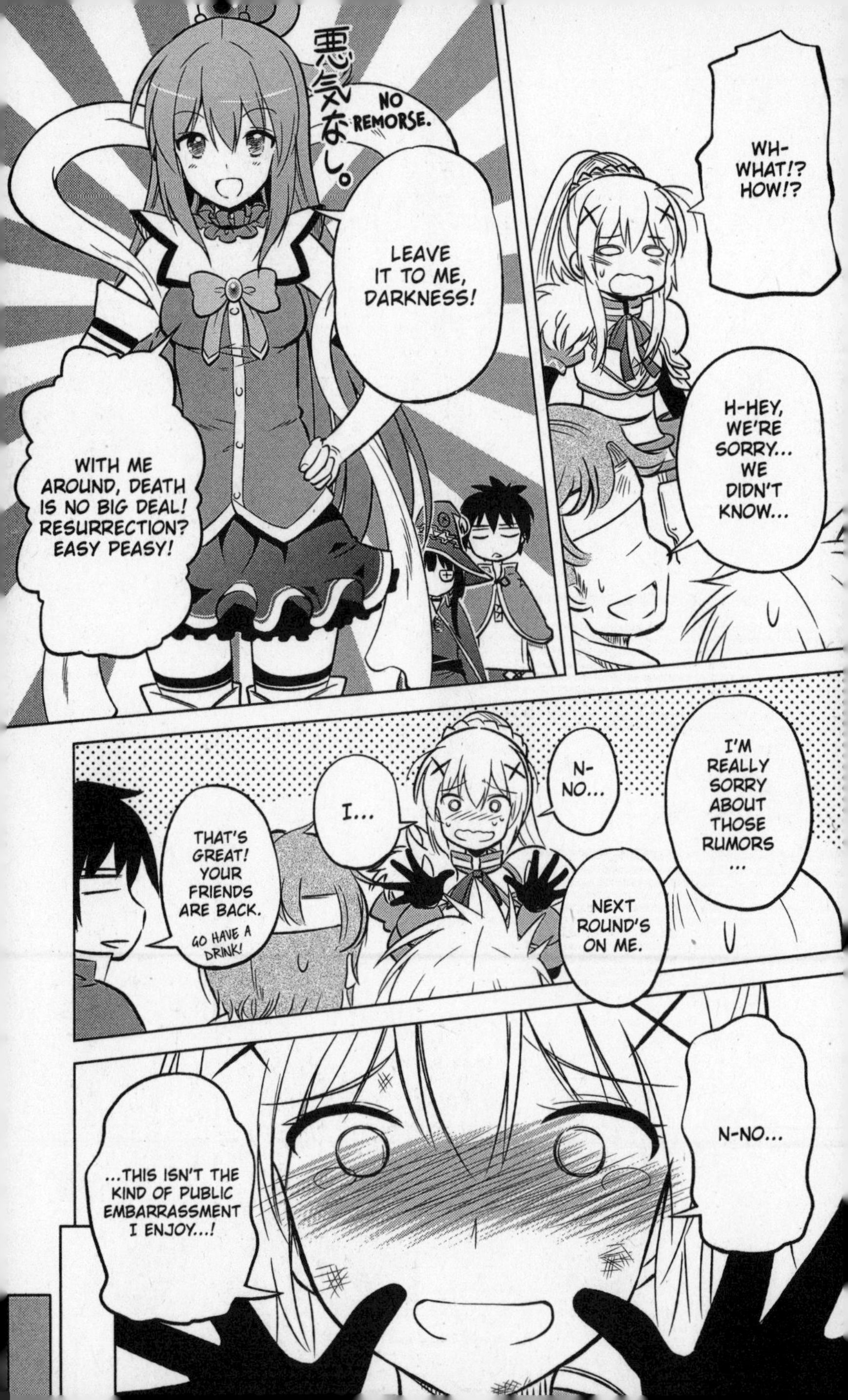
WH- WHAT!? HOW!?
H-HEY, WE'RE SORRY... WE DIDN'T KNOW...
悪気なし。
NO REMORSE.
LEAVE IT TO ME, DARKNESS!
WITH ME AROUND, DEATH IS NO BIG DEAL! RESURRECTION? EASY PEASY!
I'M REALLY SORRY ABOUT THOSE RUMORS...
N- NO...
NEXT ROUND'S ON ME.
I...
THAT'S GREAT! YOUR FRIENDS ARE BACK.
GO HAVE A DRINK!
N-NO...
...THIS ISN'T THE KIND OF PUBLIC EMBARRASSMENT I ENJOY...!

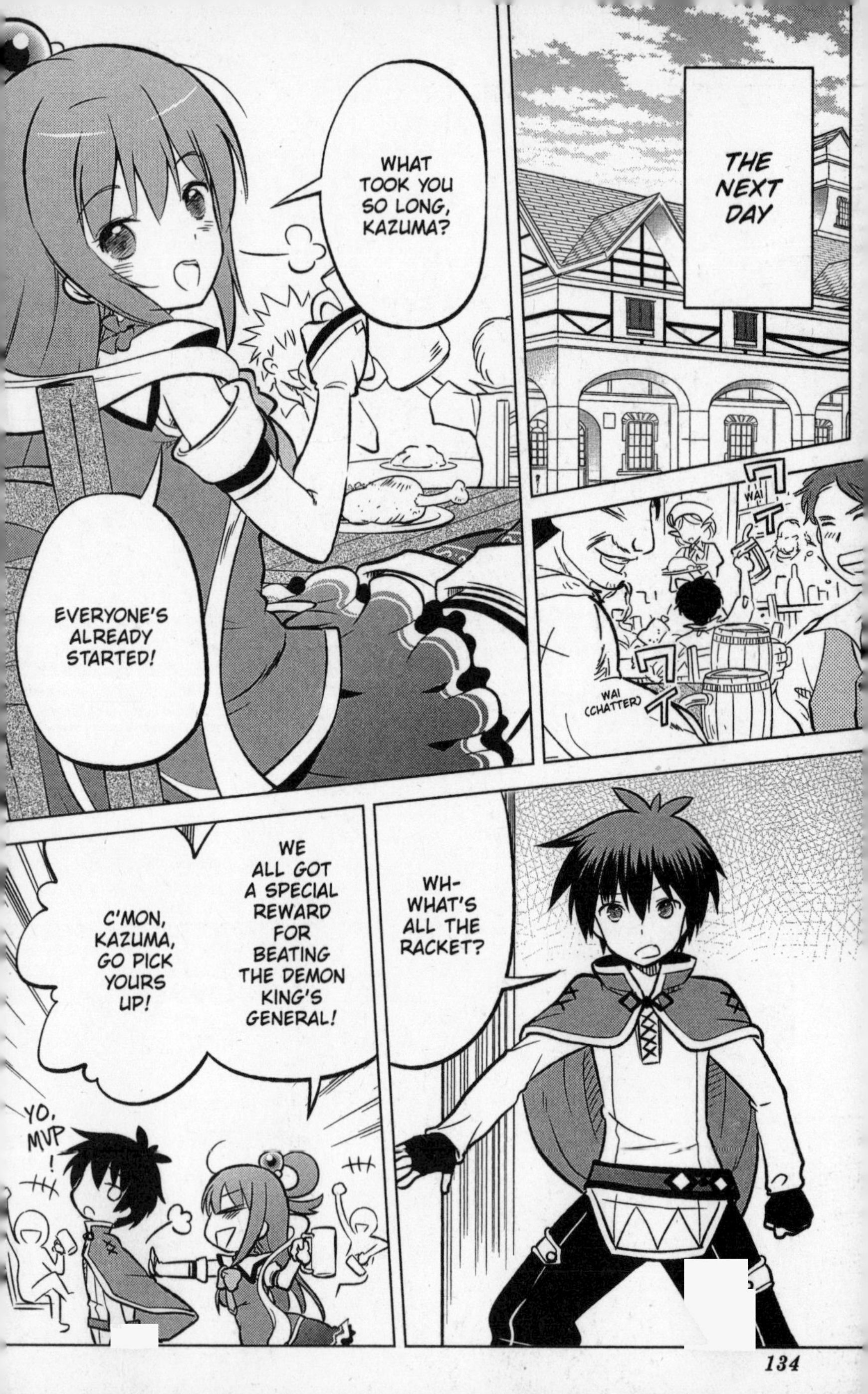
THE NEXT DAY
WAI
WAI (CHATTER)
WHAT TOOK YOU SO LONG, KAZUMA?
EVERYONE'S ALREADY STARTED!
WH- WHAT'S ALL THE RACKET?
WE ALL GOT A SPECIAL REWARD FOR BEATING THE DEMON KING'S GENERAL!
C'MON, KAZUMA, GO PICK YOURS UP!
YO, MVP!

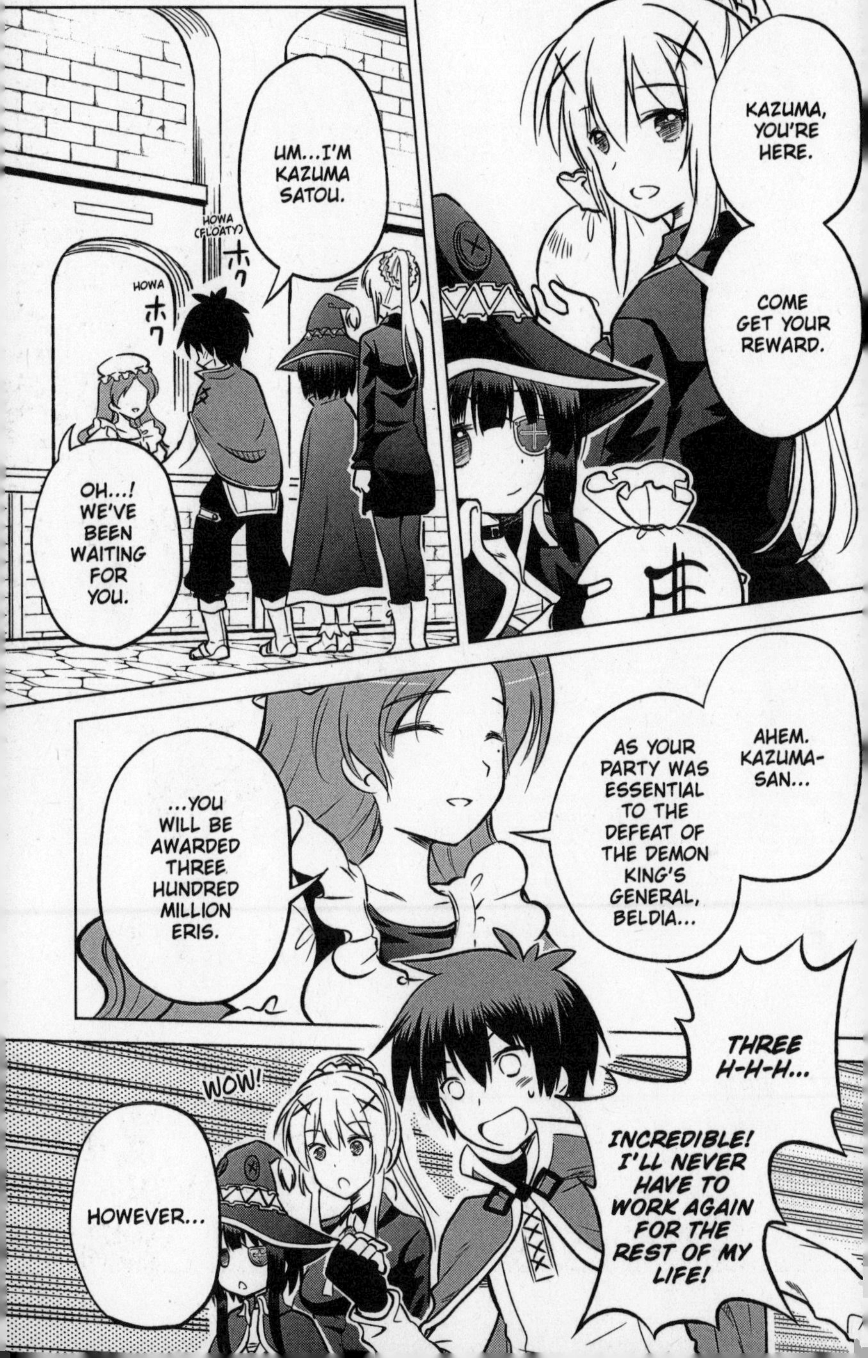

KAZUMA, YOU'RE HERE.
COME GET YOUR REWARD.
UM...I'M KAZUMA SATOU.
HOWA (FLOATY) ホワ
HOWA ホワ
OH...! WE'VE BEEN WAITING FOR YOU.
AHEM. KAZUMA-SAN...
AS YOUR PARTY WAS ESSENTIAL TO THE DEFEAT OF THE DEMON KING'S GENERAL, BELDIA...
...YOU WILL BE AWARDED THREE HUNDRED MILLION ERIS.
THREE H-H-H...
INCREDIBLE! I'LL NEVER HAVE TO WORK AGAIN FOR THE REST OF MY LIFE!
WOW!
HOWEVER...

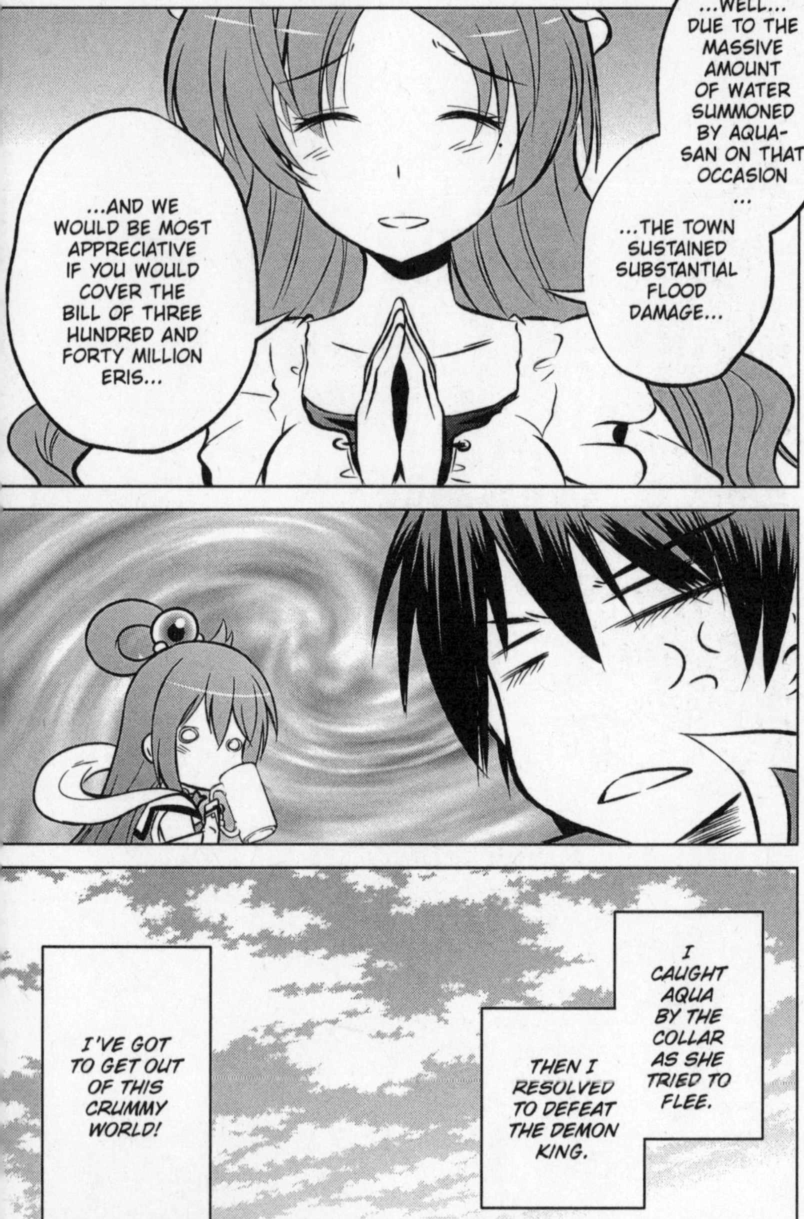
...WELL... DUE TO THE MASSIVE AMOUNT OF WATER SUMMONED BY AQUA-SAN ON THAT OCCASION ...
...THE TOWN SUSTAINED SUBSTANTIAL FLOOD DAMAGE...
...AND WE WOULD BE MOST APPRECIATIVE IF YOU WOULD COVER THE BILL OF THREE HUNDRED AND FORTY MILLION ERIS...
I CAUGHT AQUA BY THE COLLAR AS SHE TRIED TO FLEE.
THEN I RESOLVED TO DEFEAT THE DEMON KING.
I'VE GOT TO GET OUT OF THIS CRUMMY WORLD!

CHAPTER 12

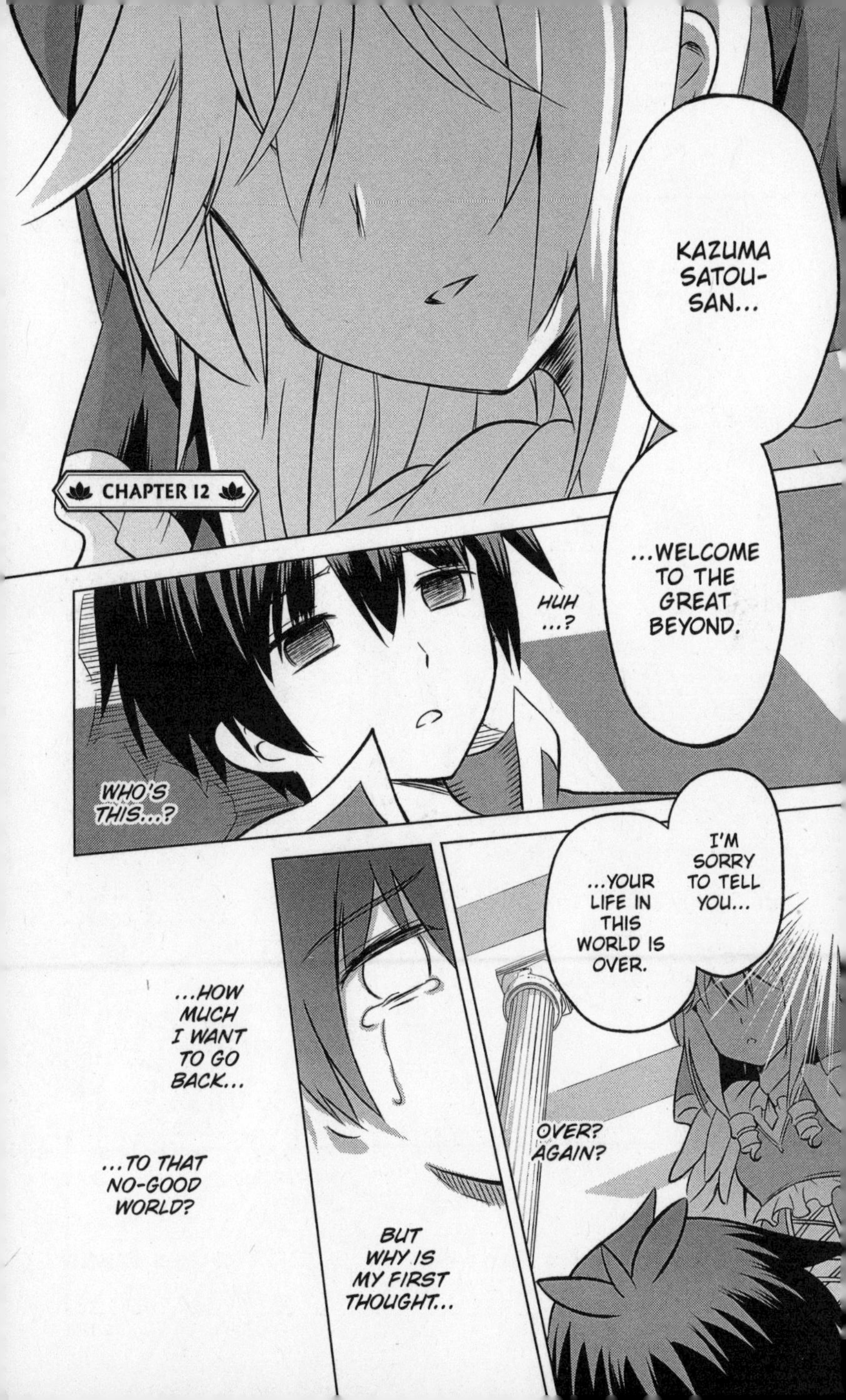
KAZUMA SATOU-SAN...
...WELCOME TO THE GREAT BEYOND.
HUH ...?
WHO'S THIS...?
I'M SORRY TO TELL YOU...
...YOUR LIFE IN THIS WORLD IS OVER.
OVER? AGAIN?
BUT WHY IS MY FIRST THOUGHT...
...HOW MUCH I WANT TO GO BACK...
...TO THAT NO-GOOD WORLD?

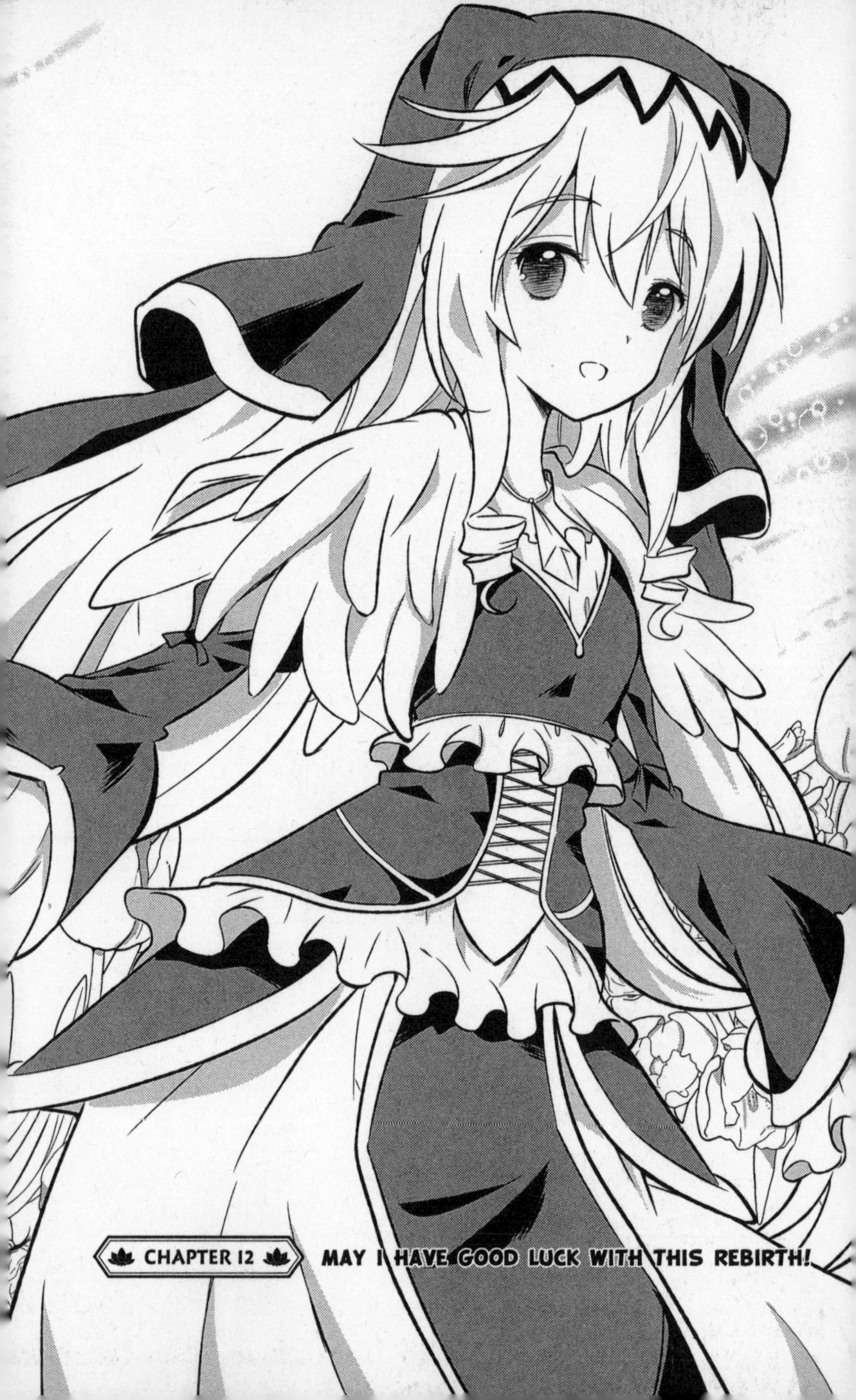
CHAPTER 12
MAY I HAVE GOOD LUCK WITH THIS REBIRTH!

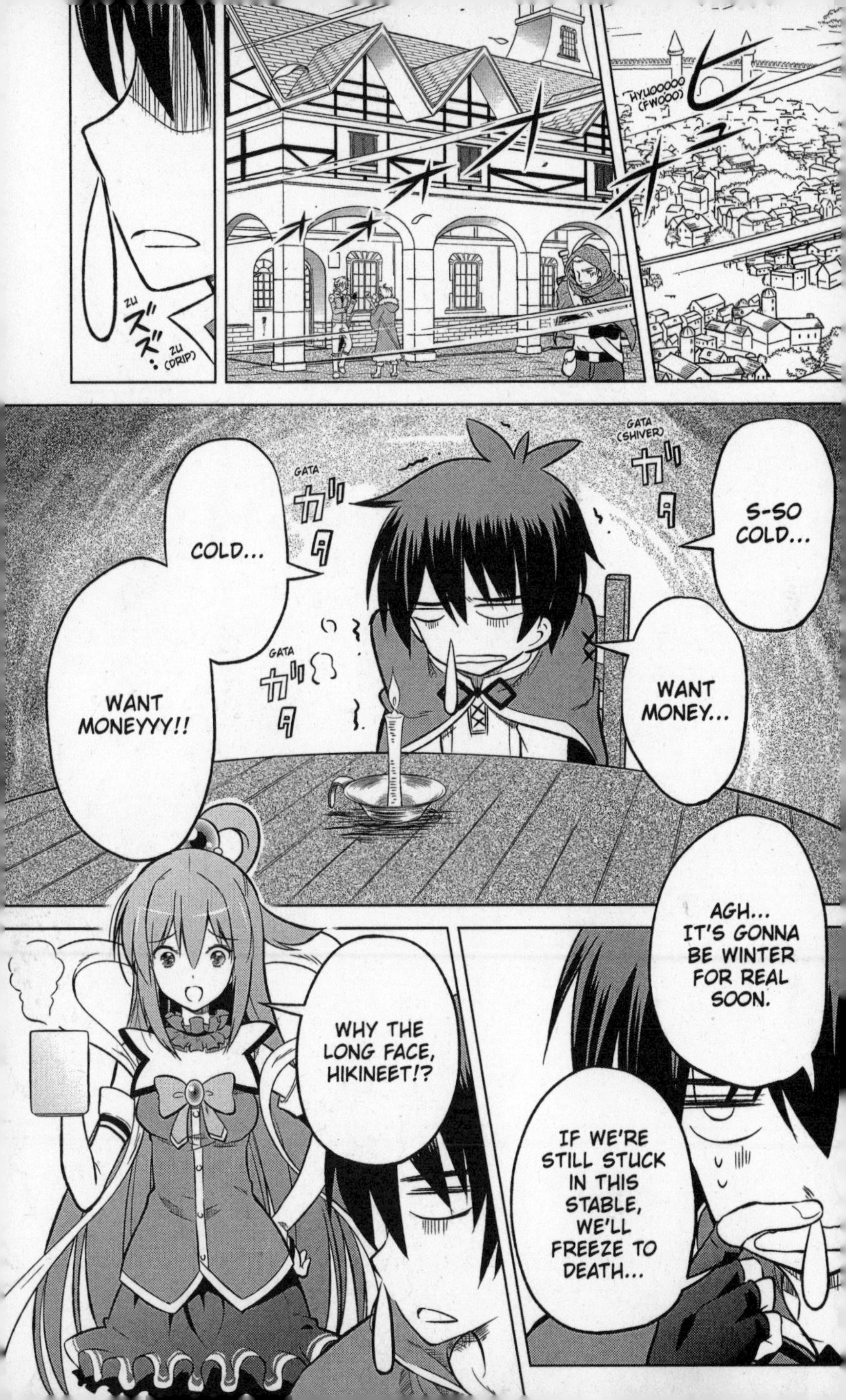
HYUOOOO (FWOOO)
ZU
ZU (DRIP)
GATA (SHIVER)
S-SO COLD...
WANT MONEY...
GATA
COLD...
GATA
WANT MONEYYY!!
AGH... IT'S GONNA BE WINTER FOR REAL SOON.
IF WE'RE STILL STUCK IN THIS STABLE, WE'LL FREEZE TO DEATH...
WHY THE LONG FACE, HIKINEET!?

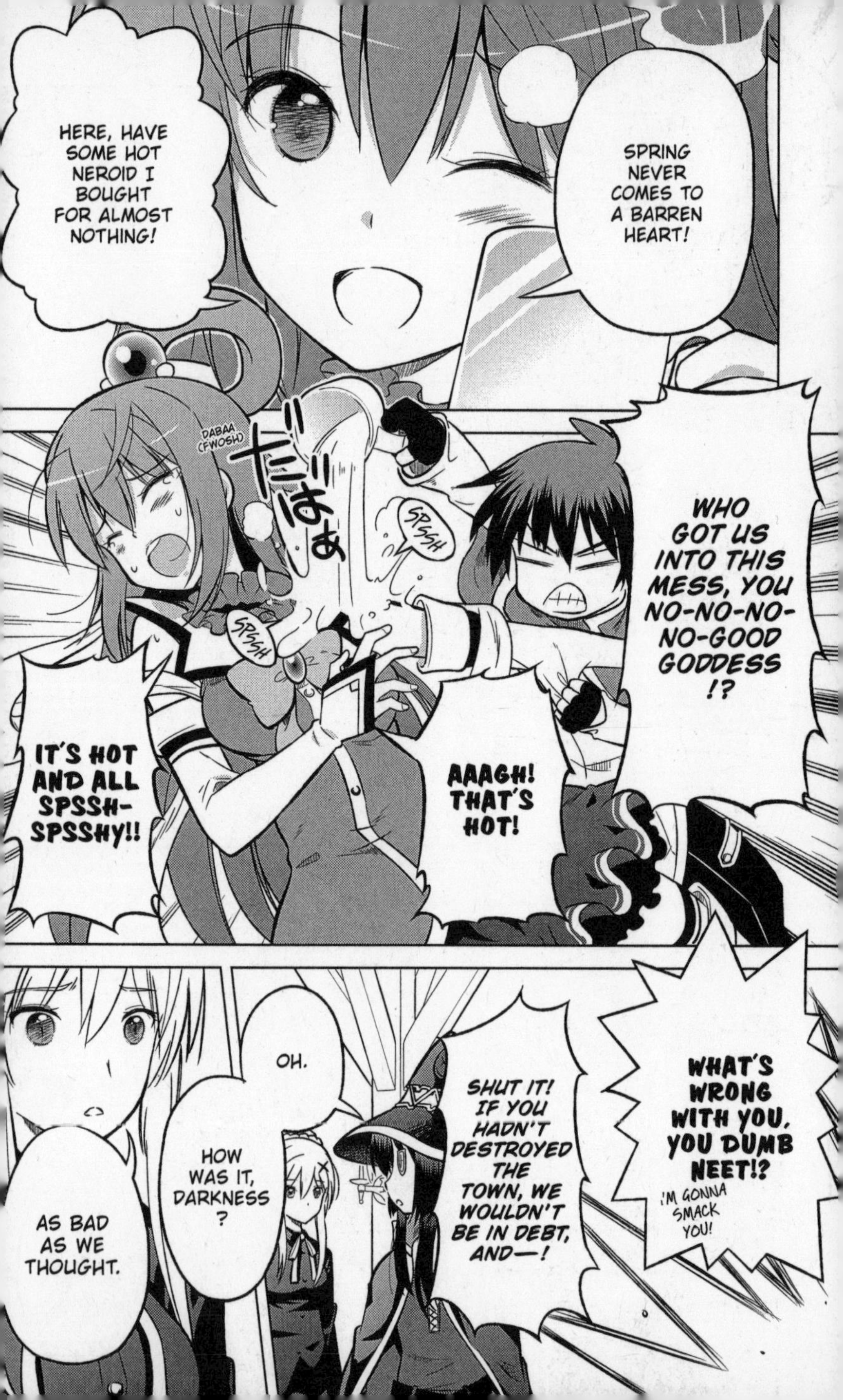
SPRING NEVER COMES TO A BARREN HEART!
HERE, HAVE SOME HOT NEROID I BOUGHT FOR ALMOST NOTHING!
WHO GOT US INTO THIS MESS, YOU NO-NO-NO-NO-GOOD GODDESS!?
だばぁ
DABAA (FWOSH)
SPSSH
SPSSH
AAAGH! THAT'S HOT!
IT'S HOT AND ALL SPSSH-SPSSHY!!
WHAT'S WRONG WITH YOU, YOU DUMB NEET!?
I'M GONNA SMACK YOU!
SHUT IT! IF YOU HADN'T DESTROYED THE TOWN, WE WOULDN'T BE IN DEBT, AND—!
OH.
HOW WAS IT, DARKNESS?
AS BAD AS WE THOUGHT.

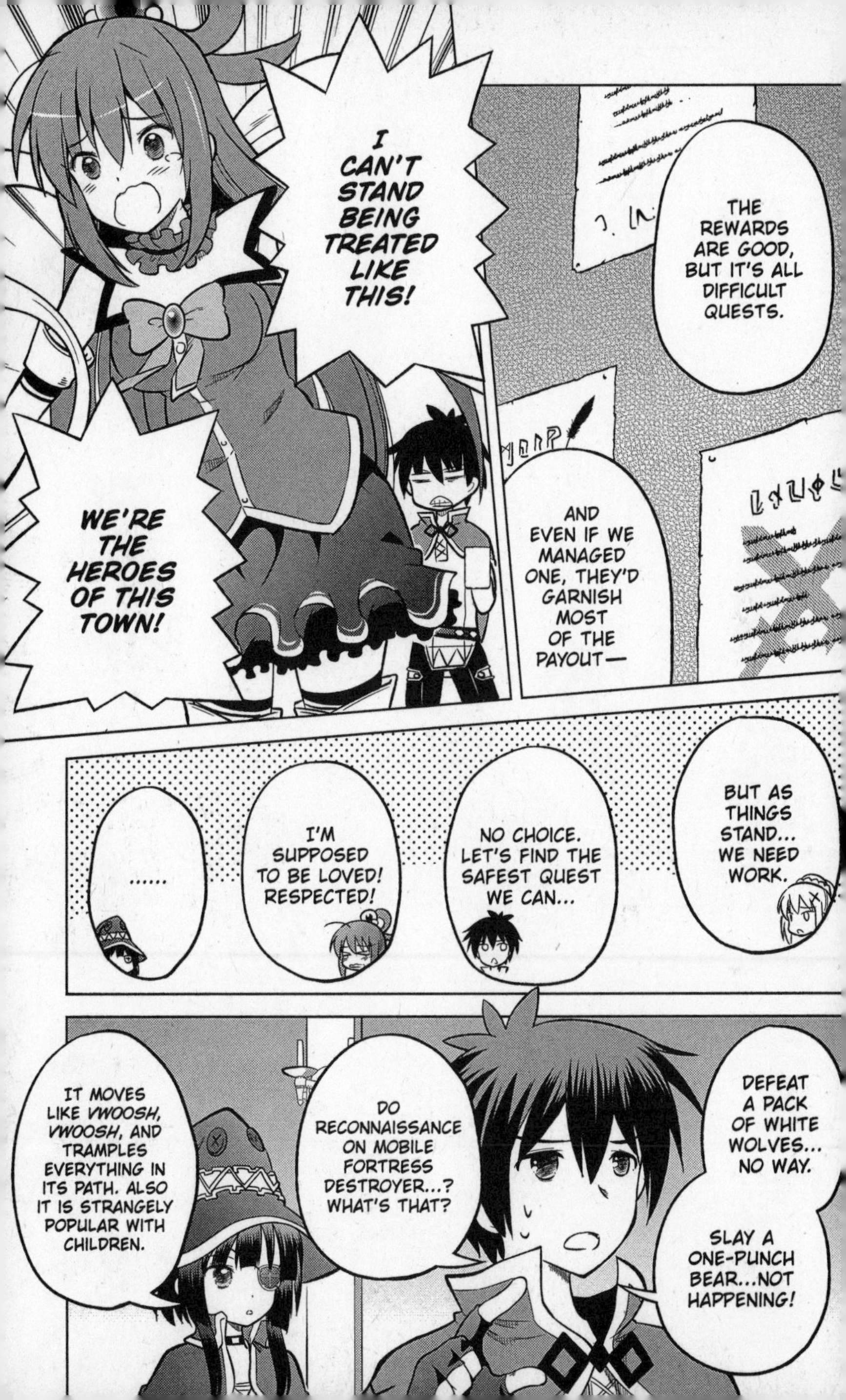
THE REWARDS ARE GOOD, BUT IT'S ALL DIFFICULT QUESTS.
AND EVEN IF WE MANAGED ONE, THEY'D GARNISH MOST OF THE PAYOUT—
I CAN'T STAND BEING TREATED LIKE THIS!
WE'RE THE HEROES OF THIS TOWN!
BUT AS THINGS STAND... WE NEED WORK.
NO CHOICE. LET'S FIND THE SAFEST QUEST WE CAN...
I'M SUPPOSED TO BE LOVED! RESPECTED!
......
DEFEAT A PACK OF WHITE WOLVES... NO WAY.
SLAY A ONE-PUNCH BEAR...NOT HAPPENING!
DO RECONNAISSANCE ON MOBILE FORTRESS DESTROYER...? WHAT'S THAT?
IT MOVES LIKE *VWOOSH, VWOOSH*, AND TRAMPLES EVERYTHING IN ITS PATH. ALSO IT IS STRANGELY POPULAR WITH CHILDREN.

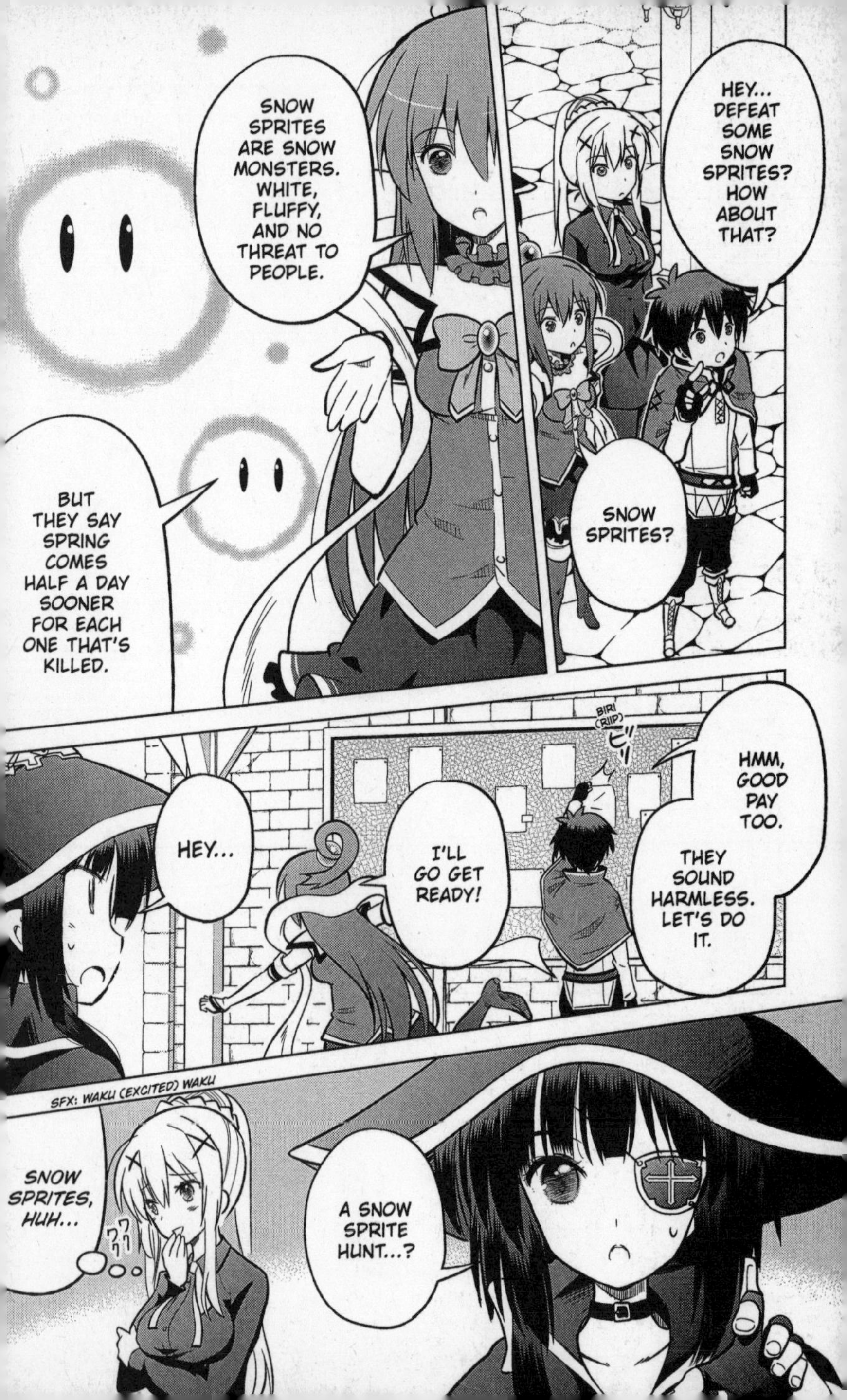
HEY... DEFEAT SOME SNOW SPRITES? HOW ABOUT THAT?
SNOW SPRITES?
SNOW SPRITES ARE SNOW MONSTERS. WHITE, FLUFFY, AND NO THREAT TO PEOPLE.
BUT THEY SAY SPRING COMES HALF A DAY SOONER FOR EACH ONE THAT'S KILLED.
BIRI (RIIP)
HMM, GOOD PAY TOO.
THEY SOUND HARMLESS. LET'S DO IT.
I'LL GO GET READY!
HEY...
SFX: WAKU (EXCITED) WAKU
A SNOW SPRITE HUNT...?
SNOW SPRITES, HUH...

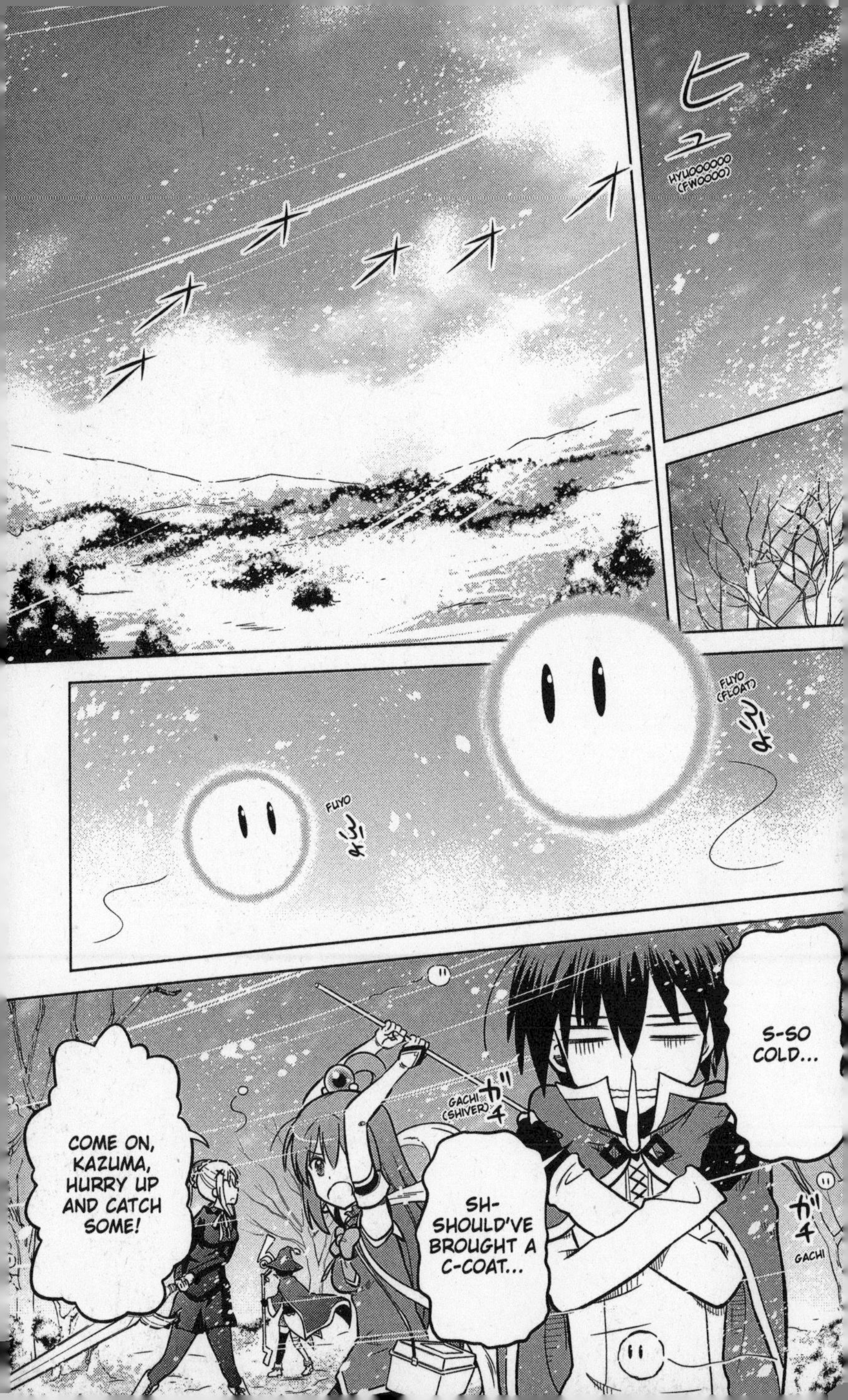
HYUOOOOO (FWOOOO)
FUYO (FLOAT)
FUYO
S-SO COLD...
GACHI (SHIVER)
GACHI
SH-SHOULD'VE BROUGHT A C-COAT...
COME ON, KAZUMA, HURRY UP AND CATCH SOME!

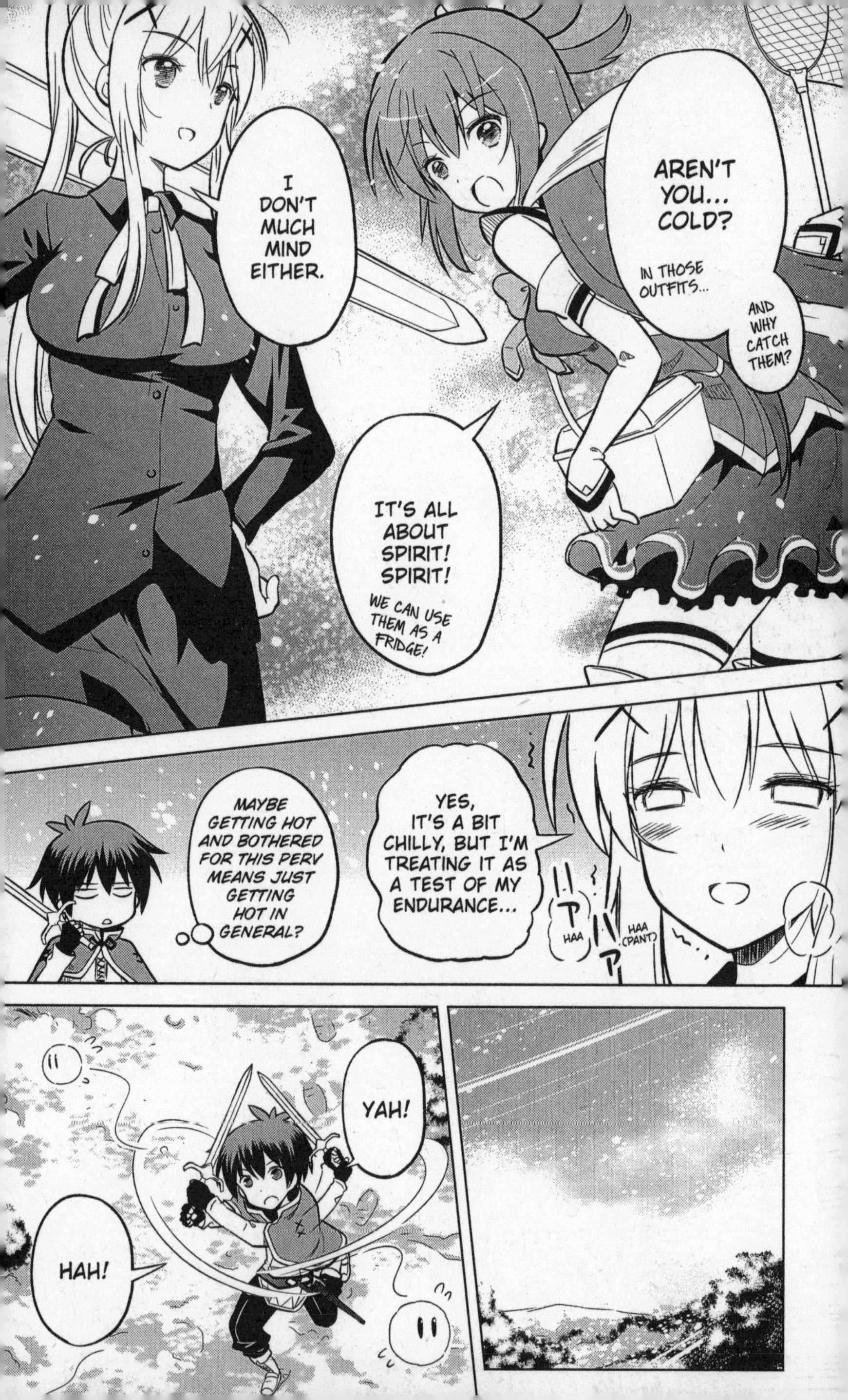
AREN'T YOU... COLD?
IN THOSE OUTFITS...
AND WHY CATCH THEM?
I DON'T MUCH MIND EITHER.
IT'S ALL ABOUT SPIRIT! SPIRIT!
WE CAN USE THEM AS A FRIDGE!
HAA
HAA (PANT)
YES, IT'S A BIT CHILLY, BUT I'M TREATING IT AS A TEST OF MY ENDURANCE...
MAYBE GETTING HOT AND BOTHERED FOR THIS PERV MEANS JUST GETTING HOT IN GENERAL?
YAH!
HAH!

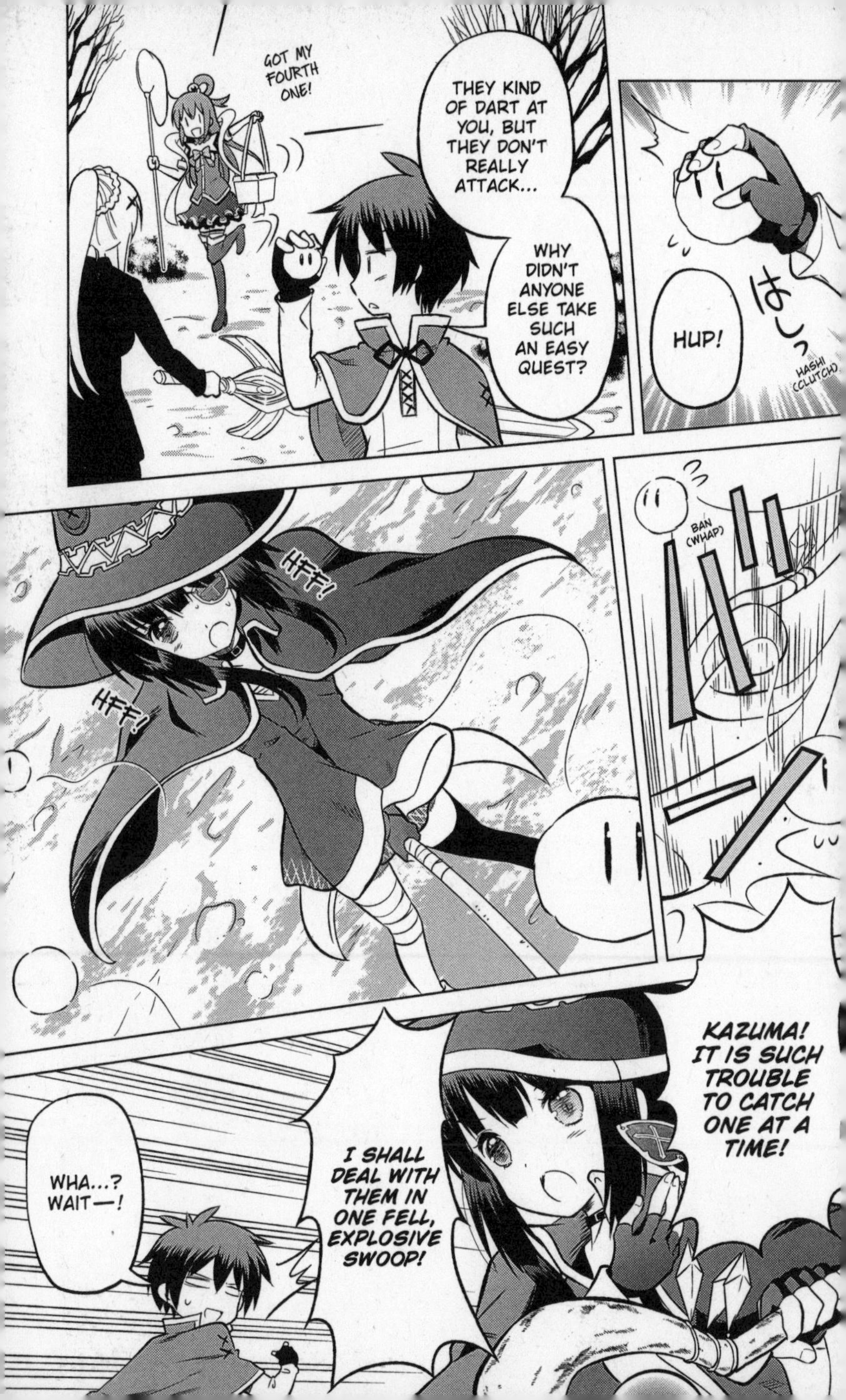
HUP!
はしっ
HASHI (CLUTCH)
THEY KIND OF DART AT YOU, BUT THEY DON'T REALLY ATTACK...
WHY DIDN'T ANYONE ELSE TAKE SUCH AN EASY QUEST?
GOT MY FOURTH ONE!
バン
BAN (WHAP)
HFF!
HFF!
KAZUMA! IT IS SUCH TROUBLE TO CATCH ONE AT A TIME!
I SHALL DEAL WITH THEM IN ONE FELL, EXPLOSIVE SWOOP!
WHA...? WAIT—!

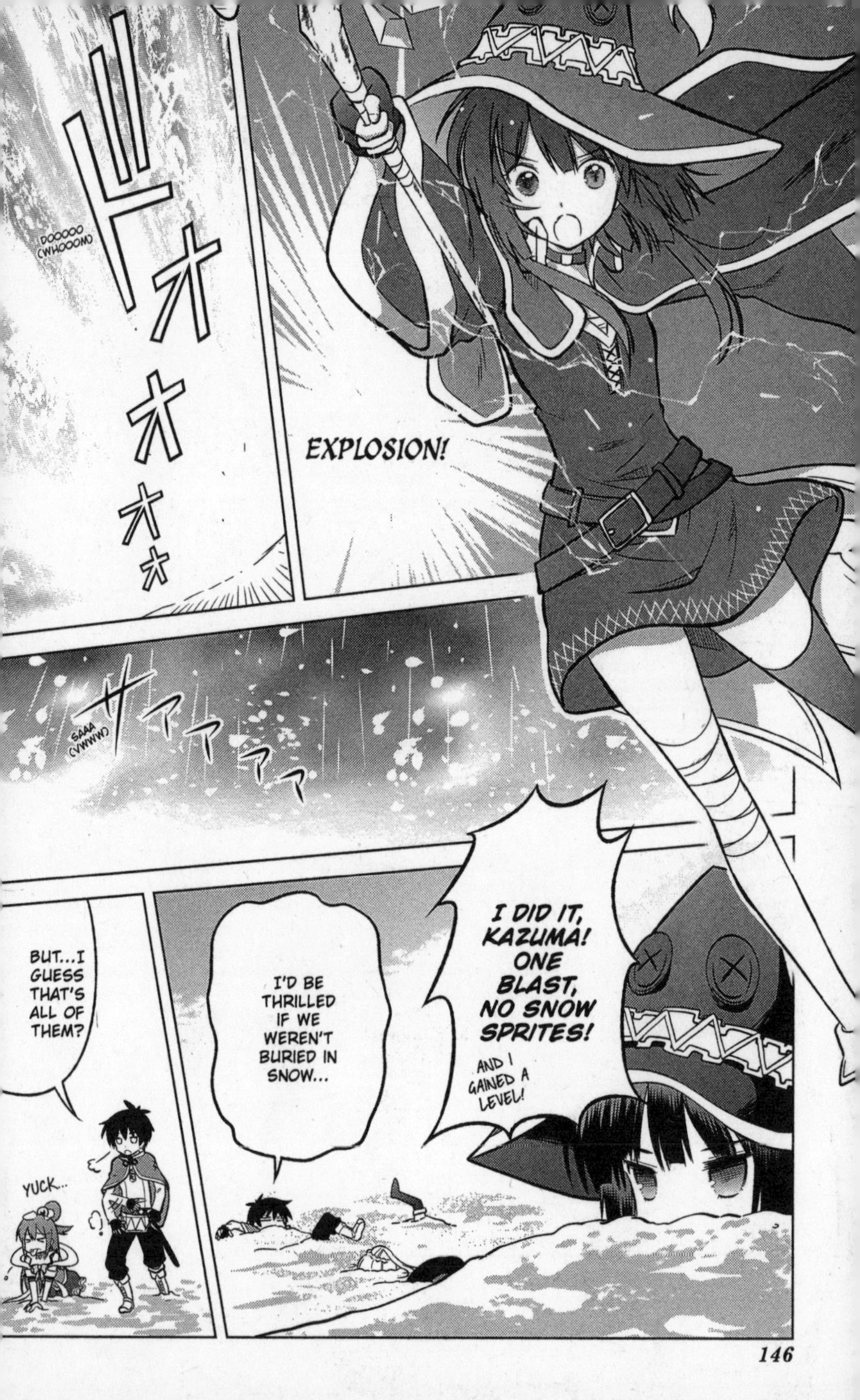
ドオオォォ
DOOOOO (WHOOOM)
EXPLOSION!
サアアアア
SAAA (VWWW)
I DID IT, KAZUMA! ONE BLAST, NO SNOW SPRITES!
AND I GAINED A LEVEL!
I'D BE THRILLED IF WE WEREN'T BURIED IN SNOW...
BUT...I GUESS THAT'S ALL OF THEM?
YUCK...

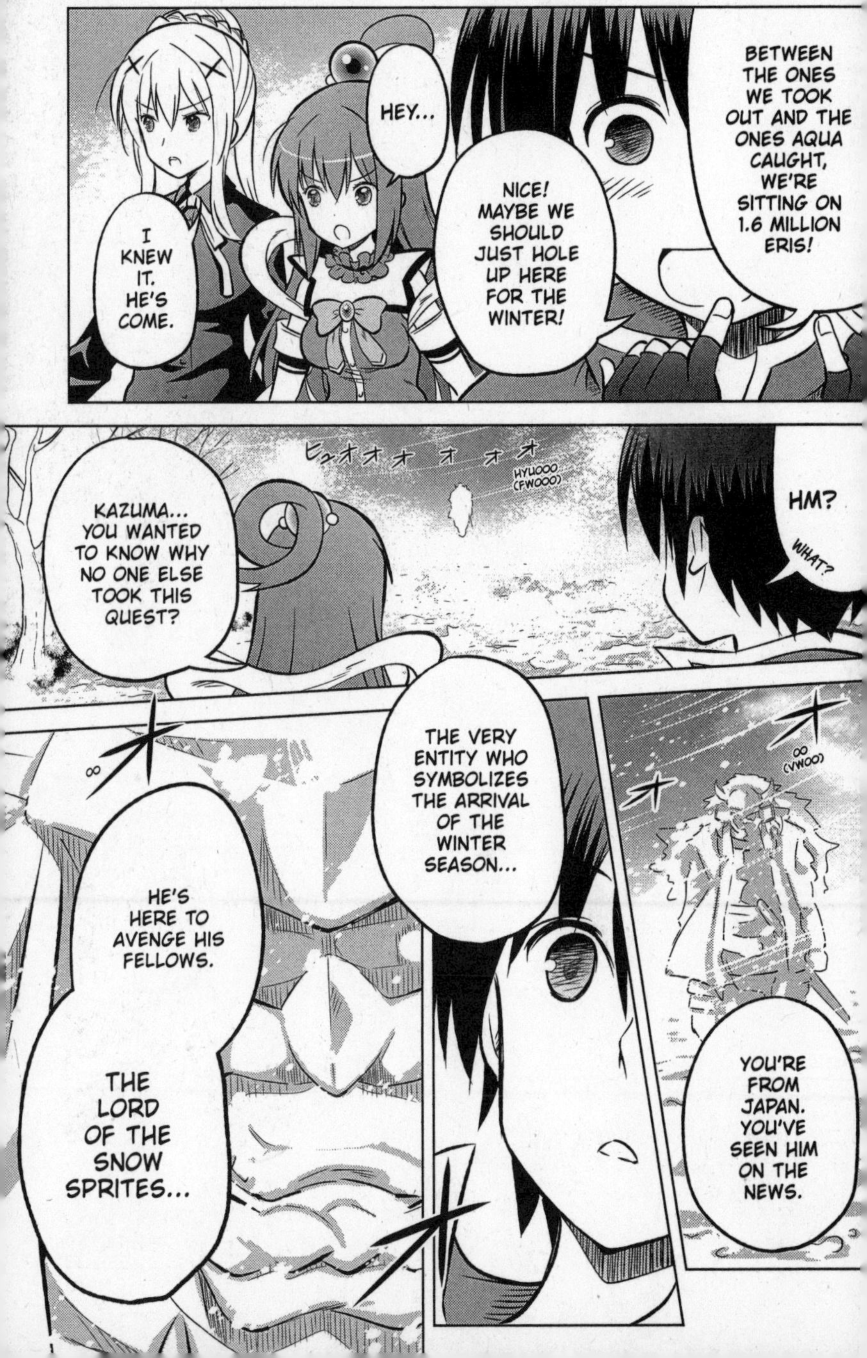
BETWEEN THE ONES WE TOOK OUT AND THE ONES AQUA CAUGHT, WE'RE SITTING ON 1.6 MILLION ERIS!
NICE! MAYBE WE SHOULD JUST HOLE UP HERE FOR THE WINTER!
HEY...
I KNEW IT. HE'S COME.
HM?
WHAT?
ヒュオオオオオオ
HYUOOO (FWOOO)
KAZUMA... YOU WANTED TO KNOW WHY NO ONE ELSE TOOK THIS QUEST?
∞ (VWOO)
YOU'RE FROM JAPAN. YOU'VE SEEN HIM ON THE NEWS.
THE VERY ENTITY WHO SYMBOLIZES THE ARRIVAL OF THE WINTER SEASON...
∞
HE'S HERE TO AVENGE HIS FELLOWS.
THE LORD OF THE SNOW SPRITES...

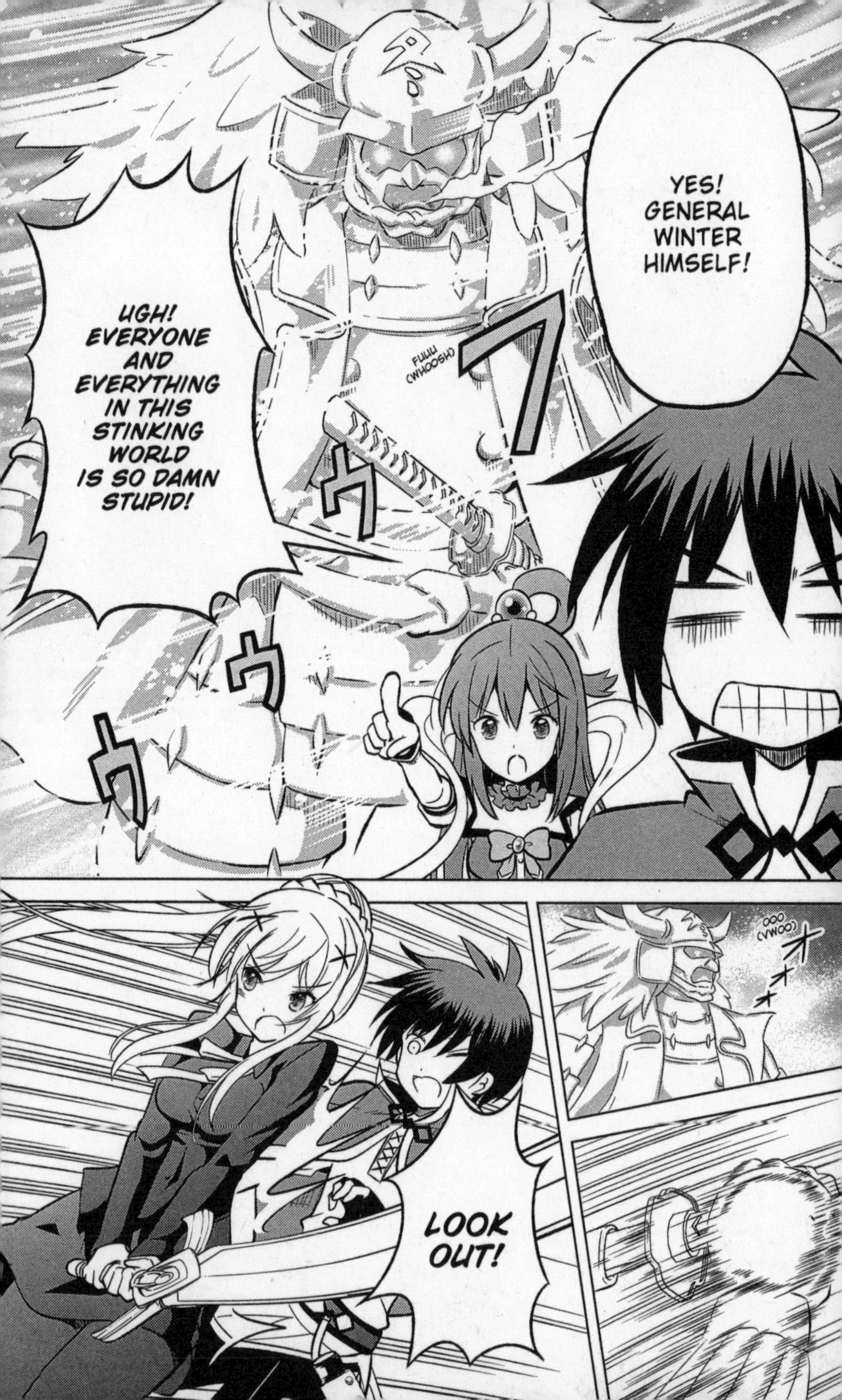
YES! GENERAL WINTER HIMSELF!
FUUU (WHOOSH)
UGH! EVERYONE AND EVERYTHING IN THIS STINKING WORLD IS SO DAMN STUPID!
OOO (VWOO)
LOOK OUT!

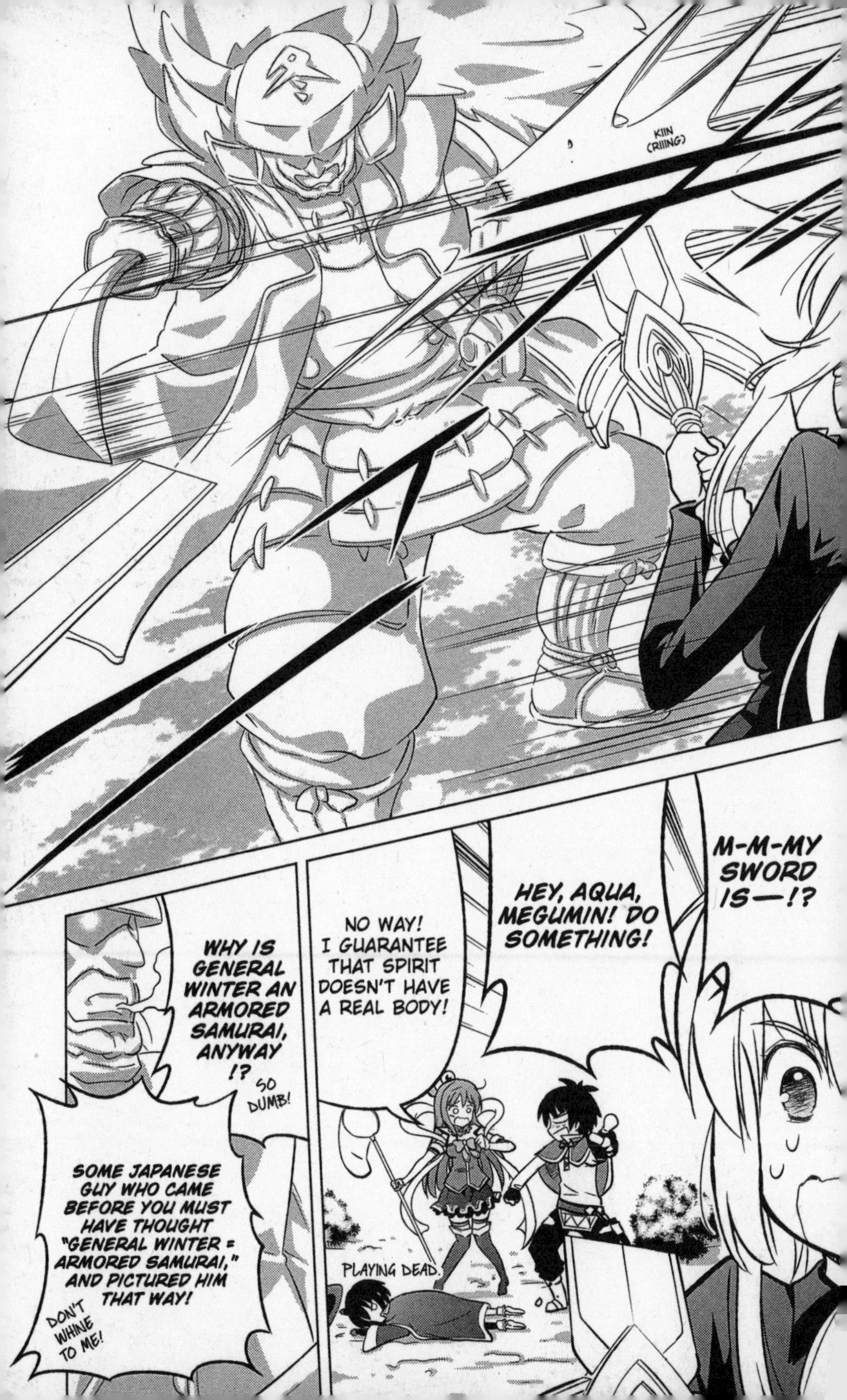
KIIN (RIIING)
M-M-MY SWORD IS—!?
HEY, AQUA, MEGUMIN! DO SOMETHING!
NO WAY! I GUARANTEE THAT SPIRIT DOESN'T HAVE A REAL BODY!
PLAYING DEAD.
WHY IS GENERAL WINTER AN ARMORED SAMURAI, ANYWAY !?
SO DUMB!
SOME JAPANESE GUY WHO CAME BEFORE YOU MUST HAVE THOUGHT "GENERAL WINTER = ARMORED SAMURAI," AND PICTURED HIM THAT WAY!
DON'T WHINE TO ME!

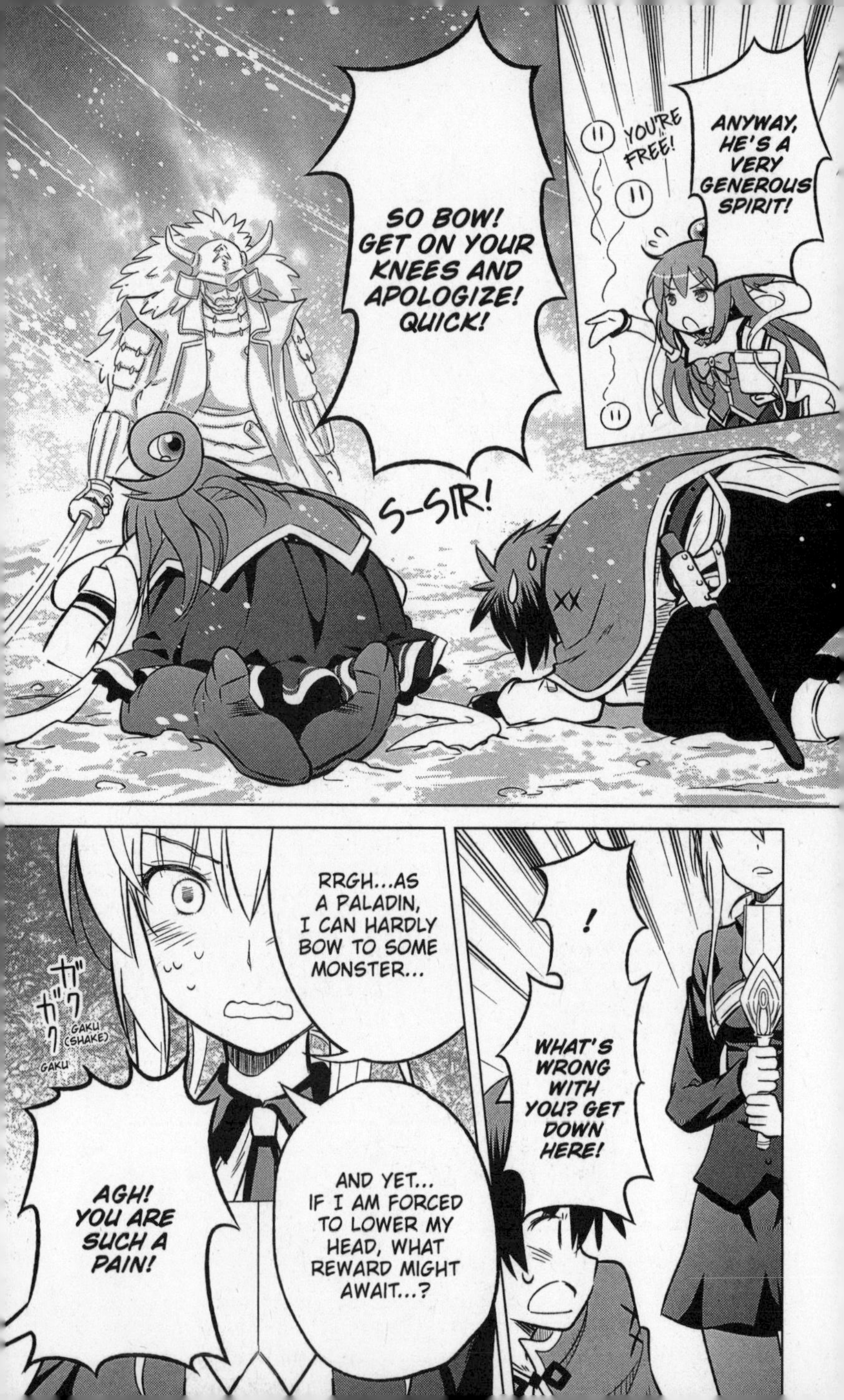
ANYWAY, HE'S A VERY GENEROUS SPIRIT!
YOU'RE FREE!
SO BOW! GET ON YOUR KNEES AND APOLOGIZE! QUICK!
S-SIR!
!
WHAT'S WRONG WITH YOU? GET DOWN HERE!
RRGH...AS A PALADIN, I CAN HARDLY BOW TO SOME MONSTER...
ガクガク
GAKU (SHAKE) GAKU
AND YET... IF I AM FORCED TO LOWER MY HEAD, WHAT REWARD MIGHT AWAIT...?
AGH! YOU ARE SUCH A PAIN!

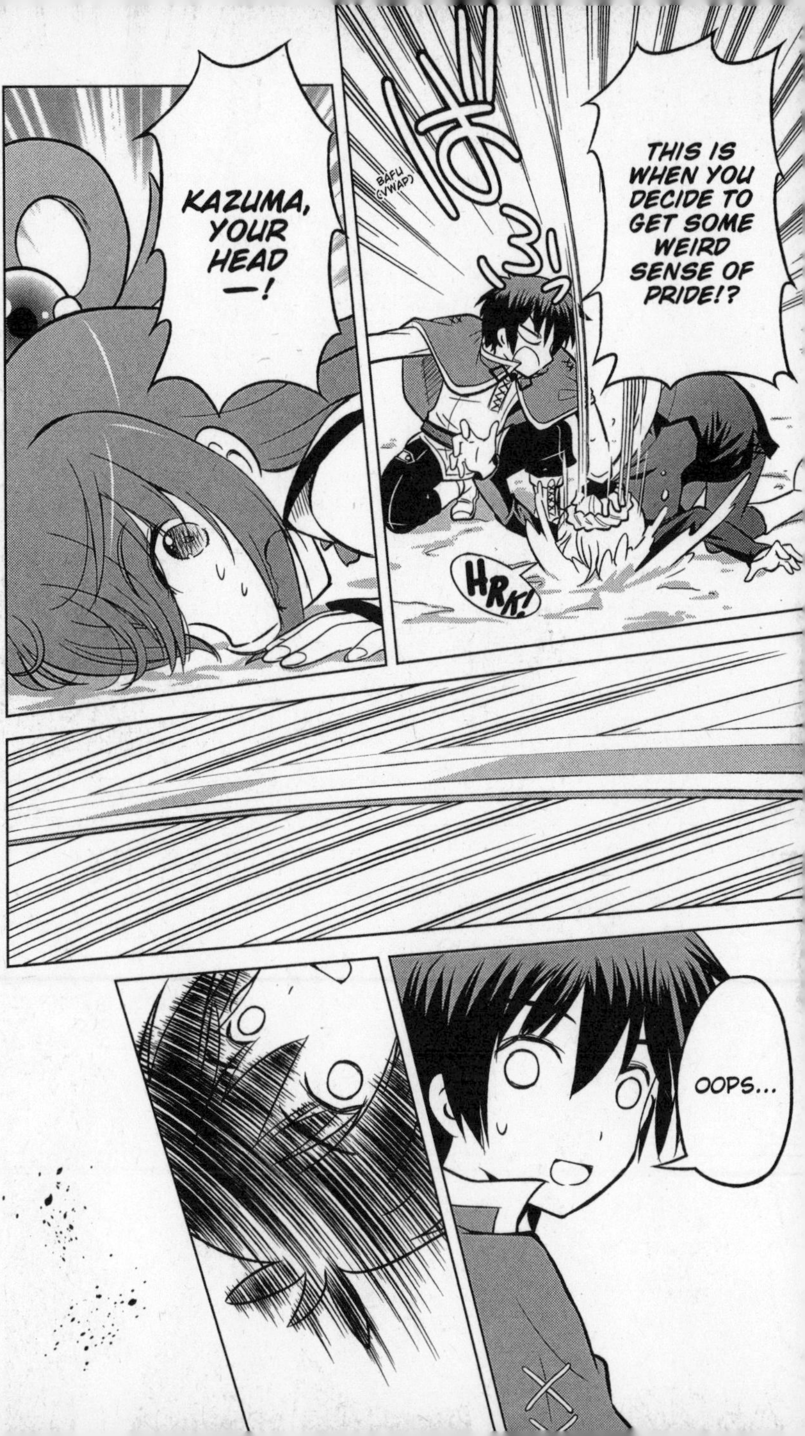
THIS IS WHEN YOU DECIDE TO GET SOME WEIRD SENSE OF PRIDE!?
BAFU (VWAP)
HRK!
KAZUMA, YOUR HEAD—!
OOPS...

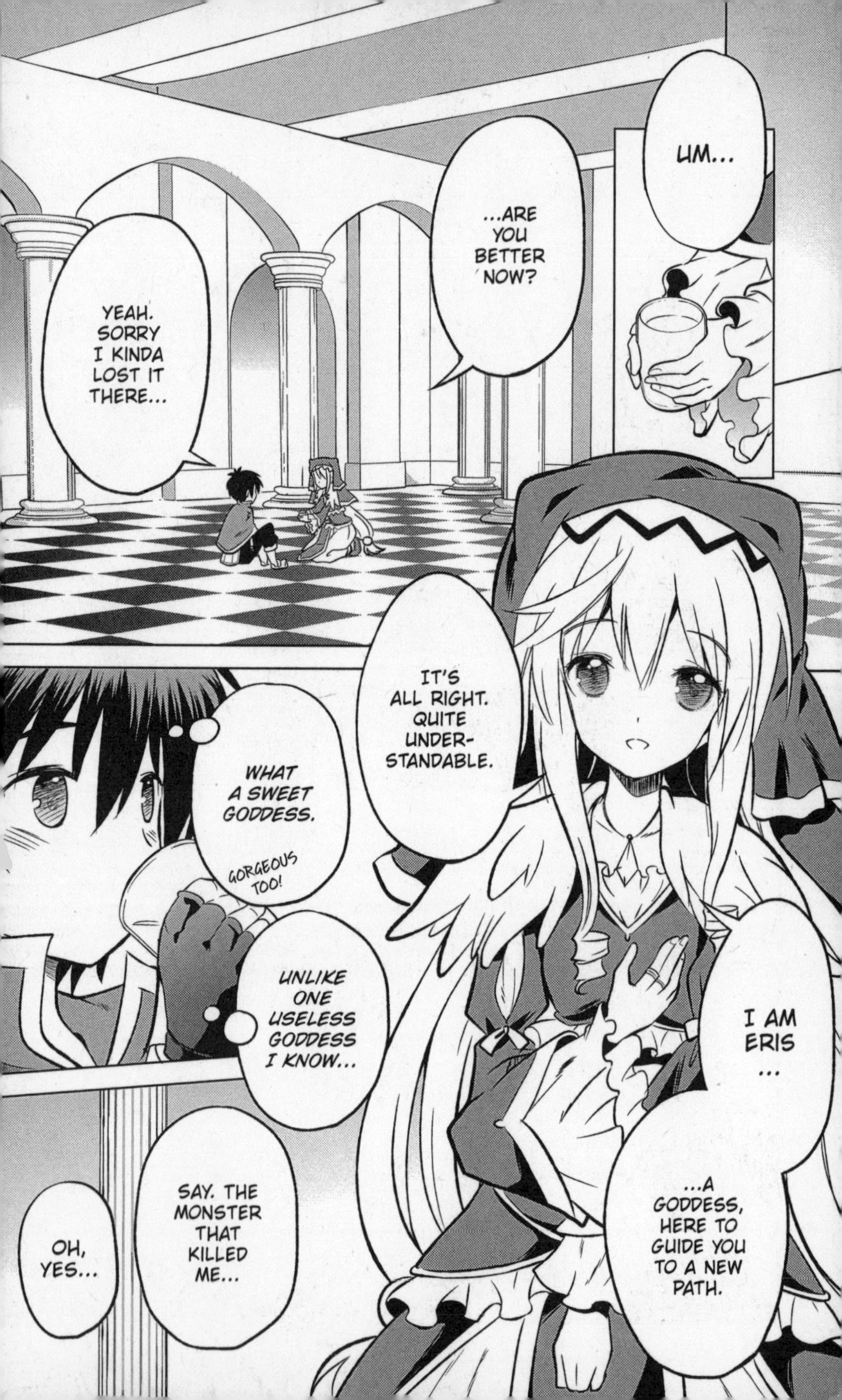
UM...
...ARE YOU BETTER NOW?
YEAH. SORRY I KINDA LOST IT THERE...
IT'S ALL RIGHT. QUITE UNDER-STANDABLE.
I AM ERIS...
...A GODDESS, HERE TO GUIDE YOU TO A NEW PATH.
WHAT A SWEET GODDESS.
GORGEOUS TOO!
UNLIKE ONE USELESS GODDESS I KNOW...
SAY. THE MONSTER THAT KILLED ME...
OH, YES...

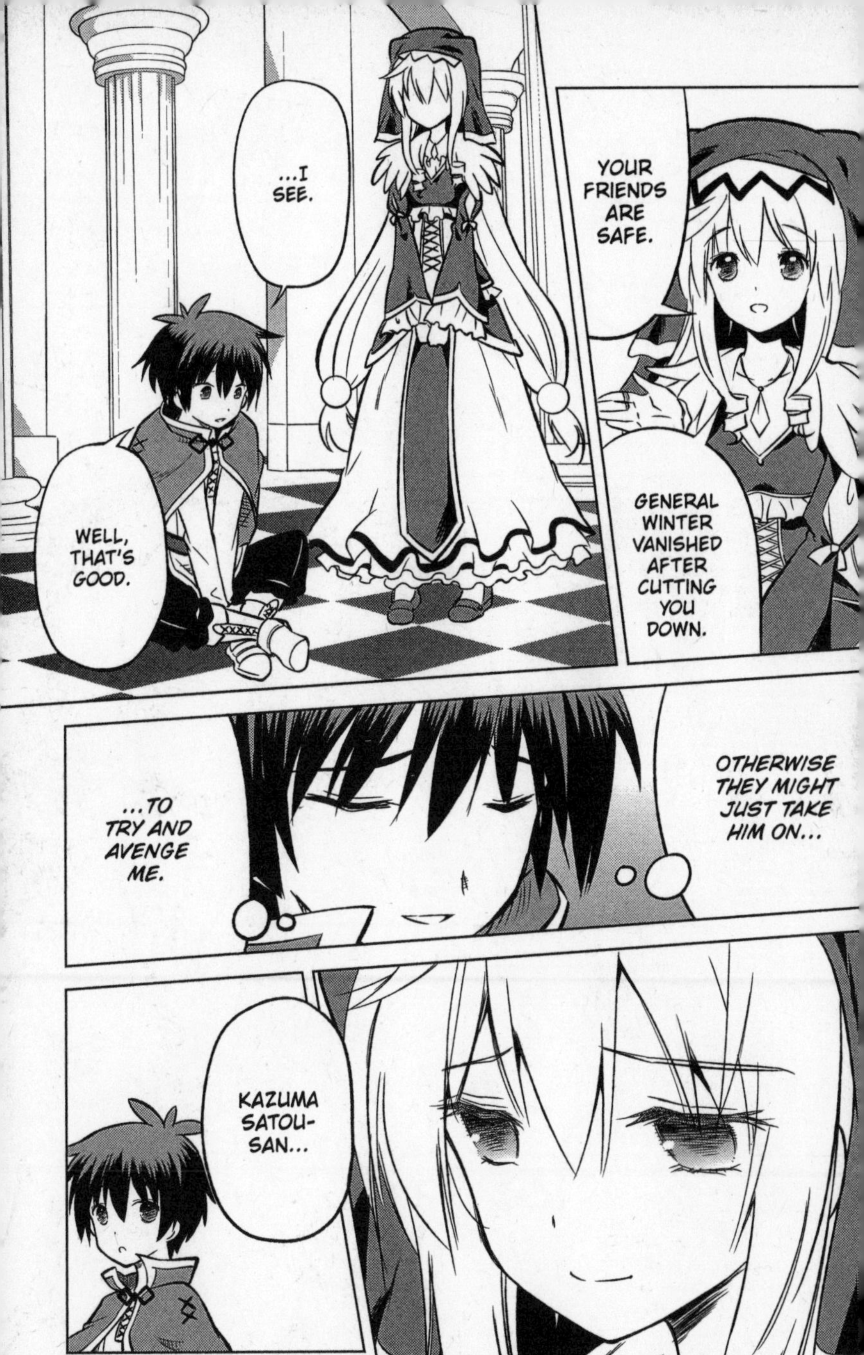
YOUR FRIENDS ARE SAFE.
GENERAL WINTER VANISHED AFTER CUTTING YOU DOWN.
...I SEE.
WELL, THAT'S GOOD.
OTHERWISE THEY MIGHT JUST TAKE HIM ON...
...TO TRY AND AVENGE ME.
KAZUMA SATOU-SAN...

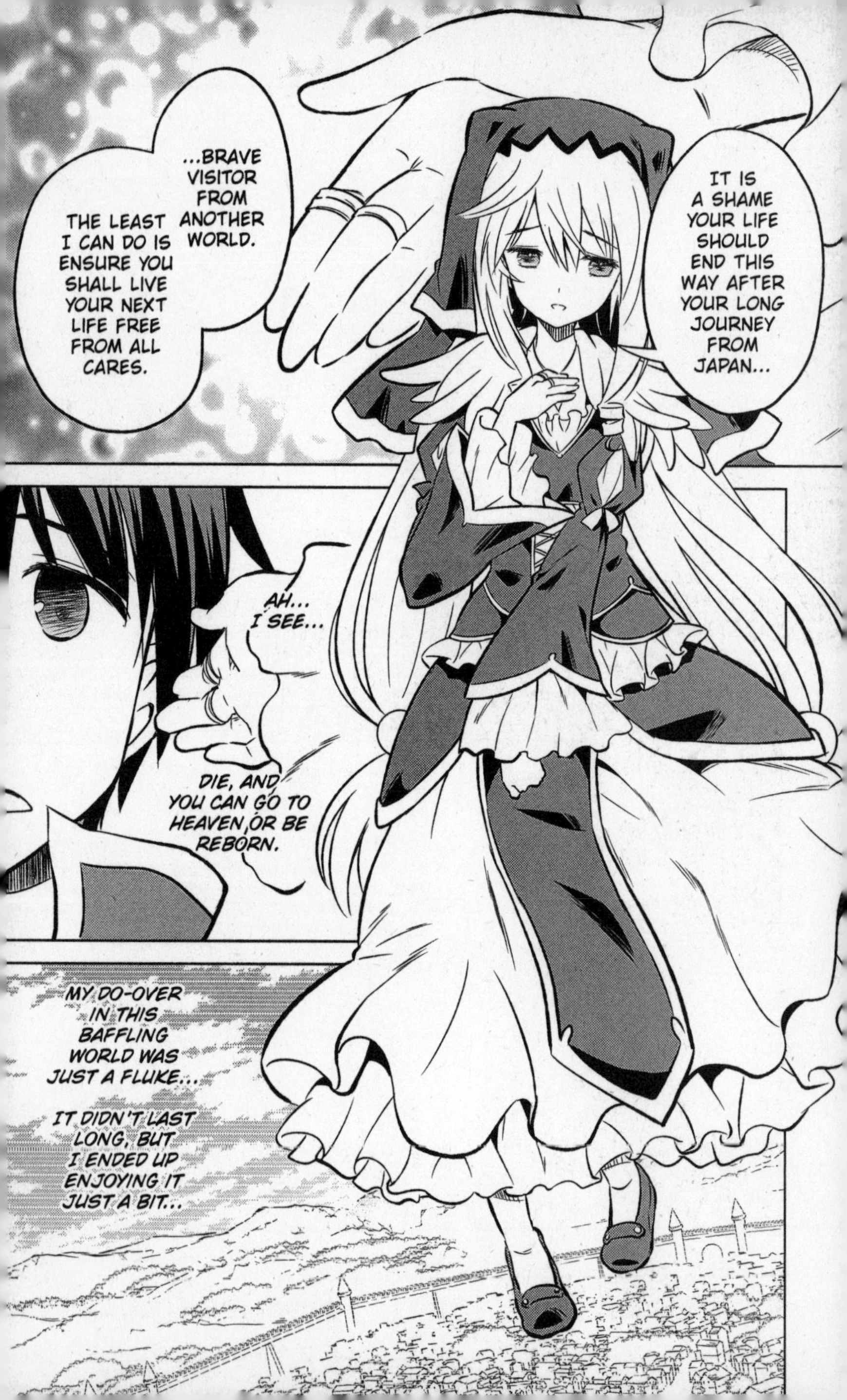
IT IS A SHAME YOUR LIFE SHOULD END THIS WAY AFTER YOUR LONG JOURNEY FROM JAPAN...
...BRAVE VISITOR FROM ANOTHER WORLD.
THE LEAST I CAN DO IS ENSURE YOU SHALL LIVE YOUR NEXT LIFE FREE FROM ALL CARES.
AH... I SEE...
DIE, AND YOU CAN GO TO HEAVEN, OR BE REBORN.
MY DO-OVER IN THIS BAFFLING WORLD WAS JUST A FLUKE...
IT DIDN'T LAST LONG, BUT I ENDED UP ENJOYING IT JUST A BIT...

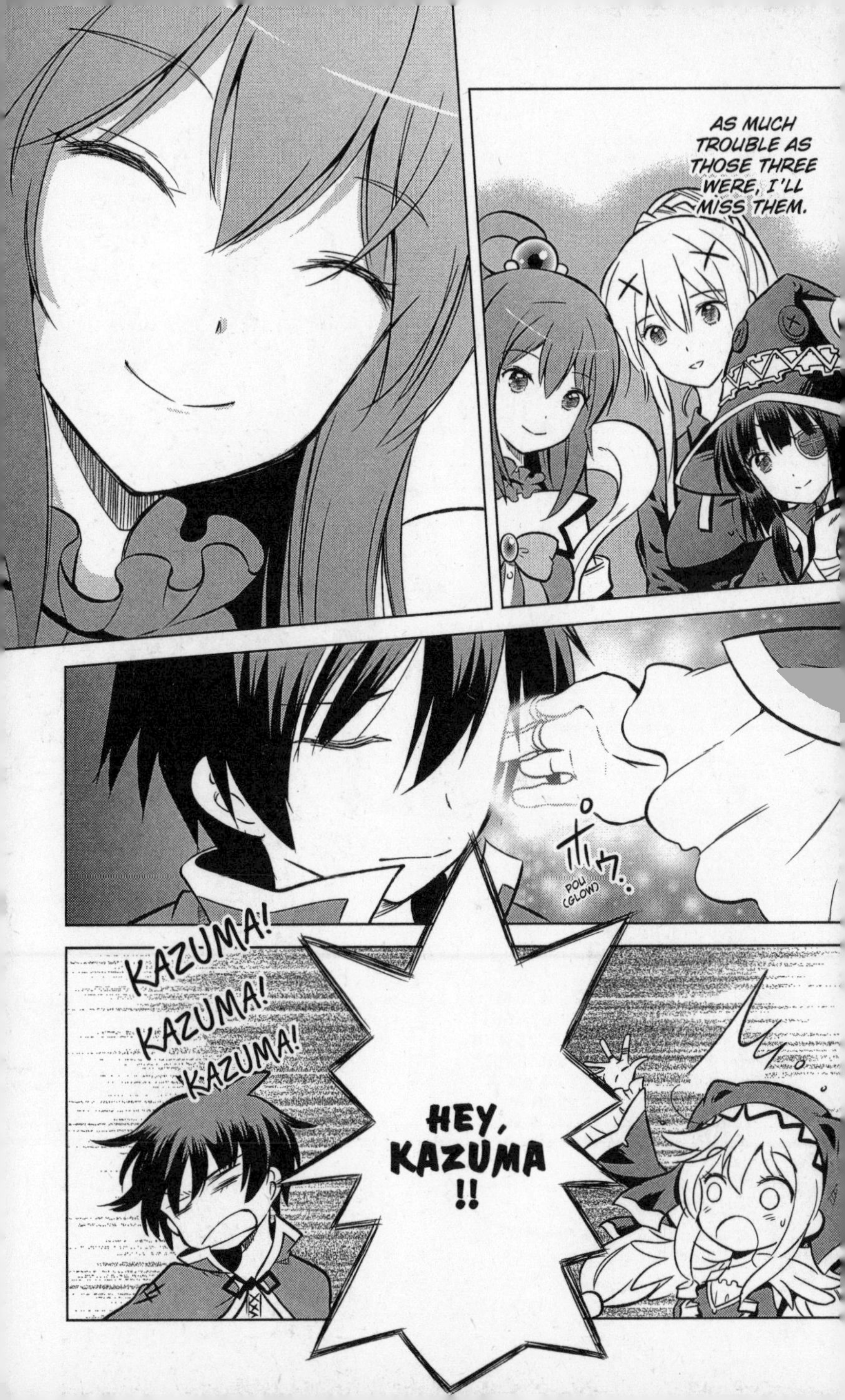
AS MUCH TROUBLE AS THOSE THREE WERE, I'LL MISS THEM.
POU (GLOW)
KAZUMA! KAZUMA! KAZUMA!
HEY, KAZUMA!!

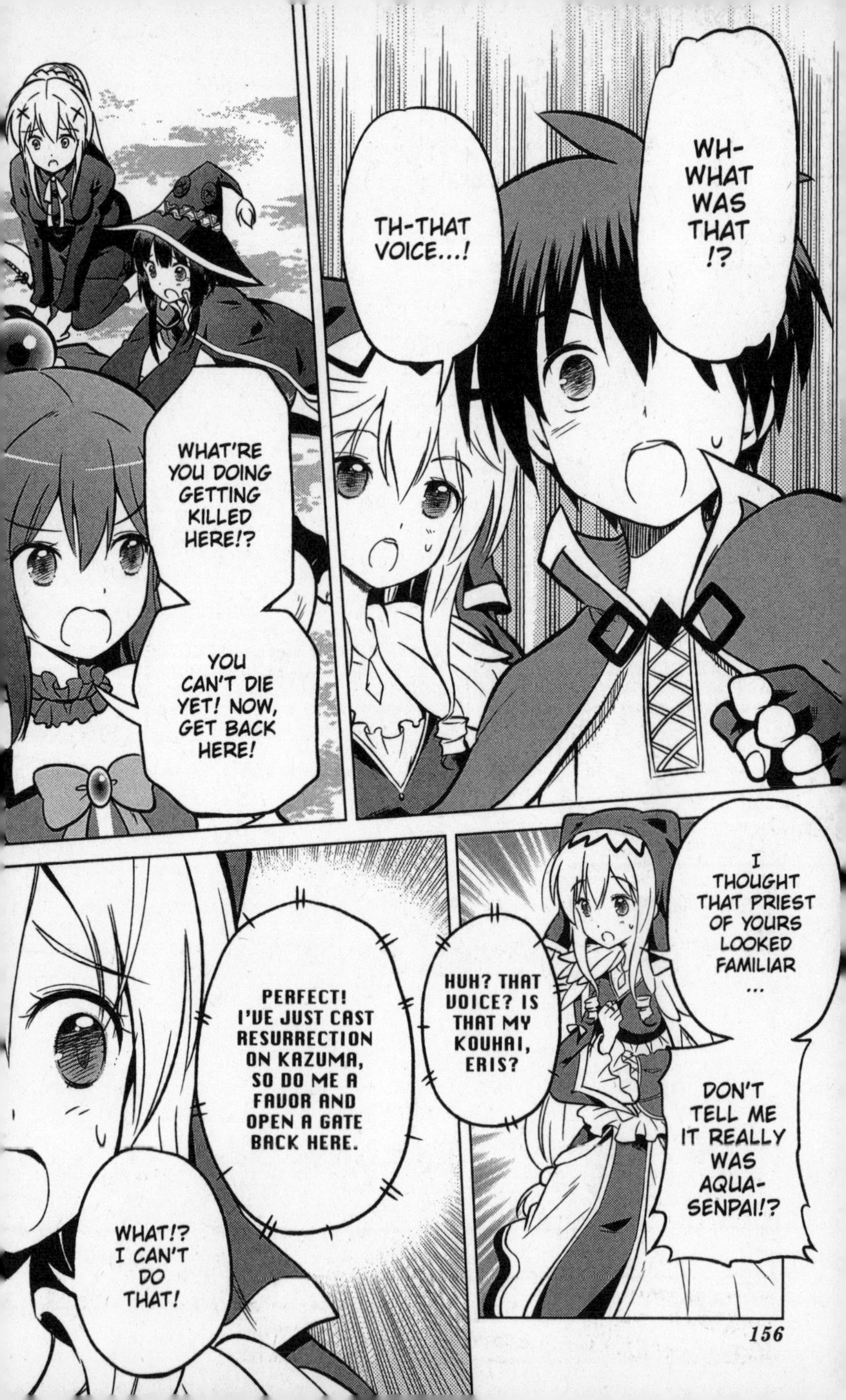
WH-WHAT WAS THAT!?
TH-THAT VOICE...!
WHAT'RE YOU DOING GETTING KILLED HERE!?
YOU CAN'T DIE YET! NOW, GET BACK HERE!
I THOUGHT THAT PRIEST OF YOURS LOOKED FAMILIAR...
DON'T TELL ME IT REALLY WAS AQUA-SENPAI!?
HUH? THAT VOICE? IS THAT MY KOUHAI, ERIS?
PERFECT! I'VE JUST CAST RESURRECTION ON KAZUMA, SO DO ME A FAVOR AND OPEN A GATE BACK HERE.
WHAT!? I CAN'T DO THAT!

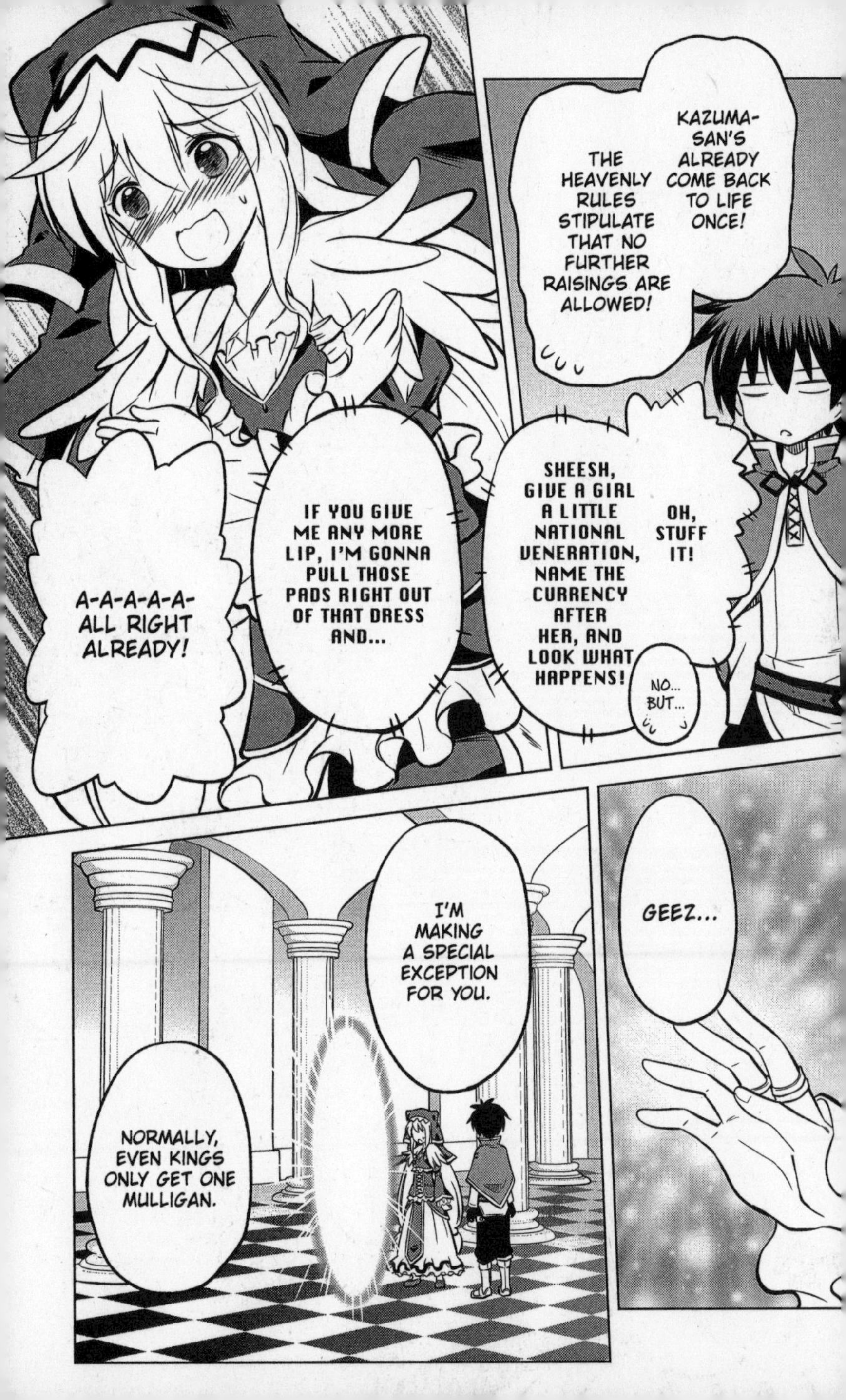
KAZUMA-SAN'S ALREADY COME BACK TO LIFE ONCE!
THE HEAVENLY RULES STIPULATE THAT NO FURTHER RAISINGS ARE ALLOWED!
OH, STUFF IT!
SHEESH, GIVE A GIRL A LITTLE NATIONAL VENERATION, NAME THE CURRENCY AFTER HER, AND LOOK WHAT HAPPENS!
NO... BUT...
IF YOU GIVE ME ANY MORE LIP, I'M GONNA PULL THOSE PADS RIGHT OUT OF THAT DRESS AND...
A-A-A-A-A-ALL RIGHT ALREADY!
GEEZ...
I'M MAKING A SPECIAL EXCEPTION FOR YOU.
NORMALLY, EVEN KINGS ONLY GET ONE MULLIGAN.

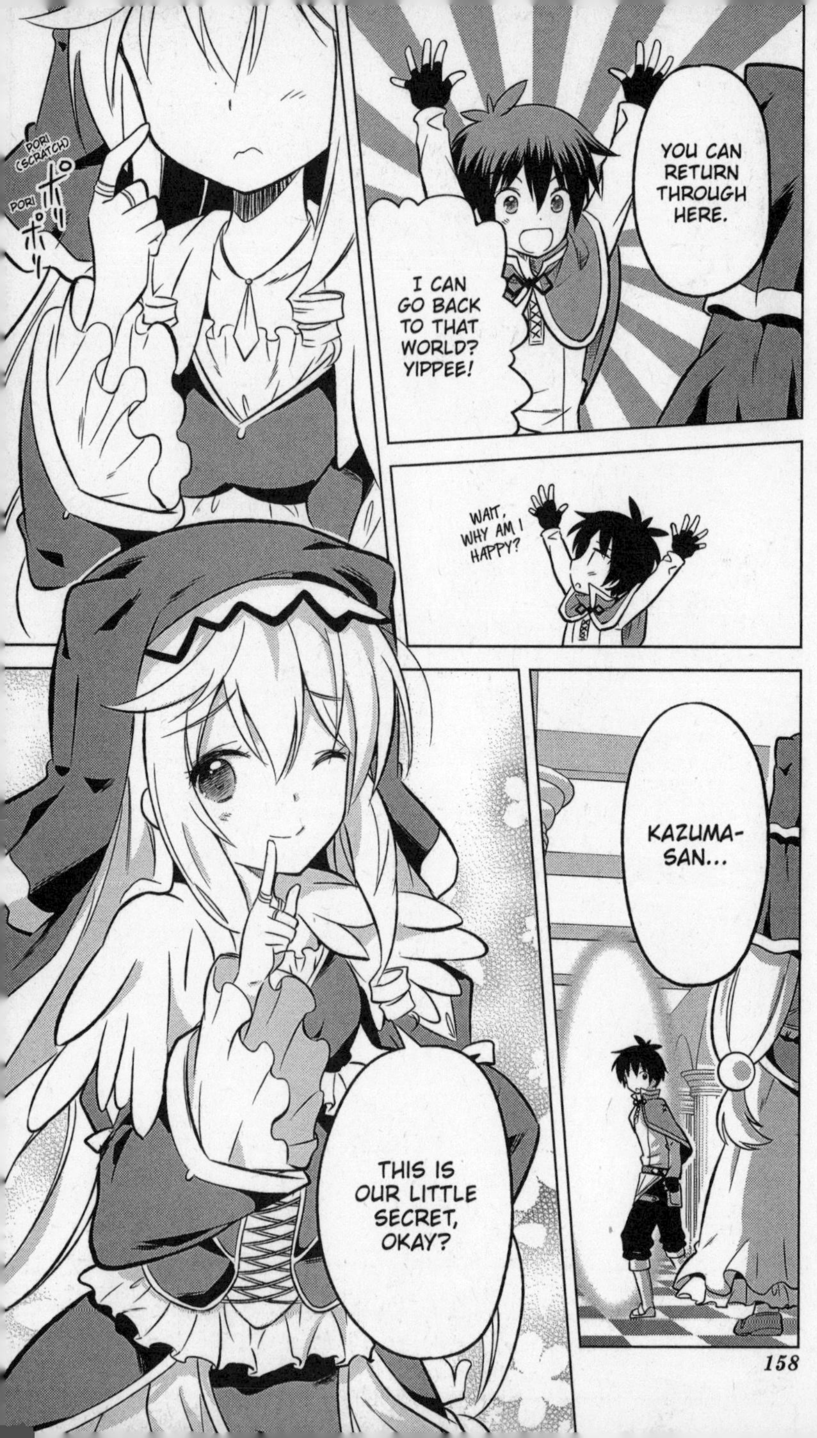
YOU CAN RETURN THROUGH HERE.
I CAN GO BACK TO THAT WORLD? YIPPEE!
WAIT, WHY AM I HAPPY?
PORI (SCRATCH)
PORI
ポリ
ポリ
KAZUMA-SAN...
THIS IS OUR LITTLE SECRET, OKAY?

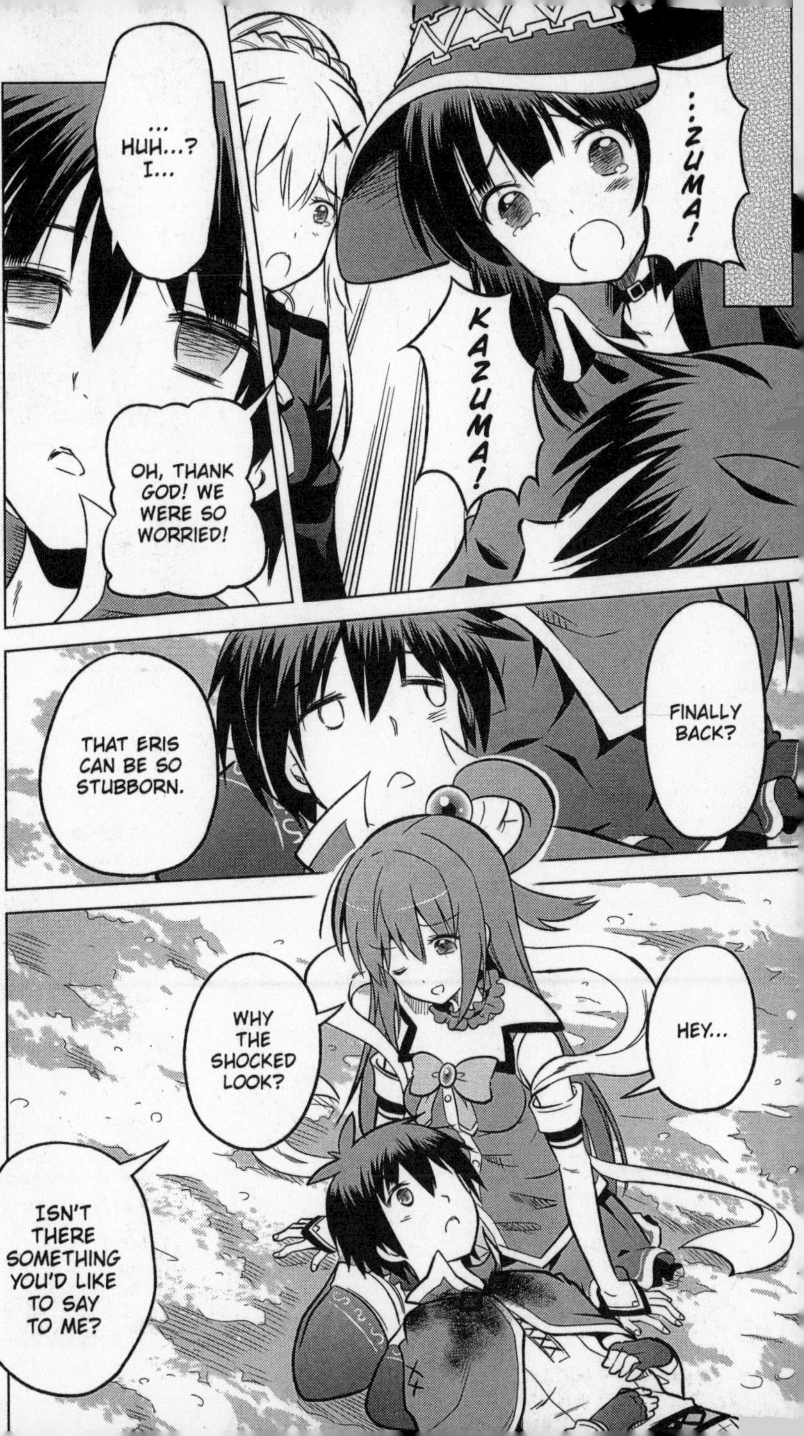
...ZUMA!
KAZUMA!
... HUH...? I...
OH, THANK GOD! WE WERE SO WORRIED!
FINALLY BACK?
THAT ERIS CAN BE SO STUBBORN.
HEY...
WHY THE SHOCKED LOOK?
ISN'T THERE SOMETHING YOU'D LIKE TO SAY TO ME?

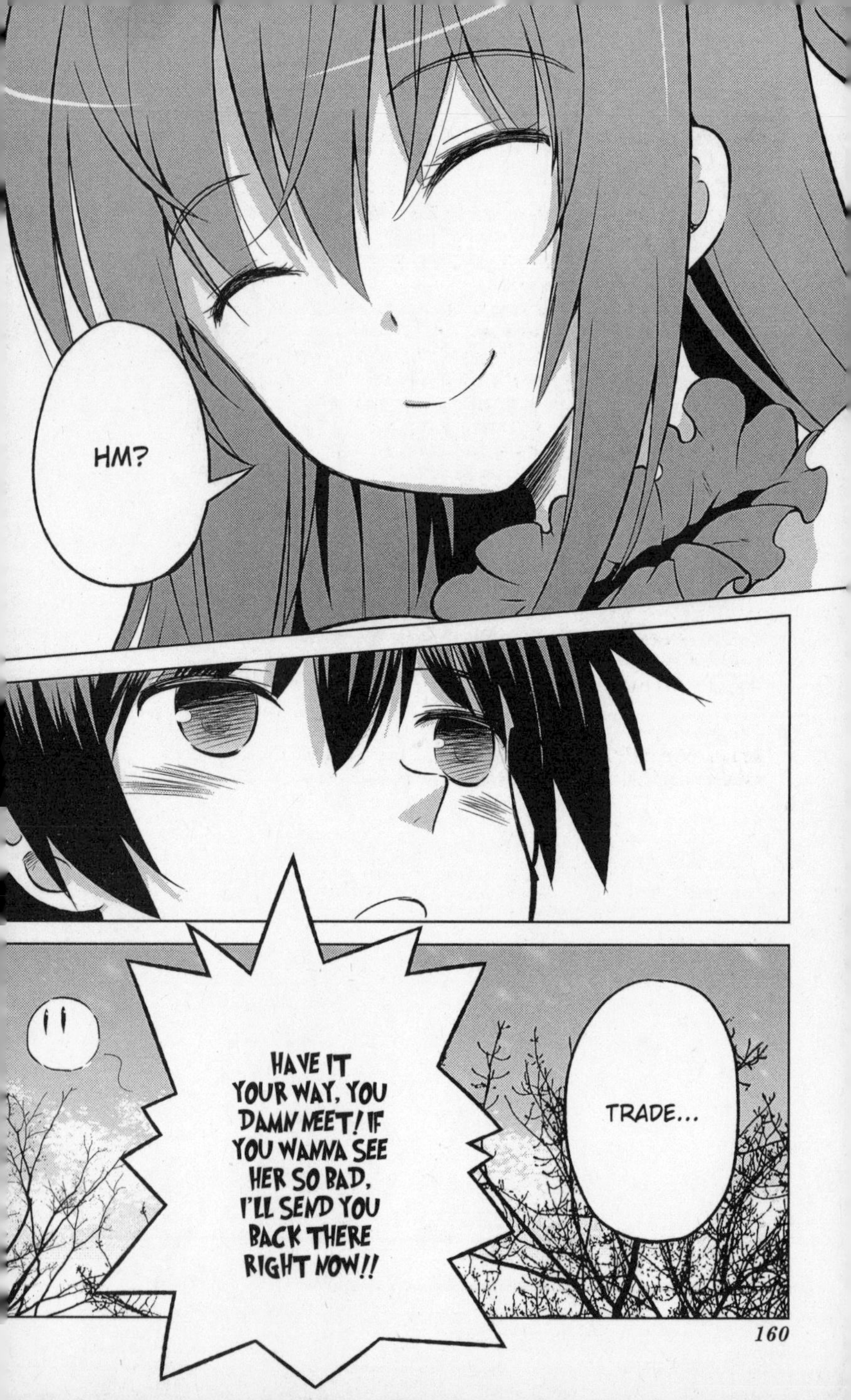
HM?
TRADE...
HAVE IT YOUR WAY, YOU DAMN NEET! IF YOU WANNA SEE HER SO BAD, I'LL SEND YOU BACK THERE RIGHT NOW!!

TRANSLATION NOTES

COMMON HONORIFICS

no honorific: Indicates familiarity or closeness; if used without permission or reason, addressing someone in this manner would constitute an insult.

-san: The Japanese equivalent of Mr./Mrs./Miss. If a situation calls for politeness, this is the fail-safe honorific.

-sama: Conveys great respect; may also indicate that the social status of the speaker is lower than that of the addressee.

-chan: An affectionate honorific indicating familiarity used mostly in reference to girls; also used in reference to cute persons or animals of either gender.

-senpai: Used with people who have seniority in an environment, such as upperclassmen or coworkers who have been at a company longer. The opposite of a senpai is a kouhai, though the term is not used as an honorific.

Page 29

HikiNEET is a combination of the terms *hikikomori* and NEET used on the fly by Aqua to bash Kazuma. *Hikikomori* refers to people who experience severe social anxiety when outside their homes or interacting with others and so, sometimes voluntarily, withdraw from society. They are often called "shut-ins" or "modern day hermits." **NEET** is originally a British term but adopted by Japan, standing for "not in education, employment, or training." It is usually used pejoratively, to look down on people who are seen as lazy or as freeloaders who won't get a job.

PAGE 147

General Winter (*Fuyu Shogun* in Japanese) is a figure in Japanese culture much like Jack Frost, a personification of the winter season.

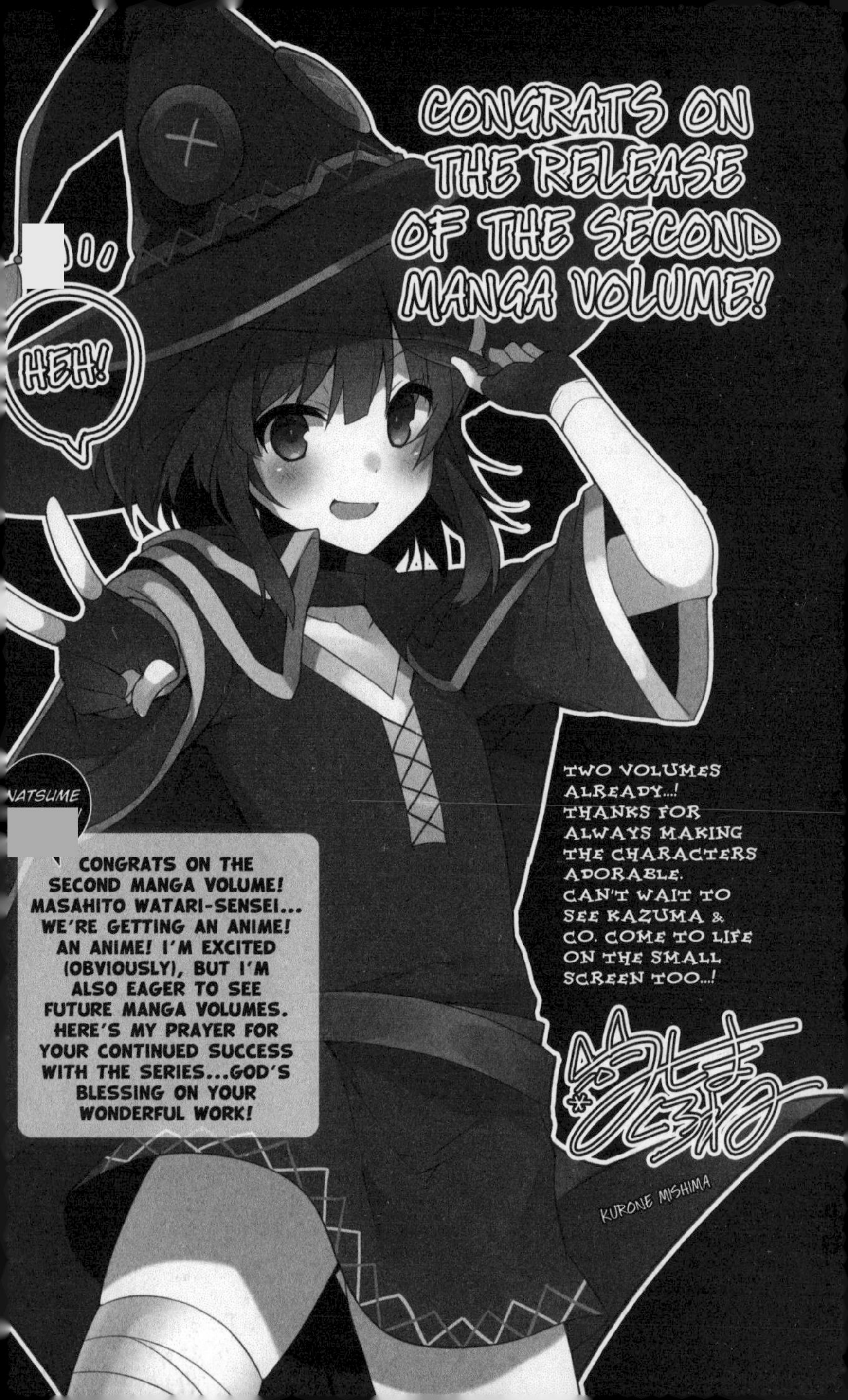
CONGRATS ON THE RELEASE OF THE SECOND MANGA VOLUME!
HEH!
TWO VOLUMES ALREADY...! THANKS FOR ALWAYS MAKING THE CHARACTERS ADORABLE. CAN'T WAIT TO SEE KAZUMA & CO. COME TO LIFE ON THE SMALL SCREEN TOO...!
KURONE MISHIMA
NATSUME
CONGRATS ON THE SECOND MANGA VOLUME! MASAHITO WATARI-SENSEI... WE'RE GETTING AN ANIME! AN ANIME! I'M EXCITED (OBVIOUSLY), BUT I'M ALSO EAGER TO SEE FUTURE MANGA VOLUMES. HERE'S MY PRAYER FOR YOUR CONTINUED SUCCESS WITH THE SERIES...GOD'S BLESSING ON YOUR WONDERFUL WORK!

VOLUME 2 IS SAFELY OUT THE DOOR (YAY!), AND AN ANIME ADAPTATION WAS RECENTLY CONFIRMED. I'M THRILLED TO BE WORKING ON A SERIES WITH AS MUCH POTENTIAL AS KONOSUBA: GOD'S BLESSING ON THIS WONDERFUL WORLD!

I PRAY THAT THE ANIME WILL BE BROADCAST IN MY AREA (LOL).

渡真仁

MASAHITO WATARI

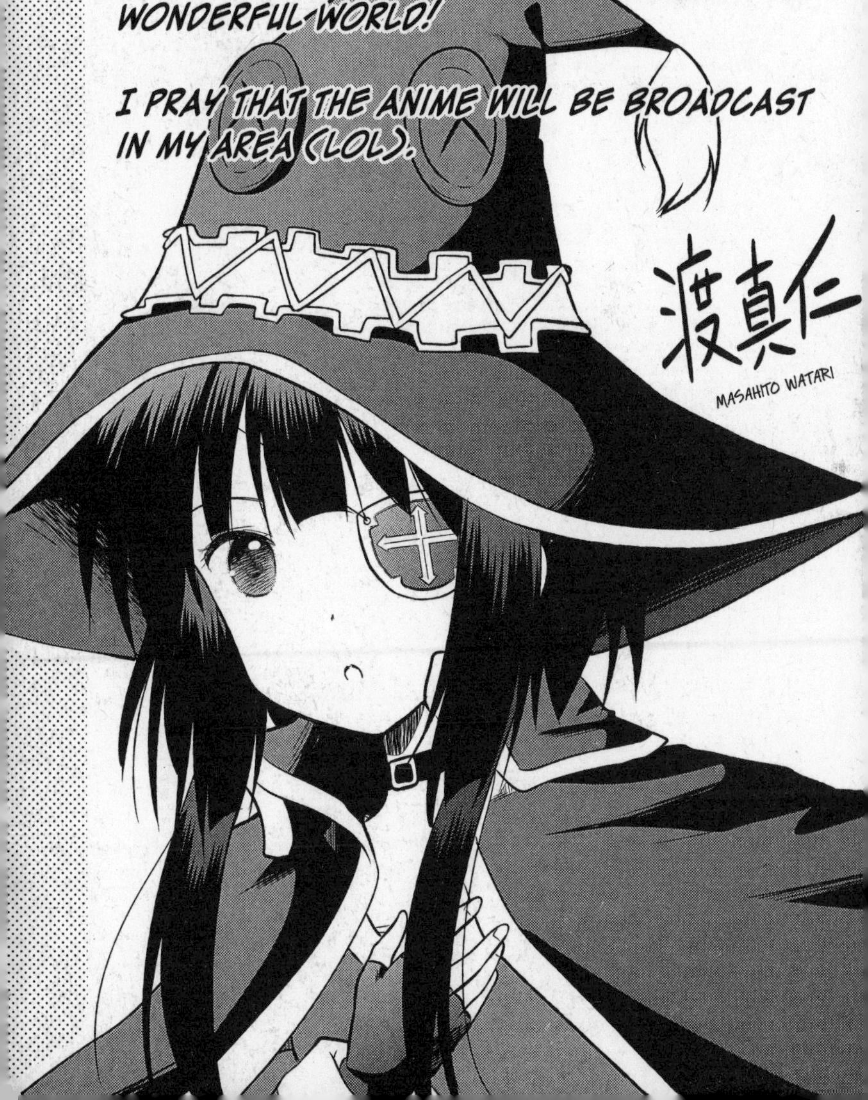

KONOSUBA: GOD'S BLESSING ON THIS WONDERFUL WORLD! 2
Natsume Akatsuki

TRANSLATION: Kevin Steinbach ● **LETTERING: Bianca Pistillo**

KONO SUBARASHII SEKAI NI SYUKUFUKU WO! Volume 2
©MASAHITO WATARI 2015
©NATSUME AKATSUKI, KURONE MISHIMA 2015
First published in Japan in 2015 by Kadokawa Corporation, Tokyo. English translation rights arranged with KADOKAWA Corporation, Tokyo through Tuttle-Mori Agency, Inc., Tokyo.

English translation © 2017 by Yen Press, LLC

Yen Press
1290 Avenue of the Americas
New York, NY 10104

Visit us at yenpress.com
facebook.com/yenpress
twitter.com/yenpress
yenpress.tumblr.com
instagram.com/yenpress

First Yen Press Edition: February 2017

Yen Press is an imprint of Yen Press, LLC.
The Yen Press name and logo are trademarks of Yen Press, LLC.

Library of Congress Control Number: 2016946112

ISBNs: 978-0-316-55332-2 (paperback)
       978-0-316-46868-8 (ebook)

10 9 8 7 6 5 4 3 2 1

BVG

Printed in the United States of America